The Sanhuri Code, and the Emergence of Modern Arab Civil Law (1932 to 1949)

Studies in Islamic Law and Society

(*Founding Editor*: Bernard Weiss)

Edited by
Ruud Peters and A. Kevin Reinhart

VOLUME 29

The Sanhuri Code, and the Emergence of Modern Arab Civil Law (1932 to 1949)

By

Guy Bechor

BRILL

LEIDEN • BOSTON
2007

Library of Congress Cataloging-in-Publication Data

Bechor, Guy.
The Sanhuri Code, and the emergence of modern Arab civil law (1932 to 1949) / by Guy Bechor.
p. cm. — (Studies in Islamic law and society)
Includes bibliographical references.
ISBN 978-90-04-15878-8 (hardback : alk. paper) 1. Civil law—Egypt—Codification—History—20th century. 2. Civil law—Social aspects—Egypt. 3. Property—Social aspects—Egypt. 4. Obligations (Law)—Social aspects—Egypt. 5. Contracts—Social aspects—Egypt. 6. Sanhuri, 'Abd al-Razzaq Ahmad, 1895-1971. I. Title. II. Series.

KRM500.B46 2007
346.62—dc22 2007029417

ISSN 1384-1130
ISBN 978 90 04 15878 8

We are a nation in need of vitality and renewal. While we stepped slowly, the world ran ahead, so that we have been left behind, after once being at the front. How, then, can we manage in the modern era?

No type of reform or progress may be adopted otherwise than in an atmosphere of social reconciliation. Reform and progress alone cannot bring such social reconciliation.

ʿAbd al-Razzāq al-Sanhūrī

To my parents
Rachel and Heskel

CONTENTS

ACKNOWLEDGMENTS

This book is a revised and expanded version of my doctoral dissertation: "The Egyptian Civil Code: In Search of Social Order, 1936–1949" (Hebrew), submitted to Tel-Aviv University, 1999. I would like to express my sincere gratitude to my advisors, Prof. Israel Gershoni and Prof. Michael Winter, without whose continuous inspiration and dedicated guidance I could not have completed this project. Since first submitting this dissertation, I have devoted several additional years of research in Egypt to complete this present volume.

I am also grateful to Prof. Uriel Reichman, President of the Interdisciplinary Center, Herzliya, for encouraging me to study the legal systems of the Arab Middle East. I greatly appreciate his generosity and ongoing support.

Last but not least, I would like to thank my wife, Nava, and my children, Lihi, Yaara and Amit, for their love, support and understanding during what has been unquestionably my greatest professional challenge.

In my dream I saw the sun rising in the west with a shining light. I fixed my gaze on it for some time, and then turned my head to the east, and it seemed as though I were drawing a greater and yet brighter sun from the expanses of the east. I felt as though I were drawing that sun with my own hands.

There are two things I would like to establish before I die. First, to open the gate of Ijtihād in the Sharīʿa, for it will return to be a living source of legislation in the East; and second, to hold the hand of the Egyptian fallāḥ, to relieve him of his agony.

ʿAbd al-Razzāq al-Sanhūrī, *Diary*, 1921, 1933 respectively[1]

[1] Nādya al-Sanhūrī, Tawfīq al-Shāwī (eds.), *ʿAbd al-Razzāq al-Sanhūrī, min Ḥilāl ʾAwrāqihi al-Shakhṣiyya* (Cairo: al-Zahrāʾ lil-ʿAllām al-ʿArabī, 1988, Hereinafter: Diary): Lyon, 24 October 1921, pp. 52–53; 21 January 1933, p. 190.

INTRODUCTION

LAW, HISTORY AND SOCIETY

Law is nothing other than the offspring of life. It is subject to life, influenced by life and protects life.

Sanhūrī, 1936[1]

1. The Need for Interdisciplinary Study

Much has been written about the development of constitutional and criminal law in twentieth-century Monarchist Egypt and about the reforms in the court system introduced during this period.[2] The discipline of

[1] Abd al-Razzāq al-Sanhūrī, "Wujūb Tanqīḥ al-Qānūn al-Madanī al-Miṣrī wa ʿAala ʾAy Asās Yakūn Hadha al-Tanqiḥ", in *Majallat al-Qānūn wa-al-ʾIqtiṣād* 6(1936) (Hereinafter: Wujūb), pp. 93–94.

[2] Laṭifa Muḥammad Sālim, *Al-Nizām al-Qaḍāʾi al-Miṣrī al-Ḥadith, 1914–1952* (Cairo: Markaz al-Dirāsāt al-Siyāsiyya wa al-ʾIstrātijiyya bil-ʾAhrām, 1986); Shafīq Shiḥata, *Taʾrīkh Ḥarakat al-Tajdīd fī al-Nuzum al-Qānūniyya fī Miṣr* (Cairo: Dār ʾIḥyāʾ al-Kutub al-ʿArabiyy, 1961); Muḥammad Sāmī Māzin, "Al-Maḥākim al-ʾAhliyya Baʿda ʾInshāʾiha" in *Al-Kitāb al-Dhahabī lil-Maḥākim al-ʾAhliyya, 1883–1933* (Cairo: Al-Maṭbʿa al-ʾAmīriyya, Bulāq, 1938) (Hereinafter: Al-Kitāb al-Dhahabī), Volume 1, p. 151; Muḥammad Labīb ʿAṭiyya, "Taṭawwūr Qānūn al-ʿUqūbāt fī Miṣr min ʿAhd ʾInshāʾ al-Maḥākim al-ʾAhliyya" in Al-Kitāb al-Dhahabī, Volume 2, p. 5; J. N. D. Anderson, "Law reform in Egypt: 1850–1950", in P. M. Holt, *Political and Social Change in Modern Egypt* (London: Oxford University Press, 1968), p. 209; G. Badr, "The New Egyptian Civil Code and the Unification of the Laws of Arab Countries", *Tulane Law Review* 30(1955–56), pp. 299–304; K. Bälz, "Sharīʿa and Qanun in Egyptian Law: A Systems Theory Approach to Legal Pluralism", in E. Cotran, C. Mallat eds., *Yearbook of Islamic and Middle Eastern Law* 2(1995), p. 37; G. Bechor, "To hold the Hand of the Weak: The Emergence of Contractual Justice in the Egyptian Civil Law", *Islamic Law and Society* 8(2001), p. 179; J. Y. Brinton, The Mixed Courts of Egypt (New Haven: Yale University Press, 1968); N. Brown, "Brigands and State Building: The Invention of Banditry in Modern Egypt", *Comparative Studies in Society and History* 32(1990), p. 258; N. Brown, "Law and Imperialism: Egypt in Comparative Perspective", *Law and Society Review* 29(1995), p. 103; N. Brown, *The Rule of Law in the Arab World: Courts in Egypt and the Gulf* (Cambridge: Cambridge University Press, 1998); B. Cannon, *Politics of Law and the Courts in Nineteenth-Century Egypt* (Salt Lake City: University of Utah Press, 1988); C. Chehata, "Les Survivances Musulmanes dans la Codification du Droit Civil Égyptien," *Revue Internationale de Droit Comparé* 17 (1965), p. 839; C. A. Eccel, *Egypt, Islam and Social Change: Al-Azhar in Conflict and Accommodation* (Berlin: K. Schwarz, 1984); I. Gershoni, J. Jankowski, *Egypt, Islam, and the Arabs: The Search*

political history, which dominated the study of Egypt for years, naturally emphasized constitutional and criminal law, which it generally perceived as a tool for domination by colonialism or of one social class by another. The developments in the Egyptian court system were also usually perceived as part of the broader political context of the relations between Egypt and the British occupiers, other foreign powers or foreigners resident in Egypt. This research perspective overlooked civil law in Egypt, which was perceived as relating not to the collective political, national and social developments in the country, but rather to personal and a-historical relations between individuals.

This book argues that legal and social research has hitherto failed to reveal one of the most comprehensive reforms of modern Egyptian and Arab law—the New Egyptian Civil Code (*al-Qānūn al-Madanī*) of 1949, with its 1149 articles (hereinafter referred to as the New Code). This work embodied a codification of all spheres of the civil life of Egyptians—property, contracts and damages, but excluding the laws of personal status. Accordingly, this book will attempt to grant the New Code its proper place in historical, social and legal discourse, and to anchor it in the context of the social, economic and legal transformations evidenced in Egypt during the 1930s and 1940s, drawing on this background to learn more about the Code, and vice versa. Accordingly, this book perceives the Code not as a closed law book isolated from its environment, as it has hitherto generally been presented by Western research, but rather as part of the social discourse and historical context of its period.

This study will attempt to show that the New Code, as the product of the sometimes Utopian philosophy of ʿAbd al-Razzāq al-Sanhūrī, was consciously formulated on the foundation of a firm and comprehensive

---

for Egyptian Nationhood, 1900–1930 (Oxford: Oxford University Press, 1986); I. Gershoni, J. Jankowski, *Redefining the Egyptian Nation, 1930–1945* (Cambridge: Cambridge University Press, 1995); E. Hill, *Al-Sanhuri and Islamic Law*, Cairo Papers in Social Science, Vol. 10 Monograph 1 (Cairo: The American University in Cairo Press, 1987); E. Hill, *Mahkama! Studies in the Egyptian Legal System, Courts & Crimes, Law & Society* (London: Ithaca Press, 1979); E. Hill, "Majlis al-Dawla, The administrative Courts of Egypt and Administrative Law", in C. Mallat (ed.) *Islam and Public Law: Classical and Contemporary Studies* (London: Graham & Trotman, 1993), p. 207; M. Hoyle, *Mixed Courts of Egypt* (London: Graham & Trotman, 1991); N. Saleh, "Civil Codes of Arab Countries: the Sanhuri Codes", *Arab Law Quarterly* 8(2) (1993), p. 161; G. Sfeir, *Modernization of the Law in Arab States* (San Francisco, London, Bethesda: Austin and Winfield Publishers, 1998); R. Shaham, *Family and the Courts in Modern Egypt, a Study Based on Decisions by the Sharīʿa Courts, 1900–1955* (Leiden: Brill, 1997); F. J. Ziadeh, *Lawyers, the Rule of Law and Liberalism in Modern Egypt* (Stanford, Calif.: Hoover Institution, 1968).

social perception relating to the unique environment and absorptive capacity of Egyptian society, and with the goal of engendering a change in the values embodied in the social structure of the Egyptian collective: introducing a new dimension of value-based morality in Egyptian law and social structure; encouraging at one and the same time both the weak and the strong; and promoting legal and social mobility in the apparently stagnant environment of polarized Egyptian society. This is a Code that sought to narrow social gaps, while at the same time motivating the economy through legislation; a civil code that dreams of a new and better Egyptian society.

Can we learn from this Code, with its varied forms of interpretation, and from Egyptian law in general, about the Egyptian society, politics and history of the period? R. Dworkin would answer this question in the affirmative. In his article "Law as Interpretation" he wrote:

> ...Legal practice is an exercise in interpretation not only when lawyers interpret particular documents or statutes, but generally. Law so conceived is deeply, thoroughly political. Lawyers and judges cannot avoid politics in the broad sense of political theory. But law is not a matter of personal or partisan politics, and a critique of law that does not understand this difference will provide poor understanding and even poorer guidance. I propose that we can improve our understanding of law by comparing legal interpretation with interpretation in other fields of knowledge, particularly literature. I also expect that law, when better understood, will provide a better grasp of what interpretation is in general...
>
> Law is a political enterprise, whose general point, if it has one, lies in coordinating social and individual effort, or resolving social and individual disputes, or securing justice between citizens and between them and their government, or some combination of these...so an interpretation of any body or division of law, like the law of accidents, must show the value of that body of law in political terms by demonstrating the best principle or policy it can be taken to serve.[3]

I should note that several methodological interdisciplinary considerations guided me in writing this book, along the juncture between law, society and history.

The first and most immediate context is the need to integrate law and society. In recent years research of Arab and Islamic law from a social perspective has blossomed. According to this approach, technical legal research confined to the letter of the law is inadequate for understanding

---

[3] R. Dworkin, "Law as Interpretation", *Texas Law Review* 60(1982), pp. 527–530.

the essence of law. Rather, the canvas must be broadened to include the political arena, power struggles between different social groups, cultural trends and long-term historical and economic processes. Cotterell offered the following comments on the sociological perception of law, by way of an introduction; we shall elaborate on this aspect below:

> The numerous approaches to legal analysis which can be categorized as sociological in the broadest sense are unified only by their deliberate self-distancing from the professional viewpoint of the lawyer. It is implicit in the aim of empirical legal theory that law is always viewed "from the outside," from the perspective of an observer of legal institutions, doctrine and behavior, rather than that of a participant, although participants' perception may be taken into account as data for the observer. Indeed from a phenomenological standpoint the interpretation of participants' perception may be of primary importance. Yet that interpretation becomes possible only through a scientific distancing as determined and thoroughgoing as the empathy which the observer (or, better, encounterer) may seek with the observed (or encountered). Sociological analysis of law has as its sole unifying objective the attempt to remedy the assumed inadequacy of lawyers' doctrinal analysis of law.[4]

Another discipline from the family of the sociology of law that influenced the writing of this book is the anthropological analysis of law, which examines the relationship between human behavior and law, emphasizing, among other aspects, the social and legal meanings of custom and of fixed and changing modes of behavior. The well-known anthropologist L. L. Fuller even argued that without understanding the law of custom, which he termed "a language of interactions," it is impossible to understand 'regular' law:

> Law provides a framework for the citizen within which to live his own life, though, to be sure, there are circumstances under which that framework can seem so uncomfortably lax or so perversely constrictive that its human object may believe that straightforward managerial direction would be preferable.
>
> If we accept the view that the central purpose of law is to furnish base lines for human interaction, it then becomes apparent why the existence of enacted law as an effective functioning system depends upon the establishment of stable itneractional expectancies between lawgiver and subject. On one hand, the lawgiver must be able to anticipate that the citizenry as a whole will accept as law and generally observe the body of

[4] R. Cotterell, "The Sociological Concept of Law", *Journal of Law and Society* 10(1983) p. 242.

> rules he has promulgated. On the other hand, the legal subject must be able to anticipate that government will itself abide by its own declared rules when it comes to judge his actions, as in deciding, for example whether he has committed a crime or claims property under a valid deed. A gross failure in the realization of either of these anticipations—of government toward citizen and of citizen toward government—can have the result that the most carefully drafted code will fail to become a functioning system of law.[5]

This approach will attempt, for example, to examine the relationship between law, including imported Western law, and the local society. Turkey and Japan, which imported Western law as a means for modernization, are just two of the many examples of this process. In the context of this book, an interesting example is the approach by the Ethiopian government to the renowned French legal scholar René David to draft a new civil code. David performed his task without even visiting Ethiopia, and his efforts proved unsuccessful. Beckstrom found that the Code was circumvented by most of the population, and that its rejection was due to the presence of traditional means of resolving disputes, existing social institutions, the absence of a developed communications system and a high rate of illiteracy. The code itself proclaimed the annulment of "all rules, whether written or custom, that applied prior to the enactment of the law relating to the matters addressed by this code." Perhaps naively, David argued in his defense that his law was not to be applied immediately to the entire country, and that it was only a matter of time before it would come to represent the Ethiopian legal system in the way that the *Code Civil* represented the French legal system. Friedman commented on this approach that the Napoleonic Code teaches us about current law in France in the same manner as the opera Aida teaches us about Egypt.[6]

Two contrasting theoretical approaches may be seen within this sub-discipline of the anthropology of law. The first approach is based on the interpretative theoretical framework as presented by Clifford Geertz, which sees the legal arena as a reflection of the fabric of cultural significances and symbols shared by all members of society.

[5] L. L. Fuller, "Human Interaction and the Law", *American Journal of Jurisprudence* 14(1969), p. 24.

[6] Lord Lloyd of Hampstead, M. D. A. Freeman, *Lloyd's Introduction to Jurisprudence* (London: Stevens) 1985, p. 883.

L. Rosen's book on law as culture in Muslim society is a prime example of this type of analysis. The second trend tends to see the legal arena as one of contest, and the legal system as a whole as the product of power struggles between different social groups. A classic example of this approach is the sub-discipline of 'Legal Pluralism',[7] but one may criticize both approaches as partial. The former approach is a-historical, transforming culture into the sole point of reference, and lacking the capacity to locate overlapping legal systems or identify structural conflicts. The latter approach, by contrast, dismisses culture; rather than attempting to reveal the cultural significance that underlies the legal system, researchers following this approach attempt to locate and define asymmetrical power relationships that characterize the nature of the legal system. Power struggles between occupiers and occupied, between those who hold the means of production and those who lack these means, between women and men and between different social classes are credited with the development of hegemonic legal culture. It may be argued that the latter approach overemphasizes the law of custom as a means for consolidating a unique identity in the face of the state, or for opposing colonial occupation.

A further criticism, based in part on the lessons of the New Egyptian Code, the subject of this book, may be added regarding this sub-discipline of the anthropology of law in the context of these two interpretative approaches. The argument that law must be examined within the overall context of society, economy and culture is virtually self-evident. Impressive advances in research mean that it is barely possible any more to examine law as a technical structure operating in a social vacuum or independently of its society, surroundings, values and history.

---

[7] C. Geertz, *Local Knowledge*, (New York: Basic Books Publishers, 1983); L. Rosen, *The Anthropology of Justice: Law as Culture in Islamic Society*, (Cambridge: Cambridge University Press, 1989). On 'Legal Pluralism' and its applications regarding Egypt and other developing societies: J. Griffith, "What is Legal Pluralism", *Journal of Legal Pluralism* (1986), p. 1; S. Engle Merry, "Legal Pluralism", *Law and Society Review* 22(1988), p. 869; N. Brown, "Law and Imperialism: Egypt in Comparative Perspective", *Law & Society Review* 29(1995), p. 103; J. Schmidhauser, "Power, Legal Imperialism, and Dependency", *Law and Society Review* 23(1989), pp. 857–878; K. Mann, R. Roberts eds., *Law in Colonial Africa* (Portsmouth, N. H.: Heinemann, 1991); B. S. Cohn, "Law and the Colonial State in India", in J. Starr and J. Collier eds. *History and Power in the Study of Law* (Ithaca, N.Y.: Cornell University Press, 1989); A. C. Christelow, *Muslim Law Courts and the French Colonial State in Algeria* (Princeton: Princeton University Press, 1985); D. S. Powers, "Orientalism, Colonialism, and Legal History: The Attack on Muslim Family Endowments in Algeria and India", *Comparative Studies in Society and History* 31(1989), pp. 535–571.

At the same time, however, the anthropological approach to law seems to have moved too far in the opposite direction; rather than examining law, it observes it. The principal tool of this approach is the field study, which led Laurence Rosen to sit in a court of a small town in the Atlas Mountains of Morocco. Such a research pays little attention to the law *per se*, preferring to observe (a charged word in its own right) the occurrences in the corridors and courtrooms as an anthropological event. It might be argued that just as it is difficult to accept the scrutiny of law without reference to society and culture, so it is difficult to accept the scrutiny of society and culture without reference to legal norms, statutes and case law. The combination of both approaches would seem to offer the desired result: what is law, who are its authorized producers, what are its desired methods, what principles guide its application, and what is its desirable scope? In the absence of this approach, the results may in any case be artificial and even distorted.

By way of illustration, we shall take the Egyptian Civil Code of 1949—the subject of this book. To date, this Code has been examined exclusively by what one may refer to as the 'legal technician' approach, i.e. through a formalistic and closed examination of the contract, land and property laws included in the Code, thus sealing its fate as a formalistic and eclectic code. None of the researchers has to date addressed the rich social expanse embodied in the Code, nor the changes it sought to introduce—changes that amount to a clear and even utopian vision. Equally, however, it is doubtful whether any observation of the civil courts following the enactment of the Code, or even of the process of drafting the Code, could have lead a scholar from the discipline of the anthropology of law to appreciate the change in values that this Code seeks to engender. One example of this is the place of the Islamic *Shariʿa* in the Code. The technical approach simply recorded an inventory of the number of norms in the Code drawn from the *Shariʿa*, and rested its case thereon. Another approach might have identified the presence of the *Shariʿa* in the Code as the producer of the confrontation between different legal systems. In this book, however, we shall show that the function of the *Shariʿa* in the Code is precisely the opposite, serving a mediating, moderating and connecting role. Rosen's one-dimensional and somewhat crude distinction between East and West, modern and traditional may also obscure a proper understanding of the essence and innovative message of the Code. For example, we shall see how the author of the code, ʿAbd al-Razzāq al-Sanhūrī, used time-honored legal tools such as the institution of the *ḥikr* or the rules for distributing estates in order to promote progress and economic innovation.

If this research encounters a potential minefield with regard to the relationship that emerges between legal and social methodology, the same phenomenon returns in the distance created between legal and historical research—a distance that is almost physical, since, relative to the former instance, the disciplines here are further apart.

It is against this background that we can appreciate D. Sugarman's comments on this 'hybrid enterprise' on the borderlines of law and history:

> The history of law and society is a hybrid enterprise, situated on the borderlines of law, history and the human sciences. It is at once a sub-field of the discipline of law and history, and a discrete and foreign territory. Its ambiguous position on the margins of law and history illuminates the indeterminate nature of the boundaries separating law from history. Law and history have always been closely intertwined. History grew out of law, and the development of legal and historical argument and proof were ultimately connected. Both worked in tandem (alongside religion) to construct and to reconstruct an 'imagined community' of national identity and both were leading players in the construction and transmission of the 'meta-narratives' of evolution, liberty and progress. While history and law were interdependent and close cousins, they were also rivals and adversaries... The on-going battle to ensure that historians and lawyers had something to keep to themselves can only be understood in relation to the jurisdictional warfare that each waged against the other and with those other competitors who sought to control their work.[8]

Steve Hedley, who researched Victorian law, noted in this context that in any historical analysis of legal tests, we must always adopt a modest and cautious approach, since what we have before us is a black box regarding which we merely claim to know what the parties truly intended in terms of their own world of concepts and culture and their own period:

> Theory, law and the brute facts of human psychology combine to limit the circumstances in which we can truly know what others intend. It is not an accident when other values creep in. It is a black box, the content of which we cannot observe directly... in doing so we do not, of course, build up a picture of what the judges 'really thought' about the case in front of them... Perhaps the judge had only a vague yet powerful sense of how the case should go; perhaps they were as much strangers to themselves as they are to us. I do not see that it is possible, on such a point,

[8] D. Sugarman (ed.) *Law in History: Histories of Law and Society*, Vol. 1 (Aldershot: Dartmouth, 1996), Introduction, xiii–xiv.

> to go beyond informed guesswork. But we can hope that our guesses will become more and more informed as we proceed.[9]

A holistic research approach employed in this book is the Historical Analysis of Law. Legal historian Markus Dirk Dubber outlined the borders of this approach to legal research, defining it as one that researches the appearance of legal practices, assessing their development, and, in particular, their legitimacy. As one of the forms of legal research, and in common with the philosophical, economic, sociological or psychological approaches, "it is not history for its own sake, but rather history with a point".

> Historical analysis seeks to understand principles and practices in their relation to other principles and practices. Rather than rushing to socially embed ideas, historical analysis first identified and clarified the ideas to be embedded. Instead of privileging one strand of, say, sociological theory, historical analysis moves freely among disciplines. For example, it might use the philosopher's tools to help locate a particular principle both internally, within a given system of ideas, and externally, within the evolution and succession of ideas, then proceed to analyze the principle from some sociological, psychological, or economic perspective, as the availability of evidence permits... It seeks analysis, not illustration.[10]

He added that this is not the history of jurists, but rather a purposeful, dissected analysis in which the legal text is a means for securing the goal, and not the goal itself. This is a perception that departs from the narrow approach that might be dubbed 'the history of jurists' in order to reach broader conclusions. By way of example, Dubber noted the enormous contribution, in his opinion, made by Foucault, as someone who not only examined the motives behind the enlightened reforms of punishment, but explained the associations between these reforms and their application and the establishment of the modern state.

Thus it emerges that by virtue of its very purpose, a historical analysis of law must be interdisciplinary. Moreover:

> Instead of reducing legal life in its myriad manifestations to the playground of recent (and not so recent) trends in other disciplines, critical analysis of law presses these disciplines into the service of understanding and critiquing legal practices. In this way, critical analysis of law, historical and

---

[9] S. Hedly, "Superior Knowledge or Revolution: An Approach to Modern Legal History", *Anglo-American Law Review* 18 (1989), pp. 199–200.

[10] M. D. Dubber, "Historical Analysis of Law", *Law and History Review* 16(1998) pp. 160–161.

> otherwise, helps reconstitute law as the paradigmatic practical discipline, and thereby makes truly interdisciplinary exchange possible.[11]

The arena of Anglo-American law has seen the emergence of the discipline of Legal History, which links history and law. The research of law in the Arab world, by contrast, has not seen any rapprochement between these two distinct discourses. The disconnection is two-fold—between Western and Eastern research on these subjects, and between the historical and legal disciplines. If a jurist analyzes a Middle Eastern situation, his analysis will usually be formalistic and ahistorical in nature; conversely, an historian will analyze a legal issue without reference to professional juridical sources. In both cases, the analysis comes up short.

As I traveled the twilight zone between these two disciplines, I considered to what extent I should include legal doctrines and theories in my study, since these will clearly be unfamiliar to those who are not legal experts. The conclusion I formed was that these legal elements are necessary in order to prove the research thesis. If my study seeks to situate the New Code in its historical context, these legal elements themselves become raw historical material for the future use of historians. Thus law and history develop a relationship of mutual significance: the legal becomes historical and the historical legal, since it is difficult to understand legal changes without an acquaintance with their sometimes covert historical or social causes.

2. A Code as a Legal Narrative

Legal discourse has generally refrained from narratology and narrative reporting techniques. Considered ambiguous, vague and imprecise, narrative has been rejected by legal discourse due to the desire of law to root itself in the world of scientific authority.[12] This approach created a gulf between historical and legal research that must be addressed by interdisciplinary research.

---

[11] Ibid., 162.

[12] P. Ewick, S. Silbey, "Subversive Stories and Hegemonic Tales: Toward a Sociology of Narrative", *Law and Society Review* 29(2) (1995), p. 198. On the legal narrative see: R. A. Posner, "Legal Narratology Law's Stories: Narrative and Rhetoric in the Law" *University of Chicago Law Review* 64(1997) pp. 737–748.

This rejection should not be taken to imply that legal discourse does not create narratives; however, these are subject to the strict internal rules that dominate the legal sphere, and they may still be considered ahistorical by the historian. These rules are based on the belief that the most precise and reliable method for recognizing reality and discovering truth depends on the ability of the jurist to extract and isolate the simplest and clearest elements that comprise a given phenomenon within the chaotic and undistinguished flood of events, and to repackage them within given categories and in clear and distinct capsules of time and space. This legal language, in brief, acts to dismantle processes and free events in moulds that may be examined through the objective eye of the jurist.

While this narrative is usually ahistorical and asociological, this study will attempt to yield the opposite of the storytelling that has hitherto been the product of the New Egyptian Code: purely formalistic narratives, since this is how the Code has been seen to date by researchers, jurists and historians alike. Instead, for example, of extracting and isolating laws relating to a given topic, this study will consolidate the Code, viewing it as a coherent entity with a firm social message: to seek to establish a new Egypt characterized by solidarity, harmony and progress. Thus, as we shall see below, the inherent vision embodied in the Civil Code becomes a narrative.

Yet, is this possible? Is it viable to address a legal code, with its articles and sub-articles, its sections and chapters, even if it proclaims its social intentions, as a story?

A review of the literature published in recent years on the subject of narrative will be at a loss to find a single, exhaustive definition of this concept. However, several basic characteristics seem to be required of a given statement in order for it to be considered narrative:

Selective expropriation of events—selective, since any narrative is inevitably the product of a selective choice of certain events and the rejection of others. In our case, the event might be the process of enactment, or it might be a given legal article in the Code that embodies a particularly social, legal or other philosophy. A legal article itself might be seen as a narrative sequence or as an event. Thus, for example, Articles 859–862 in the Code, which address relations between the upper and lower floors in an apartment building, might be seen as a symbolic description of the desired relations between the upper and lower social strata in the country, with the voluntary and involuntary solidarity that must exist between these strata. Another example is the social arena of the doctrine of the abuse of a right as embodied in the New Code. Thousands of additional examples could be found in the Code, combining like a multidimensional puzzle to form a narrative statement.

Closure—the series of events described in the narrative must be sequenced chronologically and presented as a story with beginning, middle and end. In terms of the present study, the vision in the Code has an emerging chronological sequence: the description of the structure of the legal and social engineering in the Code has a beginning and an end, since were this not the case, the mechanism developed therein would not have functioned successfully, as I argue is the case. The Code began by establishing its two basic pillars, intended to prevent excessive social polarization: the restriction of property rights, on the one hand, and the protection of weak members of society, on the other. Only after these were in place did the Code establish its third pillar: advancing society, its future and its economy, by encouraging the stronger elements in society. Lastly, after these pillars are in place, the mechanism is created that will coordinate between all three, and between them and society: a principle I referred to above as *murūna*, i.e. legal flexibility, and the authority of the court to activate successfully this formula for social order.

Causal relationship—Lastly, the events described in the narrative must be connected by a causal relationship around a particular idea, figure or institution; again, we return to the vision that permeates the Code.

Does not the narrative I seek to outline in this book amount to a specific interpretative approach in reading the Code? Might it not even constitute an artistic or literary interpretation as discussed by Dworkin? Dworkin himself would probably answer in the affirmative, arguing that although law is not art, the science of law could do well to learn some of the developed interpretative approaches from the field of literature and art.

> I say, that a literary interpretation aims to show how the work in question can be seen as the most valuable work of art, and so must attend to formal feature of identity, coherence, and integrity as well as more substantive considerations of artistic value.[13]

[13] Lloyd's Introduction to Jurisprudence, pp. 1216–1217.

3. Existing Theses to be Addressed by This Book

Two narratives have become entrenched in the historical and legal research relating to the New Egyptian Code—the second-most important act of legislation after the Constitution—since it was enacted in October 1949.[14] The first described it as an eclectic, technical code bereft of legal or conceptual homogeneity. The fact that some twenty civil codes from East and West, alongside local case law and the Islamic *Shariʿa*, served as sources for the New Egyptian Code was the object of some ridicule from certain Western scholars. Norman Anderson, one of the most important researchers of law in the Arab world commented that "several principles and provisions [were absorbed into] the New Egyptian Code from the civil code of other countries, such as Germany, Italy *and even Japan*" (emphasis added—G. B.), implying that legal uniformity and harmony are impossible with such a range of alien legal methods.[15]

The second narrative argues that the New Code was not creative or innovative, but rather continued the legal tradition of its antecedents, the Mixed and the *ʾAhlī*, civil code without any substantive changes. As G. Sfeir wrote:

> It was more important... that the new code continue the legal tradition established by its predecessor. The new code could therefore do no more than improve on the old one which through decades of application and interpretation by the Egyptian courts had become domesticated and detached from its French origin.[16]

This approach was current not only among foreign researchers, but also in Egyptian research. In his book *The Sources of Obligation* (*Masādir al-ʾIltizām*), the Egyptian jurist Dr. ʿAbd al-Munʿim al-Ṣada wrote about the New Civil Code:

[14] On the Egyptian legal system see: Laṭīfa Muḥammad Sālim, *Al-Niẓām al-Qaḍʾi al-Miṣrī al-Ḥadith, 1875–1914* (Cairo: Markaz al-Dirāsāt al-Siyāsiyya wa al-ʾIstrātijiyya bil-ʾAhrām, 1982), pp. 29–53, 113–124; Shafīq Shiḥata, *Taʾrīkh Ḥarakat al-Tajdīd fī al-Nuẓum al-Qānūniyya fī Miṣr* (Cairo: Dār ʾIḥyāʾ al-Kutub al-ʿArabiyy, 1961), pp. 64–75; Al-Kitāb al-Dhahabī.

[15] On the claim that the Code has been eclectic and inconsistent: N. Brown, "*Sharīʿa* and State in the Modern Muslim Middle East", *International Journal of Middle East Studies* 29 (1997), pp. 359–376, 371; N. Anderson, *Law Reform in the Muslim World* (London: University of London, 1976), pp. 88–89; E. Hill, *Al-Sanhuri and Islamic Law*, p. 69.

[16] G. Sfeir, *Modernization of the Law in Arab States* (San Francisco, London, Bethesda: Austin and Winfield Publishers, 1998), p. 95.

> The legislature did not intend to alter the legal tradition that had taken root in the country, [but rather] to advance social and legal development without a sudden or exaggerated turn.[17]

The Egyptian legal historian Dr. Latīfa Sālim also presented a formalistic view of the New Code; the social purpose I propose here is completely absent from her essay.[18] The only scholar who hinted that the Code was one of change rather than continuity was the renowned Egyptian jurist Shafīq Shiḥāta, a peripheral participant in part of the process of drafting the Code.[19]

The old Egyptian Mixed Code was the subject of intense fascination among researchers in the West in the early twentieth century, it was drafted in French, and was thus perceived as the 'code of the foreigners' who settled in Egypt, and was addressed by Western attorneys who also lived in the country. By contrast, the New Code, that was drafted in Arabic, was dismissed to the margins of Western research, and even encountered a hostile reaction. It was perceived as abolishing the glory of the Mixed Egyptian Code (modeled on the magnificent *Code Civil!*), and was categorized as an offensive act of Egyptian nationalism that sought to nullify the 'contribution' of the West and the foreign presence in Egypt—a sin that could not easily be forgiven.

The British legal adviser to the Egyptian government (effectively the British legal inspector), Sir Maurice Amos, commented regarding the Mixed Courts, which ruled in accordance with the Mixed Egyptian Code, that:

> I have often taken occasion to remark that next to the Church, the Mixed Courts are the most successful international institute in history.[20]

An American judge of these Mixed Courts, J. Y. Brinton, lamented the passing of the Mixed Courts and the subsequent enactment of new laws:

> The Mixed Courts came to an end at midnight on October 14, 1949. On the morning of the fifteenth, Egypt awakened to the fact—incredible though it might seem—that the institution which for three-quarters

[17] (Cairo: Dār al-Nahḍa al-ʿArābiyya, 1991), p. 5.
[18] Laṭifa Muḥammad Sālim, *Al-Niẓām al-Qaḍāʾī al-Miṣrī al-Ḥadith*, 1875–1914, pp. 402–408.
[19] Shafīq Chiḥata, *Taʾrīkh Ḥarakat al-Tajdīd fī al-Nuẓum al-Qānūniyya fī Miṣr*, p. 67.
[20] Brinton, p. xv.

> of a century had dominated the judicial life of the country had ceased to exist... Thus came to an end an institution which had played a commanding role in the history of modern Egypt. It had brought order out of chaos... The promulgation, as of the date of the closing of the Mixed Courts, of an entirely new Civil Code began to destroy the value of judicial precedents which they had established... To this was added the complete and sudden abandonment of the use of the French language.[21]

Moreover, since its publication and through to the present day, the main focus of attention to the New Code among Western researchers has been the extent of its affinity to Islamic *Shariʿa*, since most of the researchers who have examined the Code, such as Khadurri, Ziadeh, Anderson and Hill, have been interested in the *Shariʿa* and in the extent to which it has been integrated in modern Arab legislation.[22] Accordingly, this research direction has become entrenched in historiographical legal studies, as if the New Egyptian Code could offer no other research avenues. None of the researchers has examined the sociological ideology of the Code, its international environmental context, or the sociolegal transformations it sought to advance.

Furthermore, mainstream historical literature has tended to portray the Egyptian Parliament, which, during the 1930s and the 1940s, the decades of relevance to this book, was dominated by the large landowners in the country, as impervious to social pressure and as blocking any serious attempts at social or economic reform. Nevertheless, the fact is that both the upper and lower houses of Parliament approved the Civil Code Law, though the members were quite aware of its social intent to protect weaker members of society and restrict property rights. The present analysis may offer a more balanced view of the landowners who sat in Parliament and of their feelings regarding the polarized Egyptian society within which they functioned.

---

[21] Ibid., pp. 208, 210, 211.

[22] J. N. D. Anderson, "The *Sharīʿa* and Civil Law", *Islamic Quarterly* 1(1954), pp. 29–46; J. N. D. Anderson, *Law Reform in the Muslim World* (London: University of London, 1976), pp. 83–100; J. N. D. Anderson, "Law Reform in Egypt: 1850–1950", P. M. Holt ed., *Political and Social Change in Modern Egypt* (Oxford: Oxford University Press, 1968), p. 209; C. Chehata, "Les Survivances Musulmanes dans la Codification du Droit Civil Égyptien", *Revue Internationale de Droit Comparé* 17 (1965), p. 839; M. Khadduri, "From Religious to National Law", R. N. Anshen ed. *Mid-East: World Center, Yesterday, Today and Tomorrow* (New York: Harper, 1956), pp. 220–234; F. Ziadeh, *Lawyers, the Rule of Law and Liberalism in Modern Egypt* pp. 99–147; *Law of Property in the Arab World: Real Rights in Egypt, Iraq, Jordan, Lebanon and Syria* (London: Graham and Trotman, 1978); G. Sfeir, *Modernization of the Law in Arab States*; E. Hill, *Al-Sanhuri and Islamic Law*.

Lastly, research of Egyptian 'law' in the West has hitherto focused mainly on its public-constitutional and criminal aspects. The present study will reveal the intensive developments in the field of civil law, clarifying the relevance of these developments for an appreciation of Egyptian society, and expanding, it is to be hoped, legal, historical and social discourse on this subject.

As Morton Horwitz and others have shown with regard to Anglo-American law, private civil law can depart from the attempt to perform justice between two individuals and become perceived as the emissary of social policy.[23] When this happens, those responsible for shaping private law (in that case, primarily the courts) may come to adopt an instrumentalist approach to law, seeking to improve commercial life, promote public well-being and social interests, and shape the social character of the state. Such law may therefore also become a flagship for morality, justice or, as in our case—the desire to establish a new *modus vivendi* within Egyptian society.

The question remains as to why discourse relating to the research of Egyptian law has not hitherto addressed civil law. Perhaps such an examination requires a level of legal specialization that is not usually found among historians or sociologists. Without an acquaintance with the processes undergone by private law in France and Egypt, it is difficult to identify this social and utopian aspiration to forge a different Egyptian collective.

4. Methodology: The Concealed Code

In my attempt to identify the covert purpose behind the Code, I drew on two methodological stages according to the mentioned Historical Analysis of Law: the stage of deconstruction and the stage of construction and reconstruction. In the deconstruction stage, I gathered, in no particular order, the articles and legal principles which, in my opinion, constituted innovations in the New Code by comparison to its predecessors, the old Codes. In so doing, I divorced these articles and norms from the existing structure of the formal New Code, in an

[23] M. Horwitz, *The Transformation of American Law 1780–1860*, (Cambridge, Mass.: Harvard University Press, 1977); M. Horwitz, *The Transformation of American Law, 1870–1960, The Crisis of Legal Orthodoxy*, (New York: Oxford University Press, 1992).

effort to connect them to new common denominators according to my broad impression of the social goals of the Code. An initial impression of the social ideas and thought process of the author of the Code was provided by a review of Sanhūrī's diaries, which were not intended for publication, but which were published (in part) in Cairo by his daughter seventeen years after his death.[24] The diaries emphasized the importance Sanhūrī attached to achieving social justice by favoring the weak and poor in Egyptian society; his dissatisfaction with the excessive social polarization of his country; and his consistent search for pragmatic limits in Egyptian society to avoid its ultimate dissolution into its various social and economic components—all this without changing the basic existing social order. In January 1949, Sanhūrī wrote:

> The social problem in Egypt is not how to take from the rich in order to give to the poor, but how to raise the standard of living of all, since the average individual income in Egypt is so low as to be inconceivable.

In February 1950, he added:

> Exploitation and arbitrariness on the part of the rulers brings only the humiliation of the ruled. If such a ruled person gathers the courage to fight exploitation and arbitrariness, he will prefer to suffer in his struggle rather than suffer from tyranny."[25]

After these initial guiding impressions, to which I added the Western legal, and more particularly sociological, ideologies that influences Sanhūrī, I proceeded to an examination of the collections of the preparatory processes behind the inception and formulation of the New Code (*al-Qānūn al-Madanī, Majmūʿat al-Aʿmāl al-Taḥḍīriyya*). These collections include the different drafts of the New Code, the legal origins and sources of each article, the explanatory comments for the original draft of the New Code, and protocols of the debates on the subject in both houses of parliament—particularly the deliberations of the Civil Code Committee in the Senate (*Majlis al-Shuyūḥ*).[26] These collections also include the protocols of special symposia held to discuss the drafting

---

[24] Nādya al-Sanhūrī and Tawfīq al-Shāwī (eds.), *ʿAbd al-Razzāq al-Sanhūrī min Ḥilāl ʾAwrāqihi al-Shakhṣiyya* (Cairo: al-Zahrāʾ lil-ʿAllam al-ʿArabi, 1988). ʿAbd al-Razzāq al-Sanhūrī kept a diary for some 50 years. Apparently, the diary was shortened and only sections of it were published by his daughter.

[25] Diary, pp. 218, 264, 273 (respectively).

[26] Egyptian Government, Ministry of Justice, *Al-Qānūn al-Madani, Majmūʿat al-ʾAʿmāl al-Taḥḍiriyya* (Cairo: Maṭbʿat al-Kitāb al-ʿArabī, 1949).

of the New Civil Code, and attended by senior jurists, as well as social and religious figures. At this stage I also had access to the twelve extensive volumes of the interpretation of the Code, written by Sanhūrī between 1952 and 1970 (*al-Wasīṭ fī Sharḥ al-Qānūn al-Madanī* and its abstract, *al-Wajīz fī Sharḥ al-Qānūn al-Madanī*).[27] The protocols of the parliamentary committee, the explanatory comments on the proposed Code and the interpretation of the Code do not include any structured presentation of its social goals; these must sometimes be extrapolated from between the lines, or composed puzzle-fashion by interpreting the different articles. An additional element were the doctrines and legal schools, which were described in detail in the interpretations and explanatory comments, albeit according to the formal structure of the Code rather than on the basis of the social goals I was seeking.

The review of these sources, alongside the articles of the Code itself, was intended to confirm my impression that the legal text seeks to implement the social goals presented in Sanhūrī's social and political writings. Once I was indeed able to confirm this hypothesis, the stage of reconstruction began. This entailed an attempt to determine why specific legal doctrines or norms in the Code were chosen, to identify their social purpose, and to reconstruct these considerations as a coherent entity. The social considerations of the Code gradually became clear. Ultimately it was possible to collect these together in a consolidated conceptual structure, thus revealing what might be termed 'the concealed Code'. This network of considerations thus became a cipher guiding the formal Code. Those holding this cipher could appreciate why the Code drew given norms or doctrines from a particular legal system, and hence realize that what we find in the Code is not discordant eclecticism, but a substantive and deliberate choice drawing primarily from Continental European law, but also from Islamic law, from the Egyptian case law preceding the Code, and from what are perceived as positive and appropriate elements from the old *ʾAhlī* code (I indeed found that the New Code sometimes drew on articles from its predecessor; however, these were revitalized and reinterpreted)[28]—all

---

[27] ʿAbd al-Razzāq al-Sanhūrī, *Al-Wasīṭ fī Sharḥ al-Qānūn al-Madanī al-Jadīd* (Cairo: Dār al-Nahḍa al-ʿArabiyya, 1996 (hereinafter: Al-Wasīṭ); ʿAbd al-Razzāq Al-Sanhūrī, *Al-Wajīz fī Sharḥ al-Qānūn al-Madanī al-Jadīd* (Cairo: Dār al-Nahḍa al-ʿArabiyya, 1997) (Hereinafter: Al-Wajīz).

[28] A prominent example of this is the *ʿUluww wal-sufl*—the upper floor and lower floor of one building, which became an allegory for the required social solidarity in Egyptian society, see chapter 3.

this with the goal of advancing desired social and economic goals. This approach may also offer an answer to a question that has concerned scholars for many years: why did the Code draw certain norms from the *Shari'a*, but not others?

In the complex act of constructing the New Code, Sanhūrī applied a legal theory known as 'Social Engineering', which argues that the function of the jurist resembles that of the engineer: to establish a fictional structure meeting social needs and having the external appearance of a harmonious entity. The term 'engineering' also implies that, like the engineer, the jurist must calculate the social and legal elements that will be used to establish the structure, and plan these elements before construction commences, if the structure is to endure.[29] This also explains why I felt the need to include in the book graphical descriptions, which sometimes have an engineering appearance, in an effort to explain some of the technical models employed in this act of sociolegal engineering.

In constructing the social theories, I paid close attention to *al-Wasīṭ fī Sharḥ al-Qānūn al-Madanī*, the work that establishes the legal norms in terms of the desirable interpretation of the New Civil Code. *Al-Wasīṭ* was composed in somewhat unfortunate circumstances, as we shall see below. Interestingly, this source has remained largely unexplored by most Western scholars. "The world does not know about these works (*Al-wasīṭ*), and few in Egypt indicate that they realize, other than in very general terms, what they comprehend," noted Enid Hill in her legal biography of Sanhūrī. Yet even Hill, despite her awareness of the importance of this work by Sanhūrī, did not actually examine it.[30] A scholar working in the West who did address *Al-Wasīṭ* was Farhat Ziadeh, though his attention was confined to the field of land law, and he did not examine the Code as a whole or its social dimensions—dimensions that were particularly evident in the realm of property law, the area researched by Ziadeh.[31]

Although I considered beginning this book with a summary of the essence of the Code before entering into a detailed description, I have preferred to allow the reader to encounter the vision as I did—gradually

[29] On the Theory of 'Social Engineering' see Wujūb p. 65; in general: Lloyd's Introduction to Jurisprudence pp. 565–568.

[30] Hill, Al-Sanhuri and Islamic Law p. 115.

[31] F. Ziadeh, *Property Law in the Arab World: Real Rights in Egypt, Iraq, Jordan, Lebanon and Syria* (London: Graham and Trotman, 1978).

and stage by stage, intensifying the experience of discovery. Accordingly, just as this study seeks to examine the Code in a holistic manner, so, too, should this book be read. Only on its completion will the reader see the whole picture.

In an ideological and historiographical world in which the hierarchy of sources cannot be taken for granted, and in which it is apparent that an archival document does not necessarily represent reality more faithfully than other sources, I drew broadly from the primary and secondary sources at my disposal. Quotes from the Code may be used as primary material, as a source for interpretation or as a metaphor. Sanhūrī's highly personal diaries are no less important than the learned discussions of the members of parliament about the Code, and so on.

Sanhūrī himself argued that neither realistic nor imaginary thought was sufficient on its own; only a combination of the two, he posited, offered the correct approach.[32] Adhering to this position, I have begun each chapter with a selection of quotes from Sanhūrī's writings. These quotes generally reflect the idea that finds its legal manifestation in the content of the chapter. Through this technique, I have attempted to create an internal dialogue between Sanhūrī the thinker and Sanhūrī the lawmaker; accordingly, these quotes form an integral part of each chapter.

[32] Diary, 3 February 1949, p. 256.

CHAPTER ONE

LAW AS REMEDY

Today is July 14th, Bastille Day for the French, and in the streets of Greater Cairo I saw the splendid decorations the French customarily go up each year in honor of the storming of the Bastille... Yet, as an Egyptian, I felt like a stranger among these decorations, although they are placed in the center of my own country. I felt tears flow from my eyes. I passed one decoration bearing the legend 'Vive la France!' and tried to whisper to myself "Vive l'Egypte," but could not bring myself to do so. I recalled that Egypt is not alive today; it is dying after its divided and mutually hateful sons have stabbed it through the heart.

Sanhūrī, Diary, 1928[1]

1. 'Egypt is Sick'

There is extensive research literature regarding the process of political and social radicalization that swept Egypt during the period between February 1922, when the country gained its independence, and the coup staged by 'The Free Officers' thirty years later, in July 1952. Some of this literature is biased, due to the influence of the negative portrayal by the revolution of the preceding era; nevertheless, there can be no denying that during the first half of the twentieth century, Egypt underwent dramatic and unprecedented economic, social and political changes, leading to the transformation of Egyptian society.[2]

---

[1] Diary, 14 July 1928, p. 180.

[2] G. Baer, *A History of Landownership in Modern Egypt*, 1800–1950 (Oxford: Oxford University Press, 1962); J. Beinin, Z. Lockman, *Workers on the Nile: Nationalism, Communism, Islam and the Egyptian Working Class, 1882–1954* (Princeton N.J.: Princeton University Press, 1987); J. Berque, *Egypt: Imperialism and Revolution* (London: Faber & Faber, 1972); H. Erlich, *Students and Universities in Twentieth Century Egyptian Politics* (London: F. Cass, 1989); I. Gershoni, J. Jankowski, *Egypt, Islam, and the Arabs: The Search for Egyptian Nationhood, 1900–1930* (Oxford: Oxford University Press, 1986); I. Gershoni, J. Jankowski, *Redefining the Egyptian Nation 1930–1945* (Cambridge: Cambridge University Press, 1995); A. Hourani, *Arabic Thought in the Liberal Age, 1798–1939* (Cambridge: Cambridge University Press, 1983); C. Issawi, *Egypt at Mid Century* (Oxford: Oxford University Press, 1954), p. 258; A. Lutfi al-Sayyid Marsot, *Egypt's Liberal Experiment: 1922–1936* (Berkeley: Berkeley University of California Press, 1977); N. Safran, *Egypt in Search of Political Community:*

Falling cotton prices, Egypt's principal industry (from 17.5 Egyptian pounds per kantar [45 kilograms] in 1918 to six pounds per kantar just two years later),[3] and dramatic population growth (from less than ten million inhabitants in 1900 to over 22 million in 1952) were not balanced by growth in arable land. While the population increased by 67 percent between 1917 and 1947, Arable land increased by just 20 percent in this same period.

These developments led to massive migration from rural areas to the cities in search of work and hope. The result was depressing: The population of Cairo was doubled within twenty years, creating vast, dismal slums and a large social class that was not engaged in productive employment. The standard of living and nutrition fell, poverty was rife, and the gap between rich and poor widened. Over half the peasants had no land or worked as daily hired hands, while the vast majority of those who did own land had less than one *fadān* (one *fadān* equals 0.42 hectares or slightly over an acre)—less than the area needed to feed their families. By contrast, 12,000 large landowners held 37 percent of all land. Before the Second World War, Egyptian society was likened by C. Issawi to an inverted pyramid. The top of the pyramid was occupied by the landowners, who controlled much of the national wealth and enjoyed a privileged status and selfishly exploited their power.[4]

The migrants who flooded to the cities had lived for centuries in a rural social structure. The lack of communal life and moral and social restraints led to the shattering of the personal dreams that had motivated the move to the cities. Hope was replaced by a growing sense of disillusionment, frustration, personal and social malaise and resentment.

Echoing the political malaise afflicting Europe during this period, these years also saw an unstable experiment in parliamentary constitutionalism in Egypt. During the 29 years of this regime, until it was overthrown in the 1952 revolution, ten elections were held, and 38 governments

---

An Analysis of the Intellectual and Political Evolution of Egypt, 1804–1952 (Cambridge, Mass.: Harvard University Press, 1961); R. Tignor, *State Public Enterprise and the Economic Change in Egypt 1918–1952* (Princeton N.J.: Princeton University Press, 1984); S. Shamir, "Liberalism: From Monarchy to Postrevolution", in Shamir ed. *Egypt, from Monarchy to Republic* (Boulder: Westview Press, 1995), p. 195; C. D. Smith, "The Crisis of Orientation: The Shift Of Egyptian Intellectuals to Islamic Subjects in the 1930's", *International Journal of Middle East Studies* 4 (1973), p. 409; M. Winter, "Islam in the State: Pragmatism and Growing Commitment", in S. Shamir ed. *Egypt from Monarchy to Republic*, p. 44.

[3] Bear, Landownership, p. 82.

[4] C. Issawi, *Egypt at Mid Century*, p. 262.

were formed. Only two parliaments completed their term of office (1931–1936, 1945–1950). This political experiment was perceived by many Egyptians as irrelevant to the changing realities of their lives; from here, it was only a short step to the search for alternative political means, generally of a radical and revisionist nature.

Social order in Egypt deteriorated, and the situation was exacerbated by the Second World War, which further eroded religious frameworks, social affiliation, the community and the family.

Safran and others have noted that the millions of foreign soldiers who passed through Egypt led to an erosion of public morality. Well-fed, with money in their pockets and in search of pleasures, and detached from their own social environment, the soldiers created an atmosphere characterized by the motto 'Eat, drink and be merry, for tomorrow we die.' They spread new norms regarding sex, drink and licentiousness that were alien to the Egyptian social climate and offended the moral standards of most Egyptians. Moreover, these sated foreign soldiers aroused the envy of hungry Egyptians, fueling xenophobic emotions. During the war itself, these feelings were assuaged in part by the fact that many Egyptians made a living by providing services for the Allied armies. Immediately after the war, however, 250,000 Egyptians found themselves without employment.[5]

The rampant inflation that was typical of the twentieth century, worsening shortages and a corrupt administration laid the foundation for profiteering in the black market and for financial speculation. The prevailing free-wheeling atmosphere allowed a few to grow very rich at the expense of millions of starving Egyptians, since demand in the country far exceeded supply. As a result, social restraints were weakened still further. The spirit of collective solidarity that had characterized the Egyptian village gave way to growing alienation, epitomized in the colloquial saying *ʾAnā mā lī* ('Why should I care?')[6]

Social polarization continued to increase. The older quarters of the cities were occupied by rural migrants and impoverished city-dwellers living in harsh conditions. Yet the same cities saw the growth of modern quarters with parks, luxurious apartments and villas, and modern means of communication and transport (Heliopolis was an example

[5] Safran, p. 185.

[6] For example: R. Yadlin, "The Seeming Duality: Patterns of Interpersonal Relations in Changing Environment", in S. Shamir ed. *Egypt from Monarchy to Republic*, pp. 151–170.

of such a neighborhood). The middle and upper classes lived in these neighborhoods alongside those who were considered foreigners. Religion and the institution of the family were significantly weakened in these areas.[7] Safran referred to this state of blatant polarization as 'two cities', divided by a gulf of increasing bitterness and hatred. For example, an outbreak of malaria in Upper Egypt led to tens of thousands of deaths in 1943–1945, yet Egyptian society remained unmoved and continued its life undisturbed, although debates were held in parliament on the issue, and this may have formed part of the background to the introduction of a law establishing, for the first time, a minimum wage for agricultural labor. Thousands more Egyptians died in a cholera epidemic that erupted in the south in 1947.[8]

A famous article written by Egyptian author Ṭaha Ḥusayn was entitled 'Egypt is Sick', and described the way Egyptian society responded to the cholera epidemic in the south of the country and the poor neighborhoods of the capital. With the double entendre of its title, the article was a searing indictment of the nation's political and social leaders.

Ḥusayn describes returning from Europe on a ship headed for the port of Alexandria. The sole topic of conversation among the passengers was the cholera outbreak, and the author was convinced that on disembarking, he would find an atmosphere of general concern:

> Yet behold! All the Egyptians I meet are continuing their lives in the manner to which they are accustomed. The epidemic scares them, but does not divert their attention from themselves and their own pleasures...They continue their life as usual: long tongues, small brains and hearts as hard as stone. They feel nothing of all this or they feel but pay no attention, or they feel and pay attention but care only for themselves...[9]

The most virulent manifestation of the bitterness felt by the disadvantaged members of Egyptian society was probably the day that came to be known as 'Black Saturday'. On January 26, 1952, over 7,000 hotels, clubs, restaurants, cinemas and modern offices were systematically looted, destroyed and burned in Cairo within just a matter of hours.

I. Gershoni and J. Jankowski have demonstrated that it was the middle class that had emerged in Egypt during this period—the new *ʾafandiyya*, products of the expanded education system and less Westernized

---

[7] Safran, p. 186.
[8] Ibid., 201.
[9] *Al-Miṣrī*, 30 October, 1947.

than the previous generation—that responded the most strongly to the collapse of social order and the increasingly vocal nationalist calls.[10] Educated, urban and full of expectations, this class suffered from the economic crisis, and the younger generation was pushed cruelly downwards.[11] Middle-class Egyptians were painfully aware of the economic and social woes of their country—a theme that was increasingly examined by the Egyptian press following the abolition of the Capitulation system in 1937 and a heightened focus on internal affairs. This new class was the embodiment of frustration and disillusionment.

The prevailing public atmosphere was pessimistic and hostile toward the leadership. Egyptian politics were perceived as impervious to the growing pressure from below, and cut off from the economic and social worries of the masses. The disappointment with bickering politicians and a monarchy that failed to offer any solutions was easily converted into hatred for the constitutional government in general, and its European roots in particular, as Vaticiutis noted.[12]

The decay of the existing social order created an urgent need to redefine the collective framework of Egypt. Accordingly, the frustration created led to a new political and social phenomenon—the growth of radical extra-parliamentary groups: strong trade unions, Socialist and Communist groups, on the left; the quasi-Fascist 'Young Egypt' (*Miṣr al-Fatāt*) movement on the right, led by ʾAḥmad Ḥusayn, which also spawned a semi-military youth movement known as the 'Green Shirts'; and the militant Islamic Muslim Brotherhood (*al-ʾIkhwān al-Muslimūn*), founded in 1929 by Ḥasan al-Banna.

Among the masses, socioeconomic tension and pressure were channeled mainly in the directions of nationalism and political Islam. As a result of the prevailing dissatisfaction, despair, cynicism and outrage, the Muslim Brotherhood, with their message of the holistic *Shariʿa*, seemed to offer a chance for the hope that the regime and the existing social order could no longer provide. A right-wing nationalism of a strongly xenophobic and zealous character began to surface among the public, enabling extra-parliamentary organizations, and particularly the Muslim Brotherhood, to attract hundreds of thousands of supporters

[10] Redefining, p. 11.
[11] Issawi, p. 262.
[12] *The History of Modern Egypt: from Muhammad Ali to Mubarak* (London: Weidenfeld and Nicolson, 1991), p. XX.

both among the urban poor and among the rural population, whose condition was as wretched as ever.

The Muslim Brotherhood often resorted to violence, political assassination and terror, in addition to instigating a wave of workers' strikes, demonstrations and riots that shook Egypt. The short-lived Egyptian governments seemed helpless in the face of the breakdown of social order. One prime minister, ʾAḥmad Māhir, who was one of the founders of the Saʿadist party (a strong representative of the interests of the landowners, industrialists and leading merchants)[13] alongside Maḥmūd Fahmī al-Nuqrāshi and ʿAbd al-Razzāq al-Sanhūrī, was assassinated in February 1945 after declaring war on Germany and Japan. The assassin, apparently a member of the 'Young Egypt' group, was tried and executed. Following the assassination, Nuqrāshī was appointed prime minister. In 1948, he outlawed the Muslim Brotherhood following their increasingly severe terror attacks. However, he was himself assassinated by the Muslim Brotherhood within less than a month.

This was a society in which collective characteristics and social solidarity had begun to collapse; a society plagued by doubts about its identity, torn between East and West, between secularism and Islam, between liberalism and Fascism, between the temptations of progress and the comforting protection of tradition.

However, as emphasized at the beginning of this chapter, it would be wrong to present a simplistic picture of a society so negative that the revolution of 1952 can be perceived only as an act of redemption.

This was a complex society, one that also saw the emergence of positive economic processes—a growth in manufacturing industries, particularly cotton and textiles, sugar, oil, cement and alcohol, particularly since the Second World War. Established in 1920, Bank Miṣr had helped in the development of an Egyptian-Arab financial system (as distinct from the financial system run by the foreigners who settled in Egypt). Since the outbreak of the Second World War, industrialization had accelerated considerably—a process that continued after the war. A class of industrialists and businessmen began to emerge in an economy with capitalist characteristics. By 1948, Egyptian Arabs held 39 percent of the share capital of the companies that operated in the country, compared to just 9 percent in 1900.

---

[13] More on this Political Party see: M. Deeb, *Party Politics in Egypt: The Wafd & its Rivals, 1919–1939* (London: Ithaca Press, 1979), p. 421.

Yet these positive processes struggled to make headway in an Egyptian society marred by fundamental and complex problems. This situation was described by Tignor as 'development without growth'—there were economic developments, but these were left floating in the stagnant waters of Egyptian society.[14]

2. The Desire for Legal Revision (*Tanqīḥ*)

2.1 *Liberalism*

During the first three decades of the twentieth century, Egyptian society and politics shared a broad common denominator that united the various shades of social and national opinion in the country, and which exerted an influence not only in intellectual circles, but within public discourse as a whole. This common denominator was liberalism, which colored the meeting of East and West in Egypt, the various shades of national revival, the institutions of power, economy and society.

There are disagreements among historians as to the year in which liberal discourse ceased to dominate Egyptian society, before anti-liberal forces such as the 'Muslim Brotherhood' and 'Young Egypt' as discussed above emerged on the social and political arena. The late 1930s are usually considered the twilight years of Egyptian liberalism, and as the point after which alternative nationalist and Islamicist theories expounded by those who challenged the pro-Western liberal approach began to move toward center stage. The research is also divided regarding the end of the era of liberalism. N. Safran placed this occurrence at the end of the Second World War; A. Hourani proposed 1936, as did A. Lutfī al-Sayyid Marsot; while P. J. Vatikiotis simply stated that it came during the 1930s. The different dates are of no special consequence in terms of this book, except insofar as they indicate that the liberal era came to an end during the years in which the Civil Code, the subject of this study, was being drafted.

As a broad generalization, Egyptian liberalism in this period may be seen as the desire for internal change in the face of the challenge posed

[14] R. Tignor, *State, Public Enterprise, and the Economic Change in Egypt 1918–1952* (Princeton N.J.: Princeton University Press, 1984), p. 247; R. Tignor, *Capitalism and Nationalism at the End of Empire* (Princeton N.J.: Princeton University Press, 1998), p. 36; E. Davis, *Challenging Colonialism: Bank Misr and Egyptian Industrialization, 1920–1941* (Princeton N.J.: Princeton University Press, 1983).

by Europe—the challenge of a rapidly-changing world, while attempting to adapt the various facets of life to this changing European pace in the fields of religion, legal reform, state institutions, economic life, higher education and the arts. This desire for change in itself reflected the process of Westernization that had occurred among sections of Egyptian society, and certainly among its elite. The worldview of Egyptian liberals was shaped by the Greek, French and British philosophers, and by the great humanist and rationalist novelists of the nineteenth century. Some of these liberals also addressed the ancient Islamic traditions, and saw this attempt to forge a synthesis between different worlds as a form of innovation (*tajdīd*).[15]

As for the secular orientation of this generation, M. Winter has shown that it may be more accurate to speak of 'westernization' than 'secularization'. The secular process did not focus on the separation of church and state (polity separation), but rather on a unique model of secularism that expands toward government (polity expansion). According to this model, the government expands its authority into fields of social and economic life that were formerly shaped by religious patterns.[16] S. Shamir demonstrated that this liberalism differed considerably from the European model (which fell into decline during the zenith of Egyptian liberalism), particularly in terms of the integration of Islamic tradition, the absence of any tradition of civil society in Egypt, the absence of economic dimensions and the absence of any real tension between the individual and the collective.[17] In the third edition of his classic work *Arabic Thought in the Liberal Age* (1983), A. Hourani criticized the limited use that he had made of the term 'liberal' in describing the ideas imported into the region from the West. In his new edition, he argued that these ideas related not only to democratic institutions and individual rights, but also to national resilience, unity and the strength of regimes.[18]

F. Ziadeh and D. Reid have shown that, in Egypt during this period, a new and dynamic cadre of attorneys and jurists provided an important kernel for defining and protecting secular liberalism in the country. The members of this cadre advocated the adoption of the secular liberal constitution of 1923 (which mainly followed the Belgian constitution).

---

15 Shamir, pp. 196–199; Smith, p. 409.
16 Winter, p. 44.
17 Shamir, pp. 196–197.
18 A. Hourani, p. iv.

They protected the constitution, and it protected them: by protecting personal liberties, through the perception of the state as the source of all authority, through a democratic approach that emphasized the principle of the rule of law, through pluralism of expression, and through an attempt to restrict the monarchy and transfer some of the king's legislative authorities to the legislature. Ziadeh explained the emergence of this cadre as the result of the influence of its members' legal education, which had been acquired in European schools in Egypt or during their studies in France and Britain. The reality of the Mixed Courts (*al-maḥākim al-mukhtalaṭa*) in Egypt, in which some of the judges were Westerners, and which ruled according to Western legislation, led to the emergence of generations of Egyptian attorneys and judges steeped in Western legal perceptions, including the separation of powers and the independence of the judiciary. Indeed, during the early years of the twentieth century, legal studies were considered a framework for an advanced 'liberal education' in Egypt. It is hardly surprising, therefore, to find that most of the leading figures of the period had a legal education, including ʾAḥmad Luṭfī al-Sayyid, Musṭafa al-Naḥḥās, ʿAlī Māhir, ʾAḥmad Māhir, Maḥmūd Fahmī al-Nuqrāshī, Muḥammad Ḥusain Haikal, Tawfīq al-Ḥakīm, Muḥammad ʿAlī ʿAlūba, Muḥammad Luṭfī Jumʿa, Muḥammad Najīb, Fuʾād Saraj al-Dīn, Fatḥī Radwān, ʿAbd al-Khāliq Ḥasūna and others.[19]

Leading attorneys who offered a coherent exposition of the Western political concept of the freedom of the individual include, most notably, Fatḥī Zaghlūl (1863–1914) and Luṭfī al-Sayyid (1872–1962). Al-Sayyid was the closest to the European liberal principles of the nineteenth century, with his insistence on individualism and on limiting the power of government.[20] Ziadeh wrote that leading attorneys in this context also include Qāsim ʾAmīn, ʿAbd al-ʿAziz Fahmī, ʿAbd al-khaliq Tharwat and ʿAbd al-Razzāq al-Sanhūrī.

Admiration of European liberal ideas was widespread among this cadre of jurists, and among government clerks, whose functions required them to think in terms of rights and obligations, authority and immunity,

---

[19] F. Ziadeh, *Lawyers, the Rule of Law and Liberalism in Modern Egypt* (Stanford: Hoover Institute, 1968), p. 77 (Hereinafter: Ziadeh, 1968); D. M. Reid, *Lawyers and Politics in the Arab World* (Minneapolis/Chicago: Bibliotheca Islamica, 1981), pp. 94, 134, 151, 154–155.

[20] ʾAḥmad Luṭfī al-Sayyid, *Mushkilat al-Ḥuriyya* (Beirut: 1959); ʾAḥmad Luṭfī Al-Sayyid, *Qiṣṣat Ḥayātī* (Cairo: 1960); Ziadeh, 1968, pp. 88–89.

sovereignty and personal liberty. This also explains their enthusiasm for democracy, and while European democracies faced numerous challenges in the 1930s, ʿAbd al-Razzāq al-Sanhūrī, the central character of this book, was bold enough in 1938 to define democracy as the best form of government invented by man.[21]

As early as 1952, al-Sanhūrī advocated a form of judicial review of the decisions of parliament, a pioneering position in Arab constitutional law. This demand, which is at odds with the classic concept of the separation of the powers, reflects the absorption of pluralistic concepts, the desire for democracy and a balance between the powers of government:

> The deviation from the authority of the legislature appears as the third development, following the two previous developments: the theory of the abuse of a right, and the deviation from the authority of the executive power. Just as we have described the abuse that may be committed by an individual in exercising his right, and the deviation by the executive power from its authority, what is to prevent the parliament from deviating from its legislative authorities?
>
> ...(While) our Egyptian constitution does not include the establishment of a supreme court charged with examining the constitutionality of laws, neither does it include any prohibition against such constitutional review. The court will not disqualify an act of legislation, but that same court must refrain from implementing legislation contrary to the constitution, in the case of non-constitutionality.[22]

While liberal intellectuals spoke of *tajdīd*, the cadre of attorneys preferred the term *tanqīḥ*, a word that can refer to editing, polishing or selecting kernels of wheat. They used this term to refer to a general legal reform in all areas of life, in the hope that legal change will in turn encourage the emergence of a new Egyptian society more in harmony with itself and with the world. This was a desire for social and political change to be secured through legal means—an approach characteristic of those jurists who believed that with the stroke of their pen the legislature could secure desirable social changes. As we shall see below, Sanhūrī shared this same hope, as he drafted the new Egyptian Civil Code, although his approach toward the relations between society and law was more complex.

---

[21] ʿAbd al-Razzāq al-Sanhūrī, "Al-Taʿbīr ʿan Raʾy al-ʾUmma" *Al-Hilāl* 46 (April 1938), pp. 601–603.

[22] ʿAbd al-Razzāq al-Sanhūrī, "Al-ʾInḥirāf fī ʾIstiʿmāl al-Sulṭa al-Tashrīʿiyya", in *Majmūʿat Maqālāt wa ʾAbḥāth al-ʾUstādh ʿAbd al-Razzāq al-Sanhūrī* (Cairo: Maṭbaʿat Jāmiʿat al-Qāhira, 1992), volume 1, pp. 423, 476–477.

The classical legal approach was, on occasion, too theoretical and artificial for the needs of Egyptian society (Reid noted that it was often said, semi-seriously, that these attorneys had turned the Egyptian Question into the Egyptian Case).[23] However, some members of this cadre of attorneys argued that it was also important to prepare the population for these reforms, in order to ensure their successful inculcation in society. To this end, for example, the attorney Fatḥī Zaghlūl devoted much time to translating into Arabic the liberal classics of the nineteenth century.

The political pluralism of what was dubbed the constitutional 'liberal experiment'; the animated parliamentarism; the independence of the legal system as opposed to the traditional approach of the clergy (the *'ulamā'*) who were subject to the ruler; the positioning rule of law as the basis for this cadre of attorneys; a lively and relatively free press—all these combined to create a *modus operandi* unique to this period: lobbies of attorneys who pressured the legislature by means of articles in the press, lectures and campaigns in parliamentary committees, in the hope and assumption that such pressure would yield results.

Thus, the legal struggles of these attorneys during this period were accompanied by numerous articles in the Egyptian press. Major laws were adopted by the relatively pluralistic parliament after academic, legal, public and parliamentary struggles, rather than on the dictate of an all-powerful ruler. *Tanqīḥ*, then, was founded on a culture of discourse typical of the period.

This group of attorneys led several campaigns for a broad-based *tanqīḥ* in Egyptian society, which they sought to improve and make more efficient by means of these reforms. They advocated a reform of the court system; reforms in the laws of personal status; changes in the status of the Muslim trust (the *waqf*) and a reform in civil law, including the amendment or even abolition of the twin civil codes—that of the Mixed Courts (from 1876) and that of the native (*'Ahlī*) Egyptian Courts (from 1883).[24]

These attorneys advocated a unified Egyptian legal system, free of the Mixed Courts, which ostensibly dealt with cases involving Egyptian citizens and foreigners, but actually managed the legal and commercial life of the country, and free of separate courts ruling according to the

[23] Reid, p. 103.

[24] On the Mixed Code see: J. Y. Brinton, *The Mixed Courts of Egypt* (New Haven: Yale University Press, 1968), pp. 86–96.

Sharīʿa (*al-maḥākim al-sharʿiyya*) and the laws of other recognized religions and ethnic groups (*al-maḥākim al-milliyya*). Efficiency became a principle to be fought for. The general approach was practical and liberal: Europe was perceived as role model, but also as a challenge.

2.2 *The Resurrection of the East*

At first glance, the struggle to amend the Civil Code in Egypt seems surprising, as it would appear to contradict the general direction. After all, the existing code (the Mixed and the *ʾAhlī* codes, in French and Arabic respectively) was based on the liberal French *Code Civile*, and, accordingly, might have been expected to enjoy the support of the cadre of liberal attorneys who had been educated and influenced by this code. This was not a piece of Islamic law or Islamic codification, but an example of the European legislation that should ostensibly have been a model for this circle. In 1926, Turkey abolished its civil code, which was based on the Ḥanafī school (the *Majalla*), and replaced it with the Swiss Civil Code, just the opposite of the situation in Egypt during the same period. Headed by ʿAbd al-Razzāq al-Sanhūrī, a group of Egyptian attorneys sought to abolish the legislation based on the French code and introduce new legislation incorporating elements of the Islamic *Sharīʿa* and local legal culture. Having waged a campaign to amend the status of the *Waqf* in the name of efficiency and modernity, why would the Western-oriented jurists of Egypt now agree to replace a living and successful civil code with apparently antiquated provisions liable to impair the stability of the legal system? The conclusion to be drawn from these questions is that the process of legislating the New Code differed from the other aspects of *tanqīḥ*; in other words—while the legal mechanism and operation of these social systems were, perhaps similar, the goals were distinct.

While this legal cadre spoke of individual rights, the New Code first and foremost addressed the rights of the collective, echoing the legal and socioeconomic approaches current in Europe during the first half of the twentieth century. While they spoke of individualism, liberalism and even capitalism, the New Code spoke of the weak members of society and society's duty to care for the weak within the context of a broad-based social solidarity. While they emphasized the values of the West, Sanhūrī sought to emphasize the values of the East as a more appropriate antithesis for his region—the East as a civilization that is not inferior to that of the West. This explains his respectful attitude to the Islamic *Sharīʿa*, although in the context of the Civil Code, he perceived it primarily from the point of view of culture, civilization and sociology, rather than religion.

Accordingly, while Ziadeh and Hill considered ʿAbd al-Razzāq al-Sanhūrī, the architect of the New Code, part of the same historical category as the secular liberal stream, a distinction should be made between Sanhūrī and the typical secular liberals of the 1920s and early 1930s. Such a distinction will facilitate an understanding of the distinct goals of the New Code as Sanhūrī perceived them.

I. Gershoni and J. Jankowski distinguished between various key categories within the Egyptian nationalism of the first half of the century, including, for the purpose of our discussion, territorial Egyptian nationalism, which is basically identified with those secular liberals who saw the West not only as a role model, but also as the remedy for Egypt's woes; nationalism founded on Islam; and Easternism. The latter two categories challenged the former, and it is in this context that the New Code should be examined.

The Islamic nationalist approach spoke of a return to the ancient days of Islam: the liberation of the Muslim nation, its internal cohesion and political unification. The Eastern approach argued that the East was home to a unique civilization with its own emphases and values that would enjoy a renaissance as the West fell into decline.[25]

In his personal diary, which was not intended for publication, Sanhūrī recorded a dream that may offer an explanation of his political, legal and educational approach against the backdrop of the gulf between East and West:

> In my dream, I saw the sun shining in the West with a dazzling light. I focused my gaze on it for a long time, and then turned my head to the East. I felt that I were drawing a still larger and brighter sun from the depths of the East, *and I felt as if I were drawing this sun with my own hands* [emphasis in original], while I heard whispered the phrase 'knowledge'. Then I awoke from my sleep. Perhaps it was arrogant of me to mention this dream in my memoirs, but it had a tremendous influence on me. I can still see before me the two suns, the shining sun of the West, and the still more beautiful and radiant sun of the East, overshadowing the sun of the West. God, make this dream come true and I shall be capable of anything.[26]

---

[25] Redefining, pp. 79–96, 35–53.

[26] Diary, Lyon, 24 October 1921, pp. 52–53.

Sanhūrī perceived the relations between East and West as dynamic rather than static: one rising as the other descended. This approach describes an inherent state of coexistence, with a diffusion that is perceived as relatively healthy and as vital to the progress and spiritual enrichment of humanity. As he wrote in his diary:

> The revival of the East does not imply a war against the West. The resurrection of the East in no way contradicts our benefiting from the sciences and culture of the West, since the East still requires this. The East can draw on the culture of the West in those areas that will bring benefit, just as the West drew on the culture of the East in its own revival. The West should not be afraid of the East as it attempts to revive itself, since this is in the West's own interests. Wars will be reduced by closing the gates of greed (a reference to imperialism—G. B.), thus opening up to the West young nations that will join, according to their luck, the world of culture and advanced sciences.
>
> The revival of the East does not mean the revival of one particular religion at the expense of another or the establishment of an expansive empire dominating the nations of the East and displaying animosity toward the West. Religion can only prevail in the East, because the East is the cradle of all the religions, an expansive empire of history...The nations of the East aspire to revival; each nation will attend to its own affairs, and if alliances are formed, this will be for the purpose of economic advancement and to repel enemies.
>
> I shall add a further point, namely that after independence, the peoples of the East should establish a scientific movement (to revive the sciences of the East) based on the ancient Eastern sciences, together with the spirit created through the experiences accumulated to date by the West. After all, knowledge has no homeland.[27]

What, then, does Sanhūrī consider the advantage of the East over the West that may lead to the revival of the East and an increase in its global relevance? The answer is its spirituality:

> The East is waking now from its slumber, and seeks to play a part in the happiness of the world by raising the status of culture, after it has remained silent for some while. But it wishes to make a serious effort in a manner that does not imitate the West. It seeks to maintain two unique aspects of its culture: that this culture will have an Eastern quality in the connection between past and future; and that this culture will serve as an answer to the growing materialism of contemporary Western culture. Westerners have gone too far with their materialism, and the victims of this culture exceed those who have benefited from it. The world is now

[27] Diary, Lyon, 27 August 1923, pp. 98–99.

> waiting for the East to save it from this abyss. And who can perform this task better than the East—the source of light, wisdom and the religions? Say not that the East should imitate the West and abandon religion, for this would cause the gravest damage to culture. Culture began with religion and it will end with it.[28]

It is hardly surprising, then, that Gershoni and Jankowski considered Sanhūrī and those of his ilk not among the strongly liberal public, but as a form of hybrid between Islamic and Eastern identity, within the framework of diverse national discourse. Their point of reference was the revival of the East, but on the basis of Islamic civilization. They claimed that these intellectuals set out to interpret Islamic civilization in secular terms: a civilization that is the product of a historical process reflecting a social situation, and embodying secular social meanings, and which is no longer controlled by religion. Islam, these circles argued, was indeed born in a revelatory religion, a religion formulated in the sacred texts, but the Islamic civilization has acquired a distinct, extra-religious existence, and has become an autonomous secular entity. This Islam, which is an historical and cultural creation that embodies only the slightest spark of religious faith, was seen by these individuals as a proper and fitting foundation on which they sought to establish the pan-Eastern framework. "Identification with the 'east'—while a 'spiritual' entity, nonetheless broader than Islam *per se*—provided such a framework".[29]

According to Sanhūrī's perspective, Islamic law provided a potential and authentic Eastern response to Western culture and European law, since it was in no sense inferior to the law that formed the West, whether Roman law or English common law. He addressed Islamic law from the standpoint of Islamic culture and civilization, rather than that of the Islamic religion, although he was personally a devout believer. There is ample evidence of this in his diaries, in statements such as "I believe in God with a limitless belief," and "Our bond with God uplifts heart and mind."[30]

The 'historical school' of law, headed by the German jurists Friedrich Karl von Savigny (1779–1861) and Josef Kohler (1849–1919), influenced Sanhūrī's mundane perception of Islamic law. These scholars discussed the revival of the legal system of a given society and its adaptation to

---

[28] Diary, Paris, 4 January 1924, p. 139.
[29] Redefining, pp. 35–53.
[30] Diary, pp. 54, 172.

modern society. Regardless of whether the legal system in question is Roman law, the *Shari'a* or Jewish law, its antiquity does not necessarily detract from its pertinence even in modern times. This revival may also lead to a social and cultural renaissance.[31]

The 'historical school' in German legal theory began after the defeat at the hands of Napoleon, who tried to impose French legislation throughout the German states. After his downfall, it was decided to abolish this legislation. The question that arose was similar to that facing Egypt in the time of Sanhūrī—with what should it be replaced? Savigny argued that original German law should be enacted, based on the Roman legal system, which had been used in Germany for some one thousand years; moreover, he argued that each nation adds of its own spirit to this legal system, updating it and ensuring its flexibility and relevance. Ultimately, at the end of the nineteenth century comprehensive laws were enacted in Germany that embodied a successful blending of Roman law and norms and specifically German legislative traditions. Kohler added that the function of law is to create the sociopolitical order necessary to maintain the achievements of the past and create cultural progress.[32] For Sanhūrī, there could be no better source for advancing the Muslim and Arab revival than Islamic law. In any case, his starting point was the West and European law and he searched for a local-Eastern counterpart, which he found in the form of Islamic law.

This explanation of the seam between Eastern nationalism and Islamic nationalism is important not only in order to understand Sanhūrī's world view, but also in order to appreciate his future legal intentions. An interesting analogy may be drawn between 'Abd al-Razzāq al-Sanhūrī, who used Islamic law as a screen for introducing Continental legal norms into Egyptian law, as we shall see in this book, and representative of another Middle Eastern culture, the Israeli Professor Uri Yadin, who, it has been claimed, used Jewish law to introduce norms from German law, such as the concept of 'good faith', into the Israeli legal system. The term itself is drawn from the world of Jewish law, but its sources in the Israeli context lie in the German civil code, just as Sanhūrī took the same article of good faith from the German

[31] On Savigny and Kohler see: *Lloyd's Introduction to Jurisprudence*, pp. 26, 890–985.

[32] On the 'Historical School' see H. Berman, "The Historic Foundation of Law", *Emory Law Journal* 54 (2005), p. 13.

civil code and blended it in the Egyptian Code, while arguing that it came from the Islamic *Shariʿa*. It may reasonably be assumed that both Sanhūrī and Yadin perceived Islamic and Jewish law respectively in their cultural and traditional contexts, rather than from a narrow religious standpoint.[33]

3. A Figure of Duality: ʿAbd al-Razzāq al-Sanhūrī

From the initiative to revise the existing Civil Code, through the long years of drafting, consultations to defend the proposed Code in the houses of parliament and its ultimate passage as law, the New Code of Egypt was largely the product of the mind and hand of the Egyptian jurist ʿAbd al-Razzāq al-Sanhūrī (1895–1971). This Code is widely considered a masterpiece of legal phrasing, and to this day it forms the basis of civil law in Egypt and most of the Arab world.[34]

Sanhūrī embodied the duality characteristic of the social circles from which he came: a legal scholar, yet also an experienced politician, whose path crossed with the most significant decisions in the history of modern Egypt; a man thoroughly familiar with the Western world, yet who always sought to blend this world with the environment in which he lived—the 'East' as a value-based concept; a devout Muslim in his private life, and thoroughly intimate with the *fiqh* (the Muslim law, which is part of the *Shariʿa*), yet someone who recognized the importance of mundane legislation for his society; and, lastly, a great believer in democracy who ended his life in defeat, laying the foundation for the rule of Colonel Jamāl ʿAbd al-Nāṣir, which would later evolve into an authoritarian regime.[35]

---

[33] On Uri Yadin see: Y. Meron, "Le Droit Allemand en Israël", *Revue International de Droit Conparé* 43 (1991), p. 127.

[34] N. Saleh, "Civil Codes of Arab Countries: The Sanhuri Codes", *Arab Law Quarterly* 8 (1993), p. 161.

[35] E. Hill, *Al-Sanhuri and Islamic Law*, Cairo papers in Social science, Vol. 10 Monograph 1 (Cairo: The American University in Cairo Press, 1987), (Hereinafter: Hill); E. Hill, "Islamic Law as a Source for the Development of a Comparative Jurisprudence, The 'Modern Science of Codification': Theory and Practice in the life and work of ʿAbd al-Razzaq Ahmad al-Sanhuri (1895–1971)" in A. al-Azmeh (ed.), *Islamic Law: Social and Historical Contexts* (NY: Routledge, 1988), pp. 146–197; M. Khadduri, *Political Trends in the Arab World: The Role of Ideas and Ideals in Politics* (Baltimore: Johns Hopkins Press, 1970) pp. 239–244; J. Gordon, *Nasser's Blessed Movement* (Oxford: Oxford University Press, 1992), pp. 21, 61, 146–147.

Sanhūrī was born in the cosmopolitan city of Alexandria on 11 August 1895. In 1913, he moved to Cairo to attend the Cairo Law School, where the studies were held in English under pressure from the British occupiers. Donald Reid noted that this school was the arena for struggles between the French academic approach and the attempts by the British to anglicize the school, and with it—legal life in Egypt. It was here, too, that the students developed their nationalist leanings, since anti-British sentiments were rife in the institution.[36]

After his father, a government clerk, died during Sanhūrī's second year of studies, he began to work in the Ministry of Finance in order to support himself. He completed his studies in 1917, the strongest student in his class, and began to work as a *wakīl al-niyāba*—a clerk in the prosecutor's office in the Mixed Court of al-Mansūra. After participating in the anti-British riots of March 1919, during which he initiated a strike by the clerks, he was transferred—and effectively removed—to the court in ʾAsyūṭ in southern Egypt. In 1920, he secured a position as lecturer of law at the school for *Shariʿa* judges, but left his post a year later to travel to France to prepare his doctoral dissertation. He attended the University of Lyon, the main destination for Egyptian students in France, and completed two theses—the first on contractual limitations on the freedom of vocation in English law,[37] and the second on the origins and development of the Islamic Caliphate and the prospects for its reinstatement after its abolition in 1924 in Kemalist Turkey.[38]

In all his activities relating to Egyptian society, Sanhūrī showed a high level of caring, genuine concern and a tremendous desire to contribute to the welfare of his homeland. When he was just 23, he described the types of active steps he felt were demanded of him and of all young Egyptians for the sake of their nation:

> I want every young person to know that he bears responsibility for the collapse of his nation, and that he should not confine himself to expressing revulsion or regret, since these emotions inevitably destroy hope in progress. If working hands agree to act with determination and devotion, we can see the fruits of our labor, even if only after a long time.[39]

---

[36] Reid, 18–19; Diary, p. 31.

[37] *Les Restriction Contractuelles à la Liberté Individuelle de Travail dans la Jurisprudence Anglaise* (Paris: Marcel Biard, 1925).

[38] *Le Califat: Son Évolution vers une Société des Nations Orientale* (Paris: Librairie Orientaliste, Paul Geuthner, 1926). The Book was Translated to Arabic: *Fiqh al-Khilāfa wa-Tatwīrha li-taṣbaḥ ʿUṣbat ʾUmam Sharqiyya* (Cairo: Al-Hayʾa al-ʿĀma lil-Kitāb, 1993) (hereinafter: Fiqh al-Khilāfa).

[39] Diary, 19 October 1918, p. 43.

In France, Sanhūrī encountered phenomena to which he had not hitherto been exposed—a lively pluralism of thought, dynamic political action, anti-clericalism and liberty. This liberty—which had legal ramifications, as we shall see in this book—inspired him, but he also found it alarming. He found it difficult to see how such liberty could be applied in his native East, so that his admiration of the West actually enhanced his theory of Easternism. While still a student in Lyon, he wrote:

> I am amazed by the freedom of thought and speech enjoyed by the nations of the West. I attended two meetings in France, one of Communists and the other of capitalists. On both occasions, speakers several times used the term 'revolution', and the audience called out for the overthrow of the existing regime—while this very regime listened. The storm passed without anyone showing opposition. England has its Hyde Park, a kind of latter-day Tower of Babel, where every speaker comes from a different side. One speaks in favor of the existence of God, while another preaches apostasy and denies God's existence. One criticizes the policies of the present government while another lauds them. The audience listen and applaud them all.[40]

In 1926, Sanhūrī returned to Egypt and took up a position as lecturer in civil law at the Cairo University. In 1934, he was alleged to have been responsible for a secret organization of students for political motives, and was temporarily suspended from the university, though he denied the charges in the press.[41] After this incident, Sanhūrī traveled to Iraq to head the Faculty of Law in Baghdad. On returning to Egypt in 1936, he was appointed dean of the Faculty of Law at Cairo University. A year later, he was forced to leave his position "for political reasons." His dismissal was probably due to his association with ʾAḥmad Māhir and Maḥmūd Fahmī al-Nuqrāshī, dissidents within the main nationalist party in Egypt at the time, the *Wafd*. In 1937, the three men founded the Saʿadist party. With links to the palace, the party claimed to be the true representative of the positions of Saʿad Zaghlūl, the late founder and leader of the *Wafd* (who died in 1927). The Saʿadist party was also considered the representative of the major landowners and capitalists in the Egyptian parliament. This vindictive treatment of Sanhūrī at the hands of the leaders of the *Wafd* was to reappear several times during his life. Every time a *Wafd*-led government was established, Sanhūrī

[40] Diary, Paris, 22 November 1923, p. 131.
[41] Hill, p. 84.

was dismissed or transferred from his positions, only to be reinstated after the establishment of a Saʿadist government led by his friend ʾAḥmad Māhir and, after his assassination, by al-Nuqrāshī, another colleague of him.[42] Muṣṭafa al-Naḥḥās (1879–1965), the leader of the *Wafd* movement, showed a particularly fierce hatred for Sanhūrī and pursued him during his years in office. This political animosity was also significant in the context of the New Code, explaining the fluctuations in the composition of the various committees responsible for drafting the Code. In 1937, Naḥḥās led to Sanhūrī's dismissal from his position as dean of the Faculty of Law and his membership of the committee for drafting the New Code. However, Naḥḥās' government fell later the same year, and Sanhūrī was reinstated. In 1942, Naḥḥās again persecuted Sanhūrī, who fled to Iraq and Syria, where he spent the period 1942–1944, during which he drafted the Iraqi Civil Code.[43] In 1944, Sanhūrī returned to Egypt to represent the Saʿadist party as minister of education, a position he continued to hold in several anti-Wafdist governments. In March 1949, he was appointed head of the supreme administrative court of Egypt, *majlis al-dawla*, the Council of State, modeled on the French *Conseil d'Etat*.[44] He was still in this position during the revolution of July 1952, and Sanhūrī and the Council of State sided with the rebel 'Free Officers'; indeed, ʿAbd al-Razzāq al-Sanhūrī served as legal advisor to the Revolutionary Council and helped draft some of its laws.

After the Officers' revolution, however, Sanhūrī urged a return to civilian life, a position that inevitably brought him into conflict with the Revolutionary Council. The Council of State, which he headed, rapidly became a stumbling block in the efforts by the Revolutionary Council to establish a permanent military regime. Sanhūrī's position formed part of the struggle that emerged within the Revolutionary Council between Muḥammad Najīb and Jamāl ʿAbd al-Nāṣir, and he became the target of intense pressure. The Egyptian attorneys, who had become accustomed prior to the revolution to their status as the backbone of civil life in the country and as a dynamic force for initiative

[42] Hill, pp. 84–85.

[43] Z. Jwaideh, "The New Civil Code of Iraq", *George Washington Law Review* 22 (1953), p. 176.

[44] E. Hill, "Majlis al-Dawla, The Administrative Courts of Egypt and Administrative Law", in C. Mallat (ed.) *Islam and Public Law: Classical and Contemporary Studies*, (London: Graham and Trotman, 1993), p. 207.

innovation, had not yet realized that in the new authoritarian regime, their expected role was purely technical. Sanhūrī could only watch as the most basic civil values of parliament, political parties and freedom of expression were gradually eroded.

On 29 March 1954, after an article in the daily newspaper *Al-'Akhbār* quoted 'rumors' that the Council of State and Sanhūrī were about to issue a decree denying the constitutionality of the revolution, and that Sanhūrī himself was to be appointed prime minister for a four-month transitional period pending elections to a legislative council, an outraged mob, incited by 'military elements', broke into the Council of State building and attacked Sanhūrī himself. A statement by the Ministry of the Interior claimed that Sanhūrī had been attacked by demonstrators who had been deliberately misled by certain 'opportunists'. In a cynical move, Jamāl ʿAbd al-Nāṣir, who was probably behind the incitement and certainly interested in it, visited Sanhūrī in his home to express his sympathy at the attack. Nāṣir made no effort to inform Sanhūrī of his impending political doom.[45]

On 16 April 1954, a decree was issued against 38 officials from the old regime, most of them politicians who had served as government ministers between February 1942 and July 1952. The decree stripped the officials of their political rights for ten years. The group members were charged with responsibility for the corruption and decline that was alleged to have been rife in pre-revolutionary Egypt. Sanhūrī was among the group, despite his principled support for the Officers' revolution. Thus, his political and public career was abruptly derailed at its peak.

Sanhūrī spent most of the remainder of his days in his home, denied of the right to participate in the political and social life of his beloved Egypt. In his personal diary, he wrote:

> If I have today begun to appreciate the meaning of personal liberty, freedom of expression and thought, it is not because I did not understand their meaning before now, but rather because I am like a sick man who failed to understand how agreeable life is until he fell sick. Liberty is like health, and a person cannot truly appreciate them until he has lost them.
>
> There is a merchant who is determined to burn down his shop so that his bankruptcy will remain undiscovered. Do you think this merchant has taught the politicians some of his methods?...

---

45 *Al-'Ahrām*, 30 March 1954; Hill, p. 105.

> Congratulations to our victorious government. It is always right and it always wins the horse race. The only thing is that only a single horse takes to the tracks, and the government always bets on this horse.[46]

One thing, however, could not be denied Sanhūrī: the Civil Code that he conceived, planned, drafted and managed to pass through parliament several years before the revolution. Relieved of most of his activities and closed in his home, Sanhūrī thus devoted his energies to one of the few fields permitted to him—legal research.

In April 1952, three months before the revolution, Sanhūrī published the first volume of what was to become his monumental commentary on the New Code and the obligating interpretation—*Al-Wasīṭ fī Sharḥ al-Qānūn al-Madanī* (hereinafter: *al-Wasīṭ*),[47] comprising ten sections in twelve massive volumes, extending over thousands of pages, and including details not only of the legal theories established in the Code, but also the social and economic context of these theories.

Al-Wasiṭ and work relating to the New Code were effectively the only avenue by which Sanhūrī could maintain any involvement in Egyptian public life, offering a tiny window through which, albeit indirectly and covertly, he could attempt to influence the social purpose and interpretation of the Code. For the drafters of other civil codes, such social purpose might constitute no more than an intellectual challenge; for Sanhūrī, it became the essence of his being. He managed to complete the final section of *Al-Wasīṭ* a year before his death on 21 July 1971. However, as Enid Hill, who is considered his biographer, noted somberly, "The world does not know about these works, and few in Egypt indicate that they realize, other than in very general terms, what they comprehend".[48]

Yet in an ironic twist of history, ʿAbd al-Razzāq al-Sanhūrī, who was instantaneously removed from Egyptian social and political life, continues to live in the everyday workings of courts throughout the Arab world, since *al-Wasīṭ* is still considered the normative commentary on Arab civil law, and is required reading for every attorney in Egypt and the other Arab nations. By contrast, fifty years after the raucous revolution of Jamāl ʿAbd al-Nāṣir, this event now seems less cardinal in the nation's history—a feature of its past, but less of its present or future.

---

[46] Diary, 19 August 1954, p. 288; 19 June 1967, p. 319; 17 July 1967, p. 319.

[47] ʿAbd al-Razzāq Al-Sanhūrī, *Al-Wasīṭ fī Sharḥ al-Qānūn al-Madanī* (Cairo: Dār al-Nahḍa al-ʿArabiyya, 1997) (hereinafter: al-Wasīṭ).

[48] Hill, p. 115.

4. A Model of Legal Engineering: The Islamic *Sharī'a*

In order fully to appreciate Sanhūrī's approach to domestic law from his early years as a jurist, and his conviction that it could provide the impetus for renewed growth in local society (meaning not just Egypt, but the Islamic world as a whole), we shall now examine a number of theoretical legal models, perhaps even études, that he presented in the 1920s for the use of the *Shari'a*. It would be wrong to draw a direct analogy between these models and the New Code, the drafting of which started as early as the 1930s. Though a devout Muslim and an admirer of the *Shar'ia*, Sanhūrī did not always apply this approach when drafting the Code.

4.1 *A Theoretical Experimental Model*

In his doctoral dissertation on the subject of the Islamic Caliphate, Sanhūrī discussed in depth the way in which the *Shari'a* could become the foundation for Eastern culture as a whole, after undergoing a process of 'scientific' fashioning. This was a model of legal engineering, and its principle aspects are noted here in order to illustrate the manner in which Sanhūrī perceived law, rather than to draw any conclusions regarding the New Code. Nevertheless, echoes of these models of legal engineering may, of course, be found in the Code itself.

The first stage in the revision of Islamic law, as Sanhūrī argued in his thesis, was the scientific stage, in which Islamic law must be studied in accordance with the methodology of international comparative law and in comparison to other legal theories. Within the *Sharī'a* itself, those legal norms that are not related to religious ritual and concern not only Muslims, but humanity as a whole—should be distilled. Islamic law will then become a living legal branch that is no longer isolated within the apparently closed walls of religious lawmaking, but which can become a natural part of modern life.[49]

After fashioning Islamic law as a branch of comparative law completely denuded of religiosity, faith or ritual, the legislative stage then followed, i.e., the slow and gradual transfer of provisions from Islamic law to the prevailing legislation.

Sanhūrī exemplified how this might be achieved by introducing an Islamic source of interpretation into legislation, so that in the event of

[49] Fiqh al-Khilāfa, pp. 315–318.

a *lacuna* in an existing law, the judge would turn to the *Sharīʿa*, so that Islamic law would create a form of common law, and the courts would become accustomed to consulting Islamic law, particularly when the relevant law of foreign origin was silent on a given issue.[50]

After refined Islamic law, so to speak, became familiar and accessible to the legal system and to the general public, the next stage would be to replace foreign legal norms with the norms of Islamic law, after this had undergone its scientific development. This, however, was on condition that this process would not damage the existing legal system.[51]

Sanhūrī even anticipated a broad arena of cooperation between the different Muslim countries, in which the common legal element, based on the *fiqh*, i.e. the Islamic law distilled from the *Sharīʿa*, would become a focus of Eastern cultural definition *vis-à-vis* the West and among these nations. He recommended that 'a union of perspectives' should guide the legislators of the different Muslim countries as they drew mutually from the same source of Islamic law, although it was also appropriate to address the different realities of each country. Such a union might, in his opinion, reduce the danger of legal conflicts between these Muslim countries, and hence reduce friction. For Sanhūrī, this was a form of Eastern or Muslim unity by means of the law.[52]

As part of this engineering-based approach to the *Sharīʿa*, Sanhūrī sought to undertake an adaptation of familiar Islamic institutions and terms in order to facilitate their integration in his mundane Eastern approach. I shall discuss here four key examples: the institution of the Caliphate; the tool of *ʾijmāʿ* in Islamic law; the dissection of the *Sharīʿa* into a legal/mundane realm and a religious/ritualistic realm; and, lastly, the question of interpretation, and, in particular, the question of opening the ostensibly closed gates of Islamic religious ruling. It is interesting to note that Sanhūrī strongly opposed those Islamic institutions which he felt could not undergo mundane adaptation, such as the *Sharīʿa* courts.[53] This is further evidence that he was opposed to the adoption of religious institutions *per se*, without the mundane and utilitarian transformation he sought to effect in them.

---

[50] Ibid., p. 319.

[51] Ibid., pp. 320–321.

[52] ʿAbd al-Razzāq al-Sanhūrī, "Al-Taʿāwūn al-Thaqāfī wa al-Tashrīʿī Ma Bayna al-Bilād al-ʿArabiyya", in *Majmūʿat Maqālāt wa ʾAbḥāth al-ʾUstādh ʿAbd al-Razzāq al-Sanhūrī*, volume 1, p. 327.

[53] Wujūb, p. 63.

As noted above, these are theoretical legal models that cannot be used to draw conclusions regarding the process of enacting the New Code. These models are presented in this chapter mainly in order to assist in understanding Sanhūrī's system of social and legal engineering, a concept and methodology that were central to his approach, and which would later find fertile expression in the formulation of the New Code.

4.2 *The Caliphate*

Abolition of the institution of the Islamic Caliphate in Turkey in 1924 was a subject of great interest to Egyptian intellectuals and religious figures in this period. In his second thesis, which was published in 1926 under the title *Le Califat: Son Évolution vers une Société des Nations Orientale*, Sanhūrī wrote that "the Muslim world finds itself without a Caliph... so that the question of the Caliphate has become a burning reality." The questions raised for discussion in the thesis included whether the Caliphate was a vital, important and worthwhile institution for the Muslims, and whether it was desirable and feasible to separate this institution from political authority and the organs of power. Compared to other observers, Sanhūrī placed particular importance on the Caliphate, since the institution also served as the defender of (Islamic) law.[54]

In May 1926, an Islamic congress was held in Cairo to discuss the ramifications of the abolition of the Caliphate in Turkey, and the steps that should be taken to reinstate this institution. The congress reached the conclusion that the reinstatement of the Caliphate was not possible, due to "the political weakness and division of the Muslims and the passion for the idea of particularistic nationalism." The debate on the role of the Caliphate also had a political dimension; P. J. Vatikiotis noted that the Egyptian religious leaders were alarmed by the aspirations of Ḥusayn, the king of Ḥijāz and former sharīf of Mecca. If an Arab Caliphate were to be established in place of the disposed Ottoman Caliphate, they argued that it should properly be headed by an Egyptian, i.e., by their own king.[55]

---

[54] Fiqh al-Khilāfa, pp. 35–40, 307–309. More on the debate of the Caliphate: I. Gershoni, J. Jankowski, *Egypt, Islam, and the Arabs: The Search for Egyptian Nationhood*, pp. 55–74; C. Harris, *Nationalism and Revolution in Egypt: The Role of the Muslim Brethren* (The Hague: Mouton 1964), pp. 133–135 (Hereinafter: Harris); E. Kedouri, *The Chatham House Version and the Middle-Eastern Studies* (London: Weidenfeld and Nicolson, 1970), pp. 177–207.

[55] Harris, pp. 134, 296; Redefining, pp. 145–166.

In his doctoral dissertation, Sanhūrī proposed an alternative conceptual and theoretical perception of the institution of the Caliphate, according to which the Caliphate would stand above the separation between the religious and political realms, uniting both and thus also preventing the political authority from engulfing the religious. He portrayed this religious authority as an 'Organization of Eastern Nations', in which religion served as a means of bridging the gaps between the different Muslim nations. He referred to this structure as a 'temporary Caliphate', adding that this regime should be flexible in character, since "Islamic law does not impose any particular form of government."[56]

Sanhūrī noted that he was aware of the tendency to despotism among the Caliphs. However, he drew a distinction between the corrupt individuals who had seized control of this institution over the course of history and the institution itself. According to his theoretical model, Islamic law argued that sovereignty "belonged to God alone." After the death of the Prophet, this sovereignty was placed in the [Islamic] nation as a whole, and not in the hands of the Caliph or any other privileged group. "Accordingly, the Caliph is the representative not of God, but of the nation."[57] This approach differed from the accepted religious perception. Sanhūrī seems to have been attempting to evolve an Eastern and Muslim constitutional legal theory, including the idea of an 'Organization of Eastern Nations' as an Eastern response to the League of Nations, which was established during this period.

4.3 *The Potential Application of the Tool of ʾIjmāʿ*

ʾIjmāʿ (consensus) is the third source of Islamic law, based on a saying attributed to the Prophet Muḥammad that "my nation shall never be united in error or fault." The argument is that because of this infallible and conservative doctrine, the gates of independent Islamic lawmaking and interpretation (*ʾijtihād*) were effectively closed. The term *ʾijmāʿ* was used at the turn of the century in the context of the debate among Islamic modernists in Egypt, under the leadership of Muḥammad ʿAbduh, who sought to institutionalize and restrict *ʾijmāʿ* in order to enable the renewal and adaptation of Islamic law.[58]

---

[56] Fiqh al Khilāfa, pp. 307–314.
[57] Ibid., pp. 54–57.
[58] On the Issue of ʾijmāʿ see W. B. Hallaq, "On the Authoritativeness of Sunni Consensus", *International Journal of Middle East Studies* 18 (1986), pp. 427–454; Hallaq,

Sanhūrī also discussed this concept on several occasions. As we shall claim below, however, the focus of his concern was not the internal renewal of Islamic law or the religious aspect of this issue, but primarily social, legal and political considerations. Sanhūrī discussed this Islamic interpretative tool three times, and always on the theoretical level.

His first discussion of *ʾijmāʿ* appeared in his doctoral dissertation on the Caliphate, in which context he portrayed it as a tool for political definition rather than the interpretation of religious law: "What is more democratic than the confirmation that the will of the nation is the will of God Himself?"[59] This was his theoretical answer to the question of the elected government in the Western democracies. The theoretical logic is that the will of God is equivalent to the will of the people (and, by the same logic, both are infallible), and the will of the people is equivalent to democracy. In the context of his search for a response to the Western democratic system, Sanhūrī wondered whether the principle of *ʾijmāʿ* might be seen as "the basis for a representative regime in Islamic government."[60]

The second context is Sanhūrī's desire to use *ʾijmāʿ* to elaborate the Islamic legal system and transform it into a living legal theory that can be updated in order to keep pace with modern life. Muslims, or representatives on their behalf (in an institutionalized manner) would meet to discuss their problems and make decisions in keeping with the spirit of the times. These decisions would constitute laws, and thus *ʾijmāʿ* would actually become a force for innovation in the *Sharīʿa*, maintaining its flexibility and capacity for change.[61]

It is interesting to note that in a discussion on the subject of *ʾijmāʿ* in an article from 1938, Sanhūrī referred to the Italian scholar, Giorgio Del Vecchio (1878–1970), dean of the Faculty of Law at the University of Rome, who stated, in a conference on comparative law in The Hague in 1932: "There is a mechanism by which norms of custom and law that appear necessary today, can enter the official law of Islam. It is *ʾijmāʿ*, the consensus of the community".[62] The use of a quotation from a European scholar in order to claim legitimacy in an internal and ostensibly religious Islamic context illustrates Sanhūrī's mundane

---

A History of Islamic Legal Theories: An Introduction to Sunni Usul al-Fiqh (Cambridge: Cambridge University Press, 1997), pp. 75–81.

[59] Fiqh al-Khilāfa, p. 54.

[60] Ibid., p. 63.

[61] Wujūb, p. 116.

[62] Hill, p. 54.

application of the institutions of religious law as a branch of universal comparative law, rather than in their internal religious context.

The third context is that of the New Code. Enid Hill has claimed that Sanhūrī sought to include the concept of *ʾijmāʿ* in the Code, and hence "become embroiled in the struggle to achieve that consensus in the drafting committees and in the Egyptian parliament".[63] This claim may be questioned, since in his central article on the subject, from 1936, Sanhūrī already presented the preferred possibilities for drafting a future Code, and related almost in passing to *ʾijmāʿ*, explaining that the innovation of the *Sharīʿa* according to his proposal (by means of *ʾijmāʿ*) was of limited consequence in terms of the adoption of the new Code, and that, even if the *Sharīʿa* were not renewed, it could and should be used as a source of tradition for the new Code.[64]

In the deliberations of the various parliamentary committees, the question of *ʾijmāʿ* did not arise, further suggesting that Sanhūrī saw this area as a theoretical aspiration that was not necessary for drafting a mundane civil code. It should further be noted that the tool of *ʾijmāʿ* does not appear in the drafts of the Code.

4.4 *Dismantling the Unity of the Sharīʿa*

It may be argued that Sanhūrī attempted to dismantle the unity and totality of Divine Islamic ruling (the *Sharīʿa*—the term he himself employed, rather than *fiqh*, i.e. Islamic law, which constitutes an integral part of the *Sharīʿa*), and to divide it into a religious section (*dīnī*), i.e., that which did not constitute a legal norm, but rather an ethical, moral, ritual or conscience-based instruction, on the one hand; and, on the other, mundane legal norms (*dunyawī*), that had no direct connection with Islamic religious ritual, but constitutes general legal norms.

While the former category would apply only to Muslims, the latter would also be appropriate for others, given his Easternist theory that the *Sharīʿa* is, first and foremost, a source that defines civilization and culture. He further subdivided the mundane category into two parts: variable norms of a temporary and specific character, and permanent norms. These two categories could be amended and changed just as in any other legal system.[65]

[63] Hill, 30.
[64] Wujūb, pp. 113, 115–116.
[65] Fiqh al-Khilāfa, pp. 316–318; Sanhūrī, "Al-Dīn wa-al-Dawla fī al-ʾIslām", *Majmūʿat Maqālāt wa ʾAbḥāth al-ʾUstādh ʿAbd al-Razzāq al-Sanhūrī*, volume 1, pp. 9–11.

Accordingly, it could be argued that by dismantling the ostensibly indivisible totality of the *Sharīʿa*, Sanhūrī sought to transform Islamic law into an ordinary legal system, no more Divine than any other, and capable of being developed, changed and updated and of providing a cultural response to European legal systems. All this was possible once the system was free of the burden of Divine law and of the rigid opposition to changes due to the closing of the gates of legal lawmaking.[66]

4.5 *Opening the Gates of Independent Interpretatiom* (ʾIjtihād)

Sanhūrī's conclusion, based on the application of Islamic law as a potential personal, social and political response to the challenge of the West, and on his conviction that any legal system must be open to change, was that Islamic law must also change and maintain its vitality and relevance. This conclusion was incompatible with a central concept regarding Islamic law, namely that the gates of independent lawmaking and interpretation (*ʾijtihād*) have been closed. This approach presented Sanhūrī with a challenge: perhaps the closing of the gates of *ʾijtihād* implied that Islamic law had proved unable to stand alongside Roman, French or any other legal system, and hence found it convenient to withdraw into its own four walls? "The important [Islamic] legal system fell into a state of stagnation due to the commandment not to initiate the required development. [Accordingly] we must consider the rehabilitation of principles and the revival of Islamic law," he argued.[67]

Regarding his personal ambitions in this legal, social and religious field, Sanhūrī wrote:

> When I return to Egypt, I should like, if possible, to devote myself to a special study designed to find a new way to teach the Islamic *Sharīʿa* and its comparison to other legal systems, so that it may be possible to open the gates of *ʾijtihād* in this splendid *Sharīʿa*, which were closed so long ago; so that it may be possible, after the gap of the past centuries has been bridged, that this system could influence the future laws of the Egyptian nation. I beg of God that He make this hope come true.[68]

Later, however, in the context of the New Code, Sanhūrī attacked the idea that Islamic *fiqh* was stagnant, stating: "We should not be led astray by this superficial argument leveled from some quarters against the

---

66 Fiqh al-Khilāfa, p. 318; Ziadeh (1968), p. 116.
67 Ibid., p. 308.
68 Diary, 21 January 1922, pp. 55–56.

Islamic *Sharīʿa*, as though it is unfit and frozen, since this is an erroneous theory. The Islamic *Sharīʿa* has developed greatly, and may still develop in order to adapt to existing civilization."[69] It may be that at this point, Sanhūrī was concerned that an argument about opening the gates of religious lawmaking—an issue he concerned marginal in the context of the Code—would merely delay the legislative process, and thus declared that Islamic law could be employed in its current state.

Accordingly, it may be argued that opening the gates of religious lawmaking was of interest to Sanhūrī not as an internal religious matter, divorced of other legal systems or the general challenge of the West, but rather as part of an analogy he drew between Islamic law and other, Western legal systems. This is why Sanhūrī found an element of flexibility in the tool of *ʾijmāʿ* enabling him to overcome the apparent flaw of an apparently frozen legal system.[70] It also explains why Sanhūrī's approach to *ʾijmāʿ* (in the context of the New Code), and his need to open the gates of *ʾijtihād* or to argue that they were not actually closed should be seen not in terms of the relations between the Islamic religion and domestic society, as was the case with Muḥammad ʿAbduh and others, but rather against the background of comparative law, examining domestic law and European law as part of the development of universal legal theory.

5. The New Egyptian Civil Code: Stages of Legislation

Before discussing the history of civil codification in Egypt, we should first define the concept of a 'code'. A code is a comprehensive act of legislation characterized by several characteristics, most principally totality, breadth, a systematic approach, abstraction and innovation. This is an act of legislation that seeks to establish an arrangement whereby every question has an answer. The code is not, of course, based on the assumption that it can contain no *lacuna*: as long as an act of legislation is a human act, it will include cases of omission. The totality of the code refers to the desire to regulate the full scope of legal relations in a given field, without deliberately leaving unregulated areas. The field in question is not narrow, but broad, reflecting an expansive field of

[69] Wujūb, p. 114.
[70] Fiqh al-Khilāfa p. 318.

life. The code is constructed in a systematic manner, showing organization of structure and order, in an effort to draft the act of legislation in a comprehensive manner, so that the reader may find the principal arrangements. To this end, the code is developed at a fairly high level of abstraction—this provides the proper flexibility that enables it to cope with changes in the social background—a characteristic achieved, among other means, by the frequent use of principles and stopgap terms. Sometimes, the code even repeats an existing law; sometimes, an effort is made to introduce an arrangement different from that currently pertaining. The former law is nullified, and the new act of legislation henceforth provide the source of existing law. In most cases, the code embodies a blend of new and old law.[71]

Like Cato the Elder, Sanhūrī began from 1932 to call for the replacement of the existing Civil Code in Egypt with a New Civil Code, thus unifying the double legal system created by the simultaneous application of the Mixed Code (*al-taqnīn al-mukhtalaṭ*) of 1876 and the indigenous code, based thereon (*al-taqnīn al-ʾahlī*) from 1883.

In June 1876, Egypt enacted the Civil Code, based mainly on the French Civil Code of 1804. This code was used by the Mixed Courts (*al-maḥākim al-mukhtalaṭa*) in trying foreigners in the country. In 1883, this code was translated from French to Arabic (with minor amendments) for use in the native/national courts (*al-maḥākim-al-ʾahliyya/waṭaniyya*) which judged Egyptian citizens.

The Mixed Courts were international courts that operated in Egypt under the terms of the Capitulations system between 1875 and 1949. Their judicial authority, primarily civil in scope, included the foreigners in the country, as well as 'foreign interests', with the result that they enjoyed relatively broad authority in Egypt's economic life during this period, and therefore were the object of growing disquiet among nationalist circles in the country. The native (*ʾahliyya*) courts, later renamed the national (*waṭaniyya*) courts, tried Egyptian citizens;[72] over time, however, legal and nationalist resentment developed against these codes and courts in Arab-Egyptian legal circles. In 1937, the

[71] On the codification in general: J. M. Kelly, *A Short History of Western Legal Theory* (Oxford: Clarendon Press, 1999), pp. 311–315.

[72] Laṭifa Muḥammad Sālim, *Al-Niẓām al-Qaḍāʾī al-Miṣri al-Ḥadith, 1875–1914*, pp, 29–53, 113–124; Tawfīq Shiḥāta, *Taʾrīkh Ḥarakat al-Tajdīd fī al-Nuzum al-Qānūniyya fī Miṣr*. pp. 57–64; *Al-Kitāb al-Dhahabī lil-Maḥākim al-ʾAhliyya, 1883–1933* (Cairo: Maṭbaʿat al-Bulāk, 1938), in 2 volumes.

Montreux agreement was signed between the Egyptian authorities and the nations who had citizens resident in Egypt, establishing that by October 15, 1947, the Mixed Courts would be abolished and a single system of jurisdiction would apply in Egypt. This legal independence also provided the grounds for drafting a new civil code.

On 27 February 1936, in anticipation of the expected abolition of the Mixed Courts, the Egyptian government established the first committee of jurists charged with drafting the new civil code. The committee was headed by Murād Sayyid 'Aḥmad, and its members included Sanhūrī. This committee was mixed (five Egyptians and three foreigners), and although it was dissolved by the new government established just three months later, it managed to complete part of the work of drafting the Code.

A second committee was established by the government on 20 November 1936, headed by Kāmil Ṣidqī, but Sanhūrī was not among its members (as noted above, this was a Wafdist government that resented Sanhūrī's abandoning the party to join its rival). This committee's deliberations focused mainly on the subjects of guarantees and preemption (*shufʿa*), but it, too, was dissolved on the pretext of dissatisfaction with its work. The actual reason was that the Wafdist government had fallen, and been replaced by a Saʿadist government. As a member of the new ruling party, Sanhūrī presumably hoped to return to the drafting committee. In fact, on 28 June 1938, Minister of Justice 'Aḥmad Khashba Bāshā decided to charge two experts with the task: Dr. Sanhūrī and his French colleague, teacher and friend, the renowned Professor Edouard Lambert. The Ministry of Justice recommended that just two "of the most eminent legal scholars" draft the New Code, one Egyptian and the other a foreigner. They were assisted by a legal team comprised entirely of Egyptians.

Over the years, Sanhūrī maintained contacts with two leading French legal experts who were at the forefront of the transformation in French civil law in the early twentieth century, as will be discussed below. Lambert and Louis Josserand (1868–1941), who both had a strong influence on Sanhūrī, were professors of law from the University of Lyon. These contacts were particularly important given the influence of French law in that period on Egyptian law, and particularly in the context of the goal of a sociological transformation of law, as will be presented in this book, or, for example, the theory presented by Lambert in his book on customary law such as that created in court.[73]

[73] E. Lambert, *La Fonction du Droit Civil Comparé* (Paris: V. Giard et E. Brière, 1903).

The two French experts were directly involved in the subject of law in the Arab world, which accordingly had the status not of a remote legal system but of one intimately connected to the main developments in Continental civil law. Lambert was invited to drat the general sections of the opening chapter in the Egyptian New Code, while Josserand drafted the general theory of obligations as applied in the Lebanese civil code. Lambert's involvement in drafting the Egyptian Code also had a personal historical background, and constituted a form of revenge against the British, who had ruled Egypt in the period 1882–1922. Lambert had served as director of the School of Law at Cairo, but in 1907 he became embroiled in a dispute with the British advisor to the Ministry of Education and resigned. The dispute occurred against the background of the attempts by the British occupiers to anglicize schools in Egypt and to displace French educational influences. An Englishman by the name of Hill took Lambert's place as director of the school. The incident was reported prominently in the French press, and letters were exchanged on the subject between the French and British foreign ministries. After Lambert's resignation, the school was run by the British, who saw it as an important base for influencing Egyptian nationalism. This process continued until 1923, when the Egyptians began to run the school, and French influence was again in evidence, albeit obliquely.[74]

For Egyptian nationalists, and surely for Sanhūrī, the enemies of the British were perceived as friends. It may be assumed that, for Lambert, his involvement in drafting the New Code constituted a personal triumph over the British, who had led to his removal.[75]

For Sanhūrī, the new position was the realization of his longing to contribute to his homeland and to attempt to transform this codification into a tool for legal and social change in the country. As early as 1922, while studying law in Lyon, Sanhūrī had set himself the objective of "serving my country, if God enables me so to do." His first goal was to participate in the revival of the Islamic *Sharīʿa* and to make it worthy of use in our generation; his second was to participate in Egypt's economic and financial revival; his third was to play a part in educational processes, including strengthening the status of women and improving

[74] Reid, pp. 19–20.

[75] More on the Influence of Lambert on Sanhūrī: Fiqh al-Khilāfa, pp. 29–33; "Taqrīr ʿan al-Muʾtamar al-Dawlī lil-Qānūn al-Muqārin bi-Lāhāy fī ʾIjtimāʿihi al-ʾAwal Sanat 1932", Majmūʿat *Maqālāt wa ʾAbḥāth al-ʾUstādh ʿAbd al-Razzāq al-Sanhūrī*, volume 1, pp. 23–29.

their social conditions; and his last goal—to contribute to the revival of the Arabic language.[76]

As he began work on drafting the New Code, Sanhūrī formulated a credo that alluded to the holistic role he would attribute to the Code as a bridge between law and society. In his comments, he referred to Friedrich Karl von Savigny (1779–1861), the leading German jurist of the nineteenth century. In his famous essay *The Vocation of Our Time in Legislation and Jurisprudence* (1814), Savigny had established an affinity between the community and law, according to which law must adapt itself to what he termed 'the spirit of the people' (*Volksgeist*). A law that was not consonant with the spirit of society was doomed to failure. On the relationship between the public, the legislature and law, he wrote:

> If we enquire first as to the content of written law, they are already determined by the mode of derivation of the lawgiving power; the already present people's law supplies those contents or what is the same thing, written law is the people's law. If one were to doubt that, one must conceive the lawgiver as standing apart from the nation; he however rather stands in its center, so that he concentrates in himself their spirit, feelings, needs, so that we have to regard him as the true representative of the spirit of the people... Lastly, in the history of every people enter stages of development and conditions which are no longer propitious to the creation of law by the general consciousness of a people. In this case this activity, in all cases indispensable will, in great measure, of itself devolve upon legislation.[77]

According to Savigny, custom is a public and central manifestation of law, and, accordingly, the function of jurists is to adapt law, which becomes complex and technical, to its changing social contexts.

> If one looks at the true bases of positive law, at the actual substance of it, he will see that in that view, cause and effect are exactly reversed. That basis has its existence, its reality, in the common consciousness of the people. This existence is an invisible thing; by what means can we recognize it? We do so when it reveals itself in external act, when it steps forth in usage, manners, custom; in the uniformity of a continuing and therefore lasting manner of action we recognize the belief of the people as its common root, and one diametrically opposite to bare chance. Custom, therefore, is the badge and not a ground of origin of positive law.[78]

---

[76] Diary, pp. 61–62.

[77] Lord Lloyd of Hampstead, M. D. A. Freeman, Lloyd's Introduction to Jurisprudence (London: Stevens, 1985), pp. 893–894.

[78] Ibid., p. 893.

Savigny was opposed to codification, arguing that history suggests that hasty codification has little value. For our purposes, Sanhūrī's reference to Savigny emphasizes the extent to which European legal discourse formed part of legal discourse in Egypt. Sanhūri disagreed with Savigny's comment against the idea of codification:

> Law does not confine itself to the pages of a book or to a set of articles, and this fact has become undisputed since Savigny pointed it out. The legal school he headed managed to prove that law is a living, growing and developing creation within the environment in which it was born... It might seem that the consolidation of law through articles and sections, the process we know as codification (*taqnīn*), is not consonant with this assumption, but neither does it contradict it. After all, law that is a constant state of development must at some point be written down at the point it has reached. Such consolidation need not be final, since law has no end... If Savigny was attacking the very notion of codification, time has proved him incorrect, and one cannot ignore the practical benefit of codification, as proved by the experience of many nations. A legal collection assists greatly in drawing the general public nearer to an acquaintance with law.
>
> Neither can it be claimed that such codification will restrict law in a narrow and limited space, since in such a case it would not be long before law broke through these restrictions that sought to contain it, and an unwritten law, the product of rulings and legal research, would emerge alongside written law, and, with time, would gain seniority in terms of its importance. Then the written law would remain as an inferior or vague form of positive law...[79]

On 24 April 1942, the first draft of the Code was presented in Arabic (a fact that made the debate about the proposal an internal Egyptian one for the first time, i.e., for Egyptian locals only, although it was later translated into French). In addition to the proposed Code, the Sanhūrī committee also prepared a collection of explanatory notes on the Code (*al-mudhakkara al-ʾiḍāḥiyya*) that constitute a legal work in their own right. Sanhūrī's name did not appear in the explanatory comments, but he later 'admitted' authorship.[80]

Over a period of three years, Sanhūrī distributed the proposal to jurists, judges, and leaders from the fields of religion, economics and commerce, government and administration in order to obtain their comments. This process, which he referred to as a 'referendum' (*ʾistiftāʾ*), will be discussed in depth in the next chapter.

[79] Wujūb, pp. 3–4.
[80] Al-Wasīṭ, volume 1, p. 28, note 2.

On 29 March 1945, a further committee was appointed and called the Re-examination Committee (*lajnat al-murājaʿa*). Again headed by Sanhūrī, the members of this committee included the member of the Upper House in the parliament, Musṭafa Maḥmūd al-Shurbajī; the member of the Lower House, ʿAlī al-Sayyid ʾAyūb; the Supreme Court Judge Muḥammad Kāmil Mursī; and Judge Slimān Ḥāfiẓ from the *ʾAhlī* appeal court in Cairo. These members were accompanied by a committee of ancillary experts, including the director of the Codification Department in the Ministry of Justice and director of the *ʾAhlī* court, ʿAbdu Muḥaram; Dr. Ḥasan Baghdādī, a lecturer in civil law at Faruq University; Dr. Slimān Murqus and Dr. Shafīq Shiḥāta, both lecturers of civil law at Fuad University; and Naṣīf Zakī, head of the prosecution in the *ʾAhlī* appeal court in Cairo.[81]

The role of this committee was to review the comments and amendments submitted over the three-year consultation period, and to update the proposed Code accordingly. The committee embarked on a comprehensive process of updating and modification, which it completed in November of the same year.

Accordingly, by this stage there were now two versions: the original draft Code, and the amended Code after the introduction of corrections by the Re-examination Committee.

On 4 December 1945, the amended version of the Code was tabled before both Houses of the Egyptian parliament. In the House of Representatives (the Lower House, *majlis al-nuwwāb*), the proposal was tabled by May 1946, and the house Committee for Legislative Affairs introduced numerous amendments.

The proposed Code then proceeded to the Senate (the Upper House, *majlis al-shuyūkh*), were it was again delayed, after the Senate decided to establish an additional committee of its own to scrutinize the draft thoroughly, clause by clause, and to hear the comments of legal, social and religious experts. This committee introduced dozens of additional amendments in the draft.

The committee completed its work on 28 June 1948. The amended draft of the Code was returned to the Lower House, where it was passed as a complete Code on 16 July 1948. The New Civil Code, with its 1149 articles, came into force on 15 October 1949, the same day on which the Mixed Courts throughout Egypt were abolished, and

---

[81] Ibid., p. 29.

national justice extended its scope to all of the state's residents and citizens. A new era began in the Egyptian legal system, with ramifications throughout the Arab world.

Sanhūrī's New Civil Code is still the civil code in effect in present-day Egypt, and it has exerted a crucial influence throughout the Arab world, spawning an entire family of Arab civil codes.[82] With minor changes, it has been copied in Syria (1949) and Libya (1953). Sanhūrī himself drafted the Iraqi civil code (1951), and the Egyptian Civil Code served as the principal basis of reference for the civil codes of Jordan (1976), Yemen (1979) and Kuwait (1981). It is impossible to relate to civil law in the Arab world without an acquaintance with the New Egyptian Civil Code and—this book would argue—without an appreciation of the wide-ranging transformation it generated in Egyptian civil law.

[82] N. Saleh, "Civil Codes of Arab Countries: the Sanhuri Codes", *Arab Law Quarterly* 8(2)(1993), p. 161.

CHAPTER TWO

THE STRUCTURAL ENGINEERING OF THE CODE—THE GATE TO THE CONCEALED

The realistic way of thinking lacks imagination, while the imaginative way of thinking eschews reality. Accordingly, the proper way of thinking is that which successfully blends reality and imagination.

Sanhūrī, 1949[1]

1. Sociological Law and Models of 'Social Engineering'

Before he began the work of drafting the New Civil Code, Sanhūrī published in 1936 methodological guidelines for the preparation of the Code, which he divided into the external aspect (*nāḥiya khārijiyya*), i.e. the extra-legal social preparations that should accompany and support the act of legal codification, and the internal aspect (*nāḥiya dākhiliyya*), i.e. the formal and substantive legal work itself.

Subsequent chapters in this book will all focus on the substance of the Code, while the present chapter argues that the Code cannot properly be understood without examining what might seem to be a secondary matter—the extra-legal social dimensions that Sanhūrī referred to as the external aspect—and without examining the formal dimensions of the Code. This apparently technical chapter is actually intricately connected to the following chapters—Sanhūrī himself referred to this connection as constituting a single entity.[2] "Codification is a technique that has rules and principles," he noted, "and one must not neglect the rules of this technique in such an important act of legislation as the reform of the Civil Code." It will also be argued in this chapter that attention to the technical and formal aspects is not only necessary in order to understand the substance of the Code, but is also vital in order to reveal that legal and social substance that cannot easily be identified and located from a review of the articles of the Code themselves. As

[1] Diary, 3 February 1949, p. 256.
[2] Wujūb, p. 66.

we shall see below, this essence was deliberately concealed within the Code, so that an ostensibly formalistic dilemma such as questions of phraseology and language, or the technique employed in order to 'import' foreign norms into the Code may serve as signposts indicating the presence of concealed aspects waiting to be revealed. This chapter may be seen as the gate to a legal, social and philosophical world that lies hidden among the articles of the New Civil Code. Technique and form are an essential first step in the long journey into the profound essence of the Code—and hence into the deepest realms of the soul of Egyptian society.

This chapter will identify a number of principles that develop and follow in sequence, forming a single formula, namely: the sociological school of legal theory; the principles of the theory of *takhayyur*; the theory of disengagement; the referendum (*'istiftā'*) and the distinction between the overt Code and the concealed one.

When Sanhūrī referred to the 'external aspect' of the Code, his intention was, first and foremost, to the sociological perception of law, i.e. to the essential mutual relations between law and society, as formulated by Edouard Lambert (1866–1947), Roscoe Pound (1870–1964) and Rudolf von Jhering (1818–1892), three thinkers who exerted a profound influence on Sanhūrī.[3] The New Egyptian Civil Code he created was a consciously sociological Code in which he sought to manifest in legal terms the ideas of the great exponents of this approach.

In broad terms, the sociological school of law rejected the idea that law was a unique or isolated field, and saw it as no more than a method for social control. This school rejected the approach that law formed a closed conceptual order, as evidenced by the complex experience of the twentieth century, which was not always met with an adequate and changing response from the direction of positivist law. Accordingly, social techniques should be adopted in order to improve law and adapt it to changing social reality. Sociological law rejects absolutist perceptions, preferring relativism, and shows an almost obsessive preoccupation with the meaning of the concepts of 'social justice' and 'social solidarity' and the ways in which these may be implemented.[4]

---

[3] For further details of Pound's influence on al-Sanhūrī, see his article on comparative law congress, held in Hague, *Majmū'at Maqālāt wa 'Abḥāth al-'Ustādh 'Abd al-Razzāq al-Sanhūrī* (Cairo: Maṭba'at Jāmi'at al-Qāhira, 1992), Volume 1, pp. 529–530.

[4] Lord Lloyd of Hampstead, M. D. A. Freeman, *Lloyd's Introduction to Jurisprudence* (London: Stevens, 1985), pp. 548–549.

Jhering, one of the leading German legal theoreticians of the nineteenth century, argued that the science of law must apply itself to social relations and to the social goals inherent in any legal provision. These goals should protect interests, in which context he distinguished between individual interests and societal interests. According to Jhering, the function of the legislature and of the judge is to harmonize these interests, insofar as possible, and, in the case of the judge—to look less at the legal text itself, and more at the inherent social goals that lie behind it.

Jhering believed that law constituted the totality of social conditions for life as activated by the state by means of coercion; his approach, which Sanhūrī shared, was that concern for the general social interest entailed concern for the interests of the individual, rather than vice versa. A measure of paternalism may be found in this approach, and this will be manifested in real terms in the New Egyptian Civil Code, since, according to this perspective, the common good is ultimately always in the best interests of the individual. Pound maintained that the purpose of legal research is to improve the efficiency of efforts to secure the goals of law, with an emphasis on society—its life and background, the influence on it and the individual interests of its members. Accordingly, any act of legislation should be preceded by an examination of the influences of the legal institutions, norms and theories on the life of society. To this end, a preliminary sociological study should be prepared, with emphasis on the sociological history of law, i.e. the social background and functioning of legal institutions, norms and theories. For Pound and other sociological jurists, the central goal of law was justice.

The following description details Pound's approach to sociolegal engineering and his perception of supreme social interests. The same approach characterized Sanhūrī's legal work on the New Code and the Egyptian society for which it was intended:

> For Pound, jurisprudence is not so much a social science as a technology, and the analogy of engineering is applied to social problems. He is concerned primarily with the effects of law upon society and only to a lesser extent with questions about the social determination of law...The creative role of the judiciary is in the forefront, as is the need for a new legal technique directed to social needs. The call is for a new functional approach to law.
>
> Pound took over Jhering's view of the law as a reconciler of conflicting interests, and gave it certain distinctive features. For Pound the law is an ordering of conduct so as to make the goods of existence and the means

> of satisfying claims go round as far as possible with the least friction and waste. Pound regards these claims as interests, which exist independently of the law and which are "pressing for recognition and security." The law recognizes some of these, giving them effect within defined limits... The public as a whole may both lack the means of articulating its desires, or their expression be manipulated in a variety of ways, if regard is to be paid to genuine and not 'phony' interests... Pound's answer here is that every society has certain basic assumptions upon which its ordering rests, though for the most part these may be implicit rather than expressly formulated.[5]

Pound referred to the sociological and legal structure he discussed by the term 'social engineering'. The significance of his approach is illustrated by the title of one of his books: *Social Control Through Law* (1942); it argues that the role of the jurist, legislator, judge and scholar—as of the engineer—is to establish a functional structure that should meet as many social and individual needs as possible, and should have the external appearance of a harmonious and complete unit. Like the engineer, the jurist must sketch and plan the legal structure in social terms before beginning the work of drafting, in order to ensure that the structure will not collapse and will remain intact for as long as possible. This requires legal harmony between the overall doctrines manifested in the Code in all the different fields, such as contracts, damages, property and so on and the other articles in the Code. Like the architect, the function of the jurist is to plan a structure that will be suitable for the dimensions of the society for which it is intended and will meet its interests. This structure of engineering should reflect the different social classes and the desired relations between these classes, the different spheres of civil law and their interrelationships, economic dilemmas, legal and other concerns in the country and the proposed legal solutions—all these as part of a harmonious whole. This is an almost impossible task in a Code that is supposed to offer all the answers.

We shall propose below several technical engineering structures along these lines, whose goal is social, as, it is argued in this book, is the case with the New Code. Clearly, all the structures must also be harmonious, as part of a single Code.

We may begin with the example of the manner in which Sanhūrī regarded the relations between positivist prevailing law and key social

---

[5] Ibid., pp. 565–566, 568. On the Theory of social engineering: J. H. Turner, *The Structure of Sociological Theory* (Homewood: Dorsey Press, 1978).

trends, and the manner in which these social trends can be shaped by positivist law, at the same time as it is in turn shaped by the social trends. I propose that this be referred to as a form of *perpetuum mobile*—an infinite movement of social engineering:

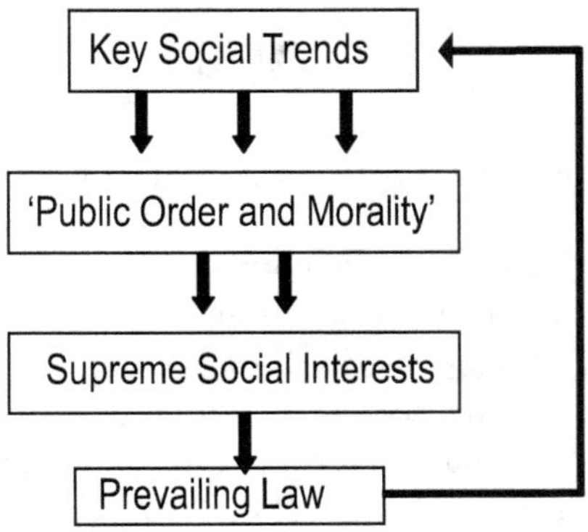

Model A: *Perpetuum Mobile* between Society and Prevailing Law

This is an example of a sociolegal structure of engineering in which diverse and even contradictory social ideas compete for admission to the field of prevailing law, i.e. positivist law. These ideas may be admitted into the New Egyptian Civil Code by means of the flexible test of 'public order and morality', which appears in the Code and will be discussed in depth below. The scholar and, to an extent, the judge are empowered to rule on this question between changing social ideas and law, and these criteria are determined in accordance with the sociological supreme doctrines of the Code as expounded below, such as the principle of protecting the weak. If a social idea secures recognition by positivist law, it then returns to the society, from which it came through court rulings, changing society accordingly. Thus law changes society, just as society changes law. The intent is to achieve a form of social 'reform', i.e. to make society more just; and this, too, is a sociological aspiration.[6]

Or take a further example that also aims to create a *perpetuum mobile* in the relations between the individual and society in the context of justice:

---

[6] G. Bechor, "To Hold the Hand of the Weak: The Emergence of Contractual Justice in the Egyptian Civil Law", *Islamic Law and Society* 8(2001) pp. 179, 197.

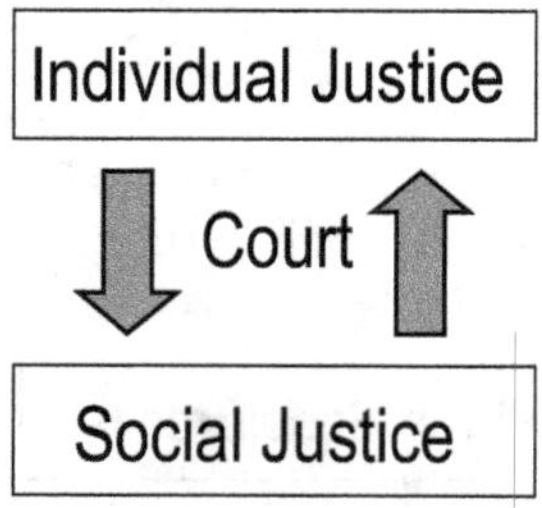

Model B: *Perpetuum Mobile* between Individual Justice and Social Justice

Through sociological law, the courts will rule in accordance with the norms of individual justice in each given case, until such point as the quantity of rulings reaches a critical mass creating broad norms of social justice. At the same time, society—as it progresses toward justice—will grant increasing legitimacy to court rulings in keeping with the norms of individual justice, and so on. Thus the individual and society will each support the other; quantity will be transformed into quality, and will then be transmuted again into quantity.

A third model of *perpetuum mobile*, in accordance with Sanhūrī's perception of the New Code, may be identified in the relations between economic and social problems, which we shall refer to as dilemmas, and the extent of the legitimacy enjoyed by the Code. Egyptian society faces its own unique and problematic dilemmas, such as the problem of irrigation using the special water channels that draw water from the Nile; problems created in the context of family joint ownership; the concept of custom and its scope, *waqf* and so on, as we shall see below. Sanhūrī was not afraid to bring such dilemmas into the Code, so that it would enjoy as extensive a legitimacy as possible, since it would be seen to be addressing such difficult problems. At the same time, Sanhūrī

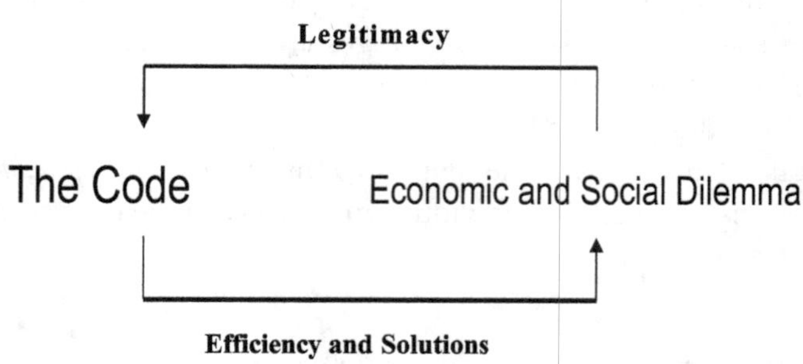

Model C: Social Needs and the Legitimacy of the New Code

improved and remedied these inherent dilemmas, so that the mention of them is far from coincidental. Thus the contribution was mutual: the dilemmas provided the Code with legitimacy, while the Code provided solutions and desirable possibilities for increasing efficiency in the context of these dilemmas. Thus society and law provide each other with mutual support.

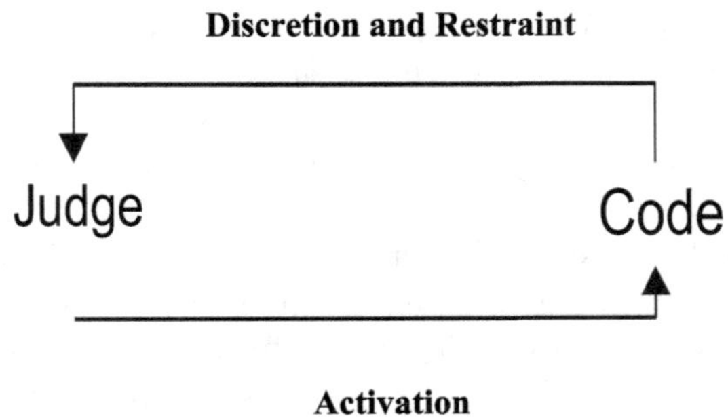

Model D: The Healthy Tension between the Judge and the Code

As will be discussed in detail in Chapter Six, which deals with the desired extent of legal flexibility, Sanhūrī developed a dimension of activation and supervision between the judge, who activates the numerous sociological doctrines embodied in the Code, and which could not be activated without him, and the Code itself. The sociological Code greatly expands the scope of jurisdiction enjoyed by the judge. However, fearing that the judge may come to believe himself to be above society, it also establishes a series of restraints on his activity, such as its insistence on an objective interpretative approach in cases in which there is concern of excessive judicial discretion. Thus the Code grants the judge extensive power, while reserving the possibility of supervising and restraining this power.

These models must interconnect harmoniously within the framework of a single Code. By way of example, we will see how two models connect: without the close supervision of the judge, it is not possible to secure individual justice, and hence the achievement of social justice will also be delayed. Concurrently, without social justice, the degree of legitimacy enjoyed by the Code will be impaired, reducing its effectiveness.

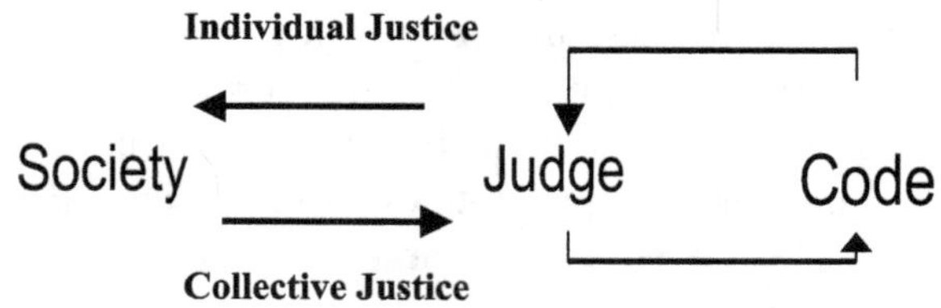

Model E: Tension between the Degree of Legal Certainty and the Degree of Justice

It may be argued that Sanhūrī also balanced the fear of damage to legal and commercial certainty and the scope of justice. The sociological approach, which advocates doctrines of equity such as good faith or the abuse of a right, is liable to impair commercial certainty and legal stability; equally, and as we shall consider below, excessively individualistic law is liable to impair the degree of justice. In order to overcome this dilemma, Sanhūrī employed a technique of balancing by means of interpretative tests imposed on the judge. The broader the potential injury to legal certainty and the potential for ambiguity, the more strongly the judge is recommended to employ an objective interpretative test, i.e., the test of the reasonable person, thus restricting judicial discretion of the court. Conversely, if a level of legal stability has been secured in a given doctrine, there is no concern at the use of Sanhūrī's preferred test, that of subjectivity, i.e., the examination of the case of an individual person who appears before the Court, rather than the test of the reasonable person. As shown in the following diagram, the triple test is seen, for example, in the doctrine of the abuse of a right and in its interpretative modalities established by Sanhūrī.

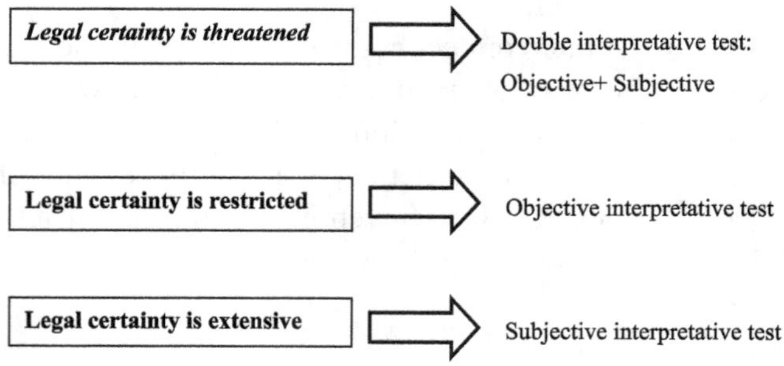

Model F: Desired Social Solidarity between Polarized Classes of the Social Home

As we shall see in the next chapter, in the context of the relations between residents of the lower floor and the upper floor of an apartment building, this book argues that Sanhūrī establishes a structure of compulsory solidarity symbolic of that needed between the upper and lower classes in society as a whole. Just as those who live on the lower floor must show solidarity with their neighbors above, since the entire building rests upon them, so those who dwell on the upper floors must show solidarity with those below them, lest undue pressure be placed on them. If each party does not support the other, the building (both physical and social) will collapse. We shall see below that Sanhūrī developed such a compulsory zone of social solidarity between the upper and lower floors. For example, the lower floor was ordered to be rebuilt if the building collapsed for any reason. This provision is a legal symbol for the need to limit social polarization. Social solidarity constitutes a key motif in sociological law, and hence illuminates its centrality in a Code of this type.

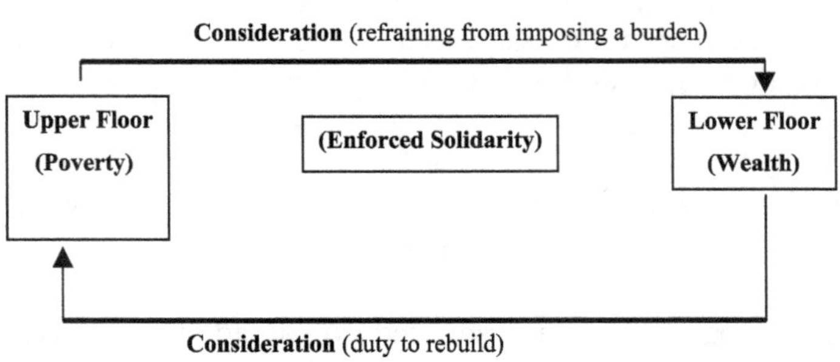

Model G: The Ideal Square of Egyptian Society

The last model, with which we shall conclude our illustration of social engineering (though the Code provides many more formulas of such ideological engineering) is the overall argument of this book—namely the structure of social forces the New Code sought to promote by means of Civil Law, which comprises four principal components: advancing and sustaining the poor, which the Code sought to achieve through the relative nature of contract law; advancing the stronger members of society, in order to allow the leading social forces to move ahead; restricting

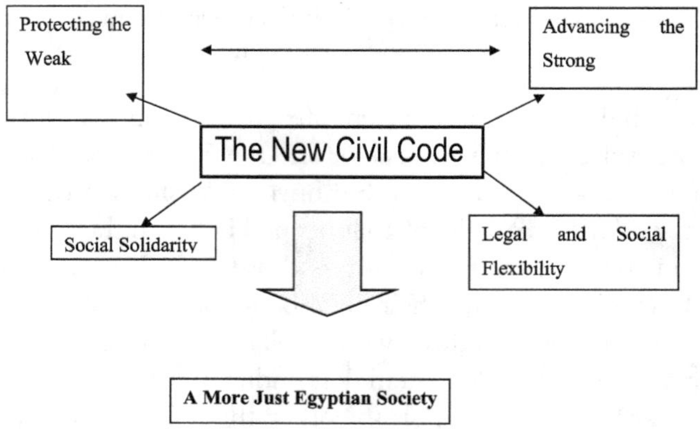

property rights in a coercive manner in order to develop models of social solidarity; and, lastly, developing models of legal and social flexibility in order to prevent such a coercive legal and social structure from leading to a social explosion and an exacerbation of the existing situation, rather than its amelioration. This is Sanhūrī's overall square model of the New Civil Code as perceived by this book—the ultimate and primary structure of social engineering. The supreme interests sometimes cross and even contradict each other. Only through their joint processing in the legal mixer of the Civil Code can they achieve synergetic merger and secure the ultimate objective—justice.

2. Teleological Interpretation and its Impact on the New Egyptian Civil Code

The sociological school is associated with an additional development in European, and particularly French law that was to have a considerable influence both on Egyptian law and on Sanhūrī.

Until the turn of the twentieth century, the historical and literal school of interpretation dominated the French legal system. According to this approach, it was unacceptable to deviate from the precise meaning of legislation and from what was perceived as the historical intention of the legislature. In the face of this conservative stance to interpretation, a new approach emerged that came to be known as the teleological approach (*interprétation téléologique*). In this approach, the meaning of a legal text is not fixed, but varies over the course of time, in accordance with the social tendencies of law. A judge interpreting an act of legislation, then, is no longer a slave to the past, and is to be guided not by criteria from past societies but by the criteria of the society in which he lives. This approach sought to examine what the contemporary legislature would seek to achieve in interpreting a given law, and determined that law serves a given ideal epitomized in the realization of social order and justice.[7]

The perception of social order and justice advanced by this approach was accompanied by a change in the perception of the role of the individual within the social purpose, of which law forms the foundations. According to this legal and social approach, the individual can no longer act freely to advance his own interests, since human rights exist primarily for the good of society and not for the benefit of those who enjoy them, and, accordingly, use of these rights is conditioned on and restricted by the social interests for which they were developed.[8]

This line constituted a clear departure from the spirit that had hitherto guided the Napoleonic codes, and principally the Code Civil of 1804. The Enlightenment, the legal philosophy of the eighteenth century and the Declaration of Human and Civil Rights (1789) all constituted a source of inspiration for these codes, lauding the function, independent will and natural rights of the individual. They perceived human rights as the absolute prerogative of the individual, in the spirit of the Latin saying "he who exercises his right hurts no person." A similar turning point occurred in Anglo-Saxon law in the late nineteenth century; however, Egyptian law remained exclusively in the influence of French and Continental law.[9]

Until the end of the nineteenth century, there were civil courts in France that applied the teleological approach to interpretation, albeit cautiously. René David (1906–1990), one of the leading historians of French law, has argued that this interpretative approach was beneath the surface. No one intended that it be presented as an explicit principle of interpretation, or that a public announcement be issued regarding the need to abandon the accepted historical form of interpretation.

[7] On the Teleological Interpretation and its influence on French law see: R. David, *French Law: Its Structure, Sources and Methodology*, trans. M. Kindred, (Baton Rouge: Louisiana State University Press, 1972)(hereinafter: David), pp. 161–164. A view from Egypt on this change see: J. Y. Brinton, *The Mixed Courts of Egypt* (New Haven and London: Yale University Press, 1968), p. 91.

[8] David, p. 200.

[9] A.V. Dicey, *Lectures on the Relations between Law and Public Opinion in England during the Nineteenth Century*, (London: Macmillan, 1962), pp. 259–302; M. Horwitz, *The Transformation of American Law, 1870–1960, The Crisis of Legal Orthodoxy*, (New York: Oxford University Press, 1992), pp. 145–167.

As the new century dawned, a doctrinal movement suddenly appeared that began to demand legitimacy for the teleological approach of interpretation. This movement was headed by leading French jurists, including Raymond Saleille (1855–1912), François Gény (1861–1959) and Louis Josserand (1868–1941), among others. This movement was European in scope, and led to the establishment of the 'Free Law' (*Freirecht*) school in Germany; changes following the spirit of the movement were introduced in the Swiss civil code of 1907 (which was also adopted by the modern Turkish state). Law was seen to be 'free' to perform justice, rather than shackled in strict norms, and the judge was required to interpret the law not in accordance with its letter alone, but above all in accordance with its content and purpose.[10]

It should be recalled that the French legal perception of the 'legal rule' (*régle juridique*) differs from what the English understood by the same term. In the English system of law, the legal rule is routinely established by the judge who faces a precise and specific question, and responds to this question by applying the legal rule. Neither does he extend the rule beyond the specific question. David claimed that this English approach reminded him of an impressionist painting—the legal rules when perceived as individual were no more than dots. The observer must move back in order to discover the overall form of the composition.

The situation in France was different, since there law is by its essence the product not of the judge, but of the jurist. French law abhors the individual case, and seeks for clarity in looking beyond individual cases toward the principles declared by the legislature and by jurists. The rules exist at a high level of abstraction, and, accordingly, the legal rule is not a dot, but a guideline.

In French law, judicial decisions do not create legal rules, but are supposed merely to apply the existing rules to a specific case. Rather than advancing in a casuist manner, French law seeks to establish general principles before entering into the details of specific cases.[11]

For our purposes, for as long as teleological interpretation was advanced by a number of courts, no major change was involved. However, when the leading jurists adopted this interpretative approach, it became a binding 'legal rule.'

---

[10] On this movement: J. Herget, S. Wallace, "The German Free Law Movement as the Source of American Legal Realism", *Virginia Law Review* 73(1987), pp. 399–455.

[11] C. Dadomo, S. Farran, *The French Legal System* (London: Sweet & Maxwell Ltd., 1993), pp. 11–13.

This transition in French law occurred, above all, because the Napoleonic codes, including the civil code, had become outmoded. A century after they were drafted, the need arose to renovate these laws in a society whose economic structure had profoundly changed. Following the establishment of the Third Republic and the development of administrative law, the leading social and legal ideas of the period had also undergone overwhelming change.

David wrote that the idea of the separation of powers was still perceived as vital for democracy, but was understood in the twentieth century in a different manner than in the past. The unpleasant memory of the pre-revolutionary courts had begun to fade, leading to a greater willingness to expand the judicial discretion within society. The idea that judges could help in legal and social development was less shocking than it would have been in the past. The judges were no longer perceived as mere pawns for implementing legislation—the 'mouth of the law,' as Montesquieu famously called them.

This period had also seen significant developments in administrative law, providing an example of the creation of case law. The *Conseil d'État*, which was responsible for the development of administrative law, was not limited by the Code Civil, and was free to choose which provisions to apply and which aspects were perceived as more just.

Adherents of the teleological school did not seek to abolish the existing civil code, but to reread it. "*Par le code civil, au-delà du code civil,*" ("through the Code Civil, beyond the Code Civil") noted the jurist Saleille, paraphrasing a saying from Roman law, a formulation that sought reassure those who were alarmed at the change and to encourage the reformists. From the turn of the twentieth century, some one hundred years after the adoption of the Code Civil, this interpretative approach "to examine the benefit to society and justice" was fully legitimized in France, without the Code itself being amended; the same approach influenced the legal system in neighboring countries.

However, David noted that the importance of this interpretative approach should not be overestimated. He claimed that the French had never taken as extreme an approach as the Germans from the *Freirecht* school. Teleological interpretation in France, he posited, continued to be subject to substantive restrictions. Firstly, it could not contradict literal or logical interpretation; in other words, a legal text could accept an interpretation motivated by the need to advance the public good and promote justice only when this was permitted by its literal meaning. In addition, the fundamental unity of principles of French law could not be disturbed or threatened. Secondly, the teleological approach did not completely displace historical interpretation: the judge could choose between the two—the original intent of the legislature, or that which was best for the public good and for justice.[12]

The legal changes that took place in Europe also reached the Egyptian legal system, beginning with the foreign jurists who worked and judged in the Mixed Courts, as evidenced in the Egyptian legal literature of the period (in European languages).[13] However, Brinton commented that the dilemma facing the French legal system was of less concern to the judges in the Mixed Courts. Although they also ruled on the basis of a code based largely on the Code Civil, the Mixed Civil Code in Egypt included a reference to 'natural law and equity' in the event of a legal lacuna or ambiguity, thus rendering it more flexible than the Code Civil, which did not include a similar provision.[14]

It was only natural that such profound changes in the French legal system also influenced the native Egyptian system, since the latter was based more on French law than on any other legal source. Sir Morris Amos, the British legal advisor, commented in this context that:

> Egypt offers an example of the reception of French law by a people totally alien to Europe in language, religion and social and political traditions. When, fifty years ago, Nubar Pasha secured the consent of the Powers to the institution of the International Courts, it was agreed without debate that the only possible law with which to equip them was that of the French Codes. Eight years later, the year after the British occupation, the French Codes were extended to the newly reorganized native jurisdictions and this became the law governing all civil causes in Egypt, excepting those relating to the family and personal status. The inevitable consequences followed: and after forty years of British occupation, British officials were administering French law in Arabic, teaching French law in English, and arguing French law in French: and today a young Egyptian who has learned English at school finds that he has to learn French when he grows up, in order to engage in business and to mix in society.[15]

Another British legal advisor to the Egyptian government, Malcolm McIlwraith, added candidly:

---

[12] David, p. 164.
[13] Wujūb, pp. 11–13.
[14] Brinton, p. 91.
[15] Ibid., p. 87.

> French law is by reason of the precision and lucidity of the language clearer in form and more congenial in substance to the mass of inhabitants of Egypt, both native and foreign, than would ever be, in my opinion, our uncodified, largely unwritten, more or less inaccessible and partly archaic system.[16]

Until 1907, the French dominated the Cairo Law School. In 1890, they opened an additional school of law in Cairo and encouraged Egyptian students to pursue academic studies in France. As a result, the legal discourse of the period in Egypt was influenced quite strongly by developments in French jurisprudence.

The transition that occurred in French law lay behind the desire, several decades later, to introduce the New Code in Egypt. An interesting transformation occurred, however: the socio-legal transition in Europe became an Egyptian shift in Egyptian discourse. A process of Egyptization occurred both in the method of transition and in its circumstances, with the result that the legal reform of the Civil Code acquired a strongly internal Egyptian significance.

As we have already seen, Sanhūrī, the architect of the New Code, completed his studies at the University of Lyon under the tutelage of his close friend, Professor Edouard Lambert, one of the scholars most closely identified with the sociological and teleological transition in French law. Accordingly, he was able to follow at first hand the changes in the French legal system.

Lambert was invited to draft the general articles in the opening section of the New Code, including important articles relating to conflicts between laws. The remainder of the Code was drafted by Egyptians.[17]

As early as 1932, Sanhūrī began to advocate a thorough revision of the Egyptian (*'Ahlī*) Civil Code. The departing point for his discussion was the debate that had taken place in France for and against the overall revision of the Code Civil. In 1936, he wrote:

> If we must decide between the arguments of both sides, we tend to the former group (those advocating an overall revision of the French Civil Code). The French Civil Code requires an overall reform (*tanqīḥ*), particularly in the current era, after the Great War changed many economic and social regimes, creating a significant gulf between the civilization of 1804 and modern day civilization. We are interested in the question of the overall reform of the French Code since this issue is also of relevance

[16] Ibid., p. 92.
[17] Reid, pp. 19–20.

> for us. If we have shown that the French Code requires an overall reform, the same will certainly be true of the Egyptian Civil Code, which was clumsily copied from the French.[18]

The New Egyptian Code sought to go one step further than French law, embodying the innovations of sociological and teleological interpretation within the text of the Code itself—something that French law, as we saw above, refrained from doing. This process was similar to that undergone by other Continental codes, such as those of Switzerland and Italy.

During the first deliberations of the Civil Code Committee established by the upper house of parliament, which functioned as a parliamentary investigating committee into the proposed Code, the proposal of the Ministry of Justice to introduce an entirely new civil code in Egypt was attacked. The committee president, Muḥammad al-Wakīl, asked why the ministry was advocating a new code rather than following in the footsteps of the French, who, despite changing social and economic circumstances, had not abolished the Napoleonic Code. These criticisms were responded to by the representative of the Ministry of Justice, ʿAbdu Muḥaram. He claimed that during the deliberations of the committee, that prepared the proposed Code, it emerged that in order to remedy the defects of the old Civil Code, three-fourths of the Code must be amended. He also argued that while the French had not abolished their Code Civil, they had collaborated with the Italians to prepare a proposed new code (that would later become the Italian Civil Code). "Were it not for the conditions and events pertaining in France, this code would also have been applied in that country. It is expected that it will be applied in France in the near future" (in reality, the proposed code was never adopted by the French).[19]

Is it possible that these modern innovations were introduced into the New Egyptian Code by the unlikely means of the ancient tools of Islamic law, such as *takhayyur*?

[18] Wujūb p. 8.

[19] The Egyptian Government, the Ministry of Justice, *Al-Qānūn al-Madanī, Majmūʿat al-ʾAʿmāl al-Taḥḍīriyya* (Cairo: Maṭbaʿat al-Kitāb al-ʿArabī, 1949), volume 1, pp. 34; 124–125; Al-Wasīṭ, volume 1, pp. 20–21, 62–63, 551.

3. *Takhayyur*: Adaptation of a Religious Concept to a Mundane Legal Use

The movement for reform and modernization in Islam in nineteenth century Egypt, founded by Muḥammad ʿAbduh (1849–1905, who served from 1899 as the Mufti of Egypt), argued that there was no contradiction between the principles of Islam and those of modern Western civilization, and that Islamic legal doctrine should be re-ordered with the goal of adapting it to meet the requirements of modern society. This group was comprised mainly of clergymen, and sought to renew Islamic law from within. Their discourse was religious and Islamic; if at all, the renewal of Islamic law was to take place using the tools of Islamic law itself.[20]

One of the most important principles introduced by ʿAbduh in order to bridge between the rapidly-developing reality of modern times and the world of Islamic law was the principle of *takhayyur* (or *talfīq*), i.e., a technique enabling the selection of a proper interpretation from the four legal schools (*madhhab*, plural—*madhāhib*) of Sunni Islam: the Ḥanafī, the Mālikī, the Shāfiʿī and the Ḥanbalī. *Takhayyur* was considered a bold concept over the centuries, since an alleged state of stagnation had emerged, and a barrier had been erected between these four systems.

Albert Hourani explained the principle of *takhayyur* in the following terms:

> The notion that in any particular case a judge could choose that interpretation of the law, whether it came from his own legal code or not, which best fitted the circumstances had been accepted within limits by some classical authorities, but what ʿAbduh suggested was something broader: not simply the 'borrowing' of a specific point from some other code, but a systematic comparison of all four, and even of the doctrines of independent jurists who accepted none of them, with a view to producing a 'synthesis', which would combine the good points of all.[21]

It may be argued that the context addressed by Muḥammad ʿAbduh was an internal one of Islamic religion; his legal tools were internal Islamic ones as was his sphere of reference. For ʿAbduh, *takhayyur* constituted

---

[20] M. H. Kerr, *Islamic Reform, the Political and Legal Theories of Muhammad ʿAbduh and Rashid Rida* (Berkeley: University of California Press, 1966).

[21] A. Hourani, *Arabic Thought in the Liberal Age, 1798–1939* (London: Oxford University Press, 1983), p. 152.

a choice between the legal schools within the *Sharīʿa* in order to meet the challenge of the West.

The concept of *takhayyur* was revisited in the twentieth century with the drafting of the New Egyptian Code. The detailed explanations to the proposed Code noted several times that its drafters had adopted the technique of *takhayyur* in selecting from among dozens of codes from around the world, in addition to Egyptian case law, the Islamic *Sharīʿa* and the Old Civil Code, with the ultimate goal of formulating the New Egyptian Civil Code. Moreover, the explanatory notes to the Code noted that:

> Alongside the Latin and German codes, a group of codes has emerged during the twentieth century that have developed the technique of *takhayyur* and cannot be identified fully with either of these schools (the Latin or the German), but rather have drawn the best from each school. The most outstanding example of these codes that have undergone a process of *takhayyur* is the Polish Civil Code, which combined the clarity and eloquence of the Latin codes with the precision and depth of the Germanic codes.[22]

Thus we can see that a term that began its life as an internal concept from the world of Islamic religious law was reincarnated in the Code not merely as a purely secular term, but as global one that could even be applied, for example, to the Polish Civil Code. The Islamic context of the term was detached, and only the essence of choice and selection remained.

The transformation undergone by the term *takhayyur* formed part of the broader approach of Sanhūrī, who drew terms from Islamic religious law and imbued them with a mundane and even secular meaning.

According to his approach, Islamic law offered an authentic local response to Western culture and law, since it was in no way inferior to the legal system that had shaped the West, be that Roman law, Latin law or English Common Law. In 1932, after returning inspired from an international congress on comparative law in The Hague, which also addressed the study of Islamic law, Sanhūrī commented:

> We must give back what may be seen as Islamic civilization (the *Sharīʿa*) the flexibility it has lost, and regard it not as a collection of customs and religious instructions, but in the original format of a civilization...[23]

---

[22] Al-Qānūn al-Madanī, volume 1, p. 17.

[23] "L'Universite Egyptienne au Congrès International de Droit Comparé de la

In 1936, as he developed the detailed proposal for the amendment of the Egyptian Civil Code, he added:

[The *Sharīʿa*] may constitute one of the pillars of (global) comparative law. We have not encountered in the history of law a legal pillar based on such solid foundations of precise legal logic, similar to the logic of Roman law, as is the case with the Islamic *Sharīʿa*.[24]

Sanhūrī drew this concept of reviving the *fiqh*, the legal core of the *Sharīʿa*, from the leading exponents of the historical school of legal history, Sevigny and Kohler, as mentioned above. The latter scholar claimed that any legal system was conditioned and dependent on the culture within which it emerged. Every culture had its own needs, and these needs and requirements must be met by law. The function of law is to draw on the past cultural strengths of each nation in order to advance society; to draw on the past and on legal and social roots in order to create a healthy social future. This adherence by Sanhūrī to the historical school may seem paradoxical: while he indeed drew on Islamic law as representing the 'national spirit', he drew far more in practical terms from the Continental legal systems, thus contradicting the national and cultural uniqueness of law.

As a faithful adherent of the Easternist approach presented in the previous chapter, Sanhūrī thus saw a fertile basis for cooperation between different Muslim nations, since they all shared a common 'Eastern' heritage and formed part of a single 'Eastern' society. The common legal component, to be based on a clarified and renewed version of the *Sharīʿa*, would come to define the Eastern culture of these nations, among themselves and *vis-à-vis* the West. Sanhūrī recommended that the unification of different perspectives guide the legislatures of the various Muslim countries in drawing mutually from the same source—Islamic law—while taking into account the divergent realities in each individual country. "Then the Islamic nations shall be able to compete with the West rather than dragging behind it."[25]

Accordingly, it may be argued that the *takhayyur* in the New Code is perceived as a sociolegal ideology: to draw on as many legal sources as possible which are best and most appropriate for Egyptian society. This

Haye", *Majmūʿat Maqālāt wa ʾAbḥāth al-ʾUstādh ʿAbd al-Razzāq al-Sanhūrī*, volume 1, p. 29.

[24] Wujūb, p. 113.

[25] *Majmūʿat Maqālāt wa ʾAbḥāth al-ʾUstādh ʿAbd al-Razzāq al-Sanhūrī*, volume 1, p. 335; Diary, p. 91.

process of selection was implemented for the first time by Egyptians, who hence faced the sole objective of the good of Egyptian society. This was of importance on the national level: after years when others had decided for Egyptians, it was now time for them to act on their own behalf. Such a process of selection should depart from a position of strength, yet be willing to reach compromises.

For Sanhūrī, *takhayyur* constituted the beginning of what will be described in this book as a journey toward a new order—an Egyptian society aware of its defects, seeking its best interests and able to exploit any source to its own benefit, whether from the East or the West, the past or the present, from the sphere of tradition or that of progress. ʿAbduh's utilitarian test may be seen here, and the fact that this benefit is intended to serve Egyptian society itself. However, while for the Islamic modernists this debate related to the delineated sources within the *Sharīʿa*, Sanhūrī argued that any legal source from anywhere in the world could participate in the process of *takhayyur*.

Within each doctrine a further difference may be noted. ʿAbduh saw *takhayyur* within the framework of the closed discourse of Islamic clergy, with the ultimate goal of influencing society at large. By contrast, Sanhūrī saw *takhayyur* in the framework of broad social discourse intended to create a new *modus vivendi* for Egyptian society. In an earlier comment from 1923, taken from his personal diaries, Sanhūrī noted:

> (There are two intellectual groups in Egypt)—the first clings blindly to an Islamic past that does not develop with time, something that is liable to encourage hatred to the Islamic nation and harm religious minorities that live in the Near East. The latter will turn to Europe for protection, so that instead of pooling their efforts alongside us, they will turn against us.
>
> On the other side, there is a group that seeks to sever the bond with the past in order to introduce European civilization into Egypt, so that it might become part of Europe, ignoring the unique traditions, history and Eastern temperament of this country.
>
> Both these groups present a danger to Egyptian society. We must admit that, at this point, we need Europe; but this does not imply that we should sacrifice our own national traditions and introduce an alien civilization into our Eastern land... That which binds us with bonds of strength is the past. A nation cannot rid itself of its past, unless it be a nation that is floundering in the dark, unable to find the path forward.[26]

---

[26] Diary, 31 October 1923, p. 125.

In a largely demonstrative act, Sanhūrī thus examined some twenty codes from around the world, as well as Egyptian case law (from both the Mixed and the *ʾAhlī* or native Courts), the principles of the *Sharīʿa* and the Old Egyptian Code in order to gather those elements that were consonant with the supreme principles established in the Code. None of these sources enjoyed substantive weight in its own right, but solely that particular principle which was taken from the source and implanted in the Code. Sanhūrī showed a measure of confidence in applying this approach due to the similar technique employed by the authors of the Franco-Italian Code of Obligations from 1928, which later became the Italian Civil Code, who also drew from different codes and legal systems. This proposed code had a profound influence on Sanhūrī in terms of its sociological tendencies, which reflected the mood of the times. Some (foreign) jurists in Egypt, such as Boyé, argued that this proposal should itself become the Egyptian Civil Code in order to maintain an affinity with Europe—a position that Sanhūrī rejected.[27]

4. The Technique of *Takhayyur*

The drafters of the Egyptian Civil Code considered the different legal sources from East and West, from the past and the present, and applied a functional test. Firstly, was a given principle consonant with the ideological approach of the Code, which was essentially a sociological one, as will be detailed in the following chapters. If the answer to this was affirmative, it was then asked whether the principle was also appropriate specifically for the Egyptian society of the mid-twentieth century.

The essence of the technique of *takhayyur* relates to the direction of the examination. The test is not whether the Code is appropriate for a given legal norm, such as the Islamic *Sharīʿa* or custom law. Rather, and contrarily, the test is to what extent a given provision in the *Sharīʿa* or in a foreign code is suitable for the New Code and the social ideology it shaped. If a principle was found to be appropriate, it secured admission. If not, it was rejected with no particular sentiments, even if it was drawn from the sanctified realm of the *Sharīʿa*.

[27] Wujūb, p. 56; Sanhūrī, "Min Majallat al-ʾAḥkām al-ʿAdliyya ila al-Qānūn al-Madanī al-ʿIrāqī wa-Ḥarakat al-Taqnīn al-Madanī fī al-ʿUṣūr al-Ḥadītha", *Majmūʿat Maqālāt wa-ʾAbḥāth al-Sanhūrī*, volume 2, pp. 21–27.

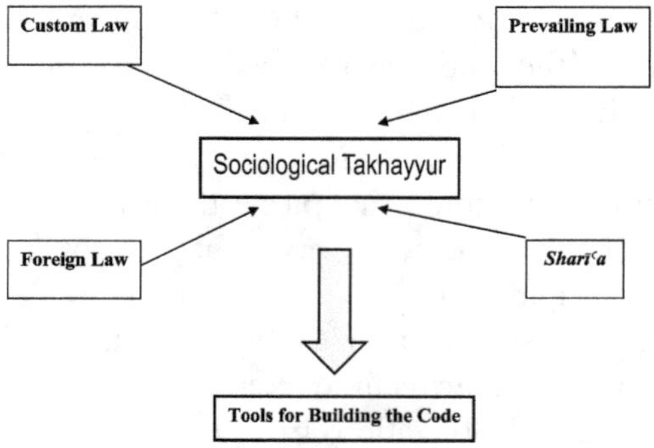

This process is thus akin to casting an arrow toward the target and then drawing circles around it. The arrow is the sociolegal ideology followed by Sanhūrī in the New Code; the circles are the various legal sources. From the standpoint of the Code, the question as to the origin of any given norm was of no particular importance. All that mattered was that the norm was appropriate in terms of the master plan for a different Egyptian society.

The multiplicity of sources did not imply any ideological confusion in the Code or any form of legal uncertainty, as might be thought. Sanhūrī's logical thought process was well-ordered, rooted in a tightly-formed social and legal approach, and the sources were integrated into the ideology.

Sanhūrī further argued that the Code should be both homogenous and harmonious. This implied coordination between the different legal sources, which were fused in order to eventually constitute the authentic sources of the Code, free of their individual legal history. More importantly still, these sources must be compatible with the broad ideology of the Code. Thus the substantive correlation has a double character, though it is still possible. "Nobody believes that the multiplicity of sources will make the Code lose its homogeneity or its internal coordination," stated the chairman of the Civil Code Committee in the House of Representatives, Muḥammad al-Wakīl.[28]

In contrast to the internal Islamic *takhayyur* of Muḥammad ʿAbduh, the *takhayyur* that lay behind the emergence of the New Code was thoroughly international, influenced by the developments in French and Continental law. The explanatory notes to the New Code noted that

[28] Al-Qānūn al-Madanī, volume 1, p. 161.

"Our [Old] Code copied the French *Code Civil* blindly, and inherited many of its faults, including internal contradictions and embarrassing errors. Much of the deficiency found in the (Old) Code is due to the fact that the Egyptian Code does not reflect the tremendous progress made in legal studies in the present generation. The (Old) Egyptian Code was taken from the French Code, which was created at the beginning of the nineteenth century. In order for our Code to close the gap with its current generation, it must cross the expanse of some 130 years, with the progress made in this time by (global) legal studies."[29]

5. *Takhayyur* and the Connection between the Code and the Islamic *Sharīʿa*

The connection between the New Civil Code and the Islamic *Sharīʿa* has constituted the principal, and often the only, point of reference for most scholars who have hitherto examined this Code from different disciplines—Sanhūrī, Norman Anderson, Muḥammad Saʿīd al-ʿAshmāwī and Shafīq Shiḥāta from the legal angle; Anderson, Majid Khadduri and Farhat Ziadeh from the historical perspective; and Enid Hill from the field of sociology.[30]

Several factors explain the intensive need of research to examine the specific point of the extent and character of the affinity between the New Code and the Islamic *Sharīʿa*:

The first factor is the express declaration by the author of the New Code himself. During his efforts to convince the Senate (*majlis al-shuyūkh*) to adopt the Code, he declared that "I can assure you that there is not one provision in the Islamic *Sharīʿa* that we could have included in this

[29] Ibid., p. 13.

[30] J. N. D. Anderson, "The Shariʿa and Civil Law", *Islamic Quarterly* 1(1)(1954) (Hereinafter: Anderson, Shari'a), pp. 29–46; J. N. D. Anderson, *Law Reform in the Muslim World* (London: Athlone Press, 1976), pp. 83–100; Ziadeh, 1968, pp. 99–147; Muḥammad Saʿīd al-ʿAshmāwī, *Al-Sharīʿa al-ʾIslāmiyya wa al-Qānūn al-Misrī*, pp. 19–27, 55–56; Shafīq Shiḥāta, *Taʾrīkh Ḥarakat al-Tajdīd fī al-Nuẓum al-Qānūniyya fī Miṣr* (Cairo: Dār ʾIḥyāʾ al-Kutub al-ʿArabiyy, 1961), p. 93; Chafik Chehata, "Les Survivances Musulmanes dans la Codification du Droit Civil Égyptien", *Revue Internationale de Droit Comparé* 17(1965), pp. 839, 839–853; J. N. D. Anderson, "Law Reform in Egypt: 1850–1950", in P. M. Holt, *Political and Social Change in Modern Egypt* (London: Oxford University Press, 1968), p. 209; M. Khadduri, "From Religious to National Law", in R. N. Anshen, ed. *Mid-East: World Center, Yesterday, Today and Tomorrow* (New York: Harper, 1956), pp. 220–234 (Hereinafter: Khadduri).

Code and did not do so... We have taken everything possible from the Islamic *Sharīʿa*, while attending to the proper principles of modern legislation, and we have not been remiss therein."[31] This maximalist declaration on the part of Sanhūrī aroused the appetite of researchers such as Anderson, since based on their discoveries it seemed to contradict reality.[32] In the following chapters we shall examine why Sanhūrī made this statement, and how he perceived the role of the *Sharīʿa* in justifying the assimilation of doctrines that were in fact drawn from European law.

Secondly, this position on the part of Sanhūrī accompanied a public debate in Egypt during the 1930s regarding the need to relate to Islamic law and the extent to which this law should be assimilated. In 1936, Judge Muḥammad Slimān advocated the replacement of the Mixed and Egyptian civil law by Muslim law, on the grounds of efficiency and greater suitability for the needs of the country and its cultural level. In order to justify his position, he showed that Islamic law provides a worthy response to French law. Slimān admitted that juridical Islamic law was not suited to modern times, but was willing to accept a solution through codification along the lines of the Ottoman *Majalla*.[33]

Thirdly, the demand to use the Islamic *Sharīʿa*, to whatever extent, as the positivist law of the state is one that has been raised by important circles within present-day Egypt, with the result that locating points of congruence between the *Sharīʿa* and positivist Egyptian legislation is of widespread interest in Egypt itself, as well as among Western researchers. Over the years, the extent of Islamic legislation has become an empirical yardstick for the degree to which a society is considered Islamic.

Lastly, the Egyptian Civil Code had a strong practical influence on relations between national law and the *Sharīʿa* in Egypt, introducing into the Egyptian statutes for the first time the charged expression 'the principles of the Islamic *Sharīʿa*' as a central source to which the judge may turn in the event that the Code is silent on a given point. This expression would appear afterwards in the modern Egyptian Constitution, creating political and legal confusion.[34]

---

[31] Al-Qānūn al-Madanī, volume 1, p. 159.
[32] Anderson, Shariʿa, p. 30.
[33] Muḥammad Slimān, "Bi-ʾAy Sharʿ Naḥkumu", *L'Egypte Contemporaine* 27(1936), p. 289.
[34] See for example: Muḥammad Saʿīd al-ʿAshmāwī, *Al-Sharīʿa al-ʾIslamiyya wa-al-Qānūn al-Miṣrī*.

One researcher who examined the individual articles of the Code in the context of the Islamic *Sharīʿa* was Norman Anderson, who attempted to understand the affinity of the New Code to Islamic law. He calculated the number of provisions from the *Sharīʿa* that were included in the articles of the Code, dividing his list into four categories. Anderson's test may be termed the positivist test; his categories were as follows:

1. The first article of the Code, which established that "...if an applicable provision is not found in the law, the judge shall decide in accordance with custom, and if this is not to be found—in accordance with the principles of the Islamic *Sharīʿa*, and if these shall not be found—in accordance with the principles of natural law and the rules of Equity." Anderson stated that "the value of this article (in terms of the reference to the *Sharīʿa*) seems more sentimental than practical", adding in a footnote: "...Its practical usefulness is limited by the fact that the phrase 'the principles of the *Sharīʿa*' is almost as nebulous as 'natural justice'".[35]
2. The *Sharīʿa* influenced the choice between legal principles concerning which disagreements were already to be found among the Western legal theories.
   In this context and specifically regarding the tension between the subjective approach (characteristic of Latin law) and the objective approach (a hallmark of the German legal system), the Egyptian scholar Shafīq Shiḥāta, who played a leading role in the study of Egyptian civil law, noted what he considered the objective (*mawḍūʿiyya*) approach characterizing the New Egyptian Code, and associated this with the similarly objective tendency of Islamic law.[36]
3. Principles drawn exclusively from the Islamic *Sharīʿa*.
4. The copying of Islamic legal principles that already appeared in the outgoing Egyptian Civil Code.

According to Anderson's positivist test, it is sufficient to count the number of rules that were apparently absorbed in the Code from the *Sharīʿa* (the *What*), as in an act of stock-taking, in order to determine the affinity of the Code to Islamic law. It might be argued, however, that without answering two further questions, namely *How* and *Why*

[35] Anderson, Sharīʿa, pp. 31–32.

[36] Chafik Chehata, "Volonté Réele et Volonté Declaré dans le Nouveau Code Civil Égyptien", *Revue Internationale de Droit Comparé* 6(1954), pp. 241–249, 243–244, notamment 6.

certain provisions from the *Sharīʿa* entered the Code, while others did not, it is impossible to properly answer the question Anderson posed.

Norman Anderson's question brings us back to the test of *takhayyur*, which, it might be argued, constitutes the answer as to *Why* the *Sharīʿa* was introduced into the Code. The same test that was applied to the foreign Western codes was also applied to the Islamic *Sharīʿa*. In this respect, then, the *Sharīʿa* was perceived not as a sublime religious entity, but as an additional regular legal source.

Sanhūrī himself emphasized that the movement between the *Sharīʿa* and the New Code was monodirectional: firstly the supreme legal ideologies and norms were formulated, and only then could the *Sharīʿa* be addressed in order to flesh out that which had already been substantively formulated by the drafters of the Code. First the overall ideological approach of the Code was consolidated, and then the principle of *takhayyur* was introduced: legal elements that were found to be consonant with this approach were adopted, while those that were not were excluded, whether they came from the Polish Civil Code or the Islamic *Sharīʿa*. The *Sharīʿa* did not enjoy any special *legal* status, though, as we shall see below, it did enjoy a special *cultural, religious* and *social* status.[37]

Sanhūrī explained this principle several times, both while he was drafting the Code and when offering guidelines to judges on how it should be interpreted:

> When drawing provisions from Islamic law, attention should be paid to adapting the provisions of the *Sharīʿa* to the principles on which the Civil Code as a whole is based. A ruling from Islamic law that contradicts any of these principles should not be adopted, in order to prevent the Code's losing its character and legal harmony... Only that which conforms to the general principles of the Civil Code should be chosen.[38]

Elsewhere, he adds: "In the event of a conflict with the law, we shall take (from the *Sharīʿa*) only that which conforms to the Code."[39]

Sanhūrī used the word *ʾistiqāʾ* (drawing water) to explain this one-dimensional flow: water was to be drawn from the well of the *Sharīʿa* in order to be poured into the Civil Code, but not vice versa.[40] In

[37] "Min Majallat al-ʾAḥkām al-ʿAdliyya ʾila al-Qānūn al-Madanī," *Majmūʿat Maqālāt wa ʾAbḥāth al-Sanhūrī,* volume 2, p. 57–58.
[38] Al-Wasīṭ, volume 1, p. 61.
[39] Al-Qānūn al-Madanī, volume 1, p. 191.
[40] Wujūb p. 114.

the context of the Code, he was not interested in an internal debate within the world of the *Sharīʿa*, or in religious renewal, despite the fact that he was a devout believer, and a great admirer and knowledgeable scholar of Islamic law. Accordingly, it would be wrong to permit his extensive knowledge of Islamic law, as reflected in his important essay *Maṣādir al-Ḥaqq fī al-Fiqh al ʾIslāmī, Muqārana bi al-Fiqh al-Gharbī*, to distort the proper perception of his introduction of the *Sharīʿa* into the New Code.

In his book on the Islamic Caliphate written in French in 1926, and mentioned in the previous chapter, Sanhūrī was bold enough to advocate a separation between the religious part of Islamic law and the secular part. In Arabic, this was translated as a distinction between the religious part and the *mundane* (*dunyawī*) part. In his programmatic essay, written in 1936 in Arabic, on the manner in which the Civil Code should be amended, Sanhūrī softened the wording still further, writing:

> In the Book of the Caliphate, we advocated the scientific and comparative study of the *Sharīʿa*. This new study will be based on a distinction between the *religious* (*dīnī*) provisions and the *legal* (*qānūnī*) provisions. We have no interest in the former, solely in the latter. We distinguish between a provision that involves religion in Islamic legal theory, which will continue to be honored in our faith and our hearts, and a provision based on pure legal logic, which will fall within the scope of our scientific research.[41]

One of Anderson's tests related to the *Sharīʿa* as a source influencing the choice between legal principles that are the subject of disagreement within the Western legal systems. He gave the example of the preference for the objective approach, which is characteristic of German law, over the more subjective position of French law. However, given the direction of flow dictated by the principle of *takhayyur*, this hypothesis must be questioned. Sanhūrī noted:

> Regarding the contract, we do not claim to have drawn from the Islamic *Sharīʿa*, for had we so drawn, we would naturally have needed to return to the theories (of the *Sharīʿa* as a source of interpretation). I would, however, argue that, in its foundation and in certain of its articles, the proposal is consonant with the provisions of the *Sharīʿa*... We have always

---

[41] ʿAbd al-Razzāq al-Sanhūrī, *Fiqh al-Khilāfa wa Taṭwirhā Litaṣbaḥ ʿUṣbat ʾUmam Sharqiyya* (Cairo: Al-Hayʾa al-Misriyya lil-Kitāb, 1993), pp. 316–318; *Le Califat: Son Évolution vers une Société des Nations Orientale* (Paris: Librairie Orientaliste, Paul Geuthner, 1926), pp. 580–581; Wujūb p. 115.

> stated that we drew this provision from our case law and statute books and—Praise be to God—it is also consonant with the provisions of the Islamic *Sharīʿa*.[42]

The significance of this is that the choice between the objective and subjective approaches, for the purpose of the given example, was made at an early stage by the drafters of the Code. The fact that the *Sharīʿa* favored one side or the other was added after the decision had already been made. Accordingly, the *Sharīʿa* neither dictated nor selected the choice from among the Western sources—a process that was guided by the substantive ideology of the Code. The *Sharīʿa* was added after the decision had been made, mainly for the purpose of enhancing its legitimacy. It might be argued that the process of subjecting a given norm to the test of the *Sharīʿa* was therefore declarative, rather than normative. Examples illustrating this argument, and which will be discussed in detail below, include the theory of the abuse of a right, which was unquestionably adopted by the Code on the basis of its development in French law, despite the fact that the explanatory comments to the Code emphasized that this doctrine also appeared in the Islamic *fiqh*; the doctrine of unforeseen circumstances; the doctrine of exploitation, and so on.

Having attempted to offer a theoretical answer to the question as to *how* the *Sharīʿa* was introduced into the New Code, we may now turn to asking *why* this took place.

The answer to this question lies beyond the realm of law, yet is intimately connected with the legal and social goals Sanhūrī sought to advance. The essence of the answer is legitimacy, and this is the closest point of affinity between the Code and the *Sharīʿa*, the answer to the question *why* and, perhaps, the answer to the question posed by Anderson.

This legitimacy faces three target populations: the international legal community; the Egyptian legislators, who were reluctant to approve certain provisions in the Code; and the Egyptian collective in general.

Regarding the first sphere, the quest for legitimacy in the eyes of the international legal world sought to prove that the 'reawakening' East could supply a legal theory that was not inferior to any other Western legal theory, and that would place the peoples of the East on an equal footing with those of the West. The *Sharīʿa* was cited as this developed

[42] Al-Qānūn al-Madanī, volume 1, p. 90.

legal theory. Sanhūrī himself noted that "(the *Sharīʿa*) can constitute a pillar among the pillars of (international) comparative law."[43]

As for the second sphere: during the legislative process, Sanhūrī used the *Sharīʿa* in a sophisticated manner in order to convince the legislators whenever opposition was expressed to adopting a given doctrine, which was almost always, in reality, drawn from European law. Sanhūrī's claims that a given provision reflected a norm in the *Sharīʿa* usually softened opposition, for who would dare to criticize the *Sharīʿa* and challenge its respected and all-encompassing status? This approach by the drafters of the Code became a permanent form of response whenever the legislators proved reluctant to introduce a legal precedent regarding which they had reservations, such as the doctrines of equity in contract law, the question of the removal of an estate, the endorsement of a debt, and so on. Whenever Sanhūrī sensed opposition in parliament, particularly from the members of the Upper House (the Senate), who showed a lively interest in the Code (perhaps more so than Sanhūrī might have wished), he turned to the *Sharīʿa* as a source of legitimacy. When criticized for including too few provisions from the *Sharīʿa*, he indignantly replied: "No one in the world loves the *Sharīʿa* more than I, and I was among the first to argue that we should take an interest in the Islamic *Sharīʿa* and study it within the framework of comparative law."[44] A study of Sanhūrī's personal diaries shows that while this claim is true, it was not manifested in the legislation of the New Civil Code. In this context, Sanhūrī saw the *Sharīʿa* as a means rather than an end.

In this respect, it emerges that everyone had his own *Sharīʿa*. By way of example, the Appeals Court judge, the Islamicist Ṣādiq Fahmī openly criticized Sanhūrī, claiming that the contract laws in the New Code contradicted the *Sharīʿa*. To prove his point, he drafted a proposed Islamic contract law together with lecturers from Al-ʾAzhar. Sanhūrī drew on his expertise in Islamic law to prove article by article that, in fact, it was Fahmī's proposal that was incompatible with the *Sharīʿa*, while the Civil Code achieved this goal.[45]

In this context, the principle of *takhayyur* ostensibly operated without any fixed regularity in selecting the sources from the *Sharīʿa*.

[43] Wujūb p. 113.
[44] Al-Qānūn al-Madanī, volume 1, p. 85.
[45] Ibid., pp. 86–87.

Sanhūrī did not hesitate to turn to the Ḥanafī *madhhab* in one case, to the Mālikī on other occasions and sometimes to additional schools of interpretation within Sunni Islam. What was important was to secure the legitimacy he sought.

Appearances notwithstanding, there were rhyme and reason to the manner in which the motif of *takhayyur* was applied in addressing the principles of the *Sharīʿa*. The determining factor was the extent to which the source in question was consonant with the general legal ideas of the Code. The most appropriate *madhhab* was that which was adopted. Accordingly, Sanhūrī would recommend the Ḥanafī *madhhab* in one case, while elsewhere emphasizing one of the other schools, if the Ḥanafī happened to be unsuitable for the ideological approach of the Code. For example, in the charged debate over granting the option of preemption to a neighbor, Sanhūrī expressed reservations with the Ḥanafī approach, which permitted such a right, despite the fact that the Ḥanafī school enjoys formal dominance in Egypt. In another case, Sanhūrī favored the Mālikī and even the Ḥanbalī schools (rather than the Ḥanafī) on the question of the requirement to secure the creditor's approval for endorsing a debt. Such cases may be found both during the process of adopting the Code and in its interpretation.

In his guiding comments for the judge, in which he sought to interpret the principles from the *Sharīʿa* found in the Code, Sanhūrī wrote in 1952:

> We should not confine ourselves to any one of the *madhāhib* of the Islamic *fiqh*. We should delve into each school and draw from it, not preferring the *madhhab* of ʾAbu Ḥanīfa and not confining ourselves to the Ḥanafī *madhhab* in general. We must (even) march further and state that we should not confine ourselves to the four recognized schools, since there are other schools that may be used, to a large extent, such as the Zaydī and ʾImāmī *madhāhib*.[46]

The third reason for emphasizing norms that were ostensibly drawn from the *Sharīʿa* was the legitimacy this could provide among the broad population of those using the Code—the Egyptian populace. According to this logic, these were not new norms imported from abroad (although most of the norms were indeed such), but rather provisions that were already familiar through the *Sharīʿa* and prevailing custom (*ʿurf*). Through such an argument, the public would be more inclined

[46] Al-Wasīṭ, volume 1, p. 61.

to accept the Code. According to this category, the *Sharīʿa* is perceived as an authentic, local element implying stability and continuity, rather than as an explicitly religious element—"a spiritual heritage that should be treasured and used."[47] It is described as the *Sharīʿa of the Country*' ('*sharīʿat al-balad*', as Sanhūrī puts it), and the closer the Code remains to this Law of the Land, the better for the Code and for the people—the better for the people since, according to this perspective, the *Sharīʿa* constitutes the default law for pluralistic Egyptian society, and hence may help assuage religious and ethnic rifts, as evidenced, for example, in the question of the removal of an estate (*tasfiyyat al-tarika*). The *Sharīʿa* may provide an invaluable common denominator for all Egyptians, regardless of whether it is applied with regard to a Muslim, Christian or Jew.[48] In this respect, the term '*Sharīʿa of the country*' resembles Savigny's term 'spirit of the people'—both of them refer to the broader social environment, and not to a certain religious or ethnic group.

The Civil Code Committee in the Senate accepted the assumption that the *Sharīʿa* was synonymous with stability. "(Islamic law) expressed and expresses the prevailing law in Egypt on many questions," noted the Committee. "The Committee does not view the return (of the judge) to the Islamic *Sharīʿa* as in any way impairing commercial and transactional stability, but rather see it as a source of stability that seeks the best practices to which those engaged in transactions have become accustomed over these centuries."[49]

6. The Stage of Disengagement and Legal Fusion

Having amassed a worthy corpus of legislation from diverse sources, according to the desired ideological thrust of the Code, the subsequent stage emphasizes the cohesive nature of the Code in terms of its content. This stage relates to the fusion of items of legislation drawn from the different sources in order to form a new, homogeneous legal creation. During this process, the different and diverse articles were disconnected from their sources. In other words, their interpretation would no longer depend on the mother source, but on Egyptian law

[47] The Report of the Civil Code Committee, The Senate, Al-Qānūn al-Madanī, volume 1, p. 131.

[48] See in this regard: Fiqh al-Khilāfa, pp. 39–40.

[49] Al-Qānūn al-Madanī, volume 1, pp. 131–132.

alone. In this stage, the legal rule drawn from a given legal theory would become a general Egyptian rule, relevant only to Egyptian society. There would be no returning to the French, Polish or other source of the law, and this constitutes a vital and principal foundation in the process of consolidating the New Code. After the disengagement, the rule stands on its own right, and hence, in this respect, it is irrelevant how many foreign codes provided various legal norms. After this stage of separation, these norms become Egyptian, and relevant primarily to the Egyptian context.

Farhat Ziadeh also discussed the 'fusion' of Western and Islamic elements in the Civil Code. However, in accordance with the test of *takhayyur*, the fusion he referred to was perceived as marginal, since its principal importance lay not in the relations between the different legal elements, be these Eastern or Western (as noted, these elements lose their origin, which was in any case insignificant from the perspective of the Code), but rather to the relations between each one of these elements and the ideological essence of the Code.[50] Once they had entered the New Code, these elements became soldiers in the service of the overall ideology of the Code. No longer the norms of the *Sharīʿa* or of French administrative law, they became the bearers of the message of the New Code, and an integral part thereof.

The explanatory notes to the Code commented that:

> The articles of the law included in this proposal have an independent entity that renders them totally independent of the sources from which they were taken. The purpose of the reference to the modern codes is not to create any affiliative affinity between the proposal and these diverse codes in interpretation, application and development, since it is obvious that each legislative text must live within the social context in which it is applied...and be completely divorced from the historical source from which it came, whatever this may be...Judges and jurists should address the text in its application or interpretation as a self-standing formula, divorced from its source, and should apply or interpret it according to the matter at hand, so that this interpretation may provide solutions for the needs of the country, and in accordance with the requirements of justice.[51]

During the deliberations of the Civil Code Committee in the Upper House of parliament, the chairman, Muḥammad al-Wakīl, mentioned

[50] Ziadeh, 1968, p. 146.
[51] Al-Qānūn al-Madanī, volume 1, p. 32.

the legal duality that had pertained prior to the enactment of the New Code: "We always said of the (Old) Code that the judge held the Egyptian Code in one hand, and the *Code Civil* in the other. If he found any lack of clarity in the Egyptian Code, he passed to the French code in order to reach the proper interpretation. Even when we were mere students of law, we were told that such-and-such an article was analogous to a given article in the French code."[52]

Regarding the New Code, however, the report of the Code Committee of the Upper House emphasized that norms drawn from other legal systems became completely Egyptian, "in accordance with the conditions of the Egyptian environment." Thus, for example, regarding the question of family joint ownership, which will be discussed in the next chapter. The source of these provisions came from the Swiss and Italian civil codes, yet give the appearance of having been created specially to meet the aspirations of Egyptian society.[53]

Another example is the ownership of floors in a building, which will also be discussed in the next chapter. This aspect refers to the ordering of legal relations between owners of apartments in a single building, and the legal provisions drawn from a 1938 French law. The Civil Code Committee reported that this section reflected a synthesis between the technical details, which were drawn from French law, and the principles of joint ownership of an apartment building, which were drawn from Egyptian case law, from the Old Code and from the *Sharīʿa* (the principles of *al-ʿuluww wal-sufl*) "in the most appropriate manner to the Egyptian environment."[54]

The only exception in which an affinity remains intact between the text and its historical sources is the reference in Article 1 to the principles of the Islamic *Sharīʿa* as one of the sources of the Code. As we have already seen, in the contest between the spirit of the Code and the *Sharīʿa*, the Code is destined to prevail. As Sanhūrī stated explicitly: "In the event of a clash between the principles of the *Sharīʿa* and the law, we shall take (from the *Sharīʿa*) in such a case, only what is suitable for the Code."[55] In other words, due to Article 1 of the Code, which refers to the principles of the *Sharīʿa* as a source on which the judge should rely, it cannot be argued that disengagement occurred here as it

[52] Ibid., volume 1, p. 55.
[53] Ibid., pp. 133–135.
[54] Ibid., p. 135.
[55] Ibid., p. 191.

did regarding the other legal sources. Nevertheless, in substantive terms, such disengagement did occur: along the interpretative path from the Code to the *Sharīʿa*, the Code placed a barrier, and only those aspects in the *Sharīʿa* that were consonant with the spirit of the Code would be permitted to pass. This, too, is a form of disengagement.

This barrier is the principle of *takhayyur* which was thus applied not only during the stage of enacting the Code, but also in its interpretation by the court. *Takhayyur* ensured, in effect, that it was not the *Sharīʿa* as an entire school of law, ruling, morality and mores that passed into the Code, in which case it might have seized control of the Code from within, but rather and precisely those norms in the *Sharīʿa* that were compatible with the Code. Thus what we see is already a synthesized and channeled *Sharīʿa*. Norman Anderson was right, then, to note, in his discussion of the principles of the Islamic *Sharīʿa* as one of the sources of the Code, that "opinions may naturally change regarding the true significance of this provision, but I must confess that I regard it as a value intended more for propaganda and sentimental purposes than for practical application."[56] The principle of *takhayyur* was, therefore, not intended solely for the proper composition of the Code by means of adopting norms from the *Sharīʿa*, and not merely to enable its proper implementation in accordance with the principles of the *Sharīʿa*, but also to defend the Code itself from the strength of the *Sharīʿa* with its infinite room.

7. The Call for Opinions (*ʾIstiftāʾ*)

After the Code had been consolidated as a collection of civil legislation, disconnected from its historical sources, unified and adapted to the realities of Egyptian life, the next step, according to its architect Sanhūrī, was *ʾistiftāʾ*—i.e., a call for opinions, or a form of public referendum. This term is also drawn from the *Sharīʿa*, and originally referred to a request for opinions on questions of Islamic law. Similar to *takhayyur*, this term also underwent a process of worldliness. As proposed by Sanhūrī, and as implemented, he sought to obtain the opinions of various groups with the leading circles of Egyptian society, such as politicians, jurists, judges, clergymen and academics, and to hear their reactions to the proposed code. The point of reference for this action

[56] Anderson, Law Reform, p. 228.

was Europe, where a similar step had been taken by those responsible for drafting civil codes in the twentieth century, rather, for example, than the form of action followed by the Islamic clerics. Sanhūrī was visibly impressed by the process whereby the French and German civil codes were submitted to expert legal committees for comment (a process he also termed *'istiftā'*) prior to their approval.[57]

Sanhūrī's call for a process of *'istiftā'* stemmed from several reasons. One factor was the desire to secure as broad a public legitimacy for the new *legal* code as possible, but still more important was his desire to secure consensus around the Code as a *social* common denominator that went alongside the legal function of the Code. Without broad social support or, at least, the semblance of such support, there was no point in enacting an ideological Code that sought to secure social transformations and even usher in a new social order. Such direct participation in the process might also reduce future opposition and obstacles, particularly due to the exclusion of individuals from the process. Accordingly, *'istiftā'* was intended to provide the Code's launching ground, and to provide protection for the future, should anyone claim that the Code had no right to introduce changes in the structure of Egyptian society.

The first draft of the Code was presented on 24 April 1942, and was sent by Sanhūrī to members of Egypt's legal and political elite in order to receive responses within a set period of three years. Members of the Upper House of parliament delayed the proposed Code by a further two years, and invited experts from outside parliament, including religious leaders such as the grand Mufti of Egypt, Sheikh Jazā'irlī and leading judges with a strong Islamic background (one of whom, Hasan al-Huḍaybī, was even widely known to be a leader of the Muslim Brotherhood). It was important to Sanhūrī that religious scholars should also participate in this *'istiftā'*, thus providing their consent if only by way of their participation in discussions relating to the Code.

In 1936, Sanhūrī wrote the following comments on his intended *'istiftā'*:

> The number of members of the Drafting Committee (of the planned Code) is limited and, as we have said, it must be limited. Accordingly, many factions and organizations are left without representation. Even highly talented individuals will remain outside, unable to participate in

[57] 'Abd al-Razzāq al-Sanhūrī, "Min Majallat al-'Aḥkām al-'Adliyya 'ila al-Qānūn al-Madanī", in *Majmū'at Maqālāt wa 'Abḥath*, volume 2, pp. 9–13, 34–35.

> the work. Accordingly, we must invite these capable factions and individuals to participate in the codification through the *'istiflā'*. The French undertook a process of *'istiflā'* in 1801 through the courts before adopting their code (the *Code Napoleon*), and these courts established committees to study the proposed code as submitted. Italy followed a similar course... Germany and Switzerland held a broad-based *'istiflā'* among legal and business circles, a process that led to many amendments to the proposals. Accordingly, we may say that the *'istiflā'* has become a pillar in the process of codification in the modern era.[58]

8. The Concealed Code

Those jurists who favored the sociological theory of law generally believed that law was, or should be, accompanied by broad social ideals. The Austrian jurist Eugen Ehrlich (1862–1922) claimed that ordinary law exists side by side with other factors in society, which may heavily influence or even override it. Such factors are equally law. François Gény (1861–1938) distinguished the 'technique', the mere knowledge of the machinery of legal rules from the 'science' which is the understanding of the non-legal, but highly relevant, values in the law's environment.[59] Roscoe Pound (1870–1964) included philosophical, political and moral ideas intended for legal goals within the components of law; the moral idea forming the foundation of the goals of law was justice. Moral and philosophical goals, he argued, are eternal and universal, although each society chooses that framework of ideas that is right at a given point in time. These ideas are not written or explicit in modern laws, yet they form an integral and, in Pound's opinion, even primary part of law. Sometimes the law explicitly empowers the judge to examine considerations of 'justice,' or opens ideological avenues of a philosophical, political or other moral nature, such as the example of the 'public order', which we shall discuss in depth below. Having done so, these principles become acts of legislation and, in Pound's classification, are no longer to be classed as 'ideas', but rather as 'provisions' awaiting implementation.[60]

---

[58] Wujūb pp. 68–69.

[59] Kelly, pp. 361–362; *Lloyd's Introduction to Jurisprudence*, pp. 562–564. Sanhūrī on the Austrian Civil Code: ʿAbd al-Razzāq al-Sanhūrī, "Min Majallat al-'Aḥkām al-ʿAdliyya 'ila al-Qānūn al-Madanī al-ʿIrāqī", pp. 29–30.

[60] *Lloyd's Introduction to Jurisprudence*, pp. 564–572, 606–609; J. M. Kelly, pp. 363–365.

Applying this perception of Sociological law the New Code sought to reestablish the principles of social order in Egypt, assuming a role that was educational and even coercive, while at the same time constituting a practical, routine code intended for everyday use. How can a code with profound ideological and philosophical perceptions, prolific in legal and social theories, be reconciled with the need for a practical code, substantive and understandable to all? How can a vision coexist with a civil code that must be practical?

It may be argued that two distinct codes, based on the same legal articles, coexist within the Egyptian Civil Code.

The first code, formalistic and positivist, addresses the rights and obligations defined by the classic confines of civil law: personal laws (legal status and legal capacity); property laws (real estate and chattel); laws of obligation (contracts and damages); and, to a very limited extent in the case of the Egyptian code, family and inheritance laws. This corpus of laws saw the regulation of these legal systems as its sole purpose. Sanhūrī referred to this category as 'the practical spirit' (*al-rūḥ al-ʿamaliyya*) of the Code.[61]

The second, concealed code, sought to transform these relationships, which are so vital to the fabric of any human society, into a tool for changing existing Egyptian society. Its goal was not merely to regulate legal relations on the individual level, but was a much broader social aim: the infinite collection of individual transactions would accumulate to form a critical social mass leading to a new dimension in relations within the Egyptian collective. This code aimed to manifest in tangible terms the range of legal theories and social intentions that was referred to by Sanhūrī as 'the spirit of legal theory' (*al-rūḥ al-fiqhiyya*)—the law of jurists.

Relations between these two codes were inseparable, since the social and philosophical schools that constitute the ideological code were manifested in the selection of legal principles in the overt code. Nevertheless, a tension developed between the two. Can mundane contract and property laws coexist with their function as ideological tools in the service of a specific philosophy? Is there not room to fear that such close contact will lead to the erosion of both sides? A surfeit of theories and philosophy may make the Code less practical; conversely, the practical elements may hamper the philosophy that lurks behind the scenes.

[61] Wujūb p. 70.

This substantive dilemma was reflected above all during the process of formulation. The question was whether these socio-philosophical schools should remain covert and behind the scenes as they directed the Code, the judge and society, or whether they should appear openly in the Code's articles. Should someone reading through the Code be able to discern the presence of a philosophical and almost Utopian structure directing the Code and even society at large?

Sanhūrī decided that the answer to this must be negative. The philosophical code, the vision, must be discrete, though experts in legal theory would be able to distinguish and decode it. The architect of the Code was aware that these two codes would be irreversibly connected, yet one would stand in the limelight on the stage of law, bearing responsibility for everyday individual law between citizens; while the other would supervise the former and connect to it through the proper functioning of the judge, while remaining hidden behind the scenes, appearing, at the most, in the interpretative works of scholars. This is the concealed code that this book seeks to reveal.

Sanhūrī made the following comments regarding these two parallel systems:

> The practical spirit overrules the spirit of legal theory, since the goal of the Code is to be equal for all, (to address) the public at large before (addressing) scholars of legal theory. The legislator of the Code should refrain from reinforcing its provisions by stating their reasons or from adding proofs or clarifying examples, since all these are the work of the scholars of legal theory, and are not acts of legislation. If there is no alternative but to mention something of these, then the legislator should leave this to the ancillary actions accompanying the Code and to the explanatory notes that usually accompany the code, but what is most important is that these remain separate.
>
> The practical spirit also overrules when the legislator refrains from introducing terms from legal theory in the Code, and eschews abstract generalizations and the inclusion of general theories; he should mention none of these unless obliged to do so. The legislator should not declare his affiliation to the material school or the personal school of obligation, nor to the school of internal will or the school of overt will of contracts—all these must be left to the legal theorists...As has already been stated (in French law): *"La loi commande; elle n'est pas faite pour instruire; elle n'a pas besoin de convaincre"*.[62]

[62] Ibid., pp. 70–71.

We find that the two different codes that underlie the New Code are also constructed in a different manner: the first follows the classic formalistic approach of civil codes—the private and legal personality, laws of obligations (Book One), special types of contracts (Book Two), and property rights (Book Three). This division is essential for the smooth functioning of the courts and the legal and civil system as a whole; in order for the Code to fill its primary function as an effective regulator of private legal relations among citizens.

The second code, as this book seeks to illustrate, is constructed in a different manner, its components crisscrossing those of the first code. It addresses property law and its social function in changing the shape of Egyptian society; it applies rules of justice and morality that traverse articles of the Code, applying a normative and binding framework; it supports the weaker members of society, while at the same time seeking to advance the strong, maintaining harmony between the two and avoiding excessive social polarization; it seeks to apply a new type of legal glue to the internal relations between the Code's articles, to relations between the Code and society, and to the functioning of society itself.

Sanhūrī was aware of the necessary distinction between the formal structures of each of these codes. "The Code necessitates a logical division into chapters (*tabwīb*), and this is not the scientific division of the scholarly works. The needs of the Code are not the same as those of legal theories...The Code (must be divided) into chapters and articles that particularly emphasize the practical importance of the legal provisions and *conceal* the legal theories that underlie these provisions."[63]

Accordingly, this book will now proceed to follow the structure of the second, concealed code, revealing it step by step. It will now be clear why we noted, at the head of this chapter, that an understanding of the ostensibly formalistic aspects described above is vital in order to understand the concealed code. *Takhayyur*, the stages of disengagement and the *ʾistiftāʾ* are all components that, above all, serve the substantive, concealed code. This book will argue that it is impossible to understand the substantive code without understanding the principle of *takhayyur*; yet, even more so, it is impossible to understand *takhayyur* without understanding the substantive code.

[63] Ibid., p. 69.

CHAPTER THREE

THE SOCIAL FUNCTION OF PROPERTY LAW

There is nothing which so generally strikes the imagination and engages the affections of mankind as the right of property

William Blackston, *Commentaries*, 1766

Man has an individual tendency and a social tendency. The latter does not appear in a person who is on his own, unless he joins with his fellow; like the positive and negative in electricity, which are not manifested unless they have joined together

Sanhūrī, Diary, 1934[1]

1. The 'Social Function' as a Theoretical Model

1.1 *'Social Solidarity'*

This chapter demonstrates how it was evident to Sanhūrī that concrete social changes and outcomes aided by the New Civil Code would be secured primarily through property law, just as existing social order in Egypt was founded on land and property laws.[2]

In the period of Egyptian history we are examining, that of the constitutional monarchy, land became not only a principal economic resource, but also a political and social one, providing secure investments and high yields, entitling its owner to elevated status and entry into the Egyptian elite, and forming a foundation of power in the governmental and administrative echelons. The Egyptian economy's reliance on cotton crops meant that industry contributed only ten percent of gross national product. In other words, during the first half

[1] Diary, p. 193.

[2] On the property law models as part of the social environment see: L. L. Fuller, *The Principles of Social Order* (Durham, N. C.: Duke University Press, 1981), p. 237. In Egypt see: G. Baer, *A History of Landownership in Modern Egypt, 1800–1950* (Oxford: Oxford University Press, 1962); K. Cuno, *The Pasha's Peasants, Land Society and Economy in Lower Egypt, 1740–1858* (Cambridge: Cambridge University Press, 1992).

of the twentieth century, land defined the principal social, economic and political systems in Egypt. Thus, for example, candidates for the House of Representatives were required to pay an extremely high tax that could only be afforded by the owners of large estates. The result was that a highly limited social class reached parliament, enacted the laws of the nation and defined social norms, on the basis and definition of the land it held.

In an Egyptian society polarized between rich and poor, urban and rural, and between an educated minority and an uneducated majority, and against the background of the collapse of the old social order, an economic crisis and rapid urbanization, the code sought to construct new definitions of social relations, and therefore of necessity related to property-based distinctions. Within a monarchist regime, there was no intention of implementing agrarian reforms or depriving the landowners of their privileges. Rather, the goal was to introduce a much more moderate legal reform in the spirit of European sociological perceptions. Above all, this reform was manifested through a changing definition of property rights.

According to the sociological approaches of the early twentieth century, as manifested in numerous civil codes, such the Swiss code, the proposed Franco-Italian code and the Soviet code, property laws were imbued with a prominent social function as a tool for securing social objectives, and above all—social solidarity.

Sanhūrī was familiar with the term 'social solidarity' and employed it frequently, since, in the legal and social world of the first half of the twentieth century, this phrase was discussed at length by the jurists and sociologists who influenced his thought, such as Gény and Léon Duguit (1859–1928), who discussed the ways to secure and realize social solidarity in the legal and social realms. In 1893, the renowned French sociologist E. Durkheim (1858–1917) offered the following analysis of the complex origins of this concept in the legal and, more particularly, the social realm:

> Social solidarity is a wholly moral phenomenon which by itself does not lend itself to exact observation and especially not measurement. To arrive at this classification, as well as this comparison, we must therefore substitute for this internal datum, which escapes us, an external one which symbolizes it, and then study the former through the latter.
>
> That visible symbol is law. Indeed, where social solidarity exists, in spite of its non-material nature, it does not remain in a state of pure potentiality, but shows its presence through perceptible effects. Where it is strong it attracts men strongly to each other, ensures frequent contacts

> between them, and redoubles the opportunities available to them to enter into mutual relationships. Stating the position precisely, at the point we have now reached it is not easy to say whether it is social solidarity which produces these phenomena or, on the contrary, whether it is the result of them... Should we go further and assert that social solidarity does not consist in its visible manifestation; that these express it only partially and imperfectly; that beyond law and custom there exist an inner state from which solidarity derives; and that to know it in reality we must penetrate to the heart of it, and without any intermediary?... Thus the study of solidarity lies with the domain of sociology. It is a social fact which can only be known thoroughly through its social effects... Since law reproduces the main forms of social solidarity, we have only to classify the different types of law in order to be able to investigate which species of social solidarity correspond to them.[3]

Following Durkheim's analysis, is it desirable or feasible for positivist law to include an allusion to its covert social intent? Notwithstanding his own recommendation that the Code should not include ideological theories, Sanhūrī sought to include directly in the New Code the term 'social function' in the context of property law. In his proposal for the Code, he defined the breadth of property rights as follows:

> The owner of a thing may use it, enjoy it and perform disposition (*taṣarruf*) in it, provided he acts within the limits of the law, without any intervention by another, on condition that this take place in accordance with the social function of property.[4]

Following the French Code Civil, the old Egyptian codes perceived property right as the absolute right of the individual, within the framework of his basic rights and liberties. These were not granted by God or king, but were present from birth and formed an integral part of his being. Accordingly, these codes employ the term 'absolute' (*muṭlaq*) to refer to property rights.[5] This approach was typical of the philosophical and legal perception of the Enlightenment, as also manifested in the French Declaration of the Rights of Man and the Citizen of 1789 and the Code Civil of 1804.[6]

---

[3] E. Durkheim, *The Division of Labor in Society*, W. D. Halls trans. (London: Macmillan, 1984), pp. 24–29.

[4] The original Civil Code proposal, Article 1162; Al-Qānūn al-Madanī, volume 6, p. 13; On the *Taṣṣaruf* right see Al-Wasīṭ, volume 8, pp. 501–509.

[5] The ʾAhlī Civil Code, article 11, Al-Qānūn al-Madanī, volume 6, p. 13. This article was based on article 544 of the French Code Civil.

[6] Kelly, pp. 249–253, 268–271.

The civil codes of the twentieth century criticized this absolutist approach, arguing that, in the century of the masses, it was no longer possible to grant each individual in society his full rights. According to the sociological approach, it was proper to examine the full scope of rights of society as a whole, and to define individual rights on the basis of this definition. This was nothing short of a legal revolution, since the liberal approach, which may be termed individualist in the legal sphere, defined collective rights on the basis of individual rights, whereas the sociological approach adopted the converse approach; and, while the individualistic approach argued that property rights were absolute, the sociological approach defined them as limited and relative. According to this approach, personal property is no longer an absolute and selfish right, regardless of the needs, circumstances and condition of society, but is a limited (*maqsūr*) right, whose owner is required to consider the benefit of the collective, the environment and society, and not merely his personal benefit.[7]

Sanhūrī was also concerned by the damage that resulted from the absolute freedom of action granted in accordance with the individualistic approach. On several occasions, he discussed what he termed 'selfishness,' questioning whether selfishness was exclusively positive or negative, and examining the extent to which it hampered social development. His conclusion was that while selfishness was a predominantly positive attribute, it must be restricted in order to contain its negative aspects. In his personal diaries, he wrote:

> The studies that are being published about the human being center on his inherent selfishness, provided you understand the meaning of selfishness as I term it, as distinct from the usual sense. Selfishness is a natural love present in man that prevents mental harm and brings peace of mind. People's perceptions of good and evil vary. In noble spirits, selfishness appears as sacrifice for the homeland, public service or pure love, and other aspects I term sublime emotions. In lesser spirits, selfishness appears in the form of lust, avarice and self-promotion, qualities I consider despicable.[8]

Sanhūrī manifested his desire to curb negative selfishness in the field of property law, as did other twentieth century codes. His assumption was that the reduction of selfishness in society would lead to a concomitant increase in social solidarity.

---

[7] On the contradiction between *Mutlaq* (absolute) and *Maḥdūd* (limited), see Al-Qānūn al-Madanī, volume 6, p. 14.

[8] Diary, 27 May 1922, pp. 71–72.

"This principle requires cooperation in society, and property is one of the important pillars on which such cooperation stands," he noted. "The owner of a property right should consider himself to be a member of the society in which he lives, as he indeed is. He takes from it and gives back. Even if the owner of property has accumulated the property through his personal labor, he nevertheless owes society for what he has accumulated. It is not only his labor that has brought him his possessions, but the community has (also) participated in his efforts in order for him to achieve what he has."[9]

In the New Code, Sanhūrī did not oppose the individual right in property law, but added that "the right to property is both individual (*ḥaqq fardī*) and a social function (*waẓīfa ʾijtimāʿiyya*)," thus transferring the weight of the property right from the individual to the collective sphere.[10] He added that "the function of property rests on two foundations: firstly, the obligations and authorities of the owner to meet his personal needs, and secondly, the use of the property and authority of the owner to meet the needs of society so that it can participate in general development."[11] Indeed, throughout the Code we see an effort to address the tension between the individual and social characters of the property right. Sanhūrī was well aware of the sociological emphases of the period, "in which the social aspect is naturally stressed at the expense of the individual aspect of this right."[12]

The explanatory notes to the proposed Code stated that the proposal did not grant the right of property the absolute character it enjoyed in the outgoing Code, "but abandons this absolute character in favor of another approach, currently dominant among modern codes, that... this is not another absolute and limitless right, but rather a social function to be met by the owner of the right; and, so long as he does so, the law shall protect him. If, however, he deviates from these limits, then the law does not consider him worthy of protection."[13]

---

[9] Al-Wasīṭ, volume 8, p. 554. It should be taken into consideration that volume 8 was written after the 1952 revolution, when socialist ideology was dominant in Egypt, so al-Sanhūrī stretched the elasticity of the 'social function' toward socialist notions and not only sociological ones.

[10] Al-Wasīṭ, volume 8, p. 549.

[11] Ibid., volume 8, p. 554.

[12] Ibid.

[13] Ibid., pp. 546–547, 494, 557.

The explanatory notes outline two possible scenarios for such dilemmas:

1. When the (individual) right to property contradicts the general interest (*maṣlaḥa ʿāmma*), the general interest will clearly take precedence. The explanatory notes presented the individual right as an obstacle to advancing the general good; accordingly, it would not be included in the context of the social function of property laws, and would be rejected in favor of general rights. For example, in the New Code, land ownership includes what is above and below the land to the extent of utilization. Accordingly, if the state undertakes works aboveground, in the air (erecting electricity power lines or telephone lines), or belowground (laying water pipes), without causing damage to the owner, he cannot claim that his rights of ownership have been infringed.
2. When an individual property right contradicts the individual property right of another person, the court will examine, in keeping with the sociological orientation of the Code, which one holds the preferential interest; the other party will receive 'just compensation.' Accordingly, priority will not be granted automatically; rather, on the basis of the sociological considerations applied by the court (as discussed in the following chapters), it will reach a value-based decision. Even in the context of the need to decide between two individuals, the decision may still be made within the framework of the social functions of property law, such as creating a balance between weak and strong, promoting mutual consideration, and adopting a didactic approach of punishing those who fail to show such consideration.

The phrasing of this article in the original proposal, which explicitly mentioned the concept of 'social function,' was adopted by the members of the House of Representatives during the various stages of legislation, but was rejected by the Civil Code Committee established by the Upper House (the Senate) of the Egyptian parliament in order to monitor the work on the proposed code. During the committee's deliberations, the president, Muḥammad al-Wakīl (himself a major landowner) opposed the inclusion of the words 'social function' in the Code, arguing that this was the "manifestation of a philosophical school" that accordingly had no place in the statute books.

The protocols available to us do not detail the precise nature of the concern of the committee president, and other members, at the use of this phrase. It may be assumed, however, that they feared that an excessively flexible interpretation of the Code might, in the future, threaten the prevailing social order. It should be recalled that the phrase 'social function' was not found only in the Italian Code which, according to the explanatory notes, was the source of its replication in the Egyptian context. A similar phrase also appeared in Article 1 of the Soviet Civil Code, stating that "the rights of citizens are protected by law, except in cases in which they are exercised contrary to their socioeconomic purpose." It may be assumed that this Communist context disturbed figures within a monarchist regime, particularly when phrased in such broad terms.[14] Despite Sanhūrī's pleadings, this phrase was omitted, producing the final wording of Article 802 of the finished Code: "The owner of a thing has alone the right to use it, enjoy it and undertake disposition of it, within the limits of the law."[15]

Thus the committee decided to omit the explicit mention of 'social function,' explaining that this was detailed in practical terms in the specific provisions of the Code, and spoke for itself. In his interpretative comments in the volumes of *al-Wasīṭ*, however, Sanhūrī continued to act as though the phrase had not been omitted from the Code. Accordingly, the term continued to hover over the property laws in the Code, albeit not explicitly, as an important source to be addressed in understanding its nature and the social change it sought to engender. Sanhūrī argued that even in its truncated form, the article restricted property rights, since the owner's actions were restricted to 'the limits of the law', and were, therefore, no longer unlimited.[16]

This approach of restricting the right of property, and of allowing the legal system to oblige the different parties within society to act considerately, was recognized as encouraging 'social solidarity,' and was characteristic of the civil codes of the twentieth century, such as the Swiss code and the proposed Franco-Italian code.[17] This is a 'carrot and stick' approach: the owner of property has an interest in taking into consideration the needs of the society of which he ultimately forms part, and from whose progress he will also benefit. If, however, he fails to understand this and to act accordingly, the law will not provide him

---

[14] On the Soviet Civil Code see Sanhūrī's: "Min Majallat al-'Aḥkām al-'Adliyya 'ila al-Qānūn al-Madanī fī al-'Uṣūr al-Ḥadītha, *Majmū'at Maqālāt wa-'Abḥāth al-Sanhūrī*, volume 2, pp. 305–308.

[15] Al-Qānūn al-Madanī, volume 6, p. 13; Al-Wasīṭ, volume 8, p. 494.

[16] Al-Wasīṭ, volume 8, p. 493.

[17] On the 'social function' in the French and European Law, see Al-Wasīṭ, volume 8, p. 545.

with protection.[18] In this context, Sanhūrī made the following comment regarding the principle of solidarity:

> Society rests on two fundamental pillars: competition and solidarity. These are contradictory foundations, since competition has its origins in love of the self, while solidarity originates in the love of one's fellow. If we think more deeply, however, we shall see that the individual also collaborates with his fellow for his own good; accordingly, solidarity is also based on the love of oneself.[19]

2.2 *The Theory of* al-ʿUluww wal-Sufl *as Metaphor for a New Egyptian Society*

Sanhūrī noted that there are cases in which 'the social function of the right of property reaches its ultimate purpose." An outstanding example of this might be the mutual relations between the *ʿuluww* (the uppermost floor) and the *sufl* (the lowest floor) in an apartment building.[20] This book argues that Sanhūrī drew an analogy between this issue and the question of the social cooperation needed in Egyptian society. As we shall see below, a number of articles address the sensitive relations between owners of different floors in a single building. The owner of the lower apartment is obliged to prevent the collapse of the upper floor, while the owner of the upper floor is prohibited from raising his apartment or placing undue pressure in order to prevent the collapse of the entire building.[21]

This mutual relationship may be seen as a metaphor for the principle of social solidarity the Civil Code seeks to apply in Egyptian society: society is an apartment building with lower and upper floors. The owners of the lower floors, which are richer in the Egyptian context, secure the existence of the upper floors and form the basis of the entire building. If they fail to understand this function and act accordingly, the entire building will collapse. Equally, the owners of the upper floors must also act responsibly toward those below them, or again the building may collapse. Thus both rich and poor, residents of the periphery or the center, country-dwellers and urbanites are all responsible for one another. Without mutual involvement and cooperation, the common

[18] Al-Wasīṭ, volume 8, p. 554.
[19] Diary, 21 October 1955, p. 296.
[20] Al-Wasīṭ, volume 8, pp. 559–560.
[21] The principles of *ʿuluww* and *Sufl* appear in articles 859–861 of the New Civil Code, and will be reviewed in detail later on.

(social) structure is liable to collapse. This approach decentralizes responsibility and means that all elements of society, greater and lesser, are of importance. This is also a good example of the relativity of the right of property as perceived by the New Code: if each owner cares only for his own apartment, and ignores the other owners in the building, the entire building—the collective—may eventually collapse. Accordingly, while restricting the right of property may seem injurious to the owner of the right, he will ultimately benefit from the proper functioning of the (physical and social) building. These provisions therefore allude to the underlying logic of the New Code as it addresses the privileged members of Egyptian society: it is worth sacrificing a little in order to gain much more.

True to the essentially paternalistic nature of the sociological approach, the New Code does not confine itself to assuming that apartment owners in the building will understand of their own accord the social transformation they are required to undergo. As we shall see in greater detail below in the context of contract law, the court is placed in the position of the supervisor of this mutual liability between neighbors, as an ever-present authority and as a guarantor of the existence of the shared property. The court can oblige each of the apartment owners to observe his role in this socio-legal contract; if he refuses, the court will force him to comply, even to the point of selling the apartment under his ownership.

This metaphor for the new social structure which, this book argues, the New Code sought to introduce into polarized Egyptian society, is strengthened in the light of the fact that the principles of the *sufl* and *ʿuluww* were essentially drawn from the Islamic *Sharīʿa*, a cultural context emphasized by the authors of the Code in order to enhance the authentic nature of Eastern law and society. The authenticity of these principles in the context of Muslim and Egyptian society emphasized that this social function is feasible since it is rooted in the traditional logic of the region. The explanatory notes to the original proposal referred to the relevant passages in the *Majalla*: "Any person controls his property as he wishes. However, if the right of another is connected to this property, this prevents him from controlling it as he wishes. In a building whose upper floor belongs to one person, while the lower floor belongs to another, since the owner of the upper floor has the right to be based on the lower floor, and the owner of the lower floor has the right to be sheltered by the upper floor, i.e., to find cover from the sun and rain under the upper floor, neither party can do anything that would harm the other without his consent."[22] The Ḥanafī *Majalla* also addressed the case of a common property that was demolished, examining the relations that are created among the owners of the various floors, and establishing a principle that was also adopted in the New Civil Code: "If a building whose upper floor belongs to one person, and whose lower floor belongs to another, is destroyed or burnt, each party shall rebuild its floor, and neither may delay his fellow. If the owner of the upper floor says, 'Build your floor so that I may also build my floor upon it,' and the owner of the lower floor refuses, he shall obtain permission from the court and build both floors, lower and upper, and he shall withhold the property rights of the owner of the lower floor until the latter has paid his expenses."[23]

Sanhūrī emphasized that these principles also appeared in the *Sharīʿa*, although, as we shall also see below in other cases relating to contract and property law, they also appeared in part in the outgoing Code (in which they were also based, in part, on the Islamic *fiqh*), albeit without the sociological ideology that characterizes these principles in the New Code.[24] Moreover, the New Code added to these principles of *sufl* and *ʿuluww* provisions drawn from a French law from 1938 that regulated not the relations among the neighbors, but those between the neighbors and the common property in the building. For Sanhūrī, this blending of property laws as a local manifestation of solidarity with progressive Western legislation constituted the most appropriate and successful model for Egypt. Elsewhere, he wrote regarding this blending: "Our needs for the old exist, as do our needs for the new... The old represents permanence and stability, while the new represents flexibility and development."[25]

1.3 *The Linear Development of the Concept of the Social Function*

As if to examine the full flexibility potential of the 'social function' of property in Egypt, the interpretation and scope of this concept underwent a transformation as time passed, and particularly after the trauma of the overthrowing of the monarchy and the revolution of the

[22] The Majalla, article 1192.
[23] Ibid., article 1315.
[24] ʿAbd al-Fattaḥ Sayyid, Muḥammad Kāmil Mursī, *Majmūʿat Qawānīn al-Maḥākim al-ʾAhliyya wa al-Sharʿiyya* (Cairo: Maṭbaʿat al-Raʿaʾib bi-Miṣr, 1921) articles 34–37.
[25] Al-Wasīṭ, volume 8, p. 1009; ʿAbd al-Razzāq al-Sanhūrī, "Al-Jadīd wa al-Qadīm", *Al-Hilāl* (1949), special edition, pp. 6–8.

'Free Officers,' just a few years after enactment of the New Code. This historical development must be taken into account when examining the precise manner in which this function was manifested in everyday life during the different periods: as the political and economic reality changed, so did the scope of the social function. This discussion ostensibly deviates from the time span of this book—viz. the period during which the New Code was prepared—but is included in order to cast light on the scope and borders of this function, which are supposed to be flexible.

The discussion of this concept by the various committees involved in the legislation of the New Code took place during the period of the monarchy. During this time, the social function of property laws sought to play a mediating role, softening social friction in order to maintain the existing social order. The intention was not to change the social order, but to preserve it. However, the political reality changed after the Nasserite revolution of 1952. Political, economic and social order took on a new tenor, and by the 1960s the revolutionary regime was involved in an attempt to apply the principles of Arab Socialism.

In 1967, Sanhūrī, in his capacity as interpreter of the Code, published the eighth volume of *Al-Wasīṭ*, which addresses the interpretation of the right of property. He was obliged to adapt the purpose of social function as manifested in the Code in order to respond to the changes that had occurred in the meantime in what was now an authoritarian regime. He extended still further the flexibility of the concept of social function in order to enable it to absorb the Socialist ideas that were being introduced in Egyptian society in this period. The dominance of the state over the individual was now apparent, in the context of nationalization. While during the 1940s Sanhūrī had emphasized the relativity of individual property rights *vis-à-vis* society, the emphasis now shifted to their relativity *vis-à-vis* the state. For example, a new emphasis was placed on Article 806 in the New Code, which stated that the owner was obliged to obey the rules, orders and regulations relating to the public good or the good of a given individual. This is an ostensibly technical article, and was not the subject of any real deliberation on the part of the various committees involved in enacting the Code. In the 1960s, however, it was emphasized as restricting the actions of the individual in the face of public administration.[26] Sanhūrī noted that this article addresses a wide range of restrictions, such as public security

[26] Al-Wasīṭ, volume 8, p. 644.

in time of war, public health, or administrative rights of *ʾirtifāq* (easement), such as restricting rights along the sides of roads, unauthorized construction, demolition of adjacent buildings, the uprooting of trees blocking the free passage of water, and so on.[27]

The 'social function' of the Code now included the Socialist ideas of the period, such as equality in the distribution of income, that would have been considered grossly illogical by those involved in drafting the Civil Code in the 1930s and 1940s, the major landowners who sat in parliament, including Sanhūrī himself.

In methodological terms, however, the flexible social function of property laws proved triumphant, in that it was able to adapt itself and the New Code as a whole, to the ideological changes that occurred in society and to avoid a disturbing dissonance with that changing reality. After all, this had been the starting point of the New Code, in keeping with the sociological and teleological approach in France, which argued that the legal text did not have a fixed meaning, but changed over time in keeping with changes in society.

In *Al-Wasīṭ* (1967), Sanhūrī made the following comments about the updated scope of the social function:

> The modern tendencies regarding the right of property are contrary to those of the past. While the individual right of property was strengthened and extended throughout the 19th century, and during the first quarter of the 20th century, it has receded in modern times under pressure from Socialist streams and economic schools that advocate state intervention in the regulation of personal property and economic life in general.
>
> The modern tendencies prevalent in many countries of the world (and the reference is not to the Communist countries) may be summarized as follows:
>
> 1. An increasing number of laws around the world place restrictions on personal property, particularly in the context of the ownership of land. The modern tendency, which transforms the right to property into a social function and is not content to leave it as an autonomous right granting its owner full freedom of action—has proved dominant.
> 2. The state has not confined itself to restrictions on property, but has moved much further, beginning to take control of personal property for the sake of the general interest, for the purpose of agrarian reform or nationalization in general, which has reached a very broad scale in current times.

[27] Ibid., p. 555.

3. The state encourages small property rights, dismantles the major rights and divides them into small plots for the benefit of the simple peasants. The state also encourages the construction of high-rise buildings and regulates the ownership of apartments, so that families may purchase the ownership of their own apartment in a high-rise building.[28]

In discussing the economic interpretation of the social function, Sanhūrī even began to employ Socialist terminology, writing:

> Social structure must exist on the basis of equality in the distribution (*tawzīʿ*) (of profit). The production system is not owned solely by the owner, but the workers are also partners in that system. (Accordingly), profit should be distributed justly between the owner and the workers... A factory owner, for example, is the owner of the capital and, at the same time, the director of the system. The profit of factories should be divided justly between capital and the workers; accordingly, capital deserves a portion; the owner, who is also the director, deserves a portion; as do the workers, each in accordance with the importance of his labor. The workers deserve a portion of the profits in addition to their wages, since they have participated in production, and since the profits were created not only from the capital, but also from the labor.[29]

This updated 1960s model of the social function later attempted to address the argument, which was being made openly at the time, that the private right of property should be completely abolished. Sanhūrī was appalled at this possibility, since it would herald the destruction of the balances he had constructed throughout the Civil Code and mark the end of the flexible capacity of that social function. Accordingly, in the section on the interpretation of the economic character of the social function in 1967, he wrote:

> The research often confuses the right of property *per se* and the non-distribution of wealth, whereas these are two autonomous and separate concepts. The non-distribution of wealth in society (excluding a narrow social class that enjoys the majority of wealth) is often exploited as grounds for proving the illegality of the right of property, as if the abolition of the right of property would ensure the proper distribution of wealth. In fact, the abolition of the right of property would abolish wealth itself, and it would then be immaterial to discuss the proper distribution or non-distribution of wealth. The right of property does not become less just if the distribution is unjust. If the distribution of wealth is unjust,

---

[28] Ibid., p. 489.
[29] Ibid., p. 567.

> the regime for the distribution of wealth should be amended, but without impairing the right of property.[30]

A further example, relating to a confrontation between the original social function and the changing circumstances of Egyptian society, is that of rental laws as formulated in the New Code.

In the explanatory notes to the law, and certainly in its interpretation, the New Code considered the rental contract to have a unique character, insofar as it has the potential to cross social classes. From the perspective of the Code, the rental contract can serve as a chain linking the 'class of lessors' and the 'class of tenants.' Accordingly, the rental contract is perceived as a social encounter that may be exploited in order to secure 'social peace' and solidarity between lessors and tenants, and hence between the different economic groups and classes within society.[31] As we shall see in the next chapter, the guiding principle behind the Egyptian code, and subsequently the other Arab codes, was to protect the weak, which in most cases means the tenant. However, it is not impossible that in some cases the weaker party in the contract will be the lessor, whose property right has been injured by tenant protection laws. Sanhūrī emphasized this possibility in the context of his criticism of the agrarian reform in Egypt and of the government restrictions imposed in the 1950s and 1960s, as we shall see below, on the period of tenancy and on the maximum payment that could be received on account thereof. "The legislature has entered (into the conditions of the rental contract) to the maximum and imposed restrictions thereon," he noted. "The balance between lessor and tenant has been reversed, the weight of the lessor has diminished and that of the tenant has increased, so that if, in the past, the tenant was inferior and victimized, he was now gained the upper hand, and the victim has become the victimizer. I proposed (in the 1930s and 1940s) solidarity between the social classes (regarding tenancy)," Sanhūrī continued, "but not confrontation between them."[32]

---

[30] Ibid., p. 562.
[31] Ibid., volume 6, pp. 26–27.
[32] Ibid., p. 29.

2. Social Solidarity in the Practical Dimension: From a Total to a Relative Right

2.1 *The Transition to Relativity*

We have seen how the concept of the 'absolute' property right was deleted from the New Civil Code. In addition, the Code imposed a series of restrictions on the right of property, which thus became relative to other surrounding rights, or to any other interest as decided by society. Ziadeh noted that this approach is far removed from the absolute character of the right of property as embodied in the Old Egyptian Code and the other codes of the nineteenth and early twentieth centuries.[33]

An example of the relative nature of the right of property may be seen in the provision prohibiting the owner of a property right from the excessive use of his right in a manner injurious to the property of his neighbor.[34] The right of response of the neighbor is also relative: the neighbor does not have the right of response against his neighbor on account of reasonable (*ma'lūf*) neighborly damages that could not have been avoided by the first owner. The neighbor may request removal of these damages if they deviate from the reasonable, in accordance with custom (*'urf*), the character of the lands, their mutual location and their purpose. The explanatory notes to the Code argued that this principle of relativity was drawn from the *Sharī'a*, and even referred to sections from the *Majalla*;[35] above all, however, this is the application of a Western doctrine—the doctrine of the abuse of a right—as shall be discussed in depth in the next chapter.

The article established a flexible criterion to be applied in examining the action of one landowner *vis-à-vis* another—'excess'—which was to be measured in accordance with the criterion of reasonable or unreasonable damage in neighborly relations. Ziadeh noted that the Egyptian courts considered reasonable damage (not granting the right of response) to include, for example, the casting of shade by a neighbor's trees over his neighbor's crops, unless it could be proved that the neighbor had planted the trees maliciously or that, in general, he had been negligent in following the accepted agricultural practice.[36]

---

[33] Ziadeh, *Law of Property in the Arab World: Real Rights in Egypt, Iraq, Jordan, Lebanon and Syria* (London: Graham & Trotman, 1978), p. 26.

[34] The Egyptian Civil Code, article 807(1).

[35] The Majalla, articles 1195–1209.

[36] F. Ziadeh, *Law of Property in the Arab World*: pp. 26–28. The same principal appeared

Another example relates to the expanse of land rights, which is presented as relative by the New Code. Land rights include all that is above and below ground, to the limit of enjoyment in height and depth. Through legislation or by agreement, ownership of the surface could be separated from ownership of what was above or below.[37] Ziadeh noted that this was a case in which the public interest was given precedence over the right of property: the state could exploit the airspace or the underground for any purpose it considered necessary, provided such use did not damage the property itself. It should be noted, however, that the New Civil Code continued to protect the right of property: property could not be taken from any person with the exception of cases to be established in law, and in return for just compensation.[38]

2.2 *Negative Actions by Owners*

Having reviewed the normative rule that a property right is not to be used to excess, i.e. the manner of its use is subject to the discretion of the court and is no longer autonomous and absolute, we shall now examine a further example—the restriction of the ownership of a private wall—as a question of principle. The owner of a constructed wall may do with it as he pleases—he may erect a structure on its area, demolish it and rebuild it as he pleases. However, the Code establishes an exception, whereby "the owner of a wall is not permitted to demolish it on his own initiative without serious justification (*ʿudhr qawwī*) if this will injure his neighbor whose property is adjacent to this wall".[39]

This case does not relate to the laws regarding a joint wall, which will be discussed below, but to a wall that is owned entirely and fully by one of the neighbors. The explanatory notes to the original proposed Code stated that this case embodies both the application of the doctrine of the abuse of a right and of principles drawn from the Islamic *Sharīʿa*. It is indeed true that Islamic law recognized the relativity of an individual's right to build on his private land. The *Majalla*, for

---

in the Majalla, article 1196: "If the branches of trees in any person's garden extend into the house or garden of his neighbor, the owner may be made by the neighbor to tie up such branches... he may not, however, cut down the tree on the grounds that the shadow of such tree is injurious to the cultivation in his garden".

[37] The Egyptian Civil Code, article 803(2)(3).

[38] The Egyptian Civil Code, article 805. This wording was taken from article 9 of the Egyptian Constitution. The explanatory notes referred to the Majalla, article 97: "No person may take another person's property without some legal reason".

[39] The Egyptian Civil Code, article 818(2); Al-Wasīṭ, volume 8, pp. 557–558.

example, established that "any person is entitled to raise his wall within his property to such height as he wishes and to use it as he sees fit, and his neighbor may not delay him, unless he is caused grave injury (*ḍarar fāḥish*) thereby."[40]

Sanhūrī explained that if the demolition of the wall was undertaken without serious justification, or secured only a narrow interest, the interest of the neighbor whose property was liable to be damaged by the demolition would unequivocally outweigh the interest of the owner in demolishing his wall. Accordingly, in such a case the demolition of the wall would be considered the abuse of a property right, imposing on the owner of the wall the appropriate liability, to the point that the court could oblige the owner to rebuild the wall, subject to just compensation on account of the injury to the right of property.[41]

2.3 *The Positive Action of Another*

The social function of the right of property also permitted another person to intervene in a positive manner with regard to the owner's enjoyment of his private property, in order that this other person might avoid damage significantly greater than that caused to the owner by the penetration of his property. Ziadeh termed this a specific action by another party that contradicts the right of property but is legitimized by society. In balancing the interests, however, the owner would be entitled to just compensation for the injury of his right to enjoy his property.[42]

The owner of a private water channel or drainage channel has the right to enjoy his property on his own. However, neighbors who need to do so are permitted to draw water from the private water channel to irrigate their land, or to use the private drainage channel, after the owner of the right has used the water to his full need. In such a case, the neighbors using the water installations must participate in the cost of their operation and maintenance.[43]

In another case, the Code established that a landowner is free to act as he sees fit in his property, and has the right to prevent another from enjoying the private land. However, a neighbor may oblige the owner,

---

[40] Al-Qānūn al-Madanī, volume 6, p. 65; The Majalla articles 1198–1212, cited article 1198.

[41] Al-Wasīṭ, volume 8, p. 691.

[42] Ibid., p. 558; Ziadeh, p. 26.

[43] Ibid. The Egyptian Civil Code, article 808(1)(2).

through the court, to ensure that water also passes through his land, if the neighbor's land is distant from the main water or drainage point, provided that the owner shall receive just compensation.[44]

A landowner has the right to prevent his neighbor from passing through his land, i.e., to deny him the right of passage (*ḥaqq al-murūr*). However, the Code established that if the neighbor's land was trapped and distant from the public way, or was not served by a suitable road, the neighbor would enjoy the right of passage through the private land of his neighbor for the purpose of using his own land, in a reasonable manner and in return for just compensation of the landowner. In accordance with the principle of balancing and minimizing damage, the Code noted that such passage would be effected only in the area causing minimum damage to the owner; were this not the case, the doctrine of the abuse of a right might be activated.[45]

While the provision in this article was drawn from the old Civil Code,[46] the New Code expanded the neighbor's right of passage. The former code recognized such a right only in the case of an area of land disconnected completely from the public way, whereas the New Code also permitted enforced right of passage through a private area in the case when the more distant land was served by a road, but this was unsuitable or inadequate. The Code further established that this right of passage was in itself relative, and would be nullified if the distant land were connected to the public way, or if the right of passage were no longer essential.[47]

It is interesting to note that the original proposal for the Code included two other cases in which it was permitted to enter private land, but these were rejected by the Civil Code Committee of the Senate, "in order not to (excessively) extend the restrictions on the right of property."[48] The first such case discussed the possibility for an 'interested party' (*shakhṣ dhī maṣlaḥa*) to enter private land, when necessary, for example for the purpose of construction or renovation via the land of another, to restore lost items or to secure another lawful interest, in return for just compensation, and on condition that this

[44] Ibid., p. 559; The Egyptian Civil Code, article 809.
[45] Ibid., pp. 559, 752–775; The Egyptian Civil Code, article 812(1).
[46] The ʾAhlī Civil Code, *Majmūʿat Qawānīn al-Maḥākim al-ʾAhliyya wa al-Sharʿiyya*, article 43.
[47] Al-Qānūn al-Madanī, volume 6, p. 50.
[48] Ibid., pp. 48–49.

would not cause grave damage to the owner.[49] In the second case, the general public was granted the possibility of passing through private land if passage via the public way were impossible, provided that such passage be effected in a logical manner, and that the administrative authority compensate the owner for the damage caused due to such general passage.[50]

These latter two articles apparently caused the major landowners in the Upper House of the parliament to feel threatened, hence their ultimately successful demand that they be deleted in their entirety. The explanatory notes to the proposed Code detailed how it was possible to ascertain the proper boundary between the right of ownership and the right of another to enter private property: if such intervention served an interest significantly broader than the damage caused.[51] The majority of members of the Senate committee evidently believed that these two articles did not meet this yardstick, despite the fact that the second case referred to an interest of the general public rather than of another landowner.

2.4 *Positive Actions by the Owner*

Al-Wasīṭ interpretation of the Civil Code noted that in this case the social function of the property right attains its maximum purpose, obliging the owner to undertake substantive positive actions in his land for the benefit of another.[52] By way of examples, Sanhūrī presented cases that will be discussed in depth below, such as when the owner of the lower floor in an apartment building is obliged to undertake vital construction and renovation work to prevent the collapse of the higher floor. If he fails to do so, the judge may order the sale of the lower floor. If both floors were destroyed, the owner of the lower floor is obliged to reconstruct his floor, so that the owner of the upper floor may build thereon. If he refrains from doing so, the judge may again order the sale of the lower floor, unless the owner of the upper floor asks to build on the lower floor by himself, at the expense of its owner.[53] A further case, also detailed below, involves the obligation on a minority of owners in a common property to accept the decision of

[49] Ibid., pp. 48, 51; article 1179 of the original code proposal.
[50] Ibid., pp. 49, 51–52; article 1180 of the original code proposal.
[51] The test appeared in the explanatory notes of the code proposal, ibid., p. 52.
[52] Al-Wasīṭ, volume 8, p. 559.
[53] The Egyptian Civil Code, articles 859–860.

the majority regarding the management, a change of purpose and even sale of the common property.

Another example the Code sought to introduce, and which aptly illustrates the spirit of solidarity it advocated, even at the cost of coercion, appeared in the original proposed Code, which stated that an owner must not prevent another from entering his property in order to use it, when such entrance was vital in order to prevent a danger graver than the damage that would be caused thereby; if damage was indeed caused, the owner was eligible for compensation. However, this article was not ultimately included in the final Code.[54] Owners were, however, obliged to permit adequate water for the irrigation of land distant from the water source to pass through their land into neighboring land, as well as drainage water, provided that they receive just compensation, as may be seen below.

2.5 *The Rules of Irrigation as a Tool for Enhancing Social Solidarity*

One of the more sophisticated mechanisms the New Code sought to establish in order to regulate the desired social relations, based on mutual waiver and solidarity, related to the system of agricultural irrigation in Egypt, i.e., the drawing of water from the Nile via channels.

The irrigation system has always been a source of solidarity in Egyptian society, since it was impossible to draw water from the Nile without conduit channels, requiring peasants to cooperate during time of flooding or during irrigation.

Until construction of the Aswan Dam, Egyptian peasants faced a limited period in September and October when they had to channel and dam water from the Nile before the floods arrived; this was achieved through the collective efforts of the rural population. The peasants would also work together during the harvest, passing as a group from one plot to the next. As an individual, the peasant was powerless; only through solidarity and the power of the collective could he work his land. Indeed, some scholars have hypothesized that it was the unique Egyptian irrigation system that maintained social solidarity in rural Egypt for thousands of years, until the modern era with its own form of collectivism. Yet, it may be argued that this same approach educated and destined the Egyptian individual to conformity from an early age.[55]

---

[54] Al-Qānūn al-Madanī, volume 6, p. 11; article 876 of the original code proposal.

[55] R. Cohen, *Culture and Conflict in Egyptian-Israeli Relations* (Bloomington: Indiana

President Anwar Sadat was born in the village of Mit Abu al-Kum in the Manufiya district of the Nile Delta. Recalling his early years, he wrote:

> (The village did not have more than two weeks each year), our 'statutory' irrigation period, during which all land in the village had to be watered. It was obviously necessary to do it quickly and collectively. We worked together on one person's land for a whole day, then moved to another's, using any *tunbur* (Archimedean screw) that was available, regardless of who owned it. The main thing was to ensure that at the end of the 'statutory' period all the land in the village was irrigated.
>
> That kind of collective work—with and for other men, with no profit or any kind of individual reward in prospect—made me feel that I belonged not merely to my immediate family at home, or even to the big family of the village, but to something vaster and more significant: to the land.[56]

The proposed Code attributed particular weight to this unique mechanism of irrigation, "whose importance is obvious in an agricultural country such as Egypt," as the explanatory notes to the Code emphasized.[57] Interestingly, the original proposal included an article relating to an irrigation method that is not common in Egypt—terraces. This article was rejected by the committee on the grounds that it was not relevant to the agricultural and geographical reality of Egypt. The original Code Civil proposal established that the owner of a low plot of land must permit water arriving naturally, such as rainwater, to descend onto his plot from higher plots, and must not establish a dam preventing the descent of the water.[58] In the Nile Valley, rainwater is a rarity, as is the presence of agricultural plots constructed in terrace form.[59]

The Code sought to realize two symbiotic goals by increasing the efficiency of mutual relations in the irrigation system: to utilize the importance attached to the issue of irrigation in order to advance social solidarity, and to use this social solidarity in the field of property to advance the subject of water—and vice versa. "Improving the private water and drainage channels is a matter that relates not only to its

---

University Press, 1990), p. 21; H. Sharabi, "Impact of Class and Culture on Social Behavior: The Feudal-Bourgeois Family in Arab Society", in L. Carl Brown and Norman Itzkovitz eds. *Psychological Dimension of Near Eastern Studies* (Princeton: The Darwin Press, 1977), p. 246

[56] 52. Cohen, pp. 21–22; Anwar el Sadat, *In Search of Identity: an autobiography* (New York: Harper & Row, 1977), p. 3.

[57] Al-Qānūn al-Madanī, volume 6, p. 43.

[58] Article 1177.

[59] Ibid.

(direct) beneficiaries, but also to the public interest in the agricultural economy," Sanhūrī noted.[60]

This book argues that in order to regulate the unique irrigation system in Egypt, i.e., the passage of water through channels passing through dense agricultural land with multiple ownerships, the Code established a legal system based on a series of restrictions on private property rights in agricultural land for the benefit of adjacent agricultural plots.[61] By so doing, the intention was that in the balance of interests between the functionality of the agricultural irrigation system in Egypt and the property rights in the land, priority should be given to the harmonious operation of the system.

Three functions are involved in this context: irrigation, in which the neighbor draws water from the owner; the passage of water; and drainage, in which the water from the neighbor's fields drains through the owner's land.[62]

Regarding the irrigation of fields, the Code established that the owner of a private water or drainage channel had the right to enjoy his property on his own. However, neighbors were permitted to use these water and drainage channels as they required, once the owner had used them to his full need. In such a case, neighbors using private channels must participate in the cost of their operation and maintenance.[63] This contrasts with the old Egyptian Civil Code, which established that "a person who establishes a water channel has the right to use it."[64] However, the Water Channels and Bridges Order of 1894 permitted a neighbor to enjoy irrigation rights on conditions similar to those established in the New Code, though not without considerable bureaucratic difficulties.[65]

Sanhūrī wrote the following regarding the irrigation arrangement: "The possibility of allowing the neighbor the right of irrigation in this manner constitutes the prevalence of a more important private interest over a less important private interest. The owner of the channel has an interest in maintaining his property right intact and without partners; accordingly, even if water goes to waste he will not give it to his

[60] Al-Wasīṭ, volume 8, p. 727.
[61] Ibid., pp. 711–712.
[62] Al-Qānūn al-Madanī, volume 6, p. 43.
[63] The Egyptian Civil Code, article 808.
[64] The 'Ahlī Civil Code, article 32.
[65] Article 8; Al-Qānūn al-Madanī, volume 6, pp. 34–35.

neighbor. However, this is a weak and rejected interest that embodies unjustifiable selfishness (*'anāniyya*)."[66]

Regarding the passage of water for irrigation and drainage, the Code established that the landowner must permit adequate water to pass through his land in order to irrigate land further removed from the water source, and to drain neighboring fields into the central drainage point, provided that the landowner receive just compensation.[67]

The explanatory notes to the proposed Code detailed two possibilities open to a neighbor with regard to the right of drainage: the use of his neighbor's private drainage channel (after the owner had used it to meet his full need), and hence participation in its maintenance costs, or construction of a drainage channel on the neighbor's land that would reach the general drainage point, in which case the neighbor would be required to pay the landowner compensation for the area occupied by the channel.[68]

Equally, and in order to complete this circle of solidarity, neighbors benefiting from their neighbors' private water and drainage channels were required to pay part of the cost of essential repairs to these channels and installations as requested by the owner; if they refused, they could be forced to pay by court order. Moreover, if damage was caused to the land through which the neighbor's water and drainage channels passed, the landowner could demand compensation.[69]

2.6 *The Relative Nature of Property Rights in Light of the Right of Privacy*

In Islamic law, great importance is accorded to the right of privacy as a basic right: in the context of women, the sanctity of the private home, and relations between neighbors. Interestingly, the *Majalla* referred to the latter as seeing the women's place (*maqarr al-nisā'*), i.e. the innermost parts of the house (thus the privacy of women and the privacy of the home are closely intertwined). A neighbor who glimpsed into these parts was considered to have caused grave injury, and accordingly someone in a position so to glimpse was obliged to remove the injury. As the *Majalla* puts it, "Seeing the women's place, such as the courtyard, the kitchen and the well, is considered grave injury. Accordingly, if a person

[66] Al-Wasīṭ, volume 8, p. 715.
[67] The Egyptian Civil Code, article 809.
[68] Al-Qānūn al-Madanī, volume 6, p. 44; Al-Wasīṭ, volume 8, p. 713.
[69] The Egyptian Civil Code, articles 810–811; Al-Wasīṭ, volume 8, pp. 725–726; Al-Qānūn al-Madanī, volume 6, pp. 41–42.

opens a new window in his home, or makes a window in a new house he constructs, and the women's place of his neighbor, next door or across the street, may be seen through these windows, he is obliged to remove the injury. He is forced to remove the injury by building a wall or barrier such that it is impossible to see the women's place. However, he is not obliged to completely block the window. The same applies to a wooden fence through whose cracks it is possible to see the women's place of the neighbor. He is obliged to seal the cracks, but he is not obliged to remove the fence and build a wall in its place."[70]

The New Code consciously followed in the steps of its predecessor, adopting the principles of privacy from the Islamic *fiqh*, while presenting these provisions as a restriction on the right of property. The general principle was that maintaining privacy requires the maintenance of physical distance.

As a rule, when constructing a building it is necessary to create openings in its walls in order to permit the entry of light and air, and enable the occupants to see outside. If the opening is intended for all three of these purposes, it is referred to in the Code as *maṭal*, such as windows, apertures, balconies and other general openings. If the opening is intended to provide light and ventilation, but not to afford a view of the outside, it is termed *manwar*. The *manwar* is an opening located above the height of a person, so that it is not normally possible to look outside through it. The *maṭal* may be direct, in which case it is possible to look at the neighbor directly without the need to turn the head to either side, or it may be indirect or diagonal, in which case it is only possible to observe the neighbor's property if one turns to either side or leans forward.

From the perspective of the neighbor, the form of opening that most gravely infringes his privacy is the direct *maṭal*, followed by the indirect *maṭal*, and lastly the *manwar*. The Code established specific provisions for each of these categories in the spirit of the *fiqh*, while also drawing on modern Western legislation.[71]

The issue of privacy is particularly acute when a neighbor wishes to build right on the border between his property and his neighbor's and to include openings facing the neighbor, as the right of property would entitle him to do. In normal circumstances, an owner is indeed

[70] The Majalla, article 1202.
[71] The introduction was taken from Al-Wasīṭ, volume 8, p. 775.

permitted to build on the border with his neighbor's property. However, if he wishes to include openings in the wall facing his neighbor, he must observe a number of restrictions. The previous Code confined the restrictions solely to the case of a direct *maṭal*.[72]

According to the New Code, in the case of a direct *maṭal*, the distance between the edge of the *maṭal* and the neighbor's property must be at least one meter. In the case of a diagonal *maṭal*, the required distance is half a meter (the old Code did not impose any minimum distance in this case); in the case of a *manwar*, no minimum distance was stated, since it is not possible to observe the neighbor's property from this opening without special devices.[73] However, the Code stipulates that the minimum height for the *manwar* is that of an average man. Sanhūrī stipulated minimum heights for a *manwar* drawn from French law: 2.6 meters on the first floor, and 1.9 meters on the upper floors.[74]

2.7 *Innovations in Land Accession* (ʾIltiṣāq)

The *ʾiltiṣāq* (accession, attachment) is a form of acquisition of a property right manifested in two principal forms: the first artificial and man-made, which is the focus of our attention here; and the second natural, through the action of water. Three forms of natural *ʾiltiṣāq* may be noted: the waters of a river gradually and imperceptibly lead to the accumulation of alluvium (*ṭamī*), i.e., a residue of sand and clay, which attaches to the plot; the river exposes or covers land; or the sea, lakes or water sources may retreat, exposing land. Only the first of these occurrences is recognized by the Code as constituting *ʾiltiṣāq*, while the latter two forms do not produce the acquisition of ownership through *ʾiltiṣāq*. The Code explicitly states that the *ṭami* may accumulate gradually and imperceptibly, in which case it will belong to the owner. The conditions of graduality and imperceptibility are substantive, since if the exposure of land occurs suddenly, for example after the river changes its course, then the land will be termed *ṭarḥ*, is considered state property and is regulated by a special law.[75]

---

[72] Al-Qānūn al-Madanī, volume 6, pp. 67–68.

[73] The Egyptian Civil Code, article 819; Ziadeh. P. 28; Al-Wasīṭ, volume 8, p. 776.

[74] The Egyptian Civil Code, article 821; Al-Wasīṭ, volume 8, p. 789. Compare with the Majalla, article 1203.

[75] Al-Wasīṭ, volume 9, pp. 243–330; Al-Qānūn al-Madanī, volume 6, pp. 302–310; Ziadeh, pp. 41–43.

For our purposes, the artificial manifestation of this right may be defined as the attachment of land belonging to two different owners without agreement between them. The basic principle is that the owner of a given piece of land acquires ownership of property attached to his land (for example, a house built on his land by a neighbor or a grove of trees planted on his land), even if the value of the attached property is greater than that of the land itself. Accordingly, construction, planting and other works undertaken on the owner's land by another become the exclusive property of the landowner on whose land they are attached, in cases when the removal of these elements is impossible since it would cause grave damage to the work. The owner who acquires the assets attached to his plot must pay their value to the person who erected them.[76] This obscure aspect of the acquisition of ownership is a characteristic feature of the land regime in Egypt, which was congested and often not regulated or marked, and was already recognized by the old Civil Code.[77]

The dilemma facing the authors of the New Code was whether to maintain the full force of the right of property, whereby a landowner acquires ownership of installations erected on his land on the basis of *ʾiltiṣāq*, or to agree to impair the right of property in order to encourage economic and social objectives, such as enhancing the transferability of land and encouraging development without constant fear of deviating from the borders of the plots. If the latter avenue were chosen, it would be necessary to establish limits to the injury to the property right, and to ensure that those whose rights were injured received due compensation. Accordingly, this flexibility in the laws of *ʾiltiṣāq*, to the point that ownership of the *ʾiltiṣāq* area could be transferred to the neighbor who erected the installation, was secured in the Code by means of two legal tools: the principle of good faith (*ḥusn al-niyya*) and the tool of just compensation.

In the case of a person who used his own materials and tools in order to build installation on land belonging to another, the Code draws a distinction between a person who did so in good faith, believing that the land was his own; or not in good faith, i.e., in the knowledge that the land was not his. The test of good faith, which is a subjective component in Egyptian law, is of great importance in terms of deciding the fate

[76] Ibid., p. 41.
[77] The ʾAhlī Civil Code, articles 60–67.

of the attached installations and the ownership of these installations and of the relevant land.

If a person built installations from his own materials on land that he knew to belong to another, without the consent of the owner, the owner may demand the removal of the installations at the expense of the person who erected them within one year from the date on which he learned of the execution of these works, with compensation if necessary, or he may demand that they be left intact, in which case he will pay the person who erected them for the cost of their removal, or an amount equivalent to the betterment they created in his land. This situation is similar to the legal provisions applying in accordance with the old Civil Code.

If, however, a person erected installations on land belonging to another while believing in good faith that he was entitled so to act, the landowner does not have the right to demand their removal. They will remain intact, while the landowner must choose whether to pay the person erecting them for materials and labor, or to pay an amount equivalent to the betterment of the value of his land as the result of their establishment. If, however, the scope of the said installations was so great that the landowner could not pay their value, he would be permitted to request that the land be transferred to the person erecting the installations, in return for just compensation.[78]

Situation A: No Good Faith

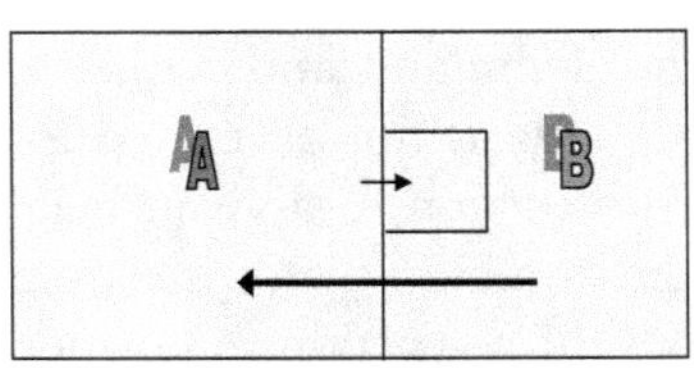

Compensation (cost)

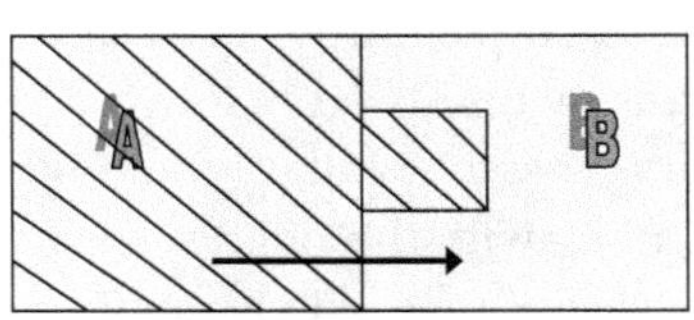

'Just' Compensation

Situation B: In Good Faith

[78] The Egyptian Civil Code, articles 924–925; Al-Wasīṭ, volume 9, pp. 284–291.

The latter condition is an innovation of the New Code, and clearly injures the property right of the landowner, who is obliged either to pay or to waive ownership of part of his property following the accidental penetration of his property by a third party. Moreover, the Code states that if, during the erection of a building on his own private property, a person encroaches on his neighbor's land in good faith, it is within the jurisdiction of the court to oblige the neighboring landowner to transfer ownership of that part of his land seized by such construction to the person undertaking the construction, in return for just compensation.[79] This is another important innovation in the New Code, and one that was intended to remove the concern among property developers that they would be obliged to remove constructions due to deviations committed in good faith. According to sociological logic, the right of property is indeed injured by such provisions, but the injury is assuaged through the provision of just compensation. A detailed discussion of the perception of justice in the Code and the essence of 'just compensation' appears in the next chapter.

2.8 *Innovations in the Laws of* ʾIrtifāq: *Limitations on the Right of Servitude*

ʾIrtifāq ('servitude') is a right that defines the enjoyment of land for the benefit of other land owned by another.[80] For example, such enjoyment may be present when the subordinate land provides the right of passage for the owner of the dominant land, or constitutes the source of water departing from the dominant land. Other examples are when the owner of subordinate land is not permitted to build on his land, or is required to limit construction to a given height, in order not to obscure the view from the dominant land. It should be noted that the rights of *ʾirtifāq* differ from the restrictions on ownership in the context of the right of passage, irrigation, and so on, as discussed above in this chapter, since *ʾirtifāq* is created primarily through consent between the parties, or by other means as discussed below.

The right of *ʾirtifāq* serves as an ancillary tool for the dominant land, and hence is transferred along with the right of ownership. It is acquired through a legal act (*ʿamal qānūnī*), i.e. a contract or testament, or is cre-

[79] Ibid., article 928; ibid., pp. 316–319.
[80] Ibid., article 1015; ibid., pp. 1279–1405; Ziadeh, p. 68.

ated through inheritance.[81] It should be noted that the right of *ʾirtifāq* in Egypt may be imposed on state property, provided that it does not contradict the purpose for which the public property was intended.[82]

As the result of decades of stagnation in land laws, and particularly due to the right of *taqādum* (prescription, the seizure of possession) as the result of protracted use, the congested agricultural lands of Egypt had become riddled with rights of *ʾirtifāq*, creating difficulties in land transactions. Islamic law recognized the possession of the old; for example, the *Majalla* stated that "Things which have been in existence from time immemorial shall be left as they were."[83] An expanded version of this by the *Majalla* was quoted in the explanatory notes to the New Code: "In the matter of the right of way and the right of ejection, the old is observed, i.e., it is left as it has been for time... And it is not to be changed unless evidence is brought to the contrary."[84] The possession of the old in the *Majalla* is reminiscent of *taqādum* in the Egyptian civil law.

The dilemma facing the authors of the Code was due to the importance of the laws of *ʾirtifāq* within the Egyptian agrarian system, on the one hand, in which context the need arose to clarify and formalize these rights in order to prevent arguments and disputes, particularly regarding *ʾirtifāq* by means of *taqādum*, which by its nature was inadequately defined; and, on the other hand, to limit the rights of *ʾirtifāq* as far as possible in order to encourage the transferability of land. As in many other cases, the Code introduced significant changes, but without causing an upheaval in the system of land ownership.

Regarding the right of *taqādum*, the Code established that *ʾirtifāq* could not be transferred by means of *taqādum* except in the case of visible (*ẓāhira*) rights of *ʾirtifāq*, including the right of passage. The word 'visible' refers to an external object suggesting the presence of the right of *ʾirtifāq*, such as a door, window or water course. If no such external sign were present, as in the case of the *ʾirtifāq* not to build on land, or not to build above a given height, then such *ʾirtifāq* could no longer be acquired by means of *taqādum*.[85]

---

[81] Ibid., article 1016(1); see also the Majalla, article 216.
[82] Ibid., article 1015.
[83] The Majalla, article 6.
[84] Ibid., article 1224.
[85] The Egyptian Civil Code, article 1016(2); Al-Wasīṭ, volume 9, pp. 1300–1303; Ziadeh, p. 69.

A further innovation in the Code established that overt *ʾirtifāq* could be created with the assistance of a mark (*takhṣīṣ*) made by the original owner. This *takhṣīṣ* was created when the owner of two separate plots established a clear sign (*ʿalāma*), thus creating relations of affiliation that might amount to relations of *ʾirtifāq* if these plots subsequently belonged to two different owners. Sanhūrī noted that this method of creating servitude was drawn from French law.[86]

For our purposes, the Code further established a series of cases in which the validity of *ʾirtifāq* would expire—innovations not found in the previous *ʾAhlī* Civil Code. *ʾirtifāq* would cease to exist, and the landowners could be released thereof, in full or in part, if the conditions changed to the extent that there were no possibility of using this right; if the purpose of the *ʾirtifāq* ceased to exist; or if its purpose diminished to the point that it were disproportionate to the burden on the land in question.[87]

For example, when the right of *ʾirtifāq* was the right to draw water from a subordinate plot, and the owner of the dominant plot excavated an artesian well in his own land, the right to draw water from the adjacent plot become unnecessary or unduly burdensome to the subordinate plot relative to the benefit accruing to the dominant land. In his interpretation of the Code, Sanhūrī added that if the owner of the right of servitude insisted on maintaining his right of *ʾirtifāq* despite the changed circumstances as explained above, the court would consider this the abuse of a right, with all this implies in light of the discussion of this doctrine in the following chapter.[88]

The Code also introduced an element of flexibility even when the *ʾirtifāq* continues to exist, if the specific location of the right of *ʾirtifāq* came to constitute an additional burden beyond the principled burden of the servitude of land, or if the *ʾirtifāq* constituted an obstacle to improvements to the land on which it was situated. In such cases, the owner of the subordinate land could request that the *ʾirtifāq* be relocated to another point in his land, or to other land owned by him or by a third party, if the latter consented to this.

The general tendency of the proposed Code authors was to reduce this right. However, the original proposal also noted that the owner

---

[86] The Egyptian Civil Code, article 1017; Al-Wasīṭ, volume 9, pp. 1333–1347.
[87] The Egyptian Civil Code, article 1028–1029; ibid., pp. 1399–1403.
[88] Al-Wasīṭ, p. 691.

of the dominant plot could also request a change in the location of the *ʾirtifāq* if he proved that such a change would benefit him without harming the subordinate land.[89] Deputy Muḥammad Ḥasan al-ʿAshmāwī, a member of the Senate Civil Code Committee, opposed this formula, arguing that it extended *ʾirtifāq* "which has become an onerous and inconvenient right that should be confined to its limited dimensions... The reason for any change in the *ʾirtifāq* must be the damage that comes from its continued presence, and not the benefit of any new *ʾirtifāq*." Accordingly, this proposed addition was ultimately omitted from the Code.[90]

Additional restrictions were made to the right of *ʾirtifāq* by the Code: If the dominant land were divided, and the right of *ʾirtifāq* subsequently served only a certain portion of these plots, the owner of the subordinate plot was permitted to request the removal of the *ʾirtifāq* from the other plots.[91] Conversely, if the subordinate land were divided, and the right of *ʾirtifāq* was no longer exercised in some of the parts, nor could be so exercised, the owner of any of these parts could request the removal of this right from his part.[92]

3. Striving for Social Harmony: Joint Ownership as a Unifying Factor

3.1 *The Dilemma of the Approach to the Idea of Cooperation*

In his theoretical discussion, Sanhūrī did not confine himself to the need to ensure social solidarity among all parts of Egyptian society, but aspired to secure the harmonious functioning of these different elements, and this was the purpose of the legal harmony the Code sought to promote. As we shall see below, the goal of encouraging coordinated social action led the Code to elevate the concept of cooperation (*shuyūʿ*) in land to the status of a prime social value.

One reason for the unsuitability of the former *ʾAhlī* Civil Code to the structure of Egyptian society was the question of common property (*al-mulkiyya al-shāʾiʿa*). True to its individualistic orientation, the *ʾAhlī*

[89] The original code proposal, article 1294(2); Al-Qānūn al-Madanī, volume 6, p. 642.
[90] Al-Qānūn al-Madanī, volume 6, p. 643.
[91] The Egyptian Civil Code, article 1024(2).
[92] Ibid., article 1025(2).

Civil Code made almost no reference to this issue, confining itself to the procedure for distributing common property—this despite the fact that joint ownership was extremely common in Egypt and in the Arab world in general, due to the Islamic inheritance laws. The property of a deceased person was inherited jointly by his heirs, and this common ownership often endured for many years without the inheritors dividing the property among them. Although Islamic inheritance laws divided the plot, the heirs had an interest in continuing to farm the plots jointly, since this ensured lower costs and substantial savings. After some of the heirs died or moved away, and their heirs in turn joined in the joint property, land transactions became difficult and family disputes often erupted. The old Code did not offer any solutions for such situations, since it did not recognize the family joint ownership that was created.[93]

Sanhūrī explained that the reason why the old Code paid virtually no attention to the issue of common property was because it mirrored the French Code, which followed Roman property laws. According to the Roman legal system, property was essentially individualistic and had a single owner who enjoyed total domain over his assets. If exceptional circumstances led to the creation of multiple ownerships, these should be dissolved. Since dissolution of a partnership, rather than its maintenance, was the rule in Roman law, there was no need to regulate rules for permanent partnerships.[94]

As a consequence of this approach, both French and Egyptian case law developed rules addressing this lack of legislative attention to the partnership.[95] In Egypt, the case law was also based on the detailed rules for joint ownership established in the *Sharīʿa* (particularly in the proposed codification *Murshid al-Ḥairān*, prepared by the Egyptian jurist Muḥammad Qadrī [1821–1886], which was ultimately not adopted; and in accordance with the *Majalla*).[96]

---

[93] The Explanatory Notes of the original code proposal, Al-Qānūn al-Madanī, volume 6, p. 9; Al-Wasīṭ, volume 8, pp. 793–800.

[94] Al-Wasīṭ, volume 8, p. 794.

[95] Ibid. Sanhūrī mentioned that joint ownership has been prevailed in Egypt much before the application of the old *ʾAhlī* code, ibid., p. 795.

[96] See the Majalla, articles 1060, 1062, 1063, 1066, 1068 and 1073; Muḥammad Qadrī, *Kitāb Murshid al-Ḥayrān ʾila Maʿrifat ʾAḥwāl al-ʾInsān fī al-Muʿāmalāt al-Sharʿiyya ʿala Madhhab al-ʾImām al-ʾAʿẓam ʾAbī Ḥanīfa al-Nuʿmān Mulāʾiman fī al-Diyār al-Miṣriyya wa Sāʾir al-ʾUmam al-ʾIslāmiyya* (Cairo: Ḥusayn Ḥasanin Ṣāḥib al-Maktaba al-Miṣriyya, 1338 h.), articles 45, 46.

By contrast, the New Civil Code discussed the issue of joint ownership in depth. Rather than merely codifying principles drawn from the *Sharīʿa*, however, it went much further: instead of simply bridging the gap created between existing social reality and the legal status quo, it actively encouraged joint property as a social value, simplifying the relevant procedures and even introducing institutions of cooperation that had not previously existing in Egyptian law. Thus the laws of joint ownership, which had lagged behind social reality in Egypt, now moved ahead and even drew that society forward. The principles of cooperation as formulated for family ownership, or regarding majority-minority relations in a partnership, for example, sought not only to overcome existing problems, but also to create a new level of joint activity.[97]

As the result of these changes, joint ownership—a common reality in Egypt—was transformed from a fact of life that was not encouraged by positive law—to a desirable social value to be encouraged as a unifying factor. In a country whose resources are limited, cooperation is essential, and the New Code could transform a necessity into a virtue.

An interesting innovation introduced in the New Code addressed the conflict between the desire of the owners of a joint property to divide it among themselves and the preference of the social function that the property remains joint and not be divided, if its purpose implied that it should remain a joint property on a permanent basis.[98] This is a classic example of the sociological approach that characterizes the New Code—the relevant provisions restrict property rights, include an element of enforced cooperation (*shuyūʿ ʾijbārī*) and draw on the terminology of the social function, for example when referring to the 'purpose' of the asset. The context here is ownership by neighbors of a bridge, joint road, common courtyard or bath house, water or drainage channels; the same principles apply in the case of a shared wall or the common portions of an apartment building.

The sociological ideology that advocated joint ownership, and even forced joint ownership, saw such cooperation between individuals as bearing the potential to promote a spirit of cooperation and harmony in society as a whole. Whereas constitutional law seeks to achieve changes through the application of broad-based and sweeping principles, particularly in the relations between the individual and authority, down to the

---

[97] The Egyptian Civil Code, articles 825–869.
[98] Ibid., article 850; Al-Wasīṭ, volume 8, pp. 986–990.

last citizen, private law applies a different logic, addressing the limited and specific relations between two fellows. If it has a social perspective, as in the case of the New Code, these personal relations may combine to create a collective element eventually leading to generalized social change. Accordingly, the direction of social change in private law is the opposite of that in constitutional law.

According to the logic of the New Code, harmonious relations between individuals, for example with regard to a shared wall shared by two owners, a mechanism regulating the relations between apartments, or various forms of partnership in general, may eventually coalesce to form a collective and unifying element in Egyptian society as a whole.

True to the approach of sociological law, Sanhūrī viewed the laws of cooperation in property as a key social value that could radiate mutual dependence throughout Egyptian society. He manifested this approach in formulating the Code, and particularly in drafting its property laws. Whereas the Code Civil, from its liberal starting point, disapproved of the concept of partnership and sought to dismantle it whenever possible, Sanhūrī mandated it as a unifying social experiment.

The liberal approach seeks to dismantle partnership since it impairs the property rights of the individual, obliging him to relate to general interests; because it encourages disputes; and because it limits the social mobility of individuals and prevents their leaving the group to which they are bound by ties of partnership.

Interestingly, both these ideological approaches—that which seeks to limit partnership and that which seeks to expand it—base their arguments on identical grounds: the need to limit disputes and arguments; transferability and land development. Sanhūrī supported a measure of injury to the right of property and believed that the law should oblige one individual to consider the interests of another; accordingly, mechanisms that were considered negative in accordance with the liberal approach were perceived as desirable from the sociological approach. Therefore, while the liberal approach sought, for example, to dismantle an imposed family joint ownership as the result of inheritance that had deteriorated into disputes, the sociological approach would seek to maintain the partnership while attempting to avoid the disputes by imposing a different regime for the partnership. A similar situation emerged in the context of contract law, as we shall see in the next chapter: rather than nullifying the contract, the social approach seeks to maintain the agreement, while finding a new form of arrangement for the relations it creates between the parties.[99]

Faithful to his social approach, Jhering addressed partnership as a desirable social model in the modern state. In his book *Law as a Means to an End* (1877), he made comments with which Sanhūrī must have been familiar:

> Partnership contains the prototype of the State, which is indicated therein in all its parts. Conceptually as well as historically, partnership forms the transition from the unregulated form of force in the individual to its regulation by the state. Not merely in the sense that it contains a combination of several for the same purpose, and thereby makes possible the pursuit of aims which were denied to the power of the individual...but in an incomparably greater measure in the sense that it solves the problem of creating the preponderance of power on the side of right. It does this by putting in place of the opposition of two particular interests fighting one another without an assured prospect of the victory of right, that between a common interest and a particular, whereby the solution comes of itself. In partnership all partners present a united front against the one who pursues his own interests at the expense of these common interests assigned by the contract, or who refuses to carry out the duties undertaken by him in the contract; they all unite their power against the one. So the preponderance of power is here thrown on the side of right, and partnership may therefore be designated as the mechanism of the self-regulation of force according to the measures of right.[100]

3.2 *Moderating the Principles of Management of Joint Ownership* (Shuyūʿ)

The New Code defined joint ownership "when two or more persons are the owner of the same thing and their relative portions are not divided, they are (considered) owners in partnership, and, in the absence of other evidence, their portions shall be considered to be equal."[101] This definition does not relate to a separate legal entity, such as a company or association, but to the joint ownership of individuals. The rights of an owner in partnership are limited to his portion of the joint property, and he is the absolute owner solely of his portion. However, his right influences the property in its entirety. Accordingly, he has the right to

---

[99] On the dilemma pro and against the idea of joint land ownership see: R. C. Ellickson, "Property in land", *The Yale Law Journal* 102(1993), p. 1315.

[100] Rudolf Von Jhering, *Law as a Means to an End*, trans. I Husik (New York: A. M. Kelley, 1968), pp. 220–221.

[101] The Egyptian Civil Code, article 825; Al-Wasīṭ, volume 8, pp. 795–796.

use the entire property and enjoy its fruits, but these usage and enjoyment are limited by the rights of the other owners in the partnership. An owner in partnership can use the property in a manner that permits the other owners to use it, such as use of a joint road or drawing water from a joint well. However, he cannot use the property in a manner that inherently prevents another from enjoy it, for example by building on joint property, sowing seeds or leasing the property.[102]

A good example of the adaptation of the principles of joint ownership as a unifying factor is the relations between the majority and minority among joint owners. The Code sought to develop a new, flexible mechanism preventing some owners from imposing dictates on others, encouraging efficiency in the partnership, enhancing its contribution to the national economy and introducing an element of justice—a key element in the Code—into majority-minority relations.

The first goal was to prevent unjustified obstinacy on the part of the minority, which the explanatory notes to the proposed Code, and Sanhūrī himself, considered a grave impediment to reforming the laws of partnership. This minority relied on the individualistic need for a unilateral (*ʾijmāʿ*) decision, and enjoyed the ability to engage in extortion due to its power to prevent or delay any decision. The joint property might, therefore, languish in stagnation for many years due to the obstinacy of a minority—in some cases, consisting of just one person.[103] The Code established that for ordinary management decisions (*ʾidāra muʿtāda*), a simple majority of the owners of the partnership was sufficient (calculated according to the value of their holdings), and this decision would bind all the partners, including those who voted against the decision. This obviated the need for a unanimous vote, "thus removing a stumbling block to reform."[104] In order to strengthen still further the efficacy of the majority decisions and avoid delays, the Code denied the minority the right to turn to the courts with regard to ordinary management decisions.

The Code went one step further, permitting a special majority of three-fourths of the owners to make substantive changes to the purpose of the joint property in order to enhance their enjoyment of it, in a manner that went beyond the limits of discretion in the context of

[102] The Egyptian Civil Code, article 826(1); Al-Wasīṭ, volume 8, p. 800; Ziadeh, p. 30.

[103] Al-Wasīṭ, volume 1, p. 79; Ziadeh, p. 31.

[104] Al-Wasīṭ, p. 79; Al-Qānūn al-Madanī, volume 6, p. 86.

ordinary management. An example of this would be the reconstruction of an apartment in order to utilize it better, or turning a restaurant into a café.[105]

In such cases, however, the Code permitted the objecting minority to turn to the court within two months of the date on which they learned of the decision. This provision was intended to prevent a dictatorship of the majority, and to ensure judicial review for majority decisions that were supposed to be taken for the sake of the general interest. However, the principle of efficiency continued to be a key social interest even in such instances. The minority enjoyed the right to address the court, but within a limited period of time. It is interesting to note that in order to enhance still further the dynamic capacity of the majority in the decision-making process in a partnership, the original proposed Code stated that special decisions could be made by the partners holding the largest portions (without the need for a three-fourths majority), although no time limitation was established for the minority to turn to the court.[106] The re-examination committee amended the wording, establishing the requirement for a three-fourths majority and imposing a limit of one month for the minority to turn to the court; this period was extended to two months in the Senate Civil Code Committee.

Lastly, the Code "promoted the maximum imposition of the majority will," enabling a special majority of three-fourths of the partners to undertake disposition (*taṣarruf*) in the joint property, such as sale or bartering. The minority was obliged to accept such a decision, though in this case the majority required substantive reasons for its implementation. Here, too, the opposing minority had the right to turn to the court within two months from the date on which it learned of the decision.[107]

3.3 *Regulating Kinship Relations: Family Ownership* (Mulkiyyat al-ʾUsra)

A further example of meeting an existing social need by means of a new family institution in Egyptian society is what was termed by the Code 'family ownership' (*mulkiyyat al-ʾusra*). Through this tool for land joint ownership the Code sought to enhance social coordination and harmony, not merely to meet an existing need in the present, but also

---

105 The Egyptian Civil Code, article 829; Al-Qānūn al-Madanī, volume 6, p. 88.
106 The Original code proposal, article 1197; Al-Qānūn al-Madanī, volume 6, p. 88.
107 Al-Qānūn al-Madanī, volume 6, p. 95; The Egyptian Civil Code, article 832.

to promote enhanced practical relations in the future. Ziadeh agreed with Sanhūrī that this type of cooperation was highly suited to Egyptian society, and to the Arab world in general, since the members of a family often inherit the father's property and agreed to continue to manage it jointly for many years.[108] A distinction should be made between joint ownership by family members after the registration of the land, which is the subject of our present discussion, and the method of *mushāʿ*, whereby the *mushāʿ* land is held jointly by the entire village.

This scenario relates to the laws of inheritance established in the *Sharīʿa*, whereby significant portions of assets that cannot easily be divided among the inheritors, such as houses, land, workshops and even animals, were held jointly by several persons, and sometimes by dozens or even hundreds. The assets continued to be divided until it became impractical to calculate the divisions. Inevitably, the greater the number of partners, the greater the difficulties and disputes. G. Baer noted that inheritance was the principal cause for the fragmentation of agricultural property in Egypt. The land was in the *mulk* category and, as such, it was covered by the Islamic rules of inheritance, which favor the parcelization of property.[109]

This type of partnership enjoyed *de facto* popularity in rural Egyptian society long before the introduction of the New Code. However, its defects caused difficulties for the joint ownership, for members of the family and hence also for the national economy. Sanhūrī explained that heirs inherited land jointly from their father and sometimes included in the partnership additional property under their ownership. In most cases, the senior partner (*al-ʿamīd*) took charge of management, although he was not necessarily the best qualified to manage the joint property. As a result, portions of the inheritance were sold, strangers from outside the family became involved, disputes developed among the family members and, in many cases, the state of the property deteriorated. Efficiency was often sacrificed to family honor and custom, resulting in stagnation and mitigating against the transferability of land.[110]

The authority of the managing *ʿamīd* was not always clear, adding further to the disputes. Management, reporting and supervision were vague and imprecise. Sanhūrī noted that custom alone regulated this

---

[108] Al-Wasīṭ, volume 8, p. 1043; Ziadeh, p. 31.
[109] Landownership, pp. 38–39.
[110] Al-Wasīṭ, volume 1, p. 80.

form of family institution, adding that the customs that had taken root in the villages "were not without defect." The senior partner managing the partnership often acted arbitrarily, sometimes without even reporting on his actions to the other partners.[111]

"Anyone who has seen how efficient plans collapse and wealth disintegrates following the death of the father of the family in Egypt recognizes the importance of the (proposed) regime for family ownership," concluded the explanatory notes to the original proposal. "According to this regime, joint ownership will continue to exist, but it will be managed in such a manner as to benefit all the owners, as well as the national economy of the country."[112] The Code sought to institutionalize this form of partnership, which actually had its origins in coercion, to improve its provisions and to ensure due supervision of its financial management; in addition, it sought to improve the ability of those partners who wished to do so to leave the partnership. Hitherto, it was rare for any partner to leave a partnership—in most cases, because they were simply unable to do so.[113]

As in other cases, the New Code introduced a mechanism from Western legal codes—in this instance, from the Swiss civil code and the proposed Franco-Italian code, "but it was influenced, above all, by the Egyptian social environment (*bī'a*) itself," as Sanhūrī explained in his commentary.[114]

In its formula for family joint ownership the Code established that members of the same family who shared a joint occupation or interest could agree in writing to establish joint family ownership. This joint ownership would include inheritance, the members of the family could decide to leave all or part of it in joint hands, or to include any other property in the joint ownership.[115]

This type of joint ownership would be created for a period not exceeding 15 years, ensuring relatively large plots in the local land market, or in different sorts of properties, managed with due commercial attention. The possibility to form larger plots also cuts costs in farming, fencing and the use of agricultural equipment.[116]

---

[111] Ibid., volume 8, p. 1053.
[112] Al-Qānūn al-Madanī, volume 1, p. 135.
[113] Al-Wasīṭ, volume 8, p. 1043.
[114] Ibid.
[115] The Egyptian Civil Code, article 851.
[116] Contemporary argument that joint ownership may bee effective by cutting costs and risks see: R. C. Ellickson, "Property in land", p. 1315.

Equally, however, the Code was careful to balance the social and communal context with the liberty of the partners, stating that each of the partners in family ownership could, if he had serious justification (*mubarrir qawwī*), address the court and request that his portion be excluded prior to the end of the period. If the partners had not agreed on the duration of the partnership, each owner could remove his portion six months after notifying the others thereof.[117]

In order to ensure cohesion and solidarity within this cooperative family unit, the Code established that no joint owner could sell his portion to a person who was not a member of the family without the consent of all the remaining partners. Even if a stranger from outside the family purchased the portion of one of the partners, with the consent of that owner or through coercion, he could not become a member of the family partnership unless he and the other partners wished him to. Indeed, during the deliberations of the Senate Civil Code Committee, the participants wondered why the first part of the article negated the possibility of the partners' selling their portion to strangers from outside the family, while the second part discussed such a scenario as a reasonable possibility. Sanhūrī replied that the second part related to the case of a partner who sold his portion despite the prohibition.[118]

Lastly, the management of family ownership was unusual in that the senior partners could (though they were not obliged) appoint one or more of their number to manage this joint ownership; after his appointment, such a partner enjoyed far broader authority than that of the director in a regular partnership. For example, the director of an ordinary partnership who decided to change the purpose of the property was subject to the provision that any of the minority partners could turn to the court—a blocking tactic that was not available to the minority or opposing partners in a family partnership.[119] The purpose of this distinction was to transform family ownership from an unwieldy and ineffective instrument delaying economic development into a valuable tool that could easily be managed and be rendered productive. However, the Code permits the director to be removed in the same manner in which he was elected, and permits each of the partners to

---

[117] The Egyptian Civil Code, article 852.

[118] The Egyptian Civil Code, article 853; Al-Qānūn al-Madanī, volume 6, p. 148.

[119] Al-Wasīṭ, volume 8, p. 1057.

ask the court to dismiss the director, albeit solely if serious cause was found justifying such a step, "if the director is incapable of performing his function or unreliable."[120] This is an additional balance introduced by the Code between efficiency and justice; as we shall see below, this balance is typical of the entire Code.

3.4 *Ownership of Floors* (Mulkiyyat al-Ṭabaqāt)

One of the principal innovations in the Code in terms of the arrangements for land management was the system of ownership of floors in a building—a subject already mentioned above in the discussion on the principles of *al-ʿuluww wal-sufl*, which also formed part of this system. These rules regulated the legal relations between owners of apartments in a single building—both among the individual owners, an area in which the Code drew on the principles in the *Sharīʿa*; and those between the owners and the common property in the building—an aspect included in the Egyptian statute book for the first time, and based on a French law of June 1938.[121] The explanatory notes to the original proposal explained that "this mechanism aims to encourage the dissemination of ownership of floors (in apartment buildings) among members of the middle class who have limited income. The individual of this class cannot purchase an entire house, and hence prefers to enter in partnership with another, transforming one of the apartments in the house into an independent unit and purchasing it. The regime for the regulation of permanent relations between this individual and his neighbors (in the building) will not only resolve the disputes that emerge in this type of ownership, but also ensure its success and dissemination."[122] Sanhūrī noted that the principles of the *ʿuluww* and *sufl*, which were already present in the outgoing Code, were in themselves sound and were hence maintained in the New Code; in addition, however, it was also necessary to introduce progressive principles regarding the modern apartment building.

The ownership of floors is divided into two types: the first is the personal and individual ownership of a floor or apartment in which the owner enjoys full property rights; the second, coercive (*ʾijbārī*) joint ownership, which includes those areas of the building intended for

[120] The Egyptian Civil Code, article 854; Al-Wasīṭ, volume 8, p. 1057.
[121] Al-Wasīṭ, volume 8, p. 1008.
[122] Al-Qānūn al-Madanī, volume 6, p. 10.

common use. Referring to the identity of the common portions, the Code established that, in the absence of any contrary provision in the certificate of property, when various floors or apartments in a building belong to different owners, these are considered the joint owners of the land and of the parts of the building intended for general use, particularly the foundations, the main walls and entrances, courtyards, roofs, passages, corridors and pipes of all types, with the exception of pipes within the floors or apartments. The internal walls dividing two apartments belong jointly to the owners of these two apartments.[123]

Regarding the financial obligations of the joint owners, the Code established that the private owner must contribute to the cost of the security, maintenance, management and renovation of the joint portions. Unless agreed otherwise, the portion of each owner in these expenses is to be calculated according to his proportionate share in the building. A management committee may be charged with the management of the apartment building (though this is not compulsory), as we shall see below.

The owner of an apartment or floor naturally enjoys all the rights of ownership. He may sell, mortgage or let the property as he sees fit, just as in the case of any other type of property ownership, and may even better the property—but in any case he may not injure the rights of others in the building. However, in keeping with the sociological approach of the Code, which made joint ownership a supreme value, there are a number of obligations imposed on such ownership, drawn from the principles of *ʿuluww* and *sufl* in Islamic law.

The main obligations are imposed on the first floor, since the remainder of the building rests on it. On the basis of a court ruling on the subject, Sanhūrī commented that if there are several owners on the first floor, they are jointly responsible for maintaining these obligations.[124]

The owner of the lower floor (the *sufl*) must implement essential maintenance and renovation work in order to prevent the collapse of the upper floor (*ʿuluww*). If he refuses to do so, a judge may order the sale of his floor. In any case, a "judge of urgent matters" (i.e. an accelerated proceeding) may order the implementation of urgent repairs. It should be noted in this context that the owner of the *sufl* is obliged to

[123] The Egyptian Civil Code, article 856; Ziadeh, p. 32.
[124] Al-Wasīṭ, volume 8, p. 1011.

renovate and maintain his floor, but not to implement renovations in the *ʿuluww* in order to prevent its collapse.[125]

The extent of responsibility of the owner of the *sufl* was even greater if the building collapsed. In this case, as Ziadeh noted, the level of responsibility could be truly 'burdensome,' since, if the entire building collapsed, the Code obliged the owner of the *sufl* to rebuild his floor. If he declined to do so, a judge could order the sale of the first floor, unless the owner of the upper floor offered to rebuild the lower floor himself, at the expense of the owner of the *sufl*. In the latter case, the owner of the upper floor could even prevent the owner of the *sufl* from using or residing on the first floor pending payment of his debt. The owner of the upper floor could also receive permission to let the *sufl* or to live in it himself—here, too, for the purpose of recovering his debt in full.[126]

The obligations incumbent on the owner of the upper floor were less weighty. He was not permitted to raise the height of the building in a manner injurious to the lower floor, and Sanhūrī added that he was not permitted to construct an additional floor if this would damage the first floor. In general, he was not permitted to undertake any action that would add to the weight of the *ʿuluww*.[127]

3.5 *Management Committee*

With the increasing prevalence of apartment buildings and high-rise buildings in Egypt, a clear need emerged for a mechanism allowing for the routine management of the common areas in each building, and regulating the *de facto* mutual relations created between different occupants of the building. Such an institution should develop the building for the benefit of its owners, nurture it and take important decisions in the name of the majority of the owners, for example following the total destruction of the entire building.[128]

The apartment building committee (*ʾittiḥād mulāk ṭabaqāt al-bina' al-wāḥid*) was a new operational tool introduced by the Code alongside the reform in the ownership of floors. The committee constituted a

---

[125] The Egyptian Civil Code, article 859; Al-Wasīṭ, volume 8, p. 1011.

[126] The Egyptian Civil Code, article 860; Al-Wasīṭ, volume 8, pp. 1009–1014.

[127] The Egyptian Civil Code, article 861; Al-Wasīṭ, volume 8, pp. 1015–1017; Kitāb Murshid al-Ḥayrān, article 68.

[128] Ziadeh, p. 32.

distinct legal entity representing the totality of owners of apartments in the building; it was established as a not-for-profit association, and its purpose was to manage the building and the common areas for the benefit of all the members. Since it was a separate legal entity, it could sue and be sued, and it bore separate financial liability. Sanhūrī noted another important aspect of this management system for the apartment building: even before the construction of the building, the future residents could establish the committee and hence construct the building through partnership. "This will encourage the establishment of apartment buildings, which may alleviate the housing crisis in overcrowded cities," Sanhūrī wrote. "The purpose of this system is to make it easier for the middle classes to build and own their own apartment, and to facilitate partnership in the construction or purchase of apartments."[129]

As in other cases, the idea itself was drawn from European law, in this case—the French law of 1938 already mentioned above. However, as explained in Chapter Two, the concepts were transposed into Egyptian parameters through the use of principles drawn from Egyptian case law and from the *Sharīʿa*, which were blended into the original French legislation. Indeed, the Senate Civil Code Committee noted with satisfaction in its concluding report that, in this case, the details drawn from the above-mentioned French law and the general principles of land partnership taken from local case law and from the *Sharīʿa*—had been blended "in a manner more appropriate to the Egyptian environment."[130]

The Code establishes that this mechanism, whose creation was dependent on the will of the occupants, could, with the agreement of all the occupants, establish regulations ensuring the better use and proper management of the common property.[131] Sanhūrī noted that the greatest contribution of this mechanism lay in the fact that a simple majority was sufficient to adopt all types of decisions, both regarding routine management and in the case of exceptional decisions, such as the decision to rebuild the building if it were destroyed for any reason. These decisions by the committee bound all the occupants, even those who had not agreed to them, provided that all of the occupants were

[129] Al-Wasīṭ, volume 1, p. 80.
[130] Al-Qānūn al-Madanī, volume 1, p. 135.
[131] The Egyptian Civil Code, article 863; Al-Wasīṭ, volume 8. pp. 1039–1043.

invited in writing to the meeting that made the decision. It was also necessary that the majority be comprised of all the occupants, and not merely of those who attended the meeting. The majority was calculated according to the proportionate value of the occupants' properties.[132]

The Code deliberately granted the committee and the paid director (*maʾmūr*) who could direct it greater freedom of action than was given to any other cooperative body, in order to encourage the development, maintenance and management of apartment buildings. Accordingly, one of the committee's functions would be to insure the common areas of the building, and it could oblige the minority to accept such a decision. "The bridle of managements rests with the majority," Sanhūrī established.[133]

The committee could also make a binding decision following the building's total or partial destruction, and a regular majority of the occupants was also sufficient for this purpose. If, in this case, the committee decided not to rebuild the building, each owner would receive his portion of the insurance and of support provided by the government by way of compensation. The committee itself would be dissolved, since it was no longer needed. If the committee decided to rebuild the building, all the occupants would be bound by the decision.[134]

3.6 *The Rules of the Shared Wall*

A further type of joint ownership not sufficiently addressed in the old Civil Code was the question of a wall shared by two owners. The New Code drew from the Islamic *fiqh* (or, as the explanatory notes put it, from the *Sharīʿa*).[135] These laws are particularly relevant to the Egyptian context, both in the country and in the cities: the shortage of land and the dense nature of construction mean that such examples of forced joint ownership are inevitable.

This is a further example of the value-based perspective applied by the New Code, which argues that the principles of cooperation can create or encourage harmony in social relations. Sanhūrī himself quoted the example of the shared wall as a classic case in which the 'social

[132] Al-Wasīṭ, volume 8, p. 1032.
[133] Ibid., volume 1, p. 91.
[134] The Egyptian Civil Code, article 868.
[135] The explanatory notes of the Code's proposal relied on the Majalla, articles 1210–1211, 1317–1318, and to Kitāb Murshid al-Ḥayrān articles 69–70, 771–772.

function' of property laws was applied.[136] This was true both on the individual level and for society as a whole. Without the harmony that rests on functional cooperation, neither of the owners of the shared wall—and none of the partners in society at large—could properly manage their own affairs without dispute. In the case of the shared wall, the issue is not merely solidarity between the neighbors, but the creation of an effective mechanism for essential joint actions.

The rules of the shared wall in the Code address two key issues: the principles relating to the legal arrangements for the ownership of a wall shared by two owners, and the question of raising the height of the wall.

The Code established that the owners of a shared wall had the right to use it for the purpose for which it was constructed, and, in particular, to rest on it beams for the support of the ceiling, provided that the wall would not be required to bear an excessive weight beyond its capacity. If the joint wall was no longer suited for the purpose for which it was established, the costs of repair and renovation would be borne by each partner in accordance with his portion therein.[137] Sanhūrī and the collection *al-Qānūn al-Madanī* noted that this formula did not appear in the outgoing Civil Code, but was based mainly on Egyptian case law, which had applied this principle without any textual legal reference.[138] Sanhūrī noted that this wording implies that the owner of a shared wall may use it in accordance with the purpose for which it was established, and that no openings of the *manwar* type are to be made—i.e., the only openings are for light and ventilation, without affording a view. Naturally, openings of the *maṭal* type were also prohibited without the consent of the other owner.

These provisions may be viewed as a lesson in mutual consideration. In accordance with the laws specified above, if, for example, one of the owners placed beams above the wall, he must take into account that his partner was also entitled to place beams for a roof, so that he could only place beams amounting to half the weight that could be borne by the wall, in order to permit his partner to enjoy his right. Since the joint ownership in a shared wall is a coercive one, the partners cannot request that the wall be divided, cannot sell their share in the shared

[136] Al-Wasīṭ, volume 8, pp. 557–558.
[137] The Egyptian Civil Code, article 814.
[138] Al-Wasīṭ, volume 8, p. 993; Al-Qānūn al-Madanī, volume 6, p. 56.

wall separately from the property to which it is attached, and a debtor cannot seize the shared portion as an independent entity.

On the basis of the rules for shared walls in the Islamic *fiqh*, the question of raising the height of the wall and the ensuing rules were a key focus of attention. The former Civil Code had not addressed these issues in depth, while the *Majalla* noted: "In a shared wall, neither partner may raise the wall height without his partner's consent, and he may not build a bower or such like thereon, whether or not this damages the other owner. If, however, one partner wishes to build a room within his plot and to place the heads of the beams on that wall, the other partner may not prevent this. However, since his partner is also entitled to rest the heads of his beams on the wall in the same number as he does, he may place only half the number of beams that the wall can bear, and no more. If beams were placed on the wall in equal numbers from the outset, and one partner seeks to increase the number of his beams, the other may prevent his so doing."[139] On this matter, the New Code established that if one of the owners had an interest in raising the height of the joint wall, he could do so, provided that his actins not cause serious damage to his partner. He alone would bear the cost of raising and maintaining the raised portion of the wall, and was required to undertake the work in such manner that the wall could withstand the additional weight without being weakened.

The Code further established that if the shared wall could not support the extension, the partner who wished to increase the wall height was required to rebuild the entire wall at his expense, in such manner that the increased width of the wall would fall within his plot, insofar as possible. The reconstructed wall, without the raised portion, would continue to be a shared wall, and the neighbor who raised the wall would not be entitled to any compensation.

[139] The Majalla, article 1210.

CHAPTER FOUR

CONTRACT LAW AS IDEOLOGY—THE EMERGENCE OF CONTRACTUAL JUSTICE

Last week, my gaze fell on a sight that I still cannot forget. As I left the club at midnight, I saw two small children in a dark corner. They had cleared a small piece of ground, were leaning on each other and were sleeping as if in embrace. These two miserables, whose home was the street, did not have what God has granted others: a comfortable bed and furniture. They had only their arms to rest on. As the two boys slept, people passed by, as if not noticing them. And those who live lives of pleasantry and comfort in their palaces sleep soundly, unaware that such miserables exist.

The Just should also be Strong

Sanhūrī, Diary, 1920 and 1944, respectively[1]

1. The Transition to 'Contractual Justice'

The Old Egyptian Civil Codes, both the Mixed and the *ʾAhlī*, disfavored judicial or legislative interference in the freedom of contracts and the use of the concept of 'justice' as a substitute for written legal rules; as explained above, this reflected their origins as replications, with certain amendments, of the Napoleonic Code Civil of 1804. In this respect, the codes reflected the *laissez-faire* approach of individualistic philosophy as embodied in the Code Civil, which regards economic and contractual liberty as the natural right of the citizen.[2] In these individualistic codes, which might even be characterized as capitalist and bourgeois in character, the idea that there are limits to the contractual freedom of an individual seem alien, since they tend to sanctify personal autonomy and contractual freedom.[3] In addition, these codes established that the

[1] Diary, 23 February 1920, pp. 45–46; 21 October 1944, p. 249.

[2] On the Theory of Personal and Economic Liberty see: ʿAbd al-Razzāq al-Sanhūrī, *Al-Wajīz fī Sharḥ al-Qānūn al-Madanī al-Jadīd* (Cairo: Dār al-Nahḍa al-ʿArabiyya, 1997)(Hereinafter: Al-Wajīz), p. 35.

[3] On the Rulings of the Egyptian Courts, regarding the Sanctity of Contracts according the Old Codes see: Al-Wasīṭ, volume 1, p. 713.

ownership of possessions is 'absolute' (*muṭlaq*).[4] In this chapter, we will argue that the New Code abandoned the individualistic approach, following in the steps of French and Continental law in the early twentieth century and opining that the *laissez-faire* approach was not appropriate for Egyptian society, since it encouraged the growing social and economic polarization, arbitrariness, social apathy and exploitation of the weak, inflaming these woes and potentially bringing Egyptian society to the brink of calamity. In place of the individualistic and capitalist approach, which Sanhūrī considered wanton selfishness (*ʾanāniyya*), and even 'the unruliness of the strong,'[5] the legal pendulum now swings toward a paternalistic and altruistic approach to contract law, one that places the interests of society and the general good at the center, even at the expenses of individual interests,[6] intervening in the contractual freedom of the individual.[7] Not only were the interests of the individual now subservient to the common good, but these interests were now perceived in a different manner. In the long term, it was argued, it was in the individual's interests if the legal system intervened in what was once considered his exclusive contractual or property right; he might be required to give some ground, but he would benefit from a healthier and more stable society. If the party to the contract or the owner of the property right failed to understand this, the court would impose the general good (and the social solidarity this was supposed to bring), according to the principle that a person may be coerced not to act selfishly toward his fellow.

The contractual transformation realized by the New Code was therefore manifested in the new perception of contract law. In place of the old approach, which argued that the function of contract law was merely to ensure the formal propriety of the process, the new approach gave contract law an altruistic and moral function, by virtue of which the law could also intervene in the content of the contractual

[4] *Majmūʿat Qawānīn al-Maḥākim al-ʾAhliyya wa al-Sharʿiyya*, article 11.

[5] Al-Wasīṭ, volume 1, p. 435.

[6] Al-Wasīṭ, volume 8, pp. 546–547, 494, 557.

[7] On the Philosophical Aspects of the 'Freedom of Contracts' in Anglo-Saxon Law see: P.S. Atiyah, *The Rise and Fall of Freedom of Contract* (Oxford: Clarendon Press, 1979). It should be noted that the Anglo-Saxon Law was not a Direct Reference to Egyptian Law, Which has been influenced mostly by Continental Law. See for example: Sanhūrī, "Min Majallat al-ʾAḥkām al-ʿAdliyya ʾila al-Qānūn al-Madanī al-ʿIrāqī wa-Ḥarakat al-Taqnīn al-Madanī fī al-ʿUṣūr al-Ḥadītha", *Majmūʿat Maqālāt wa-ʾAbḥāth al-Sanhūrī*, volume 2, pp. 3–58.

relationship. The New Code acknowledged the principle of contractual freedom, noting that a contract was analogous to a law applying to the contracting parties (*al-ʿaqd sharīʿat al-mutaʿāqidin*), and it can be nullified or amended only with their consent.[8] Immediately thereafter, however, the Code went on to introduce a series of doctrines of justice drawn from contemporary French law. These not only permitted the court—and hence society—to intervene in the contractual autonomy of the individual, but also extended moral influence over the entire spectrum of contract law, and law as a whole, in the hope that this would eventually extend across society. According to this approach, the concept of social justice thus establishes contractual justice, and, conversely, contractual justice is expected to strengthen social justice.

The first of the doctrines to be imported was the doctrine of the abuse of a right (*al-taʿassuf fī ʾistiʿmāl al-ḥaqq*). Four key doctrines of justice from Continental law were added: exploitation and discriminatory conditions in uniform contracts—at the time of making the contract; unforeseen circumstances and the obligation to observe the contract in good faith—in implementing the contract.[9] Together, they composed the altruistic and moral purpose of the Code, which extended a supportive and protective hand to weaker members of society.

1.1 *Definition of the Term 'Weak'*

In examining the social purpose that underlies contract law in the New Code, we encounter two significant and recurrent expressions: 'weak' (*al-ḍaʿīf*) and 'justice.' The explanatory notes to the proposed New Code explicitly stated that the proposal "stands by the weak in order to protect him," and that the proposed Code "will not allow the strong to overturn the weak on the grounds of respecting individual liberty, and no man will be able to exploit the power granted him by social and economic systems in order to abuse his right or act arbitrarily therein".[10] Elsewhere, the explanatory notes clarify that the New Code

[8] The Egyptian Civil Code, article 147(1), influencing the other Arab Civil Codes: Syrian, article 148(1); Libyan, article 147(1)); Iraqi, article 146(1); Kuwaiti, article 196; Jordanian, article 241; Yemenite, article 208.

[9] This Division of the conclusion of a Contract and its Performance appeared in Al-Wasīṭ, volume 1, p. 706.

[10] The Explanatory Notes of the Code's Proposal, Al-Qānūn al-Madanī, volume 1, p. 24.

has modalities for "adjusting the balance (*al-tawāzun*) that has been disrupted in the contractual association: either to strike the hand of the strong party (in punishment or deterrence), or to seize the hand of the weak party (in support)." And elsewhere: "When the balance between the two parties to the contract is disrupted, and one of them stands handcuffed against the other, society has an interest in protecting the weaker party as he stands against the stronger."[11]

The report of the Legislation Committee in the lower house of parliament went a step further, announcing that "this Civil Code is an outstanding buttress (*daʿāma*) for declaring justice in the country."[12] The explanatory notes to the Code responded in kind: "The proposed Code faithfully implements the principles of social justice born of the twentieth century..."[13]

Sanhūrī's personal philosophy adopts a compassionate view of society's weaker members, presenting a dichotic and harsh perception of the relations between the strong and the weak and the flow of power between them. This perception undoubtedly guided him later as he sought to amend and improve the relations between strong and weak:

> What am I thinking about now? What rages within me? I am thinking about power and its influence in this world, and the fact that only the strong secure this influence. Power is everything. It is hollow to speak of the 'power of the law' in honoring contracts or in relations between nations. These are terms conceived by the intellectually or physically strong in order to mock the weak and the dispossessed. The weak has only one remedy: to get stronger. And the only way for the usurped to cease to be usurped is for him: to usurp.
>
> In this multifaceted and wide world, man can only be either a servant or a master. Choose which of the two you wish to be.[14]

On the philosophical and theological level, Sanhūrī was apparently preoccupied by the question as to whether evil is an inherent characteristic of human beings. His pessimistic assessment is that if left unsupervised, people will exploit and usurp each other. Sanhūrī sought to facilitate freedom of human action, but, at the same time, to limit it

[11] Al-Wasīṭ, volume 1, p. 706, 111.
[12] Al-Qānūn al-Madanī, volume 1, p. 26.
[13] Ibid., p. 25.
[14] Diary, 17 August 1917, p. 38.

in the ways we shall examine below, due to his fear of the inherently exploitative and dominating character of the human soul. His diary offers a pessimistic and disappointed assessment of human nature (the original appears in the form of a poem):

> What are the people if not the individual? If you sought morality for the people with all your might, you who desire it and you who are disappointed. The people for whom you long, when they see a strong man they are afraid, and when they see a weak man they usurp him. These are their characteristics and morality—what morality then do you ask of them?[15]
>
> God said (from the *Qur'ān*): 'Exploitation is inherent in the soul—power reveals it, and weakness conceals it'. Al-Mutanabī said: 'The exploitation exists by human nature; if a man is modest, it is possible that he does not usurp'. Would that God grant me the power of money with high status, the power of beauty, knowledge and wisdom, to be able to struggle against the evil that often stems from these forces in impure souls. I fear, however, from this exploitation, which is ingrained in the human soul.[16]

Having discussed Sanhūrī's underlying approach, we shall now examine the term 'weak' and consider why it was necessary to hold his hand.

The first possible definition is a social and class-based, referring to the wretched and disfavored individuals who lived on the margins of Egyptian society. This usually referred to the peasants (*fallāḥūn*) in their villages, or to those of them who had come to the cities in search of transient employment, as hard-working laborers employed for a daily wage or working through contractors, deprived of social rights.

Another definition could be socioeconomic, referring to weak individuals who had found themselves in this condition due to temporary hardship. Examples of this might include a debtor unable to repay his loans; an individual obliged to sign a contract with a monopoly on unfavorable conditions; or, in general, an employee or consumer. Lastly, a legal definition could be offered from the field of contract law, whereby the weak party is that party that is contractually inferior to the other. As we shall see below, the terms 'weak' and 'strong' as employed by the Code in this legal context are relative, not absolute. In a given situation, the weak may define the strong, or vice versa; this is the motif of balance (*al-tawāzun*) which will be discussed below. The distance between weak and strong varies; it may be extensive or limited, and, accordingly, the definition of 'weak' and 'strong' must be

---

[15] Ibid., 2 February 1933, p. 191.
[16] Ibid., 19 May 1922, p. 71.

commensurately flexible. Indeed, all the examples given above may find their place in the definition of 'weak' as addressed from the altruistic perspective of the New Code.

1.2 *Justice as Proper Equilibrium*

Any attempt to define our second term, 'justice', encounters difficulties, since its linguistic and conceptual uses are numerous, and belong to diverse disciplines, such as law, philosophy, religion, morals and society.[17] In the theory of law, equality heads the list of the values of justice, as a yardstick or goal for the execution of justice, just as inequality is the hallmark of injustice.[18] This yardstick of equality guided the 1789 Declaration of the Rights of Man and the Citizen, in accordance with which "all men are born free and equal in rights," and "all men are equal before the law and entitled, without any discrimination, to the equal defense of the law," and the French Code Civil of 1804. However, the legal experts of the Roman law had already warned that the application of absolute and pedantic equality between people who are unequal, and in matters that are unequal, may actually lead to appalling injustice (*summum ius summa iniuria*). According to Aristotle, there are two kinds of equality, numerical and proportional. A distribution is equal *numerically* when it treats all persons as indistinguishable, thus treating them identically or granting them the same quantity of a good per capita. That is not always just. In contrast, a distribution is *proportional* or relatively equal when it treats all relevant persons in relation to their due. Just *numerical* equality is a special case of proportional equality. Numerical equality is only just under special circumstances, viz. when persons are equal in the relevant respects so that the relevant proportions are equal. Proportional equality further specifies formal equality; it is the more precise and detailed, hence actually the more comprehensive formulation of formal equality. Plato believed that the democratic system was distorted in its claim to grant equality both to those who are unequal and to those who are not. Aristotle also showed that equality between the unequal is no less iniquitous than inequality among equals; and that justice is proportion while injustice is disproportion.[19]

---

[17] Kelly, pp. 26–27, 30–31, 284.

[18] Among the Well-known 12 Maxims of Equity: 'Equity is Equality', where two Parties have an Equal Right, the property will be divided equally.

[19] Aristotle, *Nicomachean Ethics*, in: *The Complete Works of Aristotle*, J. Barnes ed.,

Sanhūrī was deeply concerned by the gulf between humans and the ways to bridge this gulf. Early entries in his personal diaries, from his period of studies in France onward, suggest that he did not believe in equality as an absolute yardstick, but advocated active intervention by society and the state in order to minimize social gaps.

> We cannot deny that there are natural differences between human beings in terms of their body, intellect and soul. While we cannot remove these differences in order to render men equal, we may at least do two things: refrain from adding to these differences by means of the natural differences we create through our social organizations; and reduce, insofar as possible, the influence of these natural differences in terms of the material and spiritual lot of individuals.[20]

Even in this preliminary question of the perception of justice, the New Code can already be seen to depart from the perspective embodied in the Code Civil and the two previous Egyptian codes. The New Code did not relate to equality as its preferred criterion for justice. My study argues that it chose to apply a more flexible theory of balance and correcting imbalance respectively. According to this approach, which may be more appropriate for polarized Egyptian society, people are indeed not equal, and, accordingly, the Code is positioned as the supreme supervisor of the legal civil relations between different individuals—not in order to make them equal, but in order to create balance among those who are not equal. This may be likened to unbalanced scales, whereby the doctrines of justice enable the law to raise the lower side or lower the higher side; in either case, this will be a form of justice. Accordingly, this balance does not imply total and automatic equality, and it may be justly maintained even in cases of relative balance. As the explanatory notes to the Code elaborate: "(Some doctrines of justice) correct the (disrupted) balance by striking the hand of the strong party in making the contract, while (other doctrines) corrects the balance by seizing the hand of the weak party in implementing the contract."[21]

(Princeton: Princeton University Press, 1984); Kelly, p. 26; A. Biscardi, "Epieikeia and Aequitas: History of Law", in A. M. Rabello, *Aequitas and Equity: Equity in Civil Law and Mixed Jurisdiction* (Jerusalem: the Hebrew University of Jerusalem, 1997), 8–11.

[20] Diary, 27 February 1924, p. 146.

[21] Al-Wasīṭ, volume 1, p. 706.

Model A: Legal Equality—As Justice
(Justice by the Court)

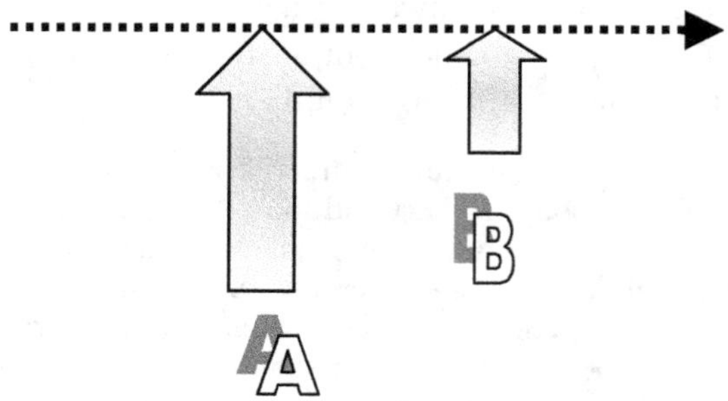

Model B: Desirable Relativity—As Justice
(Justice by the Court)

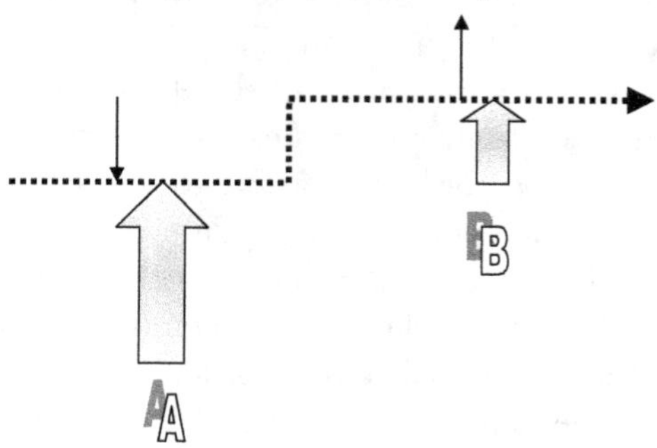

It may, therefore, be argued that justice, in terms of the New Code—and particularly justice in contract law, which forms the heart of any civil code—is the proper equilibrium, as desirable in each particular case, since, as Sanhūrī notes, "Justice derives no benefit from its having laws and traditions."[22] In contrast to the Napoleonic codes of France and Egypt, which evaluated justice according to the exclusive rights of the individual, the sociological approach means that at least two individuals must be involved in order to define what is justice—namely, the desired proportion between them. The tools for achieving this desired balance between the two parties to a contract are firm in the case of the stronger party and understanding and compassionate in the case of the weaker party. Despite this approach, the New Code did not set itself the goal of striking the stronger party; on the contrary, it aimed to

[22] Diary, 22 June 1922, p. 73.

advance and encourage the strong, but by deterring or 'striking' (to use Sanhūrī's terminology) the strong, it sought to maintain the interests of the weak, who was often unable to do so by himself—"to protect him from the strong, and even from himself."[23]

This study argues that the Code and its interpreters addressed and defined this element of the desired balance, which constitutes justice, on the basis of what might be termed the 'deprivation test' (*ghabn*). The term *ghabn* is usually translated as discrimination or injustice on the basis of an accounting test, *lésion* in French legal terms.[24] However, the explanatory notes to the New Code defined the legal concept of *ghabn* in a scientific and conceptual manner, as 'the absence of balance (*ʿadam taʿādul*) between what a party in a contract gives and what he receives'.[25] They explained that a civil code based on the individualistic approach, such as the Code Civil or the old Egyptian Code, had no room for the broader theory of *ghabn*, referring to the proper balance. In an altruistic and moralist code, however, in which the individualist component is tempered, "law enters to prevent *ghabn*."[26] The explanatory notes to the Code expanded on this theory of *ghabn* as a yardstick for justice, emphasizing that it had undergone several transformations over the course of legal history. As an individualistic legal system, Roman law does not include this principle in its perception of justice, but this position changed in the medieval canonic law, which prohibited excessive interest rates in loans, established a just price (*juste prix*) for merchandise and a just wage (*juste salaire*) for labor.[27] As a religious and moralistic legal system, the *Sharīʿa*, which, like canonic law, embodied an element of forgiveness and penitence, applied this theory in part, such as in the strict restriction on interest (*riba*). The wheel then turned again, with a renewed rise in individualism, shaping the Code Civil in the wake of the French Revolution, and leading to a concomitant decline in the significance of *ghabn* as a defining concept of justice. Following the Code Civil, the old Egyptian Code also restricted this principle, which

---

[23] Al-Wasīṭ, volume 1, p. 435.

[24] On the *Lésion* and its transformations in French Law see: B. Nicholas, *The French Law of Contract* (Oxford: Clarendon Press, 1992), pp. 137–140.

[25] Al-Wasīṭ, volume 1, p. 386.

[26] Ibid., p. 387.

[27] Ibid. On the Development of Equity in the Canonic Law see: P. Landau, "'Aequitas' in the 'Corpus Iuris Canonict'", in A. M. Rabello, *Aequitas and Equity*, pp. 128–139.

it preferred to address in terms of material (*māddī*) equality. Accordingly, this code perceived imbalance as an accounting term relating to the given product or asset. For example, if the balance deviated from the agreed amount by one-fifth or one-sixth, this constituted *ghabn*.[28] The more modern perception of the concept of *ghabn*, which began to appear at the beginning of the twentieth century, and is the approach embodied in the New Code, was not materialist and technical in nature, but was a flexible and psychological approach that examined the unique conditions and considerations of the parties to the contract at the time of its making (for example, whether they acted frivolously).[29] The new Continental codes developed the perception of balance, which became a broad principle applied to all aspects of contract law.[30] The German Civil Code, for instance, mandated the annulment of a legal disposition if one person had exploited the distress or needs of another, in cases when the circumstances showed a clear imbalance in the conditions of the transaction (pecuniary advantages which are in obvious disproportion of the performance).[31] The Swiss Obligations Law (which was strongly influenced by contemporary developments in French civil law) established that, in the event of a clear imbalance (*disproportion évidente*) between the parties' undertakings, the disfavored party could annul the contract within one year and regain any sums he had paid, if any.[32] A similar logic (*hors de toute proportion*) was also applied in the proposed Franco-Italian civil code of 1928 (which had a major influence on the Egyptian New Code).[33] This Continental European point of reference was discussed at length in the explanatory notes to the New Code and in its interpretation. In the discussion below on the doctrine of exploitation (*al-ʾistighlāl*), we shall also see how this principle was positioned and drafted in the Code. The New Code also employed the flexible terms 'balance' and 'distortion of balance' in a series of specific clauses where imbalance is a predetermined risk from the outset, such as the field of contractual labor (*muqāwala*). It established, for example, that if the financial balance between the provider of work and the contractual

[28] On the Material Approach of *ghabn* in the *ʾAhlī* Code, al-Wasīṭ, volume 1, pp. 388–389.

[29] See details later on, in the *ʾistighlāl* doctrine.

[30] Al-Wasīṭ, volume 1, p. 389.

[31] The German Civil Code (*Burgerliches Gesetzbuch*), article 138(2).On this code: Sanhūrī, "Min Majallat al-ʾAḥkām al-ʿAdliyya ʾila al-Qānūn al-Madanī", pp. 34–37.

[32] The Civil Code's Proposal, article 21.

[33] Ibid., article 22.

worker (i.e. the person working for a fixed and predetermined fee for the entire work) collapsed due to unexpected financial circumstances not envisaged in making the contract, thus eroding the foundation of the financial system established therein, the court could order an additional fee for the work, or even nullify the entire contract. On this aspect, the court does not intervene to amend the distribution of risks as determined by the parties, even if the calculations of one of the parties prove improvident. The court intervenes to restore the contractual balance when this has been disrupted due to occurrences that go beyond the risks accepted by the parties, and which cause the collapse of the contractual fabric.[34]

1.3 *Diffusion between Individual Justice and Collective Justice*

In keeping with the altruistic logic that underpins the entire New Code, including its property and obligations parts, it might be argued that even individual justice is perceived as having a social purpose, insofar as it may coalesce in countless individual cases to form a critical mass and thus be transformed into 'social justice' (*ʿadl ʾijtimāʿī*). As early as 1923, Sanhūrī noted that he wished to transform the legal system into the supreme authority in the country, "inspecting and supervising the remaining two authorities."[35] In this respect, individual justice was ultimately supposed to serve society as a whole, and not merely the specific individual involved. This logic is the opposite of the approach of constitutional law, in which general rules are applied and then divide and descend to the individual level, whereas in our case individual norms combine and may rise to the general level. The relationship between individual and social justice, a subject of great concern to the authors of the New Code, may be perceived as a symbiotic and harmonious one, whereby a random and infinite series of cases lead individual justice, as secured through the court, to crystallize and form social justice; at the same time, the social justice that is fitting for a given society at a given time guides and consolidates the infinite field of individual legal cases, again through the court. Thus, we argue, a new public order is expected to emerge as the product of the Code, a

[34] The Egyptian Civil Code, article 658(4).

[35] The Explanatory Notes, Al-Qānūn al-Madanī, volume 1, p. 25; Diary, 2 January 1923, pp. 82–83.

desirable *modus vivendi*, by means of the *perpetuum mobile*, or, at least, by means of a system of diffusion between individual justice and social justice. However, as in any altruistic and paternalistic system, these two components are not always complementary; often, they may even be contradictory: social justice may cause individual injustice, as we saw in the previous chapter in the context of the restrictions imposed on the property rights of the individual in favor of social interests. The New Code favored this option over the opposite situation, which it attributed to its predecessor, whereby complete individual justice and liberty created social injustice. As noted in the explanatory notes to the Code: "The legal principles included in the framework of social order are principles through which we intend to secure a public, political or social interest... and this supersedes the individual interest. All individuals are obliged to follow and apply this interest; even if they have personal interests, these do not outweigh the public interest."[36]

Due to the constant diffusion between individual justice and general justice, and vice versa, the logic of the New Code rejects a static relationship between the two, since "public order itself is a changing entity, contracting and expanding according to what is perceived as a public interest in a given civilization."[37]

It could be argued that, in order to enable and legitimize this component of dynamism in practical terms, Article 1 of the New Code established 'natural law and the rules of equity' (*al-qānūn al-ṭabīʿī wa qawāʿid al-ʿadāla*) as a source for filling a legal *lacuna* if the court could not find an appropriate provision for application in the Code itself, in custom or in the Islamic *Sharīʿa*. This is a source of legitimacy of both individual and collective justice; simultaneously a judicial discretion and a social manifesto. In the outgoing Egyptian code (more precisely, the Law for the Establishment of *al-maḥākim al-ʾahliyya*),[38] the foundations of equity were mentioned as a source for filling a lacuna, and, in this context, even a primary source; in the New Code, however, this legal source was imbued with an emphatic social and legal conscience in keeping with our review here of the motif of justice.

Sociological jurists such as Gény and Duguit, with both of whom Sanhūrī was thoroughly familiar, indeed tended to interpret the term

---

[36] Al-Wasīṭ, volume 1, p. 434.
[37] Ibid., p. 435.
[38] Article 29.

'natural law' as a source of social solidarity, a moral standard accepting or rejecting the actions of the individual in keeping with the norms of social justice and order.[39]

This was one of the more significant sources of the differences between the old Egyptian codes and the Code Civil. In the Law for the Establishment of *al-maḥākim al-ʾahliyya*, it was established that natural law and equity would serve as a source for filling a lacuna, and even a primary source. This would have been unthinkable from the perspective of the Code Civil. This was a logical provision in the Egyptian context, since the Mixed Courts were staffed by Western judges, some of whom came from backgrounds of the Common Law. With a measure of pride, the American judge Jasper Brinton, who served in the Mixed Courts, wrote the following comment regarding the approach to justice of the French civil judge as distinct from his own dilemma as a judge in the Mixed Courts:

> In Egypt, however, this dilemma did not disturb the judges of the Mixed Courts. It was foreseen and solved by the framers of the charter in that provision of the article cited at the head of this chapter, which declared that when the written law was silent or obscure the judge should have resort to 'natural law and equity'. As we shall see, this principle played an important role in the development of the law of the Mixed Courts. But it was intended to supplement and not to divert attention from the written law.[40]

In an effort to legitimize the inclusion of the 'rules of equity', which were essentially alien to the French civil code, as a source for filling a lacuna, the explanatory notes to the proposed Code emphasized that the term 'principles of natural law and the rules of equity' in the old code had already enabled the Egyptian courts to enjoy a considerable measure of discretion and flexibility with regard to Egyptian law that could not otherwise have been adopted. "(The courts) drew from the principles of Egyptian law, from certain provisions of the Islamic *Sharīʿa*, sought for the principles embodied in foreign codes or agreements or innovated provisions as required by the social contexts, without these having precedents in the Code or in custom." Naturally, the New Code readily adopted those isolated elements of equity already present in the old Code, while dressing them in its own social purpose—a dimension

---

39 Lloyd's, pp. 128–129; Kelly, p. 378.

40 Brinton, p. 91.

that had not previously been present. (The original proposal placed the rules of equity in third place in filling a lacuna, after the text itself and custom law, as opposed to fourth place in the final Code, in which the *Sharīʿa* occupied the third place).[41]

1.4 *Removing the 'Shackles of the Law': Judicial Discretion as Justice*

Since the court was ultimately expected to apply this standard of justice, and to bind it to reality, between individual justice and social justice, it may be asked what dilemmas faced the court in implementing justice. These dilemmas will be imbued with a double significance here: they sharpen the guidelines applied by the court in applying justice, and they also permit a better understanding of the manner in which the Code and its authors perceived justice in the specific context of Egyptian society. The authors of the Code were aware of the dissonance between the sophisticated character and legal complexity of the New Code and the Egyptian society to which it was to be applied—a society that was largely uneducated and acted in accordance with customs and usage that were sometimes more entrenched and powerful than the norms of any written code.

Judge Brinton made the following comments regarding the weight of custom law in Egyptian society:

> Apart, however, from the written law, as expressed in the codes and in the subsequent legislation, there was a second source of law in Egypt, which stood upon an equal footing with the edicts of the legislator. This was usage—*la coutume*, as it was known, an element which plays an extraordinarily large role in regulating the relation of people in Moslem countries.[42]

For this reason, the element of justice was perceived by the authors as of special importance, since, in a polarized society most of whose members could not, and perhaps would never, understand the complexities of the law, there must be substantial room for judicial discretion in order to adapt the law to changing social developments. The explanatory notes to the proposed Code emphasized that the proposal granted the judge broad freedom of discretion, in which context he could examine the different conditions emerging in a given issue, ensure the proper

---

[41] Al-Qānūn al-Madanī, volume 1, pp. 189, 183.
[42] Brinton, p. 90.

balances, and adapt general principles to meet the specific case—"and this is the closest to securing justice."[43] The identification of judicial discretion with justice is a well-established approach that may already be seen in Aristotle's Nichomachean ethics.[44]

According to this approach when a judge applies his judicial discretion, he 'weighs' the pertinent circumstances and facts, determining, evaluating, classifying and ranking them to the best ability of his conscience. In light of these considerations, he determines the issue before him, guided by his inner sense of justice. Consciously or otherwise, any act of judicial discretion embodies an effort to realize justice.

Accordingly, the explanatory notes to the proposed Code employed the term 'legal shackles' (*ʾaghlāl al-qānūn*)[45] to express their negative view of excessively restricted judicial discretion. As the notes remark: "Let no person think that the judge who rules in accordance with a frozen foundation, and whose hands are bound by the shackles of a restrictive text, will be able to adapt the legal provisions for just application in changing circumstances. Accordingly, he will either (in his ruling) achieve justice while breaking the shackles of the law, or remain committed to the limits of the law but secure only partial justice. It has already been proven that it is not long before a frozen legal foundation breaks under the pressure of practical needs. (Accordingly,) flexible criteria that anticipate possible events and a continuing course of development are preferable."[46]

In other words, the restriction of the judicial discretion enjoyed by the courts (as embodied, for example, in the Code Civil) was perceived as hampering the quest for justice. This explains why many articles in the New Code mention 'justice' or 'equity' as a comprehensive term referring to an extensive discretion of the court.

Does the use of legal valves such as 'justice', 'pubic order', 'general interests' or the 'abuse of a right' imply that Egyptian law thereby became imprecise? This question may be answered through the response of French law, address the same dilemma. David agreed that French law might appear imprecise, since the theories of the abuse of a right, of public order and or morality are liable to be perceived as imprecise and as endangering the security of legal relations. The French jurist does not share this view, does not fear such a situation and does not

[43] Al-Qānūn al-Madanī, volume 1, p. 23.
[44] Lloyd's, p. 149; Kelly, pp. 26–28.
[45] Al-Qānūn al-Madanī, volume 1, p. 24.
[46] Ibid., pp. 23–24.

believe that it will destabilize legal systems. His perception of legal rules allows him a measure of flexibility in expressing and applying the legal rule. His intuition and his review of judicial decisions will enable him to recognize when he can convince a judge to consider aspects of justice, public order or morality.[47]

An example of the perception of justice in the New Code in the context of broad judicial discretion may be found on the question of the definition of the scope of a contract (*taḥdīd niṭāq al-ʿaqd*). The New Code established that the contract does not merely bind the agreeing partner to its content, but also includes anything that is required by the nature of the obligation, in accordance with the law, custom and justice.[48] The explanatory notes stated that the judge should 'seek guidance' from the rules of justice in completing the conditions of the contract and in defining its scope. Thus, for example, the seller is not committed solely to what is necessary in order to transfer the right in the sold asset to the purchaser, but is also obliged to refrain from any action which, by its nature, renders the transfer of the right impossible or difficult, and justice requires this obligation even if it was not mentioned in the contract.[49] A further example: someone who sells a business is obliged to refrain from enticing the employees to work for him after the sale, "and this obligation also stems from justice, even if it was not mentioned in the contract." A further example is a technical worker who has learned the industrial secrets of a factory in which he was employed: he may not sell these secrets to a competing factory, even if he did not make such a commitment in his contract;[50] a person entitled to life insurance may not conceal information about his illnesses from the insurance company, and so on. Article 95 of the New Code establishes that if a dispute develops regarding details that were not agreed upon in the contract, the court may complete these details in keeping with the character of the transaction, the legal provisions, custom and justice. Article 203(2) states that the court may award financial compensation, even if the parties agreed on specific compensation, if such compensation is too burdensome for the debtor; the court may also reduce the level of agreed compensation stipulated as a punitive condition in the contract if it considers this to be excessive,

[47] David, p. 204.
[48] The Egyptian Civil Code, article 148(2).
[49] In this case the Code included specific article 428.
[50] See also the Egyptian Civil Code, article 686.

in accordance with Article 224(2) of the Code; and Article 149 of the New Code grants the court broad discretion "in accordance with the requirements of justice" in amending or abrogating unduly disadvantageous conditions in a uniform contract.

The social purpose of the Code thus assumed that broad judicial discretion ensuring that justice would be done in court serves a bridge between society and the law, and also constitutes a source of legitimacy for the Code and for the legal system as a whole. This discretion and measure of justice are vital, therefore, not only for the citizen who enters the court in search of justice, but also for the Code and for law themselves. Equally, however, individual justice may constitute a negative element on the broader level, for example by impairing economic stability and predictability, which plays such a central role in maintaining functional economic and commercial life. Accordingly, the New Code delineated limits for the judicial discretion of the court, as we shall see in Chapter Six, thus balancing the element of justice with the element of economic and social stability. In the context of this chapter, this may be seen, *inter alia*, in the context of the theory of unforeseen circumstances. The proposed law feared that excessive judicial discretion might impair stability and economic expectations, and create the background for arbitrary rulings (*taḥakkum*) by the judge. Accordingly, the expanse of judicial discretion enjoyed by the court was restricted, for example, in defining an unexpected event and in reducing burdensome undertakings to 'reasonable' (*maʿqūl*) proportions. The proposed Code further noted that this was to be effected if justice so required.[51] We shall also see this point below in the limitation imposed by parliamentary representatives on the mental foundations of the doctrine of exploitation.

2. The Manifestation of the Doctrines of Equity

2.1 *The Transformation in French Law: Equity as an Intervening Factor in Contractual Freedom*

'Equity' is a system of law designed to furnish remedies for wrongs, which were not legally recognized under positive law, or for which no adequate remedy was provided by the prevailing law.[52]

[51] Al-Qānūn al-Madanī, volume 2, pp. 280–282.
[52] Kelly, pp. 28–29.

The term equity (*équité* in French, and the two words are not necessarily synonymous) had a poor reputation in France, since it was attributed mainly to arbitrary rulings by the courts. "God save us from the equity of the *parliaments* (the pre-revolutionary courts)" was a common saying among French jurists. Indeed, these courts enjoyed a royally-recognized right to deviate from the written law in the name of justice. This power reflected their status as the replacements of the old *curia regis*, and like the prince they advised, they were considered *legibus solutus* (above the law).[53] The basic rule in French law was that the French judge rules in accordance with the written law—*la loi*—a concept that was supposed to be consistent and clear, and not in accordance with equity, which was perceived as a erratic and inconsistent legal element whose arbitrary application could lead to injustice. In this respect, France was indeed a *pays de droit écrit*. The Code Civil itself made very few references to the concept of 'equity' as a substitute for a legal rule.[54] Ostensibly, only legislation was considered as the source of civil and criminal law in French; this principle was particularly stark with regard to criminal law, as summarized in the epithet *nullum crimem, nulla poena, sine lege* ("only a law can define an offense and order a penalty for he who commits it"). David noted that this principle was also dominant in civil law. Judges in the civil courts almost always relied on the written law, only rarely referring to other legal sources, such as rulings, custom or the sense of equity.[55]

As we saw in the previous chapter, the relations between law and the rules of equity in France began to change in the early twentieth century. Nowhere in the Napoleonic codes was it stated that a human right has limits. This reflected eighteenth century legal philosophy (such as the Declaration of the Rights of Man and the Citizen of 1789), which lauded the independent will and natural rights of the individual. The individual had the full right to freedom of contract and property; the content of his contracts could be whatever he agreed with the other party, at his free will, and society was obliged to honor his contracts (*pacta sunt servanda*) and his private property. This same spirit of almost unbridled rights was also manifested in the Egyptian civil codes that preceded the New Code, both that of the Mixed Courts and that

[53] David, p. 196; Pierre Mayer, "Équité in Modern French Law", in A. M. Rabello (ed.) *Aequitas and Equity: Equity in Civil Law and Mixed Jurisdictions*, p. 365.

[54] Mayer indicates articles 565 and 1135 of the Code Civil as the only cases of that.

[55] David, p. 155.

of the Native National Courts. From the turn of the century, however, as the individualistic world view increasingly clashed with more socially-based and even Socialist ideas, changes began to take place in French law. While the Code Civil had seen the role of contract law as being to supervise the propriety of the contractual process, the new moralistic approach extended the purview of contract law to include intervention in the content of the contract. This change was reflected as French civil law began to be influenced by doctrines developed in French administrative law, according to which the government and its agents have 'authorities' and 'functions' to perform, as distinct from the classic 'rights' and 'obligations' of civil law.[56] Administrative law in France was developed by the Council of State (*Conseil d'Etat*), a judicial mechanism parallel to the civil court system that was not bound by the norms of the Code Civil, enabling the development of rules of equity by the judges. These rules then permeated the entire legal system, and hence influenced the interpretation of the Code Civil.

This ideological transformation of law was manifested in general terms in a new interpretative approach to the Code Civil, and a doctrinal school began to seek legitimization for this approach. The approach was the teleological school of interpretation, as mentioned above, which was headed by leading jurists such as Raymond Saleille, François Gény and Louis Josserand. This was a trans-European movement in scope, and changes in the spirit of the teleological approach were introduced in the Swiss civil code of 1907 and in the proposed Franco-Italian code. The movement also had a personal connection with legal developments in the Arab world. Josserand served as dean of the Faculty of Law at the University of Lyon, where Sanhūrī wrote his two doctoral dissertations. He was a member of the team that drafted the proposed Franco-Italian code and had a strong influence on Sanhūrī. Josserand also drafted the general theory of obligations in the Lebanese civil code.[57]

This context saw the development of the doctrine of the abuse of a right (*abus de droit*), one of the most important altruistic doctrines in

[56] Ibid., 199. See also: L. R. Brown, J. S. Bell, *French Administrative Law* (Oxford: Clarendon Press, 1993), pp. 245–250.

[57] J. Herget, S. Wallace, "The German Free Law Movement as the Source of American Legal Realism", *Virginia Law Review* 73(1987), pp. 399–455; H. J. Liebesny, *The law of the Near and Middle East, Readings, Cases and Materials* (Albany: State University of New York Press, 1975), p. 92.

the Continental rules of equity (particularly in the field of property law, though it also impacted on contract law) in the twentieth century. This doctrine means that the individual is no longer free to act to advance his own interests, but is also restricted and limited by other interests, particularly through the prohibition against his abusing his rights.[58] The abuse of a right is an action or failing that is permitted by law, but which becomes prohibited if committed on the basis of an improper motive. The doctrine of the abuse of a right had a clearly moralistic foundation in the French legal system. In order to establish whether a person was abusing his rights, it must be asked whether the person is exercising the right in order to behave in an unfair and unjust manner. This definition may include an action intended solely to injure another person, or an action that ignores another person or the interests of society. The question here is not what are the objective limits of the right and whether the person has transgressed them, as was the case in the administrative doctrine of the abuse of authority (*détournement de pouvoir*); rather, the test is of subjective intent. Accordingly, the doctrine of the abuse of a right may be said to have introduced a dimension of equitable appraisal in litigation. In order to decide whether a person had abused his rights, it must be decided whether he has committed any culpability; though imbued with legal consequences, this is essentially a moral concept.[59]

The Code Civil itself was not amended, and its formulation remained faithful to the old concepts of individual liberty. However, this doctrine had a significant impact on the positivist law of other Continental nations, finding a place in the civil codes of Germany, Italy and Switzerland. For example, Article 226 of the German code (*BGB*): "The use of a right is unlawful if its purpose is solely to cause damage to another;" Article 2 of the Swiss civil code: 'Every person is obliged to use his rights and perform his obligations in accordance with the pro-

[58] L. Josserand, *De l'Abus des Droits* (Paris: Rousseau, 1905); L. Josserand, *De l'Esprit des Droits et de Leur Relativité*, 2e éd. (Paris: Dalloz, 1939); On this Doctrine in other Continental legal systems see: A. Al-Qasem, "The Unlawful Exercise of Rights in the Civil Codes of the Arab Countries of the Middle East", *The International and Comparative Law Quarterly* 39(1990), pp. 396–410; A. M. Rabello (ed.) *Aequitas and Equity: Equity in Civil Law and Mixed Jurisdictions*: A. Gambaro, "Abuse of rights in Civil law Tradition", p. 632; Paul-A. Crépeau, "Abuse of Rights in the Civil Law of Quebec", p. 582; E. Özsunay, "Abuse of Rights under Turkish Civil Law", p. 645; F. Sturm, "Abuse of Rights in the Swiss Law, A survey of Recent Jurisprudence", p. 672.

[59] David, p. 201.

visions of good faith. Any abuse of a right shall not be entitled to the protection of the law;" and Article 74(2) of the proposed Franco-Italian code: "Furthermore, any person, who caused damage to another while deviating, in exercising his right, from the confines of good faith or from the purpose for which this right was granted—shall be obliged to pay compensation." It should be noted that Sanhūrī was already influenced by these articles in the early stages of drafting the New Code.[60]

2.2 *The Doctrine of the Abuse of a Right* (Taʿassuf fī ʾIstiʿmāl al-Ḥaqq)

Sanhūrī's world view argued that "society has an interest in protecting the weaker party as he stands against the stronger party."[61] Accordingly, the architect of the New Code decided to follow 'contemporary changes' in terms of the doctrine of the abuse of a right, introducing this concept in the code even though it did not appear in the French Code Civil:

> This is not a new theory, since it was already recognized by Roman law, from where it gravitated to ancient French law and was also absorbed in the Islamic *fiqh*. After the emergence of the individualistic principles of the French Revolution, however, this doctrine disappeared for some time, since the Revolution declined to adopt it. It thus remained concealed throughout the nineteenth century, eschewed by jurists, until God appointed it two French jurists—Saleilles and Josserand—to dust it off. Not long would pass before it would return at the head of the principles of legal theory. It was also later adopted by the modern codes (though not the French code), such as the Swiss code.[62]

This doctrine indeed featured prominently in the New Code,[63] and the explanatory notes to the proposed Code stated that this would permit it to influence not only property and contract law; it was also appropriate that it be applied to Egyptian public law.[64] Prior to the enactment of the New Code, Egyptian law had not included any specific provisions restricting the use of a right, with the exception of a single reference in the previous code relating to a shared wall. The Mixed and *ʾAhlī* court

[60] Wujūb, p. 97.
[61] Al-Wasīṭ, volume 1, p. 111.
[62] Ibid., p. 948.
[63] Ibid., Al-Wajīz, p. 355.
[64] The Explanatory notes of the Code's proposal, Al-Qānūn al-Madanī, volume 1, p. 207.

systems completed the missing elements through cautious rulings—similar to those in France—based on general and negligent liability. The old Civil Code established that "any action on account of which damage is cause to another requires the perpetrator to pay compensation for the damage, and requires the perpetrator (to pay compensation) for damage caused to another relating to the ignorance of matters subject to his supervision . . . or non-supervision."[65]

The New Code established that "a person who exercises his right lawfully shall not be liable for damage accruing therefrom." The exercise of a right is considered unlawful in the following cases:

1. If the sole intention is to cause damage to another;
2. If the desired interests are of negligible importance and are disproportionate to the damage caused to another on account thereof;
3. If the right is used in order to secure unlawful interests.[66]

This clause sought to declare that the Code had an altruistic purpose, which it perceived as sublime, namely to regulate relations between people on a moral basis. The norm of sublime behavior permeates the entire Code, providing a yardstick for gauging the legality of the application of its articles. Accordingly, any interest or purpose that is perceived by the Code as embodying a measure of culpability or unfairness on the part of the owner of the right, or discrimination and injustice from the injured person's perspective, is defined as unlawful. Any legal situation in the civil realm that fails to meet the moral norms developed by this article is considered unlawful. This provision could be likened to a moral traffic light that determines which rights, transactions and legal actions may pass through to the destination of legality and which will be halted and prevented from continuing their course. Accordingly, the New Code established from the outset (Article 5) that it is a 'gate' in two senses of the word, technical and substantive. As Sanhūrī wrote in his diaries, relating to the obligation to fight evil:

> He who forgets people's wickedness should forget their good. I cause bad to those who cause bad, and treat evil in the same manner, in order to curb the action of evil and evilness. I know that in so doing, I am not avenging the past but repairing the future.[67]

---

[65] The *ʾAhlī* Code, *Majmūʿat Qawānīn al-Mahākim al-ʾAhliyya wa al-Sharʿiyya*, article 151.
[66] The Egyptian Civil Code, article 5.
[67] Diary, 8 August 1944, p. 249.

In complete contrast to the previous Egyptian Code, in which the individual enjoyed liberty in making contracts (or in using his land), regardless of aspects of unfairness or discrimination that emerged thereby (although the Mixed and *ʾAhlī* courts occasionally intervened to modify this rule, restricting the unfair actions of the individual; they did so, however, without any explicit statutory authorization),[68] the 'traffic light' placed at the gate to the New Code could engender a transformation in society's perception of such actions, establishing that they constituted the unlawful use of a right, a determination that could end in the nullification or abrogation of the contract.[69]

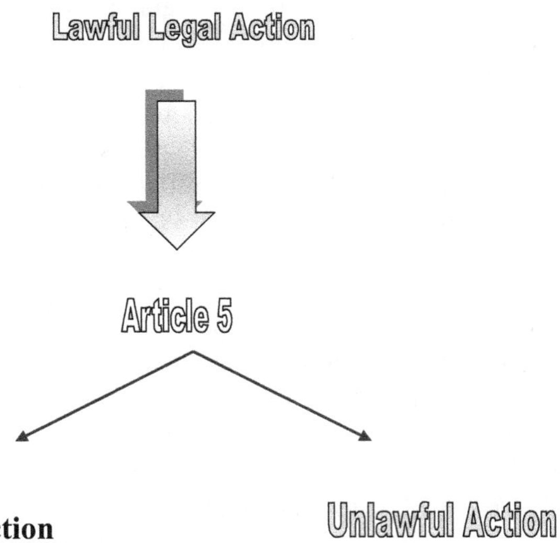

A normative clause such as this, establishing the rules of equity, obliges any legal system to determine the rules for this traffic light. In other words, how is the judge to interpret these principles?—in accordance with the subjective/mental approach, in which case this will be "the closest application to the realization of justice," as the early definition made by Sanhūrī[70]—i.e. weather the specific person had malicious intent—or will it be in accordance with an objective approach, examining each case according to the definable parameters of a 'reasonable person' or 'reasonable damage', "an approach that ensures greater stability in

[68] Al-Wasīṭ, volume 1, p. 967.
[69] Ibid., p. 127.
[70] Wujūb, p. 97.

commercial life."[71] One must keep in mind that the evidential elements are easier to secure in the objective approach.

French law examined such cases in accordance with a subjective approach, while the interpretation of the New Code preferred a combination of both subjective and objective tests, taking into consideration both commercial stability and social justice. We shall examine this according to the three categories itemized in the article. In the first case, where the sole intention is to cause damage, it is not sufficient to show that the individual intended to cause damage—the subjective test—but it must also be shown that in his behavior, he deviated from the normative behavior of the reasonable person (*al-shakhṣ al-ʿādī*)—the objective test.[72] In the second case, the examination of interests and their relative damage, the criterion for assessment is objective,[73] and *Al-Wasīṭ* explains that it is not the behavior of a reasonable person to exercise his right in a manner that causes grave damage to another, when he himself has only a paltry interest in the matter that is disproportionate to the damage he causes. A person who acts in this manner acts rashly, with disregard for the grave damage he causes to others, or conceals an intention to injure another, dishonestly presenting himself as someone acting for some particular purpose.[74] In the last case, of the unlawful securing of interests, the explanatory notes to the proposed Code noted that "the interest will be considered unlawful not only if the individual broke the law, but also if he disregarded public order and morality."[75] The interpretative test in this case is essentially subjective; the explanatory notes confirmed that it was not appearances that were the standard here, but the intention of the owner of the right should provide the basis for determining whether the right had been abused.[76] The explanatory notes provided examples of unlawful interests cloaked in the ostensibly legitimate use of a right: dismissing an employee who joined a trade union; the dismissal of an employee for personal or political reasons; a landowner who places barbed wire

[71] Ibid.

[72] Al-Wasīṭ, volume 1, p. 958.

[73] The Explanatory notes of the code's proposal, Al-Qānūn al-Madanī, volume 1, p. 34; Al-Wasīṭ, volume 1, p. 958.

[74] Al-Wasīṭ, volume 1, p. 959.

[75] The Explanatory notes of the code's proposal, Al-Qānūn al-Madanī, volume 1, p. 209.

[76] Al-Qānūn al-Madanī, volume 1, pp. 209–210.

on an area of land in order to force an airline whose airplanes land nearby to purchase the land at an inflated price, and so on.[77]

Sanhūrī noted that in this sub-section, which blends morality and society—both fluctuating and fluid elements—he preferred to use the term 'unlawful interest' rather than the two other terms encountered in French law—'unlawful purpose' and 'social goal'. His reason was that 'interest' is a clearer guide for judicial interpretation and application by the court than 'purpose'. In light of my argument that the Code sought to advance a specific social purpose, it might be asked whether it would not have been preferable to employ this specific term here. The answer is that there is a distance between the broad social goals that Sanhūrī sought to achieve through the Code, and the "theory of the social goal" as this existed in France, which argued that the law granted rights to their owners in order to secure social goals: accordingly, every right has a specific social goal, and if the owner of the right deviates from this specific social goal, he has thereby abused the right. This theory has two disadvantages that made its use unviable in the Egyptian context: the difficulty in defining a social goal for every right, and the dangers of such rigid definition in a pluralistic, polarized and constantly-changing society.[78] Indeed, a review of early drafts of the Code shows that an additional sub-section was originally included that defined the use of a right as unlawful if such use "contradicted a substantive general interest". This proposed clause was based on the theories raised in France at the time regarding the social goals of law in this context (*intérêt sérieux et légitime*), and ostensibly also on the Islamic *Sharī'a*, particularly Article 26 of the *Majalla*, which states: "One chooses damage to the individual in order to remove damage to the many." The proposal also mentioned Articles 27–29 of the *Majalla* as a source of legal influence: "One removes the grave damage by means of lesser damage" (27); "one commits the lesser of two offenses in order to avoid the graver" (28); "one chooses the lesser of two evils" (29).[79] The explanatory notes to the proposed Code explicitly stated that this referred to the test already mentioned, according to which any right was restricted by the social and economic purpose for which it was created.[80] However, as mentioned above, this provision was deleted by

---

[77] Al-Wasīṭ, volume 1, pp. 959–960.

[78] Ibid., p. 961.

[79] Al-Qānūn al-Madanī, volume 1, pp. 201, 209.

[80] The Explanatory notes of the code's proposal, Al-Qānūn al-Madanī, volume 1, p. 21.

the authors of the Code in the early stage of drafting, since "social purpose is a broad gate through which political considerations, social trends and different schools may enter, and which is liable to make the use of a right subject to divided and contrary approaches, something that is dangerous."[81] To return to the metaphor of the traffic light, there must be uniformity in the moral norms that shape the legality of the use of a right; otherwise, the traffic light will be unable to operate effectively. And if the traffic cannot function properly, the entire Code may lose its purpose and vitality.[82]

In addition to functioning as a traffic light permitting or prohibiting the exercising of rights—or, to change the metaphor, a lighthouse disseminating the general norms of justice in the New Code—the doctrine of the abuse of a right also appears in several specific clauses scattered throughout the Code; usually, this is designed to prevent in advance the damage liable to be caused due to the abuse of a right, and to deter and alert attention to such possibilities. These are cases in which the probability of the abuse of a right is considerable, and where there is *a priori* inequality, as, for example, in working relations or in the relations between an Egyptian and a foreign citizen. The Code established, for example, that if a work contract was nullified through the abuse of a right (*taʿassuf*) by one of the parties, the other party would, in addition to his right to substantive compensation, also have grounds for compensation for the act of the nullification of the contract by *taʿassuf*.[83] The explanatory notes to the Code elaborated that this was a case of "protecting the rights of the worker," who is in an inferior position relative to the provider of work.[84] Accordingly, employers would henceforth be wary of dismissing a worker in a shameful, immaterial or unlawful manner, since they would be liable to pay punitive compensation for such action. To take an example from a different field: A transaction takes place in Egypt between an Egyptian citizen and a foreign national, and it emerges that the foreigner is legally incapacitated (in accordance with the laws of his country), or that his legal capacity is defective, without it having been easily possible to know this fact in Egypt. If the legally

[81] Al-Wasīṭ, volume 1, p. 961.
[82] Like in other substantive doctrines all of the Arab Civil Codes has adopted the theory of abuse of rights. Articles 4–5 of the Egyptian civil code appear in articles 5–6 of the Syrian civil code; 4–5 of the Libyan; 6–7 of the Iraqi; 30 of the Kuwaiti; 66, 292 of the Jordanian.
[83] The Egyptian Civil Code, article 695(2); Al-Wasīṭ, volume 1, p. 966.
[84] Al-Qānūn al-Madanī, volume 6, p. 167.

incapacitated foreigner seeks to nullify the contract on the basis of this fact, he will be abusing his right, and the Code was quick to prevent such a possibility.[85] This clause seeks to protect the Egyptian citizen (who here represents the 'weak') in his contacts with the foreigner, to shelter him and to stabilize transactions with foreigners without fear of deception. The explanatory notes to the proposed Code stated that "it is difficult (for an Egyptian) dealing with a foreigner to know the details of his legal state," adding that this legal norm was originally drawn from the Italian and German codes, principally in order to protect the national interest.[86] Another provision relates to the laws for a private wall, stating: "The owner of the wall is not permitted to demolish it on his own initiative without significant justification (*ʿudhr qawwī*), if this will harm his neighbor whose property is adjacent to the said wall."[87] In this case, if a neighbor demolished his wall and caused damage to his neighbor, the damage was to be repaired after it occurred through the abuse of a right, and the neighbor who demolished his wall was required to rebuild it.[88] A further example comes from the field of the property right of *ʾirtifāq* (servitude), providing that the *ʾirtifāq* will cease to exist, and the landowner subject to it will be released in whole or in part, if the conditions have changed to the degree that it is no longer possible to exercise this right, if the *ʾirtifāq* has lost its purpose, or if its purpose has dwindled to the point that is disproportionate to the burden faced by the subordinate land.[89] The *taʿassuf* in this case would come if the dominant landowners refused to release the subordinate land, and the remedy could be in the form of the nullification of the right of *ʾirtifāq* by the court.[90]

As will become apparent in many other cases in which Sanhūrī sought to adopt an innovative legal or social norm that might be expected to encounter resistance, he generally relied on the Islamic *Sharīʿa* as a source of legitimacy and sanctity that could not easily be opposed. In my opinion, he adopted this approach regardless of whether the said legal norm was actually drawn from the *Sharīʿa* or even found there.

---

85 The Egyptian Civil Code, article 11(1); Al-Wasīṭ, volume 1, pp. 965–966.
86 Al-Qānūn al-Madanī, volume 1, p. 243.
87 The Egyptian Civil Code, article 818(2).
88 Al-Wasīṭ, volume 1, p. 966; Al-Qānūn al-Madanī, volume 6, pp. 63–66.
89 The Egyptian Civil Code, article 1029.
90 Al-Wasīṭ, volume 1, p. 967.

So, too, with respect to the abuse of a right, the Code ostensibly drew on the rules of the *fiqh*, using them to cloak the legal norm drawn from a European source. Was this doctrine indeed taken from the *Sharīʿa*, and indeed can it even be found therein? Opinions are divided on this question.

The proposed Code referred to Articles 26–29, 1198–1200 and 1212 of the *Majalla*. The explanatory notes added that "the provisions of the Islamic *Sharīʿa* regarding the abuse of a right assisted in the selection of this legal principle, since this doctrine is found (in the *Sharīʿa*) as a general school whose precision and provisions are in no sense inferior to those of the most modern Western theories."[91] In the preparatory discussions, Dr. Kāmil Malash added a comment regarding the connection between the doctrine of the abuse of a right and the *Sharīʿa*: "The Islamic *Sharīʿa* includes several questions in which the Western scholars assumed that they were the first, but further studies (in the West) have shown that it is the Muslims who were first. Among these, one may note the question of the abuse of a right."[92] The explanatory notes to the proposed Code added, regarding the connection between the modern Western theory and its appearance in the Islamic *Sharīʿa*, that in this manner the Code was establishing a form of 'constitution' (*dustūr*) for addressing rights, binding the principles of the Islamic *Sharīʿa* and the theory of the abuse of a right as absorbed from modern Western law. "Thus the Code has introduced the moral tendency, modern social tendencies, and Islamic legal theory."[93] By contrast, an Egyptian scholar who was a contemporary of Sanhūrī, Dr. Shafīq Shiḥāta, claimed that the idea of the abuse of a right was limited among the Hanafites, certainly less broad than in the New Code, and did not extend beyond the field of property relations among neighbors.[94]

---

[91] The Explanatory Notes of the code proposal, Al-Qānūn al-Madanī, volume 1, p. 207.

[92] Al-Qānūn al-Madanī, volume 1, p. 100.

[93] The Explanatory Notes of the code proposal Al-Qānūn al-Madanī, volume 1, p. 211.

[94] C. Chehata, "La Théorie de l'Abus des Droits ches les Jurisconsultes Musulmans", *Revue Internationale De Droit Comparé* 4 (1952), pp. 217–224, 223.

2.3 *The Motif of Forgiveness: The Doctrine of Unforeseen Circumstances* (Al-Ḥawādith al-Ṭāri'a)

This doctrine of legal frustration, "which has a prominent moral aspect",[95] provides an equitable measure of exoneration and forgiveness for a contractual party who is struck by unexpected misfortune or, according to the theory of the desired balance discussed here in the interpretation of justice, when the balance between the parties to an agreement is disturbed and this disruption was not the fault of the disrupting party. This doctrine offers a form of exemption for an obligated party in cases in which he cannot maintain his obligation due to circumstances beyond his control. The explanatory notes to the Code stated that this was originally an ancient doctrine of equity that appeared in medieval legislation under religious influence—in the ecclesiastical canonic laws and, to a degree, in the Islamic *fiqh*. In Church law, this principle fell under the definition of 'changing circumstances' (*rebus sic stantibus*),[96] and, according to *Al-Wasīṭ*, the Islamic *Sharī'a* was also capable of flexibility when circumstances changed, as, *inter alia*, the *Majalla* declares that "It is an accepted fact that the terms of law vary with the change in the times".[97] The French Code Civil rejected this doctrine due to the principle of the sanctity of contracts, which it supported, and refused to countenance such flexibility. Even the profound economic deprivation faced in France following the world wars, and the economic need to declare a moratorium on loans, did not lead the Code Civil to accept this doctrine. The examples were many: when the French court of appeals refused to amend insurance policies to reflect the risk of conscription. Originally, conscription in France took place by lottery. However, the army grew by almost one-half, meaning that the risk of being selected in the lottery was much greater; accordingly, the loss caused to the insurance company due to this sudden change in military policy was considerable. The court refused to amend an ancient

---

95 Al-Wasīṭ, volume 1, p. 707.

96 For details about the development of this doctrine see: Al-Wasīṭ, volume 1, pp. 706–714; Al-Wajīz, volume 1, pp. 252–261; R. Newman, *Equity and Law, a Comparative Study* (New York: Oceana Publications, 1961), pp. 193–194; Articles 148(2) of the Syrian civil code; 147(2) of the Libyan; 146(2) of the Iraqi; 198 of the Kuwaiti: 205 of the Jordanian; 208 of the Yemenite.

97 The *Majalla*, article 39; *Kitāb Murshid al-Ḥayrān*, article 306(2); the reference appeared in Al-Qānūn al-Madanī, volume 2, p. 279.

contract from the sixteenth century even after economic circumstances changed beyond recognition.[98]

In a precedent involving a gas company from Bordeaux (*Compagnie generale d'éclairage de Bordeaux*), the *Conseil d'Etat* intervened in 1916 and, for the first time, imposed this doctrine (known in French as *l'imprévision*) on French administrative law. This ruling had a profound influence on French law, and hence also on Egyptian law.[99]

The Bordeaux gas company was contractually obliged to provide lighting gas for the city municipality at a given price; however, the price of gas had since risen sharply due to the war, increasing from 35 francs per ton in 1913 to 117 francs per ton in 1915. As a result, the gas company faced financial difficulties and was on the verge of bankruptcy. The *Conseil d'Etat* ordered the amendment of the contract according to the new rate, establishing that the obligation could be amended not only when its execution became impossible, but also when it became excessively onerous. French administrative law (but not civil law) adopted this theory for two principle reasons: Firstly, the issues that appear before the administrative judicial system relate closely to the public interest. For example, the above-mentioned gas company played a vital public role; if it were to collapse, the public would suffer more than would be the case if the contract were amended in accordance with the doctrine of unforeseen circumstances. By contrast, the civil courts hear issues relating to private interests, ostensibly without direct affinity to the general interest. Secondly, administrative courts are not bound by the articles of the Code Civil in the manner that civil courts are. They enjoy greater discretion, and, indeed, some of the rulings of these courts have almost the quality of judicial legislation.[100] The theory of unforeseen circumstances was also rejected by the Egyptian judiciary, in both the Mixed and the *ʾAhlī* courts, during the period prior to the enactment of the New Code. According to the rulings of the Mixed Courts, an obligation does not expire unless its execution has become impossible; if execution is possible, it must be maintained even if it constitutes a grave burden on the debtor. The Mixed Court further ruled

---

[98] Al-Wasīṭ, volume 1, p. 170.

[99] B. Nicholas, *The French Law of Contract*, pp. 208–210; L. R. Brown, J. S. Bell, *French Administrative Law*, pp. 208–210; Al-Wasīṭ, volume 1, pp. 711–715; Newman, *Equity and Law*, 193–194.

[100] Al-Wasīṭ, volume 1, pp. 714–715.

that in times of war, difficulties could be expected in execution, and these should be taken into account, so that they could not be used as grounds for exemption from the obligation.[101] The *ʾAhlī/Waṭanī* system (which was responsible for judging cases among Egyptian citizens) did not, in most cases, recognize the doctrine of unforeseen circumstances. The court of appeals in Asiut ruled in 1942 that the courts should not adopt the doctrine of unforeseen circumstances, and that they should order the execution of contracts to the letter, without making any changes to the conditions agreed by both parties. The supreme (*Waṭanī*) court (*maḥkamat al-nakḍ*) reiterated in 1947 that "the (Old) Civil Code includes nothing that would permit the judge to contradict the obligations established by the contract, since this would infringe the general principle that a contract is a form of law for the parties (*al-ʿaqd sharīʿat al-mutaʿāqidīn*)."[102] The Egyptian Supreme Court recognized the importance of the doctrine and its justification, particularly in times of economic hardship, but argued that its hands were tied: "(It is obvious to us) that this doctrine is based on equity, forgiveness (*ʿafū*) and philanthropy, but this court is not permitted to act before the legislature and introduce this principle by itself (into the judicial system)." The Supreme Court nullified a given ruling of the court of appeals which sought to intervene in the conditions of a contract when circumstances had changed, even if execution was still possible. It may reasonably be assumed that the Supreme Court judges were already aware of the formula that was to be adopted by the New Code; this would explain their mention of the doctrine in their ruling.[103]

In complete contrast to the rulings of the civil courts in France and Egypt, and naturally to the French Code Civil and the old civil codes in Egypt, the New Code introduced this doctrine in its articles with the clear intention that the courts would henceforth employ it intensively.

The doctrine was placed in the same clause as the declaration of the principle of the sanctity of contracts, perhaps in an effort to emphasize its lofty normative status. Thus the Code symbolically juxtaposed the absolute contractual doctrine, according to which 'contracts are to be respected' (*pacta sunt servanda*) with the altruistic and moral approach that argues that a party that is unable to meet its contractual obligations,

---

[101] For sources from the *ʾAhlī* and Mixed courts rulings see: Al-Wasīṭ, volume 1, pp. 710–711.

[102] The reference in: Al-Wasīṭ, volume 1, p. 713.

[103] Ibid.

and hence liable to breach the contract, should be forgiven if this breach is caused through no fault of its own. This inclusion of a measure of exoneration in contract law was made during a period of severe economic depression and unemployment in post-war Egypt. Businessmen and ordinary citizens were often unable to meet their contractual obligations due to the deteriorating economic situation, and some form of moratorium was needed. Accordingly, the Egyptian Code took action where the French civil code had declined to, establishing that:

1. The contract makes the law of the parties and it is to be nullified or amended only by mutual consent of the parties, or for such reasons provided for by the law.
2. Nevertheless, if, as the result of exceptional events of a general nature that could not have been anticipated, the implementation of the contractual obligation becomes unduly burdensome for the debtor, threatening him with severe losses, even if it is still possible, the judge may, in the circumstances of the matter and having weighed the interests of the parties, reduce the burdensome obligation to reasonable limits. Any agreement negating such a possibility is void.[104]

In the discussions of the Civil Code in the Senate opposition was expressed, as might be expected, to the inclusion of this doctrine in Egyptian civil law. Some of the deputies felt that this was an excessively blatant violation of the basic principle that contracts are to be respected. The jurist Dr. Ḥāmad Zakī, who felt that the Code gave excessive weight to judicial discretion in applying norms of equity, argued in this context that the judge had no right to add conditions, but only to interpret them; accordingly, by applying such a forceful doctrine in Egyptian positive law, the judge would deviate from his authority.[105] The president of the committee, Muḥammad al-Wakīl, supported this objection, adding that such a clause would only serve to encourage disputes and thus disrupt commercial life. A minor political event or an increase or reduction in prices would suffice to lead debtors to argue that their obligations no longer stood: from this point on, every debtor would attempt to shirk his obligations under the cloak of the law, and this was something

[104] The Egyptian Civil Code, article 147(2).
[105] Al-Qānūn al-Madanī, volume 2, p. 286.

that the law should not permit.[106] Thus the individualistic world view of these deputies in parliament clashed overtly with the altruistic and moral approach of the author of the Code. It was clear to all, however, that introducing such a doctrine of equity required the definition of boundaries for the court on the question as to what events were to be considered unexpected, and what policy was to be used in applying this doctrine within a given unexpected event; otherwise, commercial stability might be impaired.

The first question, raised in the various committees responsible for drafting the Code, was whether the unexpected event was of an individual nature, such as a fire in the debtor's business, or collective, such as war or a general financial catastrophe. In the original proposal, as in the Polish and Italian codes, the reference was simply to unexpected events, apparently including both categories. However, the committee for the re-examination of the Code added the word *ʿāmma* (general) to the wording of the clause; "the intention is to general and not individual events," claimed the deputy Dr. Ḥasan Baghdādī in the Civil Code Committee of the Senate.[107] Sanhūrī also added that events specific to the debtor, such as bankruptcy, death or a fire in his business, would not be sufficient to activate the doctrine.[108] The re-examination committee emphasized that in order for the events in question to meet the definition, they must apply generally to a group of people, such as an unexpected flood covering a large area, an unexpected attack of locusts or an outbreak of plague.[109] Such an event must include an element of surprise, or at least of irregularity. By contrast, a plague of worms damaging crops, occurring in the northern Delta region, did not constitute such an event, since it was due to the neglect of the fields and could be avoided. Moreover, this was an expected event, according to the representative of the Ministry of Justice, ʿAbdu Muḥaram, director of the *al-waṭaniyya* courts (which were already known by this term at this stage, rather than *ʾahliyya*).[110] Thus the scope of the doctrine as included in the Code was narrowed. However, in order to maintain the flexible character of this doctrine, the explanatory notes emphasized that the list of exceptional (*ʾistithnāʾiyya*) events was not exclusive. *Al-Wasīṭ*

---

106 Ibid.
107 Al-Qānūn al-Madanī, volume 2, p. 283.
108 Al-Wasīṭ, volume 1, p. 721.
109 Al-Qānūn al-Madanī, volume 2, p. 282.
110 Ibid., p. 284.

added additional examples of the application of the doctrine, such as earthquake, war, a sudden strike, the introduction or abolition of an obligatory governmental tariff, a sudden and burdensome increase in prices, and so on. "The Egyptian Code did not include a closed list on this matter, and thus remained flexible," he commented.[111]

The explanatory notes to the Code itemized four vital and cumulative conditions for applying the doctrine in court: Firstly, the contract in connection with which equity was sought must be long-term, i.e., there must be a time lapse between the date of making the contract and the date of implementation; during the interim period, the unexpected events must occur; secondly, these events must appear after making the contract; thirdly, it must have been impossible to anticipate these events; lastly, these events must, during the implementation of the contract, have become burdensome on the debtor, though there was no requirement that they must render the performance of his undertakings impossible.[112] In the context of the effort to secure an element of social solidarity through property laws, as discussed in the previous chapter, it is interesting to note that one of the participants in the deliberations of the Code Committee Dr. Ḥasan Baghdādī, claimed that this aspect of equity also makes a contribution to the desired solidarity in Egyptian society. He explained that the foundation of the theory of unexpected events was the mutual sacrifice, whereby each of the parties bore part of the damage, since the situation was not that one party or the other bore all the damage while the other was exempted, if the contract were nullified or amended. He saw this element of mutuality and the distribution of risks as a desirable social and educational effect.[113]

The doctrine of unforeseen circumstances applied contract law as a whole. However, and presumably in order to emphasize this doctrine and the element of mercy and forgiveness (*ʿafū*) it embodied, it may be seen explicitly in specific clauses in the New Code, though, perhaps due to this very specificity and localized character, it varies from cases to case, and sometimes extends to include personal events. These cases relate to the termination or amendment of a contract on the grounds of justice, consideration and compassion, while deviating from the original conditions of the contract. For example, the lease regulations in the

[111] Al-Wasīṭ, volume 1, p. 720.
[112] Ibid., pp. 720–721.
[113] Al-Qānūn al-Madanī, volume 2, p. 284.

Code established that even if a lease was agreed for a fixed period, either party could request its termination prior to the end of that period, if grave (*khaṭīr*) and unexpected (*ghayr mutawaqqaʿ*) circumstances rendered the implementation of the lease excessively burdensome. Naturally, the party seeking to end the contract was required to pay the other party 'just' compensation.[114] The measure of equity here works in both directions: the lessor is asked to act justly toward the lessee, and, in the same measure, the lessee is also asked to act in the same manner toward the lessor—echoing the principle that justice is the desirable balance. The explanatory notes stated that this clause establishes an important principle—the annulment (*faskh*) of the lease on just grounds, adding that this principle is drawn from the Islamic *Sharīʿa*.

By way of evidence, the explanatory notes quoted the codification of *Murshid al-Ḥayrān*; and the *Majalla*: "If a reason emerges that prevents the execution of the contract, the lease is annulled. If a cook is hired for a wedding and one of the couple dies, the contract is annulled. If a person suffers from toothache and agrees with a dentist that he will remove the tooth for such-and-such a price, and then the pain passes, the contract is also annulled. A contract with a wet-nurse is not annulled on the death of the person hiring the wet-nurse, but it is annulled on the death of the wet-nurse or the child."[115]

This is also the application of the principle of unexpected events. The explanatory notes offered examples of such cases: a lawyer who rented an office and is then obliged to abandon his profession for reasons beyond his control; the death or bankruptcy of the lessee, or his relocation by his employer; or a lease contract that relates directly to the occupation of the lessee, or to other individual characteristics, where his inheritors may request the termination of the contract prior to the agreed date. This clause was drawn from the old Egyptian Code, which stated that "a lease shall not be annulled on the death of the lessor or the death of the lessee, provided that the lease was not on account of the occupation or expertise of the lessee."[116]

Observing the conditions of a lease contract may also be burdensome to the lessor, for example if he undertook to execute building work in the premises and, for unexpected reasons, is unable to complete the

[114] The Egyptian Civil Code, article 608(1); Al-Qānūn al-Madanī, volume 4, p. 597.
[115] Kitāb Murshid al-Ḥayrān, article 677; the Majalla, article 443.
[116] The Egyptian Civil Code, article 602; the *ʾAhlī* civil code, article 391.

work. In such cases, the lessor may request that the premises be vacated, while providing just compensation for the lessee (a further example of the element of mutuality embodied in the test of equity).[117] Lastly, if the financial balance between the undertakings of a person providing work and of a person working by contract terminated for general and unexpected reasons not taken into account when making the agreement, invalidating the foundation on which the financial reckoning in the contract was based, the court may decide to increase the fee or to annul the contract.[118] This provision differs sharply from that in the old Civil Code, which stated that a person who has signed a contract for work may not request an additional fee unless the cost of the work has increased for a reason connected to the provider of the work.[119]

In the deliberations of the Senate, and in the explanatory notes to the proposed Code, it was argued that the doctrine of unexpected events appeared in the Islamic *Sharīʿa* in an extensive form.[120] Sanhūrī wrote that it was derived from the concept of 'necessity' (*ḍarūra*), a central principle in the *Fiqh*; by way of example, he mentioned several principles from the Ḥanafī *Majalla* that relate to the principle of necessity,[121] such as: "Necessity makes the forbidden permissible;" "all that was narrowed expands, that is to say that when one sees a difficulty in a matter, one should ease up and broaden;' "a need, whether general or individual, is seen as a necessity," and so on.[122]

Notwithstanding these references, the source of this doctrine was not the *Sharīʿa*, but the rules and innovations of French law. Indeed, there would seem to be a significant gap between Islamic law and the doctrine of unexpected events. Islamic law, for example, recognizes totally individual grounds as justification (*ʿudhr*) for the termination of a contract, such as the sickness or bankruptcy of the lessee. In contrast, the New Code refers to 'general events'.[123] Why, then, was it important to Sanhūrī to mention the references to the *Sharīʿa*? There

---

[117] Al-Qānūn al-Madanī, volume 4, p. 598.

[118] The Egyptian Civil Code, article 658(4).

[119] The *ʾAhlī* code, article 418.

[120] About the alleged similarity between this doctrine and the spirit of the *Sharīʿa*, see: Wujūb, p. 133.

[121] Ibid., footnote number 1.

[122] The *Majalla*, articles 18, 21; 32.

[123] Hasbū Al-Fazārī, *ʾĀthār al-Ẓurūf al-Ṭariʾa ʿala al-ʾIltizām al-ʿAqdī, Dirāsa Taʾsiliyya wa Taḥlīliyya li-Nazariyyat al-Ẓurūf al-Ṭariʾa fī al-Qānūn wa al-Sharīʿa al-Islāmiyya* (Alexandria: Matbaʿat al-Gīza, 1979).

are two possible reasons: Firstly, on a practical level, his desire may have been to facilitate the passage of this doctrine in the various parliamentary committees, since it was difficult for the deputies to oppose a doctrine that was ostensibly drawn from sacred Islamic law (and, as we have seen above and shall see again below, this argument indeed helped convince recalcitrant deputies in many instances). Secondly, this reference constitutes a manifestation of national legal pride that a modern Western doctrine had been present in local law for centuries, thus proving that the peoples of the Orient are in no way inferior to the Westerners. As we saw above, the doctrine of the abuse of a right was also introduced into the New Code and was presented as ostensibly originating in the *Sharīʿa*.

2.4 *The Doctrine of Exploitation* (al-ʾistighlāl)

A further equitable doctrine in the New Code constituted the development of the principle of *ghabn* as discussed above, and aimed to include an overtly altruistic motive in contract law, providing sophisticated scales for weighing and balancing the parties' obligations.

Sanhūrī drew on a large number of twentieth century civil codes in this respect, selecting the elements he considered the most suited to the society in which he lived.[124] The German civil law considered this type of exploitation to be a moral defect, and hence mandated the invalidation of the entire contract. By contrast, the Egyptian New Code viewed it merely as a defect in the dimension of consent, enabling the nullification of the contract or the amendment of its conditions, as was the case in the proposed Franco-Italian Civil Code of 1928.[125]

The Egyptian New Code stated:

> If the undertakings of one of the parties associating in the contract are completely disproportionate (*lā tataʿādal al-batta*) to the benefit that party would derive from the contract, or to the undertakings of the other party, and it emerges that the exploited party (*al-maghbūn*) entered into the contract because the other party exploited his evident levity or unbridled

---

[124] Article 138 from the German Civil Code; Article 1448 from the Italian Civil Code; Article 42 from the Polish Obligations Law; Article 879 from the Austrian Civil Code; and even Article 74 from the Chinese Civil Code. *Al-Wajīz*, volume 1, p. 14.

[125] The Explanatory Notes of the code proposal, Al-Qānūn al-Madanī, volume 2, pp. 190–191.

> caprice, the judge is entitled to annul the contract in accordance with the request of the discriminated party, or to reduce the undertakings of this party.[126]

The arithmetic concept of usurpation (*ghabn*) in the old code counts how many portions each party receives and examines whether discrimination was present. In order to maintain commercial stability, Sanhūrī preserved some of these objective tests in his New Code. In order to avoid a clash between the old, arithmetic principle of *ghabn* and the new, conceptual interpretation of this term, Article 130 of the Code establishes that the principle of *ʾistighlāl* shall not derogate from those articles in which arithmetic *ghabn* remains by way of an objective yardstick. *ʾIsitghlāl* in the New Code includes two cumulative and flexible tests: the first material (*māddī*) and the second mental (*nafsī* or *dhātī*). The former test examines the imbalance between what a party to the contract gives and what he receives (a calculation that goes beyond the arithmetic, as we shall see below); the latter associates *ʾistighlāl* with the mental test—the element of exploitation of the weaker party. *Al-Wasīṭ* elaborated on these two tests for the model of *ʾistighlāl*. Regarding the material test, for example, it stated that a sale contract does not require complete balance (*taʿādul*) between the undertakings of both parties: one party may be discriminated against, and this will not invalidate the contract. If, however, the imbalance is grave (*ʾikhtilāl fāḍiḥ*), the court may intervene and the material foundation will be present. An example is a person who sells a large and luxurious apartment for a very low price. While this test is objective, it does not constitute a fixed and frozen figure, but varies as circumstances vary, depending on the subject of value.[127] As for the mental test, the interpretative notes stated that this refers to a case when one of the parties exploits the levity of the other (the reference is to desire and greed [*shahwa*], determined the Civil Code Committee in the Senate),[128] his rashness, inexperience or caprice: "And in our Egyptian life, we have (several examples) proving that exploitation is by no means rare, but occurs in daily life." *Al-Wasīṭ* quoted several examples from local case law, such as a case in which an elderly man

[126] The Egyptian Civil Code, article 129(1). The Egyptian Civil Code influenced the other Arab Civil Codes: Syrian, article 131; Libyan, article 130; Iraqi, article 124; Kuwaiti, article 163; Jordanian, article 146.

[127] Al-Wasīṭ, volume 1, p. 394.

[128] Al-Qānūn al-Madanī, volume 2, p. 201.

marries a younger woman ("something which is not uncommon"), and the woman exploits the caprice of the man in order to coerce him to sign contracts favorable to herself and her children; or, in the inverse case, a rich woman marries a young man who exploits her for her money. Other examples include a woman who is forced to 'buy' her freedom from her husband and pay a large sum in return for his consenting to a divorce; a rash young man who inherits a large sum from his parents and is tricked by others into signing contracts in their favor—"all these are examples of disputes that have occurred in Egyptian legal life."[129] Elsewhere, Sanhūrī noted that this was a veritable 'social phenomenon', creating an urgent need for legislative attention.[130]

The compromise presented by the Code in Article 129(1), which is a typical example of Sanhūrī's moral approach, was balanced by the demand for economic stability, in Article 129(2), where a one-year restriction was imposed from the date of signing the contract for the activation of Article 129(1), although the usual statute of limitation in the Code is fifteen years. It could be argued, therefore, that this restriction might substantively harm an owner of a right who was the victim of discrimination, but this illustrates the effort by the Code to create a balance between contractual liberty and equity, and between morality and stability, as the foundations of economic life.[131]

The doctrine of exploitation was the subject of considerable changes and debates during the legislation of the New Code before there was agreement on the final product. This suggests that the Egyptian legislators, particularly in the Senate, were reluctant to adopt the principle. The original proposal created a significantly broader area of defective consent on the part of the discriminated party, when "the discriminated party's need, caprice, lack of expertise or weak perception were exploited or, in general, when it emerged that his consent was not based on adequate freedom of choice."[132] The proposal thus established numerous grounds for identifying the defective consent of the discriminated party, something that naturally acted in his favor. However, this broad format was opposed by many members of the Civil Code Committee in the Senate, on the grounds that it was too generalized and sweeping,

[129] Al-Wasīṭ, volume 1, p. 398; Al-Wajīz, volume 1, p. 148.
[130] Al-Wasīṭ, volume 1, p. 47.
[131] Ibid.
[132] Article 179 in the new code proposal, al-Qānūn al-Madanī, volume 2, p. 190; Al-Wajīz, volume 1, p. 148.

and might impair commercial life and cause instability. The opponents further noted that Egyptian law already had tools for resolving "the limited problems of this type that have been encountered" in Egyptian society (as will be recalled, Sanhūrī claimed that this was no less than a social phenomenon), such as the principles of error, duress and fraud.[133] The president of the Civil Code Committee in *Majlis al-Shuyūkh*, Muḥammad al-Wakīl, argued that it was doubtful whether Egyptian society required this doctrine, since its application restricted the freedom of an individual to reach agreement with whomever he chose, on whatever conditions he saw fit.[134] Another deputy, Ḥilmī ʿĪshī, added that the clause was too general in form and content. He argued that the format should be clear, defined and evident to any person. If a few cases of this kind could be encountered in Egyptian society, this matter was covered by criminal law. He also felt that the adoption of this doctrine would lead to legal instability.[135]

As the committee continued its deliberations, it emerged that a majority of the participants favored the complete deletion of the article. At this stage, ʿAbduh Muḥarram, the representative of the Ministry of Justice (which had tabled the proposed code before the houses of parliament) intervened in the discussions and argued that the doctrine would actually encourage healthy (*salīm*) commerce, since the judge would determine what was proper and healthy for society; he claimed that the article was quite clearly defined in legal terms.[136] The president of the committee remained steadfast in his opposition to the proposed article, claiming that it would encourage legal disputes and demands to disqualify legal actions that had already been performed. When the representative of the Ministry of Justice realized that he was in the minority, he asked to postpone the discussion to another meeting. At the next meeting on the subject of the adoption of this doctrine, the deputy Muḥammad Ḥasan al-ʿAshmāwī defended the proposed clause, claiming that since it was important to protect the weak party in the contract, the Code should not confine itself to specific instances permitting nullification, but should extend these grounds and grant the judges greater discretion. He proposed that the clause be adopted as it had been submitted. Again, however, it became apparent that the

[133] Al-Qānūn al-Madanī, volume 2, pp. 194–196.
[134] Ibid., volume 2, p. 195.
[135] Ibid.
[136] Ibid., pp. 196–197.

majority of those present opposed the adoption of the doctrine, and the meeting was once again adjourned at the request of the government representatives.[137] Dr. Sanhūrī himself attended the third meeting, and the balance of opinion shifted. He argued that there was no real change in the status quo as created by the Egyptian courts; the doctrine merely included in the Code elements that were already present in Egyptian court decisions.[138] We can only note that, once again, this was not the case; the doctrine as included in the Code was more complex and advanced than the rather general and inconsistent rulings of the Egyptian courts. Prior to the adoption of the New Code, the Egyptian courts were obliged to examine the source of their authority in intervening in cases of the usurpation or exploitation of human weaknesses. Sanhūrī acknowledged that judicial attention to these aspects on the basis of the foundations of equity was 'partial; in other cases, solutions were borrowed from French law, which in turn lacked a decisive source of authority for tackling such problems. The Egyptian Supreme Court was reluctant to intervene in such cases and to establish a clear ruling in appeals, due to the legislative lacuna. Thus, for example, the Supreme Court determined that if a sale contract had been nullified due to the defective will of an elderly seller who had succumbed to dictates from his children, there was no room to intervene in the ruling. In another ruling, the Supreme Court decided that if an inferior court had ruled that a document written by a bequeather had been signed of his own free will and choice, this should be respected, and the court would not intervene in the decision. In both cases, these are basic rulings based on the general rules of equity, without the element of complexity and balance found in the sociological theory of *ʾistighlāl*.[139]

As we have seen, however, this was the approach Sanhūrī adopted when attempting to persuade the Civil Code Committee to accept doctrines it found unpalatable: to argue that they originated in the *Sharīʿa*, or were already present in Egyptian case law. In most cases, this was only partially true, but it was sufficient to convince the deputies. Accordingly, the committee decided unanimously to adopt the doctrine, while reducing the mental element: of the various grounds for exploitation, only 'levity' and 'caprice' remained. In order to restrict the scope of

[137] Ibid., pp. 197–200.
[138] Ibid., p. 200.
[139] Judgment from 2 January 1941; Al-Wasīṭ, volume 1, pp. 398–399.

the doctrine still further, it was noted that the levity must be 'visible' and the caprice 'unbridled'.[140]

The explanatory notes to the proposed Code again mentioned the *Sharīʿa* as one of the sources of this doctrine.[141] They argued that there, too, two tests—objective and mental—were applied. However, even a cursory review of the *Majalla* shows that the test in the *fiqh* was less sophisticated than the doctrine of *ʾistighlāl* in the New Code, and it is doubtful whether it can be attributed to the doctrine of exploitation. The Hanafite *Majalla* mentioned two terms in this context: gross fraud (*ghabn fāḥish*), which was supposedly the material element, and deception, which was supposedly the subjective or mental element. Here, though, the only possibilities were the nullification or the observance of the contract—the entire element of balance, which is the core of the theory of *ghabn* in *ʾistighlāl* in particular, and in the New Code in general, was absent. "If someone deceives another, and it transpires that the sale includes gross deception, the plaintiff may annul the sale," determines the *Majalla*.[142] However, "in a sale that entails gross deception but not through fraud, the plaintiff may not annul the sale."[143] These tests in the *Majalla*, which the explanatory notes attempted to attribute to the new doctrine, seem to belong more to the rules of deception, duress and fraud than to that of exploitation.

2.5 *The Principle of Good Faith* (Ḥusn al-Nīyya)

A further general principle "that extends its shadow over the law of all contracts" (and the Code's intention here seems to have been to emphasize that it did not replicate the distinction found in the Roman legal system between *contrats de droit strict* and *contrats de bonne foi*, as part of the distinction between the laws of equity and general laws),[144] and which was presented by the New Code as having preferential normative significance, is that of good faith (*bona fide*). "The contract is to be observed in accordance with its content and in a manner consonant with

---

[140] Al-Wasīṭ, volume 1, p. 397.

[141] Al-Qānūn al-Madanī, volume 2, p. 190. Reference to the Egyptian-Ḥanafi codification, *Kitāb Murshid al-Ḥayrān*, article 300, and the Majalla, article 356.

[142] Majalla, article 357.

[143] Ibid., article 356.

[144] The Explanatory notes of the code proposal, Al-Qānūn al-Madanī, volume 2, p. 288; A. Biscardi, "Epieikeia and Aequitas: History of Law", in A. M. Rabello (ed.) *Aequitas and Equity: Equity in Civil Law and Mixed Jurisdictions*, p. 8.

the obligation of good faith," stated the Code—an innovation, since the principle of good faith had not been included in the old *ʾAhlī* code.[145] The Code saw this not only as a subjective (*dhātī*) principle, constituting a basic moral restriction on the freedom of contractual association, but also as an educational norm: contracts are to be observed fairly, without intent to deceive, defraud or mislead. The logic behind this clause is important in understanding the manner in which the function of the Code as a whole was perceived: drawing a minimum moral line beyond which the court would not permit deviation. *Al-Wasīṭ* saw this moral principle as an active and even militant yardstick in opposing 'bad faith' (*sūʾ al-nīyya*, in Latin *mala fide*), the opposite of good faith. "This principle fights bad faith and strikes those who belittle the [principles of] morality," it noted.[146] Whereas in the past contract law was perceived as strict and rational, manifesting an individualistic and capitalist world view, these laws have now lost their arbitrary and sharp character and have become flexible, less sharp, and reflective of an altruistic and moral world view. The principle of perfect and precise implementation has been replaced by the demand for implementation in good faith, and, as a result, the contract is a dynamic and changing entity. The principle of good faith enables civil law to overcome the gap between the individualism of contractual liberty (and the rigidity that sometimes accompanies this) and the philosophy of the welfare state and consumer society.

Due to the less central status of this doctrine, comparing to the previous doctrines, the Code did not specify any immediate or direct sanctions against those who were declared to be acting in bad faith, as it had done in the case of the previous doctrines. Rather, the principle of good faith was positioned as meeting a service of selection and classification: one party would enjoy the advantages of observance in good faith, and might then gain benefits, or at least the support of the law; while another would be subject to the sanctions for deception or the abuse of a right.[147] The Code explicitly noted several specific cases in which the principle of good faith might support and benefit a party in observing its obligations.[148] For example, a debtor who in good faith failed to meet his obligations promptly—might be granted

[145] The Egyptian Code, article 148(1); al-Qānūn al-Madanī, volume 2, p. 288.
[146] Al-Wasīṭ, volume 1, pp. 127–128.
[147] Al-Wasīṭ, volume 1, p. 702.
[148] Ibid., p. 701.

an extension by the court;[149] or a party required by contract to pay compensation to a creditor on account of damage caused, in which the level of compensation was not determined in the contract or in law, might, if the damage were caused in good faith, pay compensation limited to the possible damage that was anticipated at the time of making the contract.[150] As in other cases, when the Civil Code Committee began to discuss the doctrine, objections were raised. The protocols note the objection of two deputies, ʿAshmāwī and ʿĪshī, who gave two reasons: firstly, the principle binds the parties to the contract to aspects that are 'between the lines', as they put it, thus creating an undesirable element of contractual uncertainty. Secondly, it granted a dangerous mandate to the court, which would be able to add to the parties' undertakings—something that contradicts the principle of the sanctity of contracts, which is also specified in the New Code. Their position was rejected and, after a minor amendment, the clause was adopted and became law.[151]

2.6 *The Need for Balance in a 'Contract of Obedience'*

A 'contract of obedience' is a dictated contract made between two unequal parties, such as an individual and a large company. The individual grants complete consent and is unable to raise arguments or introduce changes. This is a uniform contract, whose conditions were determined in advance by one party to serve as conditions in numerous contracts between itself and persons unspecified in number and identity.

Contracts of this type were first introduced into Egyptian law through the New Code, which believed that this would make a significant contribution to the Egyptian economy. The explanatory notes to the proposed Code noted that, in modern civilization, the law must recognize this type of contract due to technological advances and the need for mass contracts (e.g. for electric, water and gas companies).[152] However,

[149] The Egyptian Civil Code, article 346(2).

[150] Ibid., article 221(2).

[151] Al-Qānūn al-Madanī, volume 2, p. 289; Al-Wajīz, volume 1, pp. 251–252. The Egyptian Civil Code influenced the other Arab Civil Codes: Syrian, article 149(1); Libyan, article 148(1); Iraqi, article 150(1); Kuwaiti, article 197 (with minor addition: "and respecting commerce"); Jordanian, article 202(1).

[152] Al-Qānūn al-Madanī, volume 1 p. 245, volume 2 p. 68; Al-Wajīz, volume 1, pp. 81–83.

the ambivalent attitude of the Code to this type of contract may be seen from the Arabic name chosen to describe them: the concept of a contract of 'obedience' or 'submission' (*'idh'ān*) carries negative connotations,[153] as opposed to the positive term 'affiliation contract' (*contrat d'adhésion*) employed in French law—someone who receives such a contract affiliates to it without argument. This term was coined by the French scholar Saleilles, who exerted a strong influence on Sanhūrī, though apparently not with regard to the terminology for the uniform contract.[154] The New Code defined these contracts as ones in which acceptance was confined to consent to set conditions presented by the proposing party, which was not willing to enter into discussions on the matter. Such a definition predictably created a dilemma in terms of the aspiration to equity and contractual balance embodied in the New Code, "and due to this reason, of coerced acceptance, we have termed this type of contract a contract of obedience," Sanhūrī noted.[155]

How did the New Code reconcile its altruistic and moral purpose with the need to accept contracts of obedience, which by their nature perpetuate unequal contractual relations between strong and weak parties? As we have come to expect, the Code sought to mitigate the enormous strength enjoyed by those drafting such contracts, establishing that:

> If the contract of obedience includes discriminatory conditions (tantamount to the abuse of a right—*ta'assufiyya*—*G.B.*), the judge is entitled to amend these conditions, or to exempt the discriminated party therefrom, in accordance with the requirements of equity. Any agreement contradicting this provision is void.[156]

The explanatory notes stated that this provision provided the court with an effective tool for protecting consumers, for example, from the discriminatory conditions imposed by monopolistic companies (*'iḥtikār*). The court would evaluate and determine whether the condition constituted the abuse of a right (*ta'assuf*); if it determined that this was the case, it could amend the condition in order to remove the *ta'assuf.* It could

[153] A discussion whether a uniform contract is indeed a contract: Al-Wasīṭ, volume 1 pp. 246–247.

[154] Al-Wasīṭ, volume 1, p. 245 footnote number 1.

[155] The Egyptian Civil Code, article 100; Al-Wasīṭ, volume 1, pp. 245–246, footnote number 1.

[156] The Egyptian Civil Code, article 149. This article influences the other Arab Civil Codes: Syrian, article 150; Libyan, article 149; Iraqi, article 167(2); Kuwaiti, article 81; Jordanian, article 204.

also nullify the contract or exempt the weaker party from observance. The legislature did not establish any limits for judges in this respect, apart from the principle of 'the requirements of equity' and the parties themselves could not deprive the judge of this authority, since this would invalidate the contract as being contrary to public order.[157] Moreover, the Code further established a categorical instruction to the court that obscure sentences in contracts of obedience should not be interpreted to the disfavor of the weaker party.[158] The explanatory notes to the proposed Code noted that the stronger of the two parties (whether this was the creditor or the debtor) was obliged and able to present clear conditions to the weaker party; if it failed to do so, it would be considered responsible for this obscurity, and the interpretation of the contract of obedience would be to its disfavor.[159] Accordingly, this last provision of the Code is intended not only to provide the court with guidance in interpreting contracts of obedience, but also to function as a Sword of Damocles over the head of any strong party—any attempt on its part to obscure the formula of the contract, whether deliberate or not, will be interpreted against it. Thus the stronger party will be careful not to introduce obscure or vague clauses, or to exploit its strong or monopolistic status, since in so doing it is liable to injure itself.

2.7 *Localized Intervention of Justice in the New Code*

In addition to the five doctrines of equity presented above, which are designed to float above the contract laws in the Code, enlightening them with the glow of honesty, fairness and even compassion, the Code also left a mark of localized justice on dozens of specific articles—and, as we shall see below, this was not confined to the field of contract law. The following examples illustrate the altruistic and moral attitude of the Code, which sought wherever possible to stand by the weak, whether by eliminating norms that had previously prevailed in the law; adding new and hitherto unknown norms, such as protection of the consumer; or by altering the interpretation of existing norms.

---

[157] Al-Wasīṭ, volume 1, p. 250.

[158] The Egyptian Civil Code, article 151. This article influences the other Arab Civil Codes: Syrian, article 152; Libyan, articles 150–153; Iraqi, article 167(3); Kuwaiti, article 82; Jordanian, article 240.

[159] The Explanatory Notes of the code proposal, Al-Qānūn al-Madanī, volume 2, p. 300.

2.7.1 *Annulment of the sale subject to a right of redemption* (Bayʿ al-Wafāʾ)—this is an example of a case in which the Code intervenes in contractual liberty in order to solve an economic, social and even demographic problem. In Muslim society, a type of sale contract, known as sale subject to a right of redemption (*bayʿ al-wafāʾ*) was common, whereby the owner of the asset (usually real estate), requiring cash urgently, sold the property at a reduced value, but, in return, it was stated in the sale contract that the seller could return the money paid to the purchaser and receive possession and ownership of his asset within a given period of time, if he met agreed conditions.[160] The inclusion of this type of sale in the old Egyptian codes was one of the additions not found in the original, i.e., in the Code Civil. The period of time established in the old *ʾAhlī* civil code for this sale contract to be completed and forfeited was up to five years; the old Mixed Code limited the period of this sale to two years at the most.[161] The Ḥanafī *Majalla* recognized this sale, and defined as "a sale including a condition of the return of the sold item by the purchaser when the price is repaid."[162] The *Majalla* also detailed the laws of this institution: "In a sale subject to a right of redemption, the seller may repay the price and demand the sold item back. Equally, the purchaser may return the item and demand the price back."[163] During the period of this sale, the status of the asset is effectively frozen; hence these years are wasted in terms of the tradability and transferability of the asset: "neither the seller nor the purchaser may sell to another any item sold by (this type of) sale," and "as long as the purchaser has not repaid his debt, his creditors cannot touch assets in (this) sale."[164] It is important to note that Ḥanafī Islamic law was already less than enthralled with this form of sale, which it considered a necessity. Indeed, in the clause on the principle of need in the *Majalla* ("a need, whether general or individual, is considered an essentiality"), the *Majalla* noted that "for this reason, the sale subject to a right of redemption has been permitted. When debts abounded among the people of Bukhārā, it was considered necessary to validate such transaction".[165]

---

[160] This kind of sale was accepted in the old *ʾAhlī* code, article 338.

[161] Al-Qānūn al-Madanī, volume 4 pp. 164–168, especially p. 165. *ʾAhlī* code articles 338–347.

[162] The Majalla, article 118.

[163] Ibid., article 396.

[164] Ibid., articles 397, 403.

[165] Ibid., article 32.

In Egyptian society, and particularly from the 1930s onwards, a period of protracted economic crisis, this type of return sale became a trap for many Egyptians. Small landowners became impoverished and required cash, and offered their land for sale by the sale subject to a right of redemption method, in the hope that they would be able to repurchase it after the waiting period. Accordingly, they sold the land at a cheap price, sometimes far below its actual value. In most cases, however, in an era of inflation and frequent crises, the landowners did not manage to raise the required sum. As a result, they not only lost their land, which had defined their social status and provided a livelihood for their families for generations, but they also receive a paltry sum in return. Thus this institution became a form of exploitation, pawning in disguise, but without any protection or rules favoring the exploited seller. Speculators preferred the return sale method since they incurred no risk and could only gain, gaining control of land cheaply[166] and in what Ziadeh termed a 'devious' manner.[167] The more *fallaḥūn* that lost their land, the greater the flow of villagers forced to move to the big city in the hope of finding a livelihood. Thus a legal problem was transformed into a social and even demographic one. The authors of the Code were well aware of the lamentable economic and social results of this type of sale contract. The dilemma they faced was whether to leave the method intact, since the public would in any case continue to employ it even if it were removed from the statute books, but to regulate its rules and introduce an element of justice, or to abolish it completely. Sanhūrī advocated the former approach, for practical reasons. He explained to the Civil Code Committee that an amended arrangement, taking into account the rights of all parties, was preferable to 'unbridled illegality'.[168] Some members of parliament supported the status quo, despite the criticism of this institution, claiming to speak from the standpoint of the liberty of the weak. The deputies ʾAḥmad Ramzī and Jamāl al-Dīn ʾAbāẓa argued that this was an existing legal and commercial tool, and its elimination would restrict the economic freedom of small landowners. Without this tool, the small landowner would be obliged to sell his plot immediately and in totality, due to his need for money, whereas at least this system offered the option to

[166] Al-Qānūn al-Madanī, volume 4, p. 178.

[167] F. Ziadeh, *Law of Property in the Arab World: Real Rights in Egypt, Iraq, Jordan, Lebanon and Syria*, p. 19. On this kind of social phenomenon: Baer, Landownership, p. 34.

[168] Al-Qānūn al-Madanī, volume 4, pp. 173–174.

regain the land in the future.[169] After deliberation, a majority emerged of those seeking to eliminate this type of contract. A vote was held in which the committee members voted for the complete elimination of this sale mechanism. In its summary report, the Civil Code Committee appointed by the Senate noted:

> The committee decided unanimously that this type of sale does not meet the true need for financial transactions, and is no more than an unstable means of guarantee, a pawning in disguise, ending in the loss of the seller's assets for a low and poor price. Those who actually employ *bay' al-wafā'* do not receive a price commensurate with the value of the sold item: in most cases, they receive the amount of money they require, even if this is very low compared to the value of the sold item. They usually hope to raise funds before the end of the period, but if this passes, they have lost their land without even receiving due remuneration. Thus they are exploited, and the law should distance them from this danger. Accordingly, the texts relating to *bay' al-wafā'* were deleted (from the Code), and a general provision was added prohibiting this form of sale in any manner. Accordingly, the debtor and creditor will have no recourse but to pawning or another form of guarantee regulated by law to ensure the rights of each one, without *ghabn*.[170]

In order to discourage the unlawful use of this institution in the future, the Code explicitly established, in a general clause, that if, during a sale, the seller reserved the right to regain the sold item within a given period, the sale was void.[171] This issue also has a social lesson, from which we may learn about the world view of the authors of the Code. The elimination of the institution of *bay' al-wafā'* reflected a sense of justice and concern for the weak, and the altruistic spirit of the New Code can thus be seen to have been accepted by all those involved in the deliberations: members of parliament (all members of the landowning elite), senior jurists and judges. The arguments of both camps—those supporting the continuation of this type of sale and those opposing it—essentially related to the best interests of the weaker members of society. Each side declared that its arguments were those that would best help the weak. In other words, the social need and even imperative for the strong to intervene on behalf of the weak in the case of the *fallaḥ* and the small landowner had already come to be accepted

[169] Ibid., pp. 171–172.
[170] Ibid., volume 1, pp. 137–138.
[171] The Egyptian Civil Code, article 465.

by the elite by the last stages of the enactment of the Code, i.e. in the late 1940s, and was no longer the avant-garde position of a handful of individuals, but the dominant discourse.

2.7.2 *Doubt is to be interpreted in the debtor's favor*—in the case of doubt (*shakk*) as to the versions of the creditor and the debtor relating to the contract between them, the Code stated that such doubt was always to be interpreted in the debtor's favor (*yufsar al-shakk fī maṣlaḥat al-madīn*).[172] In most cases, the debtor was the weaker party and the one more in need of legal protection. The explanatory notes to the proposed Code, and *Al-Wasīṭ* explained that this was a fundamental principle found in most codes that argues that the norm is the absence of debt and the exception is debt, and "one does not extend the exception". Accordingly, the burden of proof rested on the creditor to prove the debt to which he was entitled. If he failed to do so, the debtor had the right to the benefit of the doubt.[173] In another context, Sanhūrī noted that "we see that the New Code, through its character, protects the debtor, and its character is thus the opposite of that of the old code, which was concerned with the protection of the creditor."[174]

2.7.3 *Restriction of the right of* ʾikhtiṣāṣ—this point relates to a judicial decision in which the creditor who is in possession of a court ruling asks to impose a lien on the debtor's land in order to guarantee payment of the debt. This is not a contractual right, but is presented here in order to illustrate the element of justice that was applied on a localized basis throughout the Code. In the past, in keeping with the individualistic and capitalist orientation of the Old Code, this right was virtually unlimited, ignored the rights of the debtor and, accordingly, was unilateral and could be accepted in court without the presence or consent of the debtor.[175] In keeping with the moral world view of

---

[172] The Egyptian Civil Code, article 151. This article influences the other Arab Civil Codes: Syrian, article 152; Libyan, article 153; Iraqi, articles 166–167; Kuwaiti, article 194; Jordanian, article 240, Yemenite, article 209.

[173] The Explanatory notes of the code proposal, Al-Qānūn al-Madanī, volume 2, p. 299; Al-Wasīṭ, volume 1, p. 686.

[174] Al-Wasīṭ, volume 1, pp. 111, 660. The source of this article is the *ʾAhlī* code, article 140.

[175] About the *ʾikhtiṣaṣ* see al-Qānūn al-Madanī, volume 7, pp. 156–188; Ziadeh, Law of Property, pp. 77–78.

the New Code, the explanatory notes to the proposed Code did not hide their disapproval at the lack of limits to this legal decision and its unbalanced nature (even if the creditor held a ruling against the debtor). They argued that it caused deprivation (*ʿanat*) to the debtor. The decision was taken in the debtor's absence, related to land that was often worth far more than the amount of the debt, and, in order to remove the lien, the debtor was required to pursue a protracted and complex legal course.[176] In many cases, the creditors were quick to seize the debtor's land in order to secure their standing both with this specific debtor, and with other creditors, since their ability to collect their debt would be reduced if they failed to seize the debtor's land.[177]

Applying its logic of balance, the Code did not abolish this procedure, but "amended its distortions;"[178] since, according to the logic of the Code, the procedure of *ʾikhtiṣāṣ* was required as a form of guarantee for the debt—something that is important—but in an amended form that also paid attention to the rights of the debtor.[179] Accordingly, the Code 'amended' the procedure for the adoption of *ʾikhtiṣāṣ*, adding a mental element of equity and restricting the form of the procedure. The court would grant the creditor the requested lien only if this request were made in good faith, due to genuine concern as to the debtor's actions, in which case he would receive his security and be reassured. The previous code had included no such condition, thus, as noted above, creating an incentive for any debtor to demand an immediate and sweeping lien on the debtor's land.[180] The Code also restricted the quantity of real estate that could be seized by the creditor,[181] and the debtor himself, or any other interested party, was allowed to request that the court confine the lien to part of the land, or transfer it to alternative land of sufficient value to ensure the debt.[182] Lastly, as an additional measure of consideration for the debtor, the court was to inform him of the *ʾikhtiṣāṣ* on the same day on which the *ex parte* decision was granted, in order to enable the debtor to appeal by an accelerated procedure (a possibility that was also absent in the former code).[183]

[176] Al-Qānūn al-Madanī, volume 7, p. 152.
[177] Ibid.
[178] Al-Wasīṭ, volume 1, p. 82.
[179] Al-Qānūn al-Madanī, volume 7, p. 153.
[180] The Egyptian Civil Code, article 1085.
[181] Ibid., article 1088.
[182] Ibid., article 1094.
[183] Ibid., articles 1091–1092.

A further substantive change introduced in the New Code was that after the death of the debtor, the creditor could not impose a lien on his land included in the estate,[184] since following the death of the debtor there was no longer any need to seize land in order to ensure the debt: a dead man cannot sell his land, and his inheritors could not do so until they had paid all the debts of the estate (in accordance with an important principle introduced by the Code that *lā tarika ʾilā baʿd sadād al-dayn*, i.e., the distribution of the estate to the inheritors shall come only after the removal of the deceased's debts).[185]

2.7.4 *Restriction on loans interest*—in difficult economic times, the New Code considered the needs of weak individuals obliged to take loans, including with regard to interest rates. In accordance with the moral approach, the Code reduced the level of legal interest from 5 percent to 4 percent in civil matters, and from 6 percent to 5 percent in commercial affairs. If both parties agreed to deviate from the legal interest, the agreed rate of interest could not be greater than 7 percent, in order to protect borrowers from excessive interest in cases when they had no choice but to agree to the proposed rate. The need to reduce interest rates and enforce the legal rate was acute, since citizens had been obliged to take loans at very high interest rates due to the exacerbating economic situation. By way of example, we learn that an interest rate of 7.5 percent was considered relatively low.[186] This issue was not only of economic importance but was also important socially, since the banks, which lent money during the 1930s and 1940s, employed harsh means in order to collect the debts on their loans. For example, Mayfild writes:

> In an attempt to ensure the success of debt collection, the Agricultural Credit Bank established Village Committees consisting of the *ʿumda*, the

---

[184] Ibid., article 1085(2).

[185] Ibid., articles 875–882; Ziadeh, p. 78; Al-Qānūn al-Madanī, volume 6, pp. 200–204.

[186] The Egyptian Civil Code, articles 226–227; J. Mayfield, "Agricultural Cooperatives: Continuity and Change in Rural Egypt," in S. Shamir (ed.) *Egypt from Monarchy to Republic, A Reassessment of Revolution and Change* (Boulder: Westview Press, 1995), p. 89. The articles mentioned were used in the 1980s by Islamists to argue that the New Civil Code is not Islamic enough, as Islamic law does not permit the charging of interest. See in this regard: ʿAbd al-Munʿim Al-Sharabīnī, *Al-Mawsūʿa al-Shāmila li-ʾAḥkām al-Maḥkama al-Dustūriyya al-ʿUlya* (Cairo: publisher and year not mentioned), volume 1, pp. 251–264, 282–293.

> *sarraf* (bookkeeper) and the *shaykh al-balad* (village headman). These officials were required to maintain detailed files on farmers borrowing money from the bank and were often quite willing to use strong-arm tactics to collect due debts.[187]

This protective measure was provided on the basis of a paternalistic principle, as noted by the authors of the Code: "To protect the weak (even) from themselves". Villagers and laborers might be tempted or obliged to take loans that they had little chance of meeting.[188] Again with the weak in mind, the Code further established that any commission (*ʿumūla*) or benefit of any kind conditioned by the creditor and which, when combined with the agreed interest rate, deviated from the set limit proscribed by law would be considered 'covert interest' (*fāʾida mustatara*) and would be liable to reduction, unless it were proved that this commission was given in return for an actual service performed by the creditor, or that the benefit was lawful.[189]

2.7.5 *Protection of the consumer in liability suits* (daʿwa al-ḍamān)—for the first time in Egyptian—and indeed Arab—law, the New Code introduced norms relating to consumer protection, which it included under the principle of protecting the weak. The old Egyptian civil code had enabled a purchaser to file a suit on the grounds of liability on account of concealed defects in a product sold, but only within eight days from the date on which he learned of the faults; thereafter, this right would be lost,[190] "and this is an excessively short period," the explanatory notes opined.[191] Indeed, the New Code reversed the approach of its predecessor adopting a consumer-oriented approach that transferred the burden from the purchaser to the seller. Henceforth, the seller, rather than the buyer, would be required to exercise caution. The 'purchaser' was now also a 'consumer'—a new collective term introduced into Egyptian civil law by the Code. The New Code changed the legal mechanism, enabling a purchaser to file a liability suit during one year from the date of delivery of the purchased item (or more, if the seller agreed); thereafter, however, the purchaser could no longer file suit for

[187] Mayfild, p. 89.
[188] Al-Wasīṭ, volume 1, p. 435.
[189] The Egyptian Civil Code, article 227(2).
[190] The *ʾAhlī* code, Article 324, Al-Qānūn al-Madanī, volume 4, p. 122 (*caveat emptor*).
[191] Al-Wasīṭ, volume 1, p. 77.

liability, even if he only discovered the concealed defect after the end of the year. If, however, the seller's behavior included an element of deception, i.e., if he deliberately concealed the defect from the purchaser, the statute of limitation would return to the usual period in the Code—fifteen years. By special agreement, the parties could extend, limit or annul the liability on a product, but any condition restricting or annulling the liability would be void if the seller deliberately and purposefully concealed defects in the product.[192]

The explanatory notes to the proposed Code clarified that, in balancing the interests, the scales tipped toward the consumer; equally, however, commercial stability would be maintained, since the seller would only face the risk of legal suit for one year. This article relates not only to the immediate protection of the purchaser, but also to the future protection of consumers in general, since the threat here to dishonest sellers is evident—through their own actions, they would be liable to extent the period in which they could be sued, and hence they would be careful to avoid deception.[193] The logic behind this mechanism recalls the principle that the interpretation of a contract favors the party bound by the obligations. In an additional balancing measure between justice and commercial stability, the New Code reckoned the one year period from the date of delivery—a fixed date on which there should not ostensibly be any debate—rather than on the date on which the purchaser learned of the defect (as in the old code), a fluid date that might, in principle, come years thereafter.[194]

2.7.6 *Protection of the* safīh—*A new legal composition*—Another form of protection of the 'weak' that may be noted relates to the rules of legal capacity (*'ahliyya*) in the Code, and reflected the realities of a society that was essentially illiterate, and most of whose members lacked sufficient knowledge of the law. The reference is to the problem of the prodigal (*al-safīh*) or the imbecile (*dhi al-ghafla*)—illiterate and naïve citizens who could easily be exploited.[195] The dilemma was how to protect these individuals in accordance with the principle of 'seizing the hand of

---

[192] The Egyptian Civil Code, articles 452–453; Al-Qānūn al-Madanī, volume 4, pp. 121–125.

[193] The Explanatory notes of the code proposal, Al-Qānūn al-Madanī, volume 4, pp. 123–124.

[194] Ibid., volume 4, p. 123.

[195] The *Safīh* does not lacking legal capacity. For this aim the Code attributed article 114.

the weak' and protect those who placed confidence in such individuals and entered into binding legal associations with them, on the one, while, on the other and, minimizing the damage to commercial stability and financial life. The old civil code remained silent on this issue, thus leaving it to the courts to protect the *safīh* without any statutory instructions. In general, the Egyptian courts tended to annul the legal actions of the *safīh*, who might enter into an agreement with a trickster or someone planning to deceive him and take his money.[196]

Before the era of the New Code, at least three legal approaches could be seen to the problem of the *safīh* in the Islamic *fiqh* (i.e. in the *Sharīʿa*). These approaches were known to the author of the Code, but he preferred to develop a legal construction of his own.

Sanhūrī noted the approach of the *fiqh* scholar, ʾImām ʿAbū Yūsif, who argued that once a *safīh* had been declared as such by the court, his actions were void; this voiding was not retroactive. By contrast, ʾImam Muḥammad ʾIbn al-Ḥasan (both these imams were disciples of ʾAbū Ḥanīfa, the founder of the Hanafite school of interpretation of the *fiqh*),[197] argued that from the moment signs appeared that the individual was a *safīh*, rather than the moment when the court declared him so to be, his actions were completely void.[198] Like ʾAbū Yūsif, the *Majalla* also relied on the court decision, which it called a 'disqualification'. Once the *safīh* had been disqualified, "his possessions are tantamount to those of a discerning minor"[199] (see below), and "his possessions do not exist, but his possessions from before his disqualification are as the possession of any person."[200] Lastly, "if a *safīh* who was disqualified sold any of his assets, the sale shall not go ahead. But if the judge thinks that any benefit may be derived from such sale, he may validate it."[201]

---

[196] Wujūb, pp. 90–91.

[197] The Ḥanafī school of law is widespread among Muslims in Egypt, Turkey, Iraq, Syria, Lebanon and Jordan. This doctrine was developed by two students of Abu Ḥanīfa, the founder of this school. The two students are ʾAbu Yūsif and Muḥammad bin al-Ḥasan. The former was the *khalīfa* Councilor and head of judges. He was responsible for new legal regulations and according to his advice, courts were established in every city. The latter student was the head of a *Madrasa* in Baghdad. He was taught Islamic law and religion for three years in Madina by Malik bin ʾAnas, and was therefore closely affiliated with the tradition, unlike ʾAbu Ḥanīfa. The two students are no less important than their teacher, and in cases of disagreements between them and their teacher their views took precedence. When there is disagreement between the two, the court will rule according to justice and equity.

[198] Wujūb, pp. 90–91.

[199] The Majalla, article 990.

[200] Ibid., article 991.

[201] Ibid., article 993.

The New Code created a new legal composition that blends and adds to all these approaches, and may be considered more flexible than its predecessors. The Code established the declaration by the court of the defective legal capacity of the *safīh* (*qarār al-ḥajar*) as the defining point in terms of his legal actions. If *taṣarruf*, i.e., legal disposition, took place after this declaration, the fate of the transactions would be the same as that of the actions of a discerning minor (*ṣabī mumayyaz*), i.e. they would be valid if they were fully in his favor, and invalid if they were fully to his disfavor.[202] If the *taṣarruf* took place prior to the *qarar al-ḥajar*, it would not be voided or open to voiding unless it was the result of exploitation (*ʾistighlāl*) or of a plot. This ensured a greater measure of flexibility, since transactions were not automatically nullified, and attention was also given to the other party and his mental foundation during the period prior to the declaration. The entire mechanism was supervised by the court in accordance with the parameters outlined above, and the *safīh* himself received due protection. Thus Sanhūrī developed a completely new model of legal engineering that blends elements from the *Sharīʿa*, the practical approach of the Egyptian courts prior to the Code, and the legal doctrines imported by the Code from Continental law.

2.7.7 *Unlawful enrichment*—the doctrine of unlawful enrichment (*ʾithrāʾ bilā sabab mashrūʿ*) is a characteristic manifestation of the sociological approach of the New Code, which emphasizes the element of equity, as opposed to the individualistic orientation of the old Egyptian civil codes and of the French Code Civil, in which this doctrine was not found. The Arab legal term *ʾithrāʾ* may be translated as 'enrichment', as in the English term and in German (*ungerechtfertigte Bereicherung*).

The New Code established that "every person, even someone who is legally incapacitated, who secures unlawful enrichment without legal cause at the expense of another, is obliged to compensate his fellow for the loss so caused, within the limits of profit. This liability shall exist even if the profit later disappears".[203] The Egyptian jurists determined that this principle comprised three components: enrichment without legal justification; the creation of a loss (*ʾiftiqār*) on the part of the other; and proof of the causal connection (*rābiṭa ṣababiyya*) between the enrich-

[202] The Egyptian Civil Code, articles 111, 115.
[203] Ibid., article 179.

ment and the loss. Unlawful enrichment might be in money, in kind or in a service; for example, a person who builds on his own land but employs the tools of his fellow. A loss must subsequently be caused to the other party; for example, if a person builds using another person's materials, and the latter person therefore suffers from a shortage of these materials.

Enrichment does not always cause a loss to another person. For example, if a company builds a shopping mall in a commercial area, land prices in the vicinity will soar. The landowners secured enrichment, but no loss was caused to the company, and hence this is not an instance of unlawful enrichment.

Lastly, there must be a causal connection between the enrichment on the one hand and the loss on the other. If a person builds on his own land using materials belonging to another, the causal connection is created by the person securing the enrichment. If a person builds using his materials on land belonging to another person (an instance of *ʾiltiṣāq*—see chapter three), a causal connection is again created, this time by the person who suffers the loss. A similar relationship is also created if a person builds with materials that no not belong to him on land that is not his, and the owner of the said land secures enrichment at the expense of the owner of the materials. Here, it is a third party who creates the causal connection. In any case, it is sufficient to prove that the enrichment would not have been caused without the loss.[204]

3. The Legal Legitimacy for Change: The Gates of Justice

Having examined the manner in which the New Code transformed the perception of 'contractual justice', which it encircled in a tight belt of rules of equity, thereby emphasizing its altruistic world view, we may now ask what sources of legitimacy the Code found for the changes it made in the approach of Egyptian law, and how it established this policy within Egyptian society, with its hitherto individualistic legal and economic agenda. We cannot find a clear or direct answer to this question in the explanatory notes or in the interpretation of the Code,

[204] Al-Wasīṭ, volume 1, pp. 1247–1338; N. Saleh, *Unlawful Gain and Legitimate Profit in Islamic Law: Riba, Gharar and Islamic Banking* (Cambridge: Cambridge University Press 1986).

though a purposeful review of the totality of comments therein may produce an answer. I would argue that, to this purpose, Sanhūrī built a system comprising three flexible components that enjoy normative importance: 'Morality and public order' as an extra-legal norm; 'justice' as a legal norm; and the court as the function charged with defining and operating this system. The dynamics created between these three are as follows: Morality and public order introduce justice into positive civil law, while the court, as the social and legal organ of supervision, must preserve this movement and amend and adjust it as required.

Here, too, the Code sought succor from French law, using the tools it borrowed and the philosophy that lay behind them to advance its purpose in the local Egyptian context. This was not a case of copying, but rather an instrumental and even creative process of borrowing. The two tools used to this end, which are also important for understanding the overall perception of the Code, were public order (*al-niẓām al-ʿām*, or *l'ordre public*) and morality (*al-ʾadāb, les bonnes moeurs*). Understanding these tools in their French context will help us understand their integration in the Egyptian context as achieved by the New Code. René David commented that French law did not see law and order as a goal in their own right, but as tools in the service of a perception of social life and justice. This legal system is careful (or at least claims to be careful) lest an excessive adherence to formalities lead to sacrificing the ends to meet the means.[205] Accordingly, 'public order and morality' (twin expressions that are usually found together in French law), as appearing, for example, in Article 6 of the French Code Civil, form a means for introducing broad value-based norms into the legal system—norms that some consider fundamental social perceptions, and others refer to as natural law.[206] In other words, the Code Civil drew on bridging terms creating connections with abstract moral, philosophical and social value-based concepts, and deliberately included these in the Code, thus casting the element of bridging within the mould of the law. Thus the judge could use these tools to invalidate problematic contracts, arguing not that the contract was rejected for formalistic legal grounds, but rather because this was justified by a general value-based interest—an approach that might provide public legitimacy for the invalidation.

---

[205] David, p. 202.
[206] Ibid., p. 207.

Public order's hallmark is the restriction of individual liberties for the sake of public needs. No society can ignore the requirements of 'public order'; indeed, there are those who argue that the entire purpose of the state is to maintain this concept. On the question of the means that may legitimately be employed in order to maintain public order, however, opinions are divided. An important distinction must be made between the English perception of public order and the French *ordre public*. French scholars and judges agree that this term is relative in nature, and that it changes with changing times and circumstances. They argue that it would be fruitless and indeed dangerous to attempt to define its limits. By contrast, English scholars and judges regularly attempt, as far as possible, to define and reduce the cases in which this concept may be drawn on. An English judge commented that public policy (or public good, in the original) is like a wild horse: once you release it and let go of the reins, you cannot catch it again.[207]

True to the Continental approach, the Egyptian New Code also introduced a normative article performing this bridging function, establishing that: "A contract shall be void if its object contradicts public order or morality".[208]

This book argues that the New Code thereby transformed public order and morality both into a gate through which the movement of justice it sought to engender would pass and into the source of legitimacy for this movement. The interpretation of the Code explained that public order and morality are the gate through which social, economic and moral factors enter (the prevailing law), influencing it and its contexts, and leading it to stride forward in tandem with the social, economic and moral developments of each given generation and society.[209] The explanatory notes to the proposed Code added that this is a 'key entrance' (*manfadh raʾīsī*) for social and moral streams, "so that they may find their way to the law" and there disseminate their ideas.[210] Sanhūrī continued (elsewhere): "the legal principles introduced in the framework of 'public order' are principles with whose help we intend to secure a public, political or social interest relating to the supreme priorities of society (*niẓām al-mujtamaʿ al-ʾaʿla*), those that precede any

[207] David, p. 202. Richardson v. Mellish (1824) 130 E.R. 294; Nicholas, *The French Law of Contract*, pp. 129–132.

[208] The Egyptian Civil Code, article 135.

[209] Al-Wasīṭ, volume 1, p. 437.

[210] Al-Qānūn al-Madanī, volume 2, p. 223.

private interest."[211] The circle is closed when the author of the Code notes that a central example of this supreme principle worthy of passing through the gate is the moral and altruistic principle of protecting the weak as a healthy interest in which all society shares a stake. It should be noted that Sanhūrī drew the element of social bridging from the Code Civil, but chose to introduce into the Egyptian New Code norms that are the opposite of the individual norms of the Code Civil. In other words, he borrowed only the legal and social tool or methodology, but not its content.[212]

Accordingly, it may be understood that to the author of the Code, morality and public order were not synonymous with justice, but were the gate and the legitimacy through which justice might enter. Morality as presented in the New Code is an extra-legal human balance that distinguishes between good and evil, legitimizing the scales of justice that operate within law. The interpretation of the Code noted that:

> This balance is flexible and subject to specific place and time according to the norms to which humans find themselves committed in accordance with the code that regulates their social relations. These behavioral norms are transmitted from generation to generation in accordance with well-rooted customs and practices. Religion exerts a strong influence on the shaping of morality, and the greater the influence of religion in a society, the greater and the more valid the moral criterion.[213]

Public order confirmed that this change was a supreme interest of Egyptian society. Through this logical composition, therefore, the New Code could secure several goals: It bound society to itself, so that it would not appear artificial or divorced; it granted legal and social legitimacy to a new world view that inverted contract law; and it granted judicial discretion to the court, the guard[214] at the gate of public order and morality that decides who may pass and who may not. "This moral gate is particularly flexible", the explanatory notes to the proposed Code proclaimed,[215] while *Al-Wasīṭ* explained that this gate for the passage of theories of justice could be expanded on occasions to permit the intensified entry of justice, or, conversely, could be narrowed.

---

[211] Al-Wasīṭ, volume 1, pp. 434–435.

[212] Ibid., p. 448.

[213] Ibid., p. 436.

[214] "The Egyptian Judgment is the best manifestation of the country's needs", The Explanatory notes of the code proposal, Al-Qānūn al-Madanī, volume 1, p. 18.

[215] Ibid., volume 2, p. 223.

> The framework of public order narrows if individualistic schools gain dominance in society. These schools grant the individual liberty, and the state does not interfere in his affairs, does not protect him if he is weak, and does not restrain his wildness, if he is strong. If, by contrast, social schools gain the ascendancy, such as the Socialist school, then the arena of public order is expanded and the state enters into personal affairs, protecting the weak from the strong and, indeed, protecting the weak from himself, as we have seen in the contracts of obedience and in the theory of *ʾistighlāl* . . . There is no firm base for defining public order, no absolute definition appropriate for every time and place, since public order is a relative factor.[216]

Accordingly, the interpretation of the Code took into account a dimension of dynamism in the gate of morality and public order; the width of this opening varied according to the zeitgeist. As we have seen, the element of justice is also dynamic, since, as defined in the interpretation of the Code, justice is the proper balance between the parties. Thus the Code created a dynamic and evolving system of mutual dependence: morality and public order depend on justice, and justice depends on them; and all three together depend on the society within which they function, which in turn is dependent on them. This entire system passes through the New Code and the court—it is dependent on them as they are on it.

Thus a system of relative social engineering is born which is relative on the horizontal plane: justice is relative, the gate of morality and public order is relative, positive law is relative to its period, the discretion of the court in implementing the Civil Code and positive law is relative; and hence society, which is certainly relative and changing, can change in accordance with the sociological goals of the Code. This is a process of value-based transformation within arenas of change.

Due to the dynamic arenas described above, it emerges that the ideological entrance gate to 'morality and public order' must not, as has been noted, be either excessively closed or excessively open, since:

> Too narrow an opening will prevent social transitions from finding their way to the court, so that the Code and law in general will be disconnected from social developments of the period. At the same time, however, it must not be too wide, since this is liable to threaten the Code's unity, and numerous political, social and moral schools are liable to burst into the legal system, competing for the Code's moral interpretation and, thereby,

[216] Al-Wasīṭ, volume 1, p. 435.

> for the definition of the term 'justice'. Thus, the interpretation of the Code is liable to evolve from one that is homogenous and harmonious to a long list of interpretations frequent in different sectors and separated from the Egyptian public, mutually divided and contradictory.[217]

Assuming that the judge is able to exercise the doctrines of equity that are included in the Code in accordance with the test of the relative balance as discussed above, how is he to analyze the correct 'morality and public order' for our purpose—components that are extra-legal, and regarding which there are no clear doctrines to guide the court? Here, too, the explanatory notes to the Code attempted to provide the judge with certain tools, explaining that there is a constant tension between the objective and conservative character of morality and its fluid and changing dimension. In their opinion, the moral norm is not a subjective criterion subject to the evaluation of the individual, but rather an objective one as customarily applied by people in that society; and customs are, by their nature, conservative and static. At the same time, this is also an unstable criterion that varies according to the development of moral thought in a given civilization, and this is the dynamic criterion. There are some matters, Sanhūrī noted, which were formerly considered contrary to morality and public order, such as life insurance or intervention in the personal affairs of couples, and are now "looked at differently." Conversely, there are matters that are presently regarded as contrary to morality and public order, such as servitude (*ʾistirqāq*) or smuggling, whereas in the past these were not perceived as immoral.[218] In making his decision, the judge should consider the static element of morality and public order, yet he must not forget its dynamic element, constantly examining whether changes have occurred. A prominent example to which the author of the Code sought to allude in the latter category was the 'selfish wildness', legal and economic, of Egyptian society, which he believed could no longer pass the test of morality and public order, thus justifying the transition from the capitalist and individualistic orientation to an altruistic one. The judge now enters "this flexible arena,"[219] and is supposed to determine the validity or invalidity of contracts, and, in so doing, to rule on normative issues of morality and society. The entry of the judge into

[217] Ibid., volume 1, pp. 161, 961.
[218] Ibid., p. 436.
[219] Ibid., p. 437.

this arena testifies, above all, to the broad measure of trust placed in the court by the New Code: it has confidence that the court will be able to translate the basic principles of the code, including the undefined model of morality and public order, into suitable judicial solutions. By virtue of its senior status in society, the court grants legitimacy to the process, while, at the same time, the Code accords added legitimacy to the court, further expanding its discretion. "Let no person think that a judge who rules on a frozen basis and whose hands are shackled to a narrow text can adapt legal provisions for applying justice in changing circumstances . . . Better than these are the flexible criteria that anticipate a future of development and change." The explanatory notes added that the provisions of the Code become tools for the judge in developing the Code on an ongoing basis, using these tools to face changing circumstances and conditions.[220]

Accordingly, the civil judge must perform several interlocking tasks: he must be aware of changing social and legal trends; define, in accordance with the constant changes, the extent of openness of the gate of morality and public order, so that only that which he finds proper and necessary shall enter; and, lastly, absorb the principles of equity that enter through the gate of morality, interpreting, clarifying and applying these principles. This is a complex and fluid arena of morality and justice, and is so flexible and shifting "that the judge [is liable to become] a legislator himself," creating *ab initio*, a phenomenon that is liable to raise alarm from the standpoint of codification legal systems such as the French or Egyptian systems. Indeed, René David notes that the French courts were aware that excessive use of the principles of public order and morality might endanger the security of law, leading to frequent changes and turbulence, and hence employed these principles "in moderation."[221] In other words, I would suggest that the question is one of rhythm and adaptation between the static element mentioned above and the dynamic element. A judge who relies excessively on the static element will create judicial conservatism; conversely, excessive reliance on the dynamic element will cause overly frequent upheavals in the legal system. The Code and its interpretation was confined to offering a warning and guidance to the judge and, in my opinion, they

[220] The Explanatory notes of the code proposal, Al-Qānūn al-Madanī, volume 1, p. 23; Al-Wasīṭ, volume 1, p. 104.
[221] David, p. 203.

did not claim to solve this dilemma for him. Accordingly, the explanatory notes to the proposed Code also stated that the flexible sources of morality and justice would themselves also constitute sources for guiding the judge in interpreting any given case. "The judge has almost become a legislator... but he is restricted to the morality of his age, to the fundamental arrangement of his nation, and to its economic interests."[222] Thus it may be seen that the New Code imposed a heavy burden on the shoulders of the civil judge.

Another source of tension may emerge here, however: a gulf may be seen between the judge's personal world view and what he or others perceive as the social consensus of the period. To this end, the explanatory notes to the proposed Code stated that the judge should be careful not to present his personal positions regarding social justice within the framework of the general principle of public order and morality. The judge should adopt a general school acceptable to society as a whole, rather than a narrow and personal position.[223] The authors of the Code were aware that judges, sometimes even unconsciously, were liable to be bound by their personal beliefs and affiliations in their perception of personal and social justice and morality. Such a situation is problematic in any judicial system, but particularly in one that operates according to a Code which claims for itself a leading social role, and in which the judge is granted the function of a legal and social commander.[224]

[222] Al-Wasīṭ, volume 1, p. 437.

[223] Al-Qānūn al-Madanī, volume 2, p. 223; Al-Wasīṭ, volume 1, p. 436.

[224] As the judge constitutes the engine that operate the Code, and link between the Code and society, Sanhūrī wrote in 1923 that "the judge must study not only the law to maintain the capacities that he needs for his job, but he must also study sociology, economics and finance in a scientific manner" See Diary, 29 September 1923, p. 108.

CHAPTER FIVE

THE DOMINION OF PROGRESS

> We are a nation in dire need of energy and innovation. Our past is like a shabby, worn-out garment that we must shed in order to enter the new world in new garb.
>
> While we advanced by slow steps, the world rushed forward, leaving us behind among the runners, at the back when we were once at the front. Do we aspire to live in the culture of the twentieth century according to the logic of the Middle Ages? Our culture is ancient, our systems are ancient, our social life is ancient, our economic patterns are ancient and our language is ancient. How, then, can we manage in the modern era?
>
> Sanhūrī, *The New and the Old*, 1949[1]

1. The Definition and Scope of Progress

1.1 *Time is Movement*

This chapter argues that alongside the establishment of its first two pillars, namely the pillar of social integrality and solidarity among individuals and classes, and the pillar of protecting and defending the weak within the framework of rules of morality and justice, the New Code also sought to establish the third pillar, one that is at first glance no less pretentious than the first two: to remove obstacles that had hindered economic and social life in Egypt for generations, and, by so doing, to enable strong, dynamic and entrepreneurial forces in the country to move forward to a new Egyptian future. The Code hoped that this would advance Egyptian society as a whole toward the goals of modernization, progress and economic development.

It may now be understood why the first two pillars preceded the third pillar, or had to appear together with it, since the sudden transformation of economic and social frameworks set in a conservative social system

[1] ʿAbd al-Razzāq al-Sanhūrī (as minister of Education), "Al-Jadīd wa al-Qadīm", *al-Hilāl* (1949), special Edition, pp. 6–8.

that operated in accordance with centuries-old customs might threaten the very fabric of that society. Although the Code believed that these frameworks were negative, their dismantling might cause foment among certain circles, such as the religious establishments, which had not only become accustomed to these frameworks, but had even come to define themselves through them.

Accordingly, the first two pillars were important for the authors of the Code, and Sanhūrī in particular, in two respects: not only in order to protect the status quo in the polarized Egyptian society of the 1930s and 1940s and to support the fabric of society, but also in order to enable the new social formula proposed by the Civil Code, which argued that if the Code protected and defended the weak, while at the same time encouraging and stimulating the strong, then it might be possible to maintain and even enhance relations between the different components of society—the strong and the weak, the rural and the urban, and the past and the future. The Code aimed to move all of these social components one step forward, but by binding them all together, social solidarity would not be dismantled, and communal coherence would be maintained and protected. All elements of society would stride forward, but the gap between them would be maintained and even narrowed.

These three pillars should therefore be examined on two distinct levels, as detailed in the next chapter: on the everyday level, in the increasingly polarized Egyptian community; and on the future level, in the vision of a new Egyptian community based on a new formula. This analysis does not claim the existence of a substantive community, in the sense of a defined group of people that may be clearly and sharply delineated; rather, as Benedict Anderson argued, a 'community' is an imaginary group of individuals who imagine a partnership in history, language and geography, and whose borders are therefore blurred and dynamic.[2]

One might argue, therefore, that the goal of the third pillar, on which the New Code was based, is to elaborate and professionalize the tools of private law, and particularly economic law, available to individuals in society, and thereby to increase the level of sophistication of society

[2] B. Anderson, *Imagined Communities: Reflections on the Origin and Spread of Nationalism* (London: Verso, 1991).

as a whole. A further goal is to institutionalize civil legal actions, facilitate their execution, and simplify and encourage economic mobility without impairing economic stability and confidence. To return to the quote from Sanhūrī at the head of this chapter, the goal is to create the revival (*nahḍa*) of Egyptian society and law.[3]

If it would prove possible to overcome the obstacles that hampered the Egyptian economy—such remnants of the past as the question of the *Waqf*, the complex laws of preemption (*shufʿa*), the confused arrangements for the removal of an estate, the absence of orderly rules for bankruptcy in a society facing a protracted economic crisis, the absence of copyright and intellectual property rights, the lack of economic mobility and the absence of mechanisms for the assignment of a debt; or the presence of legal tools that did more damage than good, such as *bayʿ al-wafāʾ*—this would, in accordance with the logic of the Civil Code as we have examined it, yield benefits not only for individual cases, but also for society at large. Commerciability would be enhanced, the economy would be vitalized, and economic, legal and social stability would be improved.

This hope was presented against the backdrop of the grave economic crisis that prevailed during the first half the twentieth century. Liberal intellectuals in Egypt, and not only they, sensed that Egyptian society suffered from social and economic stagnation, in contrast to the dynamic progress in the West; they sensed that the social tools of the Egyptian 'community' were unable to respond to the internal and external shocks that came with the passage of time—a sense that was discussed in detail in the first chapter of this book.[4]

The removal of such obstacles could be achieved only through the introduction of new legal and economic tools capable of courageously tackling the existing economic, social and legal impasse. However, the New Code typically sought to introduce changes while avoiding a full-scale revolution in the social order. The Code addressed areas it considered problematic, but did not seek to eliminate them completely, fearing that this might lead to excessive reactions, as we shall see below in this and the next chapter. "The New Code does not preach revolution

[3] Al-Wasīṭ, volume 1, p. 7.

[4] On the Egyptian lawyers distresses, concerning their social and economic dilemmas see F. Ziadeh, *Lawyers, the Rule of Law and Liberalism in Modern Egypt* (Stanford: Hoover Institution, 1968): "Lawyers as a Liberal Force", pp. 77–98.

and does not create a *coup d'état*", Sanhūrī emphasized in April 1952 (ironically, his comments were made just three months before the revolution of the Free Officers).[5]

In the context of his discussion on progress and the need to adjust to changing circumstances, Sanhūrī also examined the old Egyptian Civil Code, based on the French Code Civil. He emphasized that while the former code was appropriate for its age, it was not suited to the mid-twentieth century.

> There can be no doubt that the Egyptian generation that received this code in the late nineteenth century was happy and pleased with its new code, since this represented a substantial step forward relative to the previous situation, whereby law was in chaos, laws were ill-defined and unknown, and the allocation of justice was deplorable. Chaos was replaced by order and the nation was relieved, sensing that it had entered a new era of reform. No one would claim that the nation thereby instantaneously secured perfection in legislation and in judging. It is enough if we consider the legislation of that age as the harbinger of a new era of true progress[6] . . . And now, after fifty years' experience with the current (legal) regime, its various defects have been exposed . . . We must not accept what our fathers accepted, since time is movement, and to stay in the past is to stagnate.[7]

Sanhūrī continued to present his perception of progress:

> This is the language of progress, which must be heard modestly and with anxiety, [since] progress has a frightening power. It has a dominion before which one must bow one's head, and it has a beauty that quickens the heartbeat. As it races against the old, progress surges ahead, passes the old, waits for it and changes it.[8]

If progress is so frightening, what criteria will guide its introduction in the New Code? Will a simple replication of Western codes be appropriate? And how is the term 'progress' to be defined in the unique context of the Egyptian social environment?

1.2 Takhayyur: *The Functional Test of Progress*

As perceived by ʿAbd al-Razzāq al-Sanhūrī, and hence by the New Code, 'progress' did not, as might have been believed, imply the blind

[5] Al-Wasīṭ, volume 1, p. 6.
[6] Wujūb, p. 20.
[7] Ibid., p. 21.
[8] Al-Jadīd wa al-Qadīm, p. 7.

and automatic copying of Europe and Western modernization; in any case, the former civil code, annulled after the introduction of the New Code, was itself based on the Napoleonic Code. This approach argued that for all its attractions, there was no cause to be dazzled by the glory of Western law, and no need to copy it or to feel dwarfed by its presence. In 1926 Turkey abolished its civil code, the *Majalla*, which was based on Islamic legal codification from the Ḥanafite school, replacing it with the Swiss civil code. The initiators of the Egyptian code sought to avoid such a situation, and hence rejected the Turkish model.

This Egyptian approach argued that Europe, with its legal systems and level of progress, had certainly defined parameters that demanded a response. However, the function of 'Eastern' society (see our discussions of this concept at the beginning of this book) was to address these parameters, providing a response by means of the tools it considered appropriate.[9] "French law has been a gracious guest, but the time has come for the guest to return home," clarified Sanhūrī, emphasizing his ambivalence toward the glory of Western law as an Eastern and as a scholar educated in France. "Our law has hitherto been occupied by foreigners—French foreigners."[10]

The New Code thus perceived progress as the proper functionality for Egyptian life: the legislator was to place the functional arrow on the Egyptian target, and to draw around it the circles of sources based on Egyptian choices and interests. Such progress is a function of the needs of Egyptian society, and is implemented by the members of the Egyptian nation, and not by a foreigner or an occupier.

If we attempt to define this functionality, it appears as the 'new' (*jadīd*) manifested through the motif of *tanāfus*—the motif of movement, dynamism and competitiveness in the stagnant waters of Egyptian society. "Life is based on competitiveness (*tanāfus*), and this is what is meant by the *Qur'ān* when we read: 'Had God not pushed men against one another, the earth would have been destroyed,'" Sanhūrī wrote, once again, ostensibly, finding an Islamic source for an essentially Western idea.[11]

---

[9] On the Easternist attitude in the Egyptian nationalism and on the middle approach of Sanhūrī between Islamic identity and Easternist identity within Egyptian nationalism see: I. Gershoni, J. Jankowski, *Redefining the Egyptian Nation 1930–1945* (Cambridge: Cambridge University Press, 1995) ("Now is the turn of the East: Egyptian Easternism in the 1930s"), pp. 35–53.

[10] Al-Wasīṭ, volume 1, pp. 7–8.

[11] Al-Jadīd wa al-Qadīm, p. 7.

Accordingly, the appropriate term here is not Westernization, nor modernization, nor secularization—nor even 'Egyptization'.[12] What we see is a functionality that crosses frameworks and sources, seeking to secure efficiency and dynamism, embodying elements of all the above-mentioned terms—Westernization, modernization, competitiveness, tradability, secularization and Egyptization—but not synonymous with any one thereof.

Within the Egyptian conceptual world, and particularly in the context of the New Code, Sanhūrī referred to *takhayyur*, i.e., the selection of elements that are positive and appropriate, in terms of a security valve to counter the alarmingly endless nature of progress. While Sanhūrī uses this word in a positive sense, its customary meaning had a negative cultural tone, referring to the blending of distinct items without engaging in the full functional test as discussed in detail in Chapter Two.

This functionality is indeed flexible in character; it may be secured through the use of Western tools, as is often the case in the Code, but local tools may certainly also be employed, drawn from Islamic, Arabic or Egyptian civilization (for example, from the Islamic *Sharīʿa*), and there is no reason why the latter should necessarily give way to the former. Progress may also stem from the past, as we shall see below in several examples, provided, of course, that it meets the new parameters, just as past norms may also be a source of atrophy and decline. The past is not only stagnation—it may also be progress and represent the future, if it meets the parameters defined by the authors of the Code.

According to this test, then, there is no need to fear progress, which is based, above all, on the needs of Egyptian society, and no other society. Progress will serve society through the New Code—society will not serve progress.

This is a substantive test devoid of religious, national or cultural sentiments. Only those elements that are appropriate for the needs of Egyptian society and the removal of the obstacles impeding its economy and society will be adopted by the Code.

In other words, the New Code perceived the term 'progress' as a relative concept—not a detached island of European norms divorced from the local environment, but an ideal that is relative to Egyptian society and connected to its status quo. The Code shapes and confines progress in accordance with its own parameters, and progress in turn

---

[12] Approaching the New Code as *Egyptization* see Hill, p. 74.

shapes and confines the Code according to its parameters. "Our needs for the old exist, as do our needs for the new," Sanhūrī wrote. "The old and the new are both part of life. They may seem contradictory, but they actually complement one another."[13] In this context, Majid Khadduri rightly noted that "A sudden break with the past may not always be the sure way for a nation to leap into a modern phase of progress."[14]

An additional element in understanding the essence of 'progress' in the spirit of the New Code is dialogue as a channel for consent. In other words, progress is not only a goal, but also a way and a means.

The Code does not seek to impose revolutions or dictates, since if any of the various sections of society were to place obstacles in the path of reform, it would be unsuccessful or would later be revoked, thus losing the opportunity to secure the expected benefits for Egyptian society. Accordingly, a mechanism was required for dialogues in parliament, in the press and in the legal community. These dialogues produced agreements which in turn produced legislation. Thus the Code and its authors took into account the interconnecting and diverse interests as these were manifested with regard to each particular legal principle, attempting to forge as wide a consensus as possible—an approach that inevitably required concessions from all sides. A particular legal norm that the authors of the Code felt to be innovative and effective was not always accepted as they presented it, due to opposition in parliament; one example of this was the question of the assignment of a debt, as we shall see below. However, the Code preferred to include only part of a desired norm than to include it in full at the price of coercion or impaired legitimacy.

1.3 *Progress and the* Sharīʿa

In his capacity as the architect of the New Code, Sanhūrī adopted a negative attitude toward the religious *Sharʿī* institutions, which he believed were responsible in part for the degeneration of the Egyptian social system. For example, he would have preferred to abolish the *Sharīʿa* courts,[15] and was critical of the institution of the religious trust (*waqf*), and of the fact that matters of personal status were not include in civil codification, as is usual in civil codes around the world.

[13] Al-Jadīd wa al-Qadīm, p. 7.

[14] Khadduri, p. 234.

[15] N. Brown, "Shariʿa and State in the Modern Middle East", *International Journal of Middle East Studies* 29 (1997), p. 371.

> We see our Code as a single entity; there is no meaning to the division of civil law into two parts, one for interpersonal matters (*muʿāmalāt*) and one for personal status. The modern code must include all matters addressed by such a code, since, in the current situation, half of our (civil) law has not undergone a process of codification . . . We do not imply that our laws of personal status should be drawn from Western legislation—in our case, we must draw these from the Islamic *Sharīʿa* . . . In including the laws of personal status in the civil code, we do not wish to impair the authority of the Islamic *Sharīʿa* but, on the contrary, to expand this law to the civil portion of the Code . . . The inclusion of the laws of personal status in the civil code does not mean the merging of the *Sharīʿa* courts (*al-maḥākim al-sharʿiyya*), the *millī* councils (the courts of the non-Muslim communities) and the *ḥisbiyya* councils (tribunals established to protect persons whose legal capacity was limited for various reasons) with the civil courts. Not at all . . . Although any Egyptian interested in the reform of his legal system would wish to see such a situation . . . And if we required one court, we surely require one law.[16]

However, as we have already seen in previous chapters, during the preparation of the New Code, Sanhūrī repeatedly emphasized the role of the *Sharīʿa* as an important source for civil codification. "I can assure you that there is not one provision from the Islamic *Sharīʿa* that could have been included in the (New Civil) Code and has not been," he explained to the legislators of the Upper House.[17]

Sanhūrī's position may seem paradoxical. He detests the social institutions of the *Sharīʿa* but admires its law (*fiqh*). He writes: "There is no person in the entire world who loves the Islamic *Sharīʿa* more than I. I was among the first who urged interest in the *Sharīʿa* and its study in the context of comparative law."[18] Elsewhere, he claims: "It [the *Sharīʿa*] may constitute a pillar of (global) comparative law. We know of no other legal system based on such solid foundations of precise legal logic, similar to the Roman legal logic, than the Islamic *Sharīʿa*."[19]

This is paradoxical since in Islam, which is a holistic religion, all these blend together—both the *fiqh*, i.e., Islamic jurisprudence, which forms part of the *Sharīʿa*, and the institutions mentioned here. Can one separate the mechanism of the *Sharīʿa* from its content?

In recent years, historical research has developed still further the

[16] Wujūb, pp. 59–61.
[17] Al-Qānūn al-Madanī, volume 1, p. 159.
[18] Ibid., pp. 85–86.
[19] Wujūb, p. 113.

broad definition of the *Sharīʿa*. Timothy Mitchell, for example, takes the following approach to the question:

> *Al-Azhar*, the name of a particular mosque but also the general name for a group of mosques and lodgings gathered in the older part of Cairo, was not a school of law, but the oldest and most important centre in the Islamic world of law as a profession. As with other crafts and professions, one of the continuous and pervasive activities of those involved, was the learning and teaching of its skills. Learning was a part of the practice of law, and it was from this practice, rather than from any set of codes or structures, that it took its sequence and its form.[20]

The dilemma could also be phrased in the following terms. Is it possible to oppose strongly the institutions and practices of the *Sharīʿa* and to consider these the symptom of social degeneration and decline, while at the same time laud the legal essence of the *Sharīʿa*, i.e., the *fiqh*, characterizing it as progress and renaissance? Mitchell, Messick[21] and others have argued that the mechanism of legal instruction in the *Sharīʿa* cannot be divorced from its content, and that the *Sharīʿa* cannot be considered merely a legal system, but rather, and much more broadly, a system of institutions and practices. Nathan Brown added that the practice of the craft of law is connected not only to its unique educational institutions, but also to the way in which trials are managed in the *Sharīʿa* courts.[22]

If, however, we examine this paradox in accordance with the functional test of progress—*takhayyur*—of encouraging competitiveness and removing obstacles in Egyptian civil law, it could be argued that Sanhūrī's position is actually quite consistent: Sanhūrī did not adopt the *Sharīʿa* automatically and sweepingly in every situation and without distinction, but only in very distinct cases in which a particular norm in the *Sharīʿa* was suited to his purpose—again, according to the imagery of fixing an arrow to the target board and then drawing in the circles.

Thus it is that the final draft of Article 1 in the New Code, i.e., the interpretative sources to be used by the judge in the case of a lacuna, placed the *Sharīʿa* as the third source, after the Code itself and custom

---

[20] T. Mitchell, *Colonising Egypt* (Cambridge: Cambridge University Press, 1988), pp. 82–83.

[21] B. Messick, *The Calligraphic State: Textual Domination and History in a Muslim Society* (Berkeley: University of California Press, 1993), p. 3.

[22] N. Brown, "Shariʿa and State in the Modern Middle East", pp. 359–376.

law. The final draft noted that the principles of the *Sharīʿa* that would apply were 'those most suited to the provisions of this law'. The members of parliament chose to delete this condition, since, on the basis of the explanation they had received from Sanhūrī, "this was obvious within the framework of the principle of suitability".[23]

The same approach may be seen with regard to Sanhūrī's attitude to such Islamic institutions as the *ḥikr*, on the one hand, and the *shufʿa*, on the other. Whatever is suitable will be kept, but whatever is unsuitable will be slated for deletion. The Code and its authors did not define the principles of the *Sharīʿa*, but confined themselves to drawing whatever was relevant in terms of their goals. According to this logic, degenerate institutions had no place in the emerging Egyptian society, and their religious dimension was of no relevance in this respect. The same applied to the element of the *Sharīʿa* in the Code—these foundations were not included because they were part of the sacred *Sharīʿa*, but rather elements from the *Sharīʿa* were introduced if they met the authors' social or legal goal, and often while undergoing a mundane, substantive or cultural transformation. Moreover, in Chapter Two we saw how Sanhūrī attributed cultural and social meaning to Islamic institutions, such as the Caliphate, or the possible use of the Islamic tool of *ʾijmāʿ* (consensus) as a means for securing social accord and even democracy.

2. The *Waqf*: A Symbol of Egyptian Stagnation

2.1 *The Damage Caused by the* Waqf

The term *waqf* literally refers to the freezing of an asset and the prohibition of the execution of ordinary transactions relating to this asset, and is equivalent to the terms 'trust' and 'entail' in England and *Fideikommiss* in Central and Eastern Europe.[24] This is a form of trust

---

[23] Al-Qānūn al-Madanī, volume 1, pp. 192, 190.

[24] About the *waqf*, see: ʿAbd al-Ḥamīd al-Shawāzī, ʾUsāma ʿUthmān, *Munāzaʿāt al-ʾAwqāf wa al-Ḥikr* (Alexandria: 1997); ʾAḥmad ʾAmīn Ḥasān, Fatḥī ʿAbd al-Hādī, *Mawsūʿat al-ʾAwqāf, Tashrīʿāt al-ʾAwqāf, 1895–1997* (Alexandria: Munshāh al-Maʿārif, 1999); H. Cattan, "The Law of Waqf", in M. Khadduri, H. Liebesny eds. *Law in the Middle East* (Washington D.C.: Middle East Institute, 1955), p. 203; G. Baer, *A History of Landownership in Modern Egypt, 1800–1950* (Oxford: Oxford University Press, 1962), pp. 147–185.

that is unique to the Islamic nations: Just as Islam does not separate religion and state, so the *waqf* embodies both secular and religious elements. According to the original purpose, the registration of *ʾawqāf* (the plural of *waqf*) is supposed to be devoted to a religious, cultural or charitable purpose that is tantamount to a 'good deed' (*qurba*). A person who founds a *waqf* or who converts his assets into a *waqf* must decide who will receive the income, and specify this explicitly in the conditions of the *waqfiyya* (the certificate of trust). A further condition is that the chain of beneficiaries must never end. In order to meet this condition, the certificate must name an institution or purpose that is considered eternal. Such a purpose might be a mosque, alms for the poor, a cemetery, a soup kitchen, a *madrasa* for religious studies, and so on. In general, however, the certificate states that the income will not be transferred to this purpose immediately, but rather ultimately. The first beneficiaries are traditionally relatives. This type of *waqf* is referred to in Egypt as *waqf ʾahlī* (family *waqf*), as distinct from a *waqf khayrī*, which is a charitable trust in which the income is transferred immediately to a religious, cultural or charitable institution.

The main motives for founding a *waqf ʾahlī* were to enhance the status, influence and social standing of the family, for example by creating a *waqf* whose income was devoted to the family's guest house; preventing the loss of a property to the family; protecting a property from confiscation or seizure by various rulers or princes; circumventing the Islamic inheritance laws, and particularly preventing the daughters from inheriting, which they are entitled to do under Qurʾānic law; and avoiding a situation where the descendents fell into debt. Many founders of *ʾawqāf* explicitly stipulated that a beneficiary who borrowed money or owed more than a certain percentage of the capital thereby lost his eligibility to receive income from the *waqf*.

In light of these diverse goals, *ʾawqāf* became increasingly numerous in Egypt, and came to account for the alarmingly high figure of 11.5 percent of all privately-owned land. According to various estimates, the total area of *waqf* lands in 1900 was 300,000 *fadān* (one *fadān* is slightly over an acre). By 1914, this figure had risen to 350,000, by the end of World War I to 400,000, by 1927 to 611,203, and by 1942—the peak of this phenomenon—to 677,555 *fadān*, constituting, as noted, 11.5 percent of all private land.[25] Attorney Muḥammad ʿAlī ʿAlūba, a leading

[25] G. Bear, *A History of Landownership*, pp. 147–185, 151.

advocate of the abolition of the *ʾawqāf* who himself served for a while as Minister of *ʾawqāf*, explained in his memoirs the damage caused by the *waqf* in general, and by the family *ʾawqāf* in particular—an institution which he believed had no religious dimension. He argued that the continued creation of *ʾawqāf* restricted land reserves, removing the land from the commercial market, limiting the possibility of their use as securities in commercial transactions, and hence impairing the wealth of the nation. ʿAlūba also estimated that 11 percent of agricultural land was *waqf* land, and noted that this figure was rising rapidly.[26]

By its nature, a family *waqf* continues from one generation to the next. Since the number of beneficiaries in each generation is greater than in the preceding one, the income received by each beneficiary declines to the point where the sums involved become absurd. In his book *Basic Principles of Egyptian Policy*, ʿAlūba gave an example from 1927 of a *waqf* in Alexandria that comprised 438 beneficiaries, each of whom received 60 piasters, although the property itself yielded a high annual income of 7,500 Egyptian pounds.[27] Moreover, the portion of the *waqf* manager, the *nāẓir* (known as the *mutawallī* in the Levant), who was not usually a descendant of the founder of the trust, remained constant, regardless of the number of beneficiaries.[28]

An additional problem was that the beneficiaries desisted from gainful employment, relying exclusively on their paltry income from the *waqf*. From their standpoint, the *waqf* came to represent a mental state on which they were totally dependent, even when this drove them to abject poverty. They fell victim to black-market moneylenders, to whom they were eventually obliged to assign their portion in the *waqf*. In an effort to reduce the scope of this problem, Law No. 60 of 1942 restricted such assignments.[29]

Moreover, the purpose to which the founder of the *waqf* dedicated the trust prevented his descendents from using the *waqf ʾahlī* as they saw fit as circumstances changed, or from amending its purpose in order to render it more profitable. It was common knowledge in Cairo that *waqf* buildings were usually dilapidated and poorly maintained, and

[26] Muḥammad ʿAlī ʿAlūba, "Fī al-Waqf", *Al-Muḥāmā*, Volume 7(4)(1927), pp. 309–320; "Le probléme du wakf", *L'Egypte Contemporaine* (1927), pp. 501–524.

[27] Muḥammad ʿAlī ʿAlūba, *Mabādīʾ fī al-Siyāsa al-Miṣriyya* (Cairo: Dār al-Kutub al-Miṣriyya, 1942), p. 301.

[28] Ziadeh, 1968, p. 132.

[29] Ibid., p. 132.

thus yielded a lower income for the beneficiaries than buildings that had previously been 'free'.[30]

This state of neglect was also due to the fact that the management of *waqf* lands was the responsibility of the manager, or *nāẓir*, who received a fixed fee at the level of 10 percent of the income prior to distribution to the beneficiaries. Since the manager could be dismissed, and his son would not always inherit the position, the manager had no interest in the development of the asset, which would require the investment of part of the income in the property, but sought to maximize the income allotted to the beneficiaries. Moreover, the provisions in the *waqfiyya* were often vague and imprecise, leaving the *nāẓir* free to interpret them in accordance with his personal interests.

It could be argued that, in many senses, the *waqf* came to be a symbol for the state of Egypt as a whole—a self-created trap whereby people were unable to disconnect themselves from institutions that had become burdensome to themselves and to the national economy and to overcome obstacles that included a religious motif. Egyptians wanted reform, but found this difficult to consolidate and implement due to diverse interests that mitigated against change. The past became a force foiling and delaying the future.

Despite Sanhūrī's initial intention to include the laws of personal status in the New Code, thus unifying the entire range of civil law in the Code,[31] this idea was dropped, presumably due to opposition from conservative religious circles. Accordingly, the idea of abolishing or amending the *waqf* was also abandoned, since this was perceived as part of the sanctified aspects of personal status and subject to the authority of the *Sharīʿa* courts. It is indeed the case that the demand to reform the trusts aroused more passionate debate than any other aspect of the proposed legal reform.[32]

It is not difficult to understand why this was the case. Since the beneficiaries of a *waqf khayrī* (a charitable trust) were usually mosques, religious schools and similar institutions, the *waqf* was associated with religion, and any criticism of this institution was perceived in conservative circles as a deliberate attack on religion. Secondly, many people made a living from the *waqf*, particularly the managers and the *Sharīʿa*

---

[30] Fī al-Waqf, pp. 313–318.

[31] Wujūb, pp. 59–61.

[32] On the dispute over the *waqf* in Egypt see, *inter alia*, Ziadeh, 1968, pp. 127–135.

lawyers, who thus had an interest in preserving the institution. The managers received a fixed income, while the lawyers' income was created mainly on suits field by the *waqf* in the *Sharīʿa* courts.

The demand by reformist lawyers in Egypt at the beginning of the twentieth century to abolish the *waqf* reflected developments in several European countries, where laws had been passed abolishing or severely restricting trusts. In Egypt, the criticism focused mainly on the *waqf ʾahlī*, the family trust, whose beneficiaries were the descendents of the founder throughout the generations, despite the legal fiction that the asset would eventually be transferred to some religious institution.

Article 335 of the Swiss code of 1912 forbad the establishment of such trusts, and Article 155 of the German Constitution of 1919 completely outlawed this institution. In Turkey, the *ʾawqāf* were abolished in 1926, prior to the adoption of the Swiss civil code in this country.[33]

The campaign by the Egyptian jurists eventually yielded results, albeit limited ones. In 1946, Law No. 48 was enacted, introducing a measure of reform in the field of the *ʾawqāf*. The law constituted a compromise between the liberals, who sought to abolish the institution, and religious circles, which sought to preserve it without change.

The new law stipulated that from henceforth (i.e., the law was not retroactive and did not apply to existing *ʾawqāf*), any *waqf* (with the exception of a mosque or cemetery) could be annulled by its founder (Article 11 of the law from 1946); any *waqf khayrī* (apart from one supporting a mosque) would henceforth be perpetual (*muʾabbad*) or temporary (*muʾaqqat*, Article 5 of the law); new family *ʾawqāf* would no longer be perpetual, and would henceforth last for no longer than 60 years, or two generations after the death of the founder; the founder could include conditions enabling the amendment of the *waqf*, or the replacement of the assets of the *waqf* with assets of equal value (Article 12). The law also introduced, for the first time, strict rules of liability regarding the *nāẓir*: the manager was required to submit regular financial statements, and bore personal financial liability in the event that incompetent or negligent management were proved (Articles 50–53). A further innovation in the law was that the *nāẓir* was henceforth required to withhold 2.5 percent of the income of the *waqf* for the purpose of maintaining the property, under the supervision of the *Sharīʿa* court.

[33] Ziadeh, 1968, p. 129.

The beneficiaries could only use this sum with the authorization of the court, and on the basis of special grounds (Article 54).[34]

The explanatory notes to the law stated that although the religious aspect had certainly been diluted in the *waqf ʾahlī*, the committee had not recommended the total abolition of this institution, preferring instead to correct its defects in order to draw it back toward the goals of the Islamic *Sharīʿa* and enable it to fill its function more successfully. The committee determined that the total abolition of the *waqf ʾahlī* might cause "an earthquake that would create difficulties and financial disputes that would last for decades."

A final development, outside the timeframe of this book but worth noting in order to complete the picture, came when the revolutionary government that came to power in July 1952 chose to abolish the *waqf ʾahlī* completely and abruptly, in Law No. 180. A year later, the *waqf khayrī* was effectively nationalized. Law No. 180 of 1952, one of the first laws enacted after the revolution, stated in its first clause that "a *waqf* for other than charitable goals is prohibited'. Article 2 added that "any *waqf* whose purpose is not charitable (*bar*) shall be considered to have absolutely terminated. If the founder dedicated part of the *waqf* to charitable purposes and the remainder of the income to non-charitable purposes, the *waqf* shall be considered to have terminated." Article 3 established that the beneficiaries of the terminated *waqf* would become owners in accordance with their portion in the asset. The appropriate institution for hearing disputes relating to a *waqf* remained the *Sharīʿa* court (Article 8).

What the revolutionary government achieved through the use of brute force, the New Code had previously attempted to achieve through its typical means, as we shall see below: persuasion, the creation of a broad consensus, and inevitable compromise.

2.2 *'By Any Other Name'—Indirect Attack No. 1*

If it were impossible to abolish the *waqf*, an attempt could be made to amend it, and thus to limit the damage this institution caused. In this chapter, we argue that this is what the Code attempted to do, by means of what might be described as an indirect attack on the *waqf*.

[34] See Landownership, pp. 215–222.

In defining the term 'legal person' (*shakhṣ ʾiʿtibārī*), i.e., the artificial creations of law that have legal capacity for any purpose and matter, such as membership and associations, Article 52(3) of the New Code included the *ʾawqāf*, an innovation that was not previously present in Egyptian law.

The explanatory notes to the proposed Code stated that the previous civil code had not treated the *waqf* as a distinct legal person, while the courts had done so, permitting the *waqf* to sue and to be sued. The proposal admitted that "the recognition of the *waqf* as a legal person is not an obvious measure, since this is an Islamic institution with its own specific rules. However, the authors of the proposal preferred to adopt the approach of the courts in accordance with practical needs."[35]

This approach may be described as an indirect attack on the *waqf*, since the Code drew an ancient Islamic institution defined by its own autonomous conceptual world and imprisoned it within a framework taken from another world—that of modern Western law, viz. the concept of legal persons, which has its own rules and norms. In so doing, the Code enabled the court to interpret and consider the *waqf* not only in terms of its own rules, but also in terms of the rules of modern law, which are alien to the familiar norms of the *waqf*. The Code attributed the legal person with rules, authorities and obligations that have little in common with the traditional provisions for managing the institution of the *waqf*.[36]

Pierre Bourdieu argued that law is a field that includes a network of positions, locuses and practices distinguishing among different legal actors, and in which a constant competition is waged for the right to appropriate legitimate fields of jurisdiction and authority, and for the power to determine what is law, who are its authorized producers, what methods it should employ, what principles should guide its application, and what should be its desired scope.[37] On the basis of this sociological approach to law, the partial expropriation of the institution of the *waqf* by the Code may also be examined from a broader standpoint. The Code sought to expropriate the *waqf* and all the laws of personal status within the confines of the 'legal centralism' it represented.[38] Since it

[35] Al-Qānūn al-Madanī, volume 1, p. 375.
[36] The Egyptian Civil Code, article 53.
[37] P. Bourdieu, "The Force of Law: Towards a Sociology of the Judicial Field", *The Hastings Law Journal* 38(1987), p. 814.
[38] J. Griffith, "What is Legal Pluralism", *Journal of Legal Pluralism* (1986), p. 1;

failed to achieve this objective, it could do no more than whittle away at the laws of the *waqf* as best it could, on the assumption that once these were under its control, even partially, it would be easier to change the mechanism and function of this institution from within.

2.3 *The* Ḥikr *as Indirect Attack No. 2: Minus and Minus = Plus*

Due to the beneficiaries' lack of interest in the state of maintenance of the *waqf* assets, and since the *waqf* did not usually have ready access to cash, many *waqf* properties became sadly dilapidated, unkempt and even destroyed.[39] Accordingly, the Code searched for a mechanism that would enable the rehabilitation of *waqf* properties, but without impairing or amending the laws of the *waqf*, which, as already noted, were perceived as laws of personal status imbued with a dimension of sanctity, and hence outside the authority of the Code. True to its approach, the Code sought to find a tool through consensus, attempting, as far as possible, to satisfy conservative circles, who were highly sensitive to issues relating to the *waqf*.

The solution was found with the help of the institution of the *ḥikr*, a special form of lease of a long-term and sometimes perpetual nature. This tool is taken from Islamic law, which, in this case, was used by the Code to secure the progress it sought to introduce and to encourage competition and renewal. This is a further example of the way that an ancient legal tool may be used to secure 'progress', rather than a modern concept drawn from outside the conceptual world of the community.

The basic problem was that *waqf* properties could not be leased for a period of more than three years, unless a longer period was authorized

S. Engle Merry, "Legal Pluralism", *Law and Society Review* 22(1988), p. 869. In Egyptian Context see: N. Brown, "Law and Imperialism: Egypt in Comparative Perspective", *Law and Society Review* 29(1995), p. 103. In the context of other developing societies: S. B. Burman, B. E. Harrell-Bond eds. *The Imposition of Law* (New York: Academic Press, 1979); J. Schmidhauser, "Power, Legal Imperialism, and Dependency", *Law and Society Review* 23(1989), pp. 857–878; K. Mann, R. Roberts eds., *Law in Colonial Africa* (Portsmouth: Heinemann, 1991); B. S. Cohn, "Law and the Colonial State in India", in J. Starr and J. Collier eds. *History and Power in the Study of Law* (Ithaca, NY: Cornell University Press, 1989); A. C. Christelow, *Muslim Law Courts and the French Colonial State in Algeria* (Princeton, N.J.: Princeton University Press, 1985); D. S. Powers, "Orientalism, Colonialism, and Legal History: The Attack on Muslim Family Endowments in Algeria and India", *Comparative Studies in Society and History* 31(1989), pp. 535–571.

[39] Ziadeh, p. 64; Al-Wasīṭ, volume 6 p. 1433.

by a judge in special cases.[40] This was the ruling of the *Sharī'a*, and was adopted by the 'Mixed' judicial system in Egypt, rather than by the judges of the *'ahlī* courts, and it was taken from the Mixed case law by the authors of the New Code. The previous code had not even related to the possibility of leasing a *waqf* property. Interestingly, the proposed Code followed the Islamic *fiqh* in distinguishing between the lease of a building or shop that formed part of a *Waqf* and the lease of land in a similar condition. In the case of a building, apartment or shop, the maximum period of lease was one year, whereas land could be leased for a period of up to three years. However, the Re-examination Committee amended these provisions, setting a maximum period of three years in all cases.[41]

It is also interesting to note that the judges of the *'ahlī* courts were opposed to the inclusion in the New Code of a specific provision relating to the lease of *waqf* property. However, their objections were rejected, both in order to remove the contradictions created between the courts in different provinces regarding the provisions for the lease of *waqf* properties, and since "people have become accustomed through centuries" (to the provisions for the lease of *waqf* properties in accordance with the *Sharī'a*), and these specific provisions were adapted to the character and protection of the *waqf*.[42]

The harsh three-year limit on the lease of *waqf* properties was thus included in the Code, stating that if the period of lease exceeded three years, whether overtly or covertly, the contract was not nullified, but the termination date was automatically cut back to three years.[43]

While this possibility to lease *waqf* properties certainly introduced a measure of dynamism and *tanāfus*, this was not adequate. It was not worth the while of the lessor of a *waqf* property to invest in the property and renovate it (Sanhūrī used the word revive—*ta'mīr*), since he knew that he was limited to a lease period of just three years. Accordingly, the Code adopted the institution of the *ḥikr*.

Ziadeh noted that, over the years, the courts had permitted the development of a custom for the leasing of vacant *waqf* land for construction on a long-term or even perpetual basis, namely the *ḥikr*. The

[40] The Egyptian Civil Code, article 633; Ziadeh, p. 64; Al-Wasīṭ, volume 6 pp. 1423–1427; Kitāb Murshid al-Ḥayrān, article 579.

[41] Al-Wasīṭ, volume 6, p. 1425.

[42] Ibid., p. 1405.

[43] The Egyptian Civil Code, article 633; Al-Wasīṭ, volume 6, p. 1427.

usual form of *ḥikr* related to vacant land purchased by the lessor, who undertake to rehabilitate the site (see the contract of *ʾījāratain* below). In this way, the lessee secured *jus ad rem* in the land, built on it or bettered it, exploited the property for his sundry commercial needs, and gradually repaid his investment. Everyone benefited from this situation: the *waqf* found someone to revive the asset, which might return to the *waqf* in totality after a set number of years, in an improved state; the lessee had a chance to secure profits on his investment; and the state benefited from the return of the *waqf* property to the market, in an improved condition. It should be noted that prior to the New Code, the courts also permitted *ḥikr* with regard to non-*waqf* properties, if these required serious renovation.[44] Sanhūrī noted a social need, in addition to the economic need as already discussed: the desire of the landowning class to maintain this status, even if they had almost lost their hold on property that had deteriorated due to under-investment.[45] Land was a status symbol as well as a purely economic function. Through this mechanism, members of this class could lease *waqf* properties while remaining their owners.

The Code established restrictive rules for the tool of *ḥikr* by comparison with the provisions of the *Sharīʿa*, since, as noted, the Code considered this tool to be the lesser evil in order to limit the damage caused by the *waqf*, rather than a tool of intrinsic value. The limitation of the right of *ḥikr* was applied in the spirit of the *Sharīʿa*, which established the well-known principle (which appears, for example, in Article 27 of the *Majalla*) that "the greater damage is removed by means of a lesser damage."

Thus, *inter alia*, the Code restricted the period of *ḥikr* to no more than 60 years, in order to prevent the property from falling once again into a state of stagnation; it determined that, henceforth, *ḥikr* would no longer be applied to non-*waqf* properties (since the *ḥikr* was a positive tool for limiting the *waqf*, but was negative in the context of 'free' properties—in the absence of a *waqf*, there was no need for *ḥikr*). A *ḥikr* imposed on non-*waqf* property at the time of the enactment of the Code would be managed according to the principles for the *ḥikr* as established in the Code. In order to eliminate the ordinary *ḥikr* over the course of time, the Code established relations of *shufʿa* (i.e., preemption, priority

[44] Ziadeh, p. 64.
[45] Al-Wasīṭ, volume 6, p. 1434.

in purchasing—see below) between the owner of the property and the holder of the *ḥikr*; this would lead to the elimination of the *ḥikr*, since the holder would become the owner and the owner would be freed of the right of *ḥikr* imposed on his property.[46] It is interesting to note that the proposed Code established a maximum period of 99 years, but this was reduced to 60 years by the Re-examination Committee of the Upper House, on the grounds that nowadays it was possible to secure the renovation of the property and the recouping of the cost of lease by the lessee in a shorter period than had been the case in the past.[47]

Further provisions relating to the right of *ḥikr* also have their origins in the *Sharīʿa*. For example, *ḥikr* would be permitted by the court only in cases of need or necessity. The lessee had an actual *in rem* right, could act with his right as he saw fit and could even bequeath the right.[48] Additional construction, planting or other works undertaken by the lessee belong exclusively to him, and he can execute dispositions in these elements freely, separately or together with his right of *ḥikr*. The Code seeks to protect rental fees in the case of *ḥikr*; contrary to rental fees in other cases, it established in this case that the rental fees would not be less than those for similar properties, and would be linked to this level whether it rose or fell. The right of *ḥikr* is eliminated if it is not employed for a period of 15 years, except in the case of a *ḥikr* on a *waqf* property, in which case expiry due to non-use comes after 33 years. As noted, the right of *ḥikr* is a need the Code imposed on itself due to the disadvantages of the institution of the *waqf*; accordingly, the *ḥikr* is subject to the *waqf*; if the 60-year period in accordance with Law No. 48 of 1946 expires and the *waqf ʾahlī* on the land is annulled, the right of *ḥikr* also expires at that point.[49]

Presumably in order to make this tool more acceptable and functional, the Code detailed two specific *ḥikr* contracts: the first is known as *ʾijāratain* (i.e. 'two leases'); and the second—*khulūū al-ʾintifāʿ*.

The *ʾijāratain* contract is a private case of *ḥikr* whereby the *waqf* creates a *ḥikr* on land on which a building requiring renovation already stands (as opposed to a regular *ḥikr*, which is made with regard to vacant land), in return for a sum of money equivalent to the value of

[46] The Egyptian Civil Code, articles 1012, 936(4).
[47] Al-Qānūn al-Madanī, volume 6, pp. 568, 570.
[48] The Egyptian Civil Code, articles 1000, 1001; Al-Wasīṭ, volume 6, pp. 1443–1448.
[49] The Egyptian Civil Code, articles 1002, 1004, 1011, 1008(3).

the above-mentioned building (this is the 'first lease'), as well as annual rental fees equivalent to the value of a similar lease of similar land (this is the 'second lease'). In all other respects, the general rules of the *ḥikr* apply here. This is essentially an urban form of the *ḥikr*. In a regular *ḥikr*, the lessee can build on the *waqf* land he has leased, and the building then belongs exclusively to him. Here, too, the building purchased by the lessee on the *waqf* land belongs exclusively to him.

With the first full payment, the owner acquires full ownership of the building; however, in this type of contract he cannot demolish the building, but must continue to renovate it, and the payment of rental fees is for the right of *ḥikr* he received to the trust's land. The *ʾijāratain* contract requires the authorization of the court, as do the other types of *ḥikr*.[50]

The *khulūū al-ʾintifāʿ*, by contrast, is a contract in accordance with which the *waqf* leases its property, even without the court's authorization, in return for fixed rental fees for an indefinite period. According to this contract, the lessee must rehabilitate the property and make it fit for use. The special feature of this type of *ḥikr* is that the *waqf* can cancel the contract at any time, with appropriate notice, provide it compensates the lessee for the expenses he has invested in the property. *Al-Wasīṭ* notes that this mechanism is not actually a form of *ḥikr*, granting *jus ad rem* to the lessee, but rather a form of personal lease that may be nullified at any time. Whereas in the classic *ḥikr* and the *ʾijāratain*, the buildings and trees on the *waqf* land belong to the lessee, here they belong to the *waqf*. Accordingly, there is no need for court authorization for this type of contract.

Contrary to a regular *waqf* lease, the lessee in this case must renovate the building. He will not suffer damages in any case, however, since, if the contract extends over a considerable period, the lessee will be able to recoup his investment by exploiting the property, and if it finishes prior to this point—he will be compensated by the *waqf*.[51]

2.4 *The End of the* Ḥikr

The *ḥikr* played an important role in the economic history of Egypt, but this ended abruptly several years after the New Code was enacted, following the revolution of the Free Officers in 1952. Although this

[50] Ibid., article 1031; Al-Wasīṭ, volume 6, pp. 1497–1498.
[51] The Egyptian Civil Code, article 1014; Al-Wasīṭ, volume 6, p. 1500; ziadeh, p. 65.

development lies outside the timeframe of this book, it is important in that it illustrates the nature of the decision-making process regarding the New Code.

Most of the rights of *ḥikr* were cancelled after the enactment of Law No. 180 (amended in Law No. 342) of 1952. This law abolished the family *ʾawqāf*, and hence also abolished the rights of *ḥikr* imposed on these *waqf* lands, since the Code itself had established the condition that the right of *ḥikr* would expire if the land to which it applied were no longer *waqf* land. The exception to this was when this cessation was the result of the dissolution of the *waqf* by its founder, in which the *ḥikr* would continue to apply until its original expiry date.[52]

Law No. 649 of 1953 empowered the Minister of *ʾawqāf*, with the consent of the Supreme Council of the *waqf*, to terminate *ḥikr* rights that had become cumbersome for the land of a *waqf ḥayrī*, i.e. a charitable *waqf*, if they believed that such termination was in the best interests of these *ʾawqāf*.[53] Following the annulment of the *ḥikr*, the rights of the parties to the buildings and trees on *waqf* land were regulated by Article 1010 of the New Code, in the case of a *waqf ʾahlī*, and by Law No. 92 of 1960 (which replaced Law No. 295 of 1954) with regard to a *waqf ḥayrī*. This law established that any *ḥikr* on the land of a *waqf ḥayrī* would terminate within a period not exceeding five years from the date on which the law came into force. The only rights of *ḥikr* not treated in this manner were *ḥikr* on land not dedicated as a *waqf*—these would terminate on the agreement of the parties, or on the expiry of the period of *ḥikr*; in any case, such cases of *ḥikr* were few and of limited importance.[54]

According to the logic of the Code and its authors, and according to the logic applied by the leaders of the Egyptian revolution several years later, the *waqf* was perceived as one of the causes of degeneration in the country; accordingly, it should be abolished, and once there is no *waqf*, there would be no need for the 'lesser of two evils', i.e. for the *ḥikr*. Accordingly, the revolution led to the abolition both of the *waqf ʾahlī* and of the *ḥikr* itself.

Here, however, we see the essence of the difference between the mechanism adopted by the New Code and the mechanism of revolution.

[52] The Egyptian Civil Code, article 1008(3); Ziadeh, p.65; Al-Wasīṭ, volume 6, p. 1407.

[53] Ziadeh, p. 65.

[54] Ziadeh, pp. 65–66.

The Code sought to introduce legislation through a process of consensus encompassing as many sectors of Egyptian society as possible, without coercion, through persuasion and understanding. This is the essence of the theory presented up to this point as adopted by the authors of the Code: to promote social solidarity, whereby the strong support the weak and vice versa, through persuasion rather than coercion. The imposition of a measure by one sector and the unilateral change of reality were diametrically opposed to the social philosophy of the Code. This process of persuasion included religious circles; accordingly, it was important that the basis of the laws of *ḥikr*, drawn from the *Sharīʿa*, be included in public discourse as a motif intended to soften opposition. The *ḥikr* was an Islamic element whose adoption was intended to soften opposition to the injury of another element from the *Sharīʿa*—the *waqf*, as if in accordance with the mathematical principle that two minuses create a plus.

By contrast, the leaders of the revolution imposed their decision without any attempt to forge social or national consensus. Since they had no need for consensus, they also had no need for any form of authority or legitimacy from Islamic law.

2.5 *The* Muʾassasa—*The 'New* Waqf'—*Indirect Attack No. 3*

Much has already been written about the struggle by liberal, secular lawyers in Egypt to abolish the institution of the *waqf*, both the *ʾahlī* and the *khayrī*, which many of them perceived as a tangible symbol of the problems of Egyptian society.[55] It could be argued that the New Code also participated in these efforts, in its own unique way—a way that has not hitherto received due attention. The reference is to the institution of the *muʾassasa*—the foundation.[56] In some ways, this indirect form of attack as adopted by the Code was more effective than other approaches.

The essential logic of the Code was that while the *waqf* could not be abolished, it might be possible to locate an alternative legal institution that would be more effective and flexible, so that, in time, use of the *waqf* would decline of its own accord. In this way the *waqf* would be attacked and the national economy would be revived through the

[55] For example: Ziadeh, 1968, pp. 127–135.
[56] The Egyptian Civil Code, articles 69–80.

use of modern tools. This chapter argues that, to this end, the Code presented Egyptian civil law with a new institution: the *mu'assasa*. This is a financial foundation constituting an independent legal person, that devotes (the explanatory notes used the word *ḥabs*, which means to set aside, just as in the case of the *waqf*) a sum of money for objectives other than profit.[57] This definition includes charitable and scientific activities, research, religion, art and sport, for the benefit of the public and on a not-for-profit basis. The *mu'assasa* differs from the *jam'iyya* (association) since it is based on an allocation of money (*ḥabs*), whereas the latter institution is based on and comprised of a group of people who associate for the purpose of a common activity.[58]

Even before the beginning of the deliberations on the New Code, Sanhūrī explained the need for an institution to replace the *waqf*. In 1936, he wrote that neither Egyptian nor French law include specific provisions regarding the institution of the foundation. "The *waqf* in Egypt has enriched us greatly, insofar as anyone who wished to do so could devote it to such purpose as he intended. Despite this, however, we still strongly need the institution of a foundation that is more flexible than the system of the *waqf* with which we are familiar. The *mu'assasa* will be managed in a manner consonant with practical (modern) needs, thus enabling a wide circle of people to participate in the establishment of foundations (for purposes) not permitted by the *waqf*. At present, people are obliged to establish associations of individuals, when their real intent is to establish financial foundations. Special legislation for the foundations will enable administrative supervision, whereas the supervision of the *waqf* is provided by the *Sharī'a* courts" (i.e., a judicial tribunal which, in accordance with the functional test, was perceived as unworthy, and which Sanhūrī did not hide his intention to abolish—G.B.)[59] Sanhūrī added that, contrary to the *waqf*, the *mu'assasa* could change the purpose of its financial support and move from one goal to another, "if it emerged that the goal for which the *mu'assasa* was established has lost its significance, become outmoded or contradicts public order. All these are aspects of flexibility not found in the institution of the *waqf*, so that the *waqf* is not suited to the allocation of money in favor of social or economic purposes that have

[57] Al-Qānūn al-Madanī, volume 1, p. 371; The Egyptian Civil Code, article 69.
[58] Al-Qānūn al-Madanī, volume 1, p. 427.
[59] Wujūb, pp. 97–98.

a beginning and end, and since these do not fall under the definition of charity."[60] Moreover, "the subject of foundations has now become more important, both for disseminating charitable matters and due to the increasingly level of economic activity in the country."

It was important to the proposed Code to emphasize that the *mu'asasa* permitted a much broader definition of enterprises and fields than the *waqf*. Firstly, the *mu'assasa* differed from the *waqf* in that the latter applies only to real estate; accordingly, it was not possible to devote a *waqf* in favor of hospitals, orphanages or associations in the fields of health, sport and education. The explanatory notes showed that private welfare institutions in Egypt had been established as associations since they could not be formed as foundations. The example was given of a Jewish orphanage by the name 'Drop of Milk' (*quṭrat al-ḥalīb*) that had the structure of an association, although its founder intended to establish it as a financial foundation.[61]

The means for creation of the *mu'assasa* was the desire of the donor allocating the money, expressed through an official certificate—if the founder were alive, or through a testament, if it was established after his death. The institution of the foundation was not subject to the approval of the executive branch, as in the German and Belgian codes, but the *mu'assasa* was subjected to the administrative supervision of the state, through the Ministry of Social Affairs, the state attorney's office or any other organ of state. If necessary, the court would rule between the *mu'assasa* and the state. The court also enjoyed broad authority to amend the guiding constitution of the *mu'assasa*, to reduce expenditures, or to delete conditions mentioned in the certificate of establishment of the *mu'assasa*, if such deletion were necessary in order to protect the funds of the *mu'assasa* or to realize the goal for which it was established. The court could even order to liquidation of the entire *mu'assasa* if it had become unable to secure the purpose for which it was established, or if this purpose had become impossible or inconsonant with the law, morality or public order.

Due to the highly flexible nature of the foundation, for example in terms of amending the goals for the allocation of the money, it became a convenient tool and a type of 'new *waqf*' (this is my term and does not appear in the Egyptian sources) symbolic of a new, progressive and

---

[60] Ibid.

[61] Al-Wasīṭ, volume 1, p. 71; Al-Qānūn al-Madanī, volume 1, p. 371.

efficient Egypt characterized by financial dynamism, competition and creativity. The *mu'assasa* is a secular and functional tool that is devoid of any dimension of sanctity or religion, unlike the *waqf*. In keeping with the unique approach of the New Code, this creativity was not introduced by means of a sudden threat to existing institutions, but was introduced alongside them. At the most, the *mu'assasa* might be seen as an indirect attack on the *waqf*, but not as a direct attempt to abolish or usurp this ancient institution.[62]

3. Preemption (*Shuf'a*)—A Disliked Right

3.1 *The preemption in Islamic Law*

One of the ways to secure ownership of land in Islamic law is through preemption (*shuf'a*), i.e. first right to purchase. Preemption is defined in the New Code as "the opportunity for a person to position himself in place of the purchaser in the sale of real estate..."[63] The *Majalla* defined the *shuf'a* as "the acquisition of [real estate] property sold at cost price to the purchaser".[64] According to the formula for *shuf'a*, if a person sold his land to a given purchaser, the holder of the right of *shuf'a* enjoyed an opportunity to displace the purchaser, moving him aside and purchasing the land in his place. "If the land were sold through a sale contract, the gate is opened to *shuf'a*."[65]

The right of *shuf'a* was granted by the court solely in defined cases. In the *Majalla*, for example, it may be granted in three cases: the first is a partnership—i.e., a partner enjoyed the right of refusal in purchasing his partner's portion, and if the partner sold his portion to a third party, the preemptioner (i.e., the holder of the right of *shuf'a*) could displace this third party. A lesser status was enjoyed by a person who had a right to the sold plot, such as a right of passage or irrigation; and lastly, a neighbor who owned an adjacent plot of land.[66] This

---

[62] The Egyptian Civil Code, articles 70, 74; Al-Wasīṭ, volume 1, p. 72.

[63] The Egyptian Civil Code, article 935; More on the institution of *Shuf'a*: F. Ziadeh, "Land Law and Economic Developments in Arab Countries", The *American Journal of Comparative Law* 33(1985), pp. 93, 99–101.

[64] The Majalla, articles 950, 1008–1044.

[65] Ibid., article 950. The *shuf'a* articles in the Majalla: 1008–1044; On the right, Ziadeh, 46–48; F. Ziadeh, "Shufah: Origins and Modern Doctrine", *Cleveland State Law Review* 43(1985–6) p. 35; Al-Wasīṭ, volume 9 p. 481.

[66] The Majalla, article 1008.

latter situation created problematic relations of dependence between neighbors, since one neighbor could intervene in the private affairs of his fellow, enter into a sale that the latter had decided to initiate and even take control of the process.

Accordingly, Islamic law regarded the right of *shufʿa* as a weak right, and among *Sharīʿa* jurists it was classified as a repugnant right (*ḥaqq makrūh*). It was even permissible to resort to a ruse (*ḥīla*) in order to thwart the use of *shufʿa*.[67] The right of *shufʿa* not only enabled gross interference in the freedom of contractual association, but also encouraged stagnation and immobility in real estate, for reasons that will be detailed below.

Indeed, the *Majalla* attempted to restrict this right, imposing technical limitations on the *shafīʿ* and stating that this right would expire if its conditions were not scrupulously observed. For example, a *shafīʿ* who was tardy in claiming his right "and was in a situation testifying to distraction, such as engaging in another matter or in another conversation for another purpose, or if he stood up and left before demanding the properties for himself, then he loses his right." The *shafīʿ* must not agree to the sale in any circumstance; as the *Majalla* states, "if he hears rumor of the sale, and says, 'Very good!'—his right of pre-emption is nullified and he is not entitled to displace the taker. And if, after hearing of the association for the sale, he wished to purchase or rent the property from the taker—his right of pre-emption is nullified."[68]

3.2 Shufʿa *in Egypt*

In a highly normative land regulation system such as Egypt, which defines not only economic relations, but also the social and political foundations of the community, *shufʿa* was of particular importance. By controlling land law, this right also held control of society and economic life. Stagnation in land law due to the negative impact of *shufʿa* in Egypt thus inevitably led to stagnation in the national economy and society. The reason for this was that *shufʿa* could prevent new owners from acquiring land, increasing the power of large landowners to dictate conditions to smaller owners in the vicinity. The large landowner could control the price of land among his neighbors, since his mere

[67] Al-Qānūn al-Madanī, volume 6, p. 378.

[68] The Majalla, articles 1032, 1024.

declaration of his intention to exercise his right of *shuf'a* in any instance would be sufficient to deter potential buyers, thus reducing the value of his neighbors' land. This situation also mitigated against mobility in the acquisition of new land or the entry of new owners into a village or residential area.

The removal of *shuf'a* from land law, particularly in the context of the neighbor's right of *shuf'a*, which constituted the most intrusive example of the damage caused by this right to the freedom of association, was thus perceived by the authors of the New Code as an essential reform in order to secure the goals discussed by this chapter.

Prior to the introduction of modern civil codes, in the latter half of the nineteenth century, the right of *shuf'a* in Egypt was applied by the courts in accordance with Islamic law and custom. Both the Mixed and the *'ahlī* codes, at the time of their enactment, included provisions for implementing *shuf'a*, drawn from the *Sharī'a*, though with a number of differences. The confusion created between the two codes that applied simultaneously in Egypt led the Egyptian government to promulgate two laws: the first dated March 26, 1900, for the Mixed courts, and the second dated March 23, 1901, for the *'ahlī* courts. These laws regulate the issue of *shuf'a* and replace the provisions of the civil codes on this matter.[69]

The authors of the New Code based their approach on these two laws, and again included *shuf'a* in the New Code, though, as shall be seen below, they did not hide their disapproval of this mechanism.

The New Code defined the list of those enjoying the right of *shuf'a* as follows, in descending order of priority:

Firstly, the owner himself, in the case of the sale of a right of use (*ḥaqq 'intifā'*) to any or all of his land (the New Code does not define what is a right of use to another's land; the Syrian civil code defines as a *jus ad rem* a person's right to use or exploit something that belongs to another);[70] secondly, the owner of the right of use in the event of the sale of part or all of the land on which it is situated; thirdly, the partner in ownership in the case of the sale of part of the common property to a third party; fourthly, the owner himself in the event of *ḥikr*, if the right of *ḥikr* were sold, and, on an equal footing, the owner of the right of *ḥikr*,

[69] Ziadeh, p. 46. *Shuf'a* 'ahlī law appears in 'Abd al-Fattāh Sayyid, Muḥammad Kāmil Mursī, *Majmū'at Qawānīn al-Maḥākim al-'Ahlīyya wa al-Shar'īyya*, p. 94.

[70] The Egyptian Civil Code, articles 985–998; Syrian Civil Code article 936; Ziadeh, pp. 61–62.

if the sale was of the land itself (this is an innovation by the New Code since, as we have seen above in this chapter, the use of *ḥikr* itself is an innovation that did not exist hitherto); and, fifthly, neighboring landowners in the following cases (the list narrows the provisions relative to the *Majalla*, which granted sweeping rights of *shufʿa* to the neighbor):

1. In the case of buildings or land for construction situated in a city or village;
2. If the land enjoyed the right of servitude (*ʾirtifāq*) over the neighbor's land, or vice versa—if the neighbor's land enjoyed the right of *ʾirtifāq* over the sold land;
3. If the neighbor's land were adjacent (*mulāṣaqa*) to the sold land on two sides, and had a value at least half that of the sold land;

If several persons enjoying the same ranking sought to enjoy the right of *shufʿa*, it would belong to each one in proportion to their share, unless one of them were the purchaser, in which case he would enjoy priority over others at the same priority ranking.[71]

As we shall see below, Sanhūrī and the proposed code (particularly in its amended version, see below) expressed reservations regarding the *shufʿa*, above all since it created a situation that was the opposite of the element of *tanāfus* mentioned at the beginning of this chapter. It restricted the commerciability of land, prevented renewal and the entry of new owners, and perpetuated stagnation and the status quo where the Code sought to encourage dynamism.

Secondly, *shufʿa* encourages a process of conglomeration and the endless acquisition by landowners of their neighbors' land, since there will always be another neighbor whose land can be controlled. Indeed, *shufʿa* encouraged the development of a practice of land speculation (*muḍāraba*). Thirdly, *shufʿa* severely restricted the freedom of contractual association, and, lastly, it embodied an element of coercion, in that landowners were obliged to sell to someone against their original intentions. Accordingly, the proposed Code sought to restrict the right of *shufʿa*, although, as we have seen in other instances, without resorting to unnecessary revolutions. The Code hoped that significant procedural and substantive restrictions would minimize this phenomenon and the problems it caused.[72]

---

[71] The Majalla, article 1008; The Egyptian Civil Code, articles 936–937.
[72] Al-Qānūn al-Madanī, volume 6, p. 378.

3.3 *The Procedural Restriction of* Shufʿa

The New Code consciously and deliberately adopted the approach of the *Sharīʿa*, which viewed *shufʿa* as a weak right that expires immediately if the conditions established for its activation are not strictly observed, in order to interpret the right in a restrictive manner. Again, we see how rules from the *Sharīʿa* could be used by the Code to meet its needs, in keeping with its modern approach, when these rules were appropriate for this purpose. The fact that these were centuries-old provisions was no demerit—on the contrary, their inclusion as consensual and accepted elements of the *Sharīʿa* served only to provide legitimacy, albeit indirectly, for the intention of the Code to introduce progress and competitiveness in the Egyptian legal instruments of the twentieth century. Paradoxically, therefore, it was through the old that the Code hoped to achieve the new. Again, though, it must be recalled that the Code chose from the *Sharīʿa* only those rules that were consonant with its spirit and suitable to its purpose.

We argue that the Code adopted two procedural techniques in order to restrict and limit the right of *shufʿa*: preventing the exercising of this right, in certain cases; and imposing conditions on the *shafīʿ* which, if not observed, led to the expiry of the right.

Firstly, the Code adopted several restrictions on the application of the right of *shufʿa* from the outgoing civil code: if the sale took place by means of auction; there was no *shufʿa* among relatives, and, in detail, if the sale took place between the head of a family and his offspring (*al-ʾuṣūl wal-furūʿ*), between spouses, between relatives up to the fourth degree, or between relatives by marriage up to the second degree (the last provision, excluding relatives by marriage up to the second degree, is an innovation, emphasizing the effort by the Code to extend the interpretation of the term 'relative' to its maximum); if the property were being sold in order to serve religious purposes, or to be annexed to land already used for such purposes; and a *waqf* could not exercise the right of *shufʿa*.[73]

Secondly, the Code extended the strict formal conditions required in order for the *shafīʿ* to realize the *shufʿa*, and the slightest failure to meet these conditions would lead to the immediate expiry of the right. The *shafīʿ* must announce his intention to exercise *shufʿa*, both to the

---

[73] The Egyptian Civil Code, article 939; Al-Wasīṭ, volume 9, pp. 534–538.

seller and the purchaser, within 15 days from the issue of the warning notice by the court (*ʾindhār*). If he fails to do so, his right expires. This provision was taken from the previous law of *shufʿa*, but the New Code restricted the right still further, requiring the *shafiʿ* to deposit the actual price of the transaction at the court before demanding *shufʿa*. The *shafiʿ* must deposit the money within 30 days from the date on which he informed the court of his interest in the right and, in any case—prior to the commencement of the hearing on his demand. Any deviation from this timetable and any delay will lead to the expiry of the right. It should be noted that the proposed Code also required the *shafiʿ* to deposit at least one-third of the final sale price with the court exchequer within 15 days; however, this provision was amended in the *al-qānūn al-madanī* Committee of the Senate.

This condition, requiring a financial deposit, was intended not only to present the *shafiʿ* with the challenge of obtaining the sale price within a limited period of time, but also to prevent empty threats against the parties to the sale, for example in order to extort money from them in return for a promise not to intervene, where after he would ostensibly announce that he was declining to exercise his right.

The date by which the *shafiʿ* must inform the court that he is interested in exercising *shufʿa* creates an additional race against time: the claim must be submitted to the court, accepted and scheduled for a hearing within 30 days from the date of notification, or the *shufʿa* expires. The explanatory notes to the proposed Code emphasized that it was not sufficient for the claim to be submitted and accepted: a hearing must also be scheduled, "in order to prevent the *shafiʿ* from delaying the legal proceedings unnecessarily." Lastly, the *shufʿa* would expire if four months passed from the date of official registration of the sale contract. In the previous *ʾahlī* code, *shufʿa* expired after six months; the proposed Code stipulated a three-month period, and the eventual compromise stated four months.[74]

3.4 *The Substantive Restriction of* Shufʿa

The question as to whether *shufʿa* constituted a land 'right' (*ḥaqq*) was relevant in the context of the extent to which it was possible to execute

[74] The Egyptian Civil Code, articles 940, 942–943, 948(2); Al-Qānūn al-Madanī, volume 6, pp. 424–425, 442–446; Ziadeh, p. 47.

disposition in this right, as with any other property right. The various schools of Islamic law were uncertain as to whether *shufʿa* should be considered a personal right or a substantive *jus ad rem*.[75] The New Code rejected both positions in this famous debate among the *fuqahāʾ*—the jurists of the *fiqh*, establishing that *shufʿa* was not a right of any type. The Code established that *al-shufʿa—rukhṣa*—i.e. that it is an opportunity, permission or a reason to win a right. Sanhūrī distinguished between the property right itself, *inter alia*, purchase, *ḥikr* or right of use, and the reason enabling the securing of this right. This distinction is significant, for example, in terms of the transfer of *shufʿa* by inheritance or by assignment.[76]

In its amended form, the proposed Code included an explicit provision declaring that the right of *shufʿa* could not pass through assignment or inheritance, based on the logic that this was not a right *per se*, but rather a reason for a right. However, this provision was deleted during the final deliberations on the article in the *Majlis al-shuyūkh*, and the matter was left to judicial interpretation. It should be noted that the original draft of the proposed law, before Sanhūrī became involved (in the short-lived committee of *Kāmil Ṣidqī*, which mainly discussed matters relating to *shufʿa*) noted that while *shufʿa* could not be transferred by assignment, it could be inherited.[77]

As the interpreter of the Code, Sanhūrī restricted the *shufʿa* still further, ruling that this was not a generic 'opportunity', but rather a personal one that could only be activated by the *shafīʿ* himself. These distinctions are significant in operative terms. For example: (1) The creditors of the *shafīʿ* cannot acquire his status as such; (2) The *shufʿa* cannot be transferred by way of assignment from the *shafīʿ* to another person; (3) The *shafīʿ* can waive (*nazl*) his right *vis-à-vis* another even before this right has crystallized; (4) The *shufʿa* cannot pass by bequeathal to the inheritors, if the *shafīʿ* died before declaring his intention to realize the *shufʿa*.[78]

In addition, however, the (amended) proposed Code also attempted, albeit unsuccessfully, to reduce significantly the scope of the criteria

---

[75] Al-Wasīṭ, volume 9, pp. 260–262; Sanhūrī, Maṣādir al-Ḥaqq fī al-Fiqh al-ʾIslāmī, volume 5 p. 22.

[76] Al-Wasīṭ, volume 9, p. 447.

[77] The Explanatory notes of the code proposal, amended article 1007; Al-Qānūn al-Madanī, volume 6, p. 345.

[78] Al-Wasīṭ, volume 9, pp. 452–460. For third option see the Egyptian Civil Code, article 948(1).

permitting the possibility of *shufʿa*. The reference is to the gravest possibility in terms of the injury to the freedom of association—the granting of the option of *shufʿa* to a neighbor. While the Code includes conditions restricting the receipt of this right, since the neighbor's land must be adjacent (*mulāṣaqa*) to the sold agricultural land on two sides, and must be worth at least half the value of the sold land, there is still no substantive affinity between the plots, as there is in the case of *ʾirtifāq*.[79]

In the original proposal, before Sanhūrī became involved, the possibility was included of granting *shufʿa* to a neighbor, further to the appearance of this possibility in the *shufʿa* law annexed to the outgoing code. Over the various stages of legislation, however, the Examination Committee (headed by Sanhūrī) decided to omit entirely the possibility of granting this right to a neighbor in any context (i.e., to omit the entire fifth possibility as itemized above).[80]

The Legislative Affairs Committee of the Lower House (*Majlis al-nuwwāb*) declined to approve the complete abolition of the laws regarding a neighbor's right of *shufʿa*, preferring instead to eliminate just one possibility—the sub-section relating to the adjacent land of a neighbor. This aspect was deleted from the proposed law before it was forwarded for ratification by the plenum of the Lower House.

In a discussion held on May 15, 1946, this key omission was the subject of extensive debate among the deputies in the Lower House. The main points raised in this debate are interesting, reflecting the discourse of the period in the Egyptian parliament: concern at excessive shocks to the system, combined with an internalization of the need for change and for enhanced mobility in economic and social life. The Islamic *Sharīʿa*, particularly in the case of *shufʿa*, constituted an authority and a basis for reference, and occupied a central position in public discourse. The insistence of the parliamentary deputies that a neighbor must enjoy the possibility of *shufʿa* might be seen as evidence that the elite class of major landowners represented in parliament was unwilling to relinquish this tool as part of the concessions introduced by the Code. The Egyptian landowning class probably attached importance to this right, which not only enabled them to seize control of neighboring land, but also to determine whether new neighbors could move into the region, the village or the surroundings of their estate, and if so—who.

---

[79] The Egyptian Civil Code, article 936(5)(3); Al-Wasīṭ, volume 9, pp. 575–579.

[80] Al-Qānūn al-Madanī, volume 6, pp. 366–369.

In this respect, the *shufʿa* enjoyed by the landowners constituted not only an economic privilege, but also a tool for social, and perhaps even political, control.

While the major landowners constituted a small class, it was one that was heavily represented in parliament.[81] The largest estates sometimes extended over hundreds of thousands of *fadān*s (acres) each, and the owners continued to control political institutions until well into the 1940s. In this respect, there was no difference between the *Wafd*, the Saʿadists or the constitutional liberals, although the latter two parties operated as the overt representatives of the major landowners. With the rise of the middle class and the expansion of education, middle-class and intellectual parties and movements were founded in Egypt that were divorced from land assets. As noted, however, during the 1930s and 1940s, parliament continued to be dominated by the major landowners. In this respect, the need for progress clashed with what were perceived by the landowners as more vital interests.

Accordingly, the summarized protocols quoted here offer an opportunity to understand the discourse among Egyptian lawmakers, and particularly among the owners of the large estates, as they attempted to cope with the issue of *shufʿa* in particular, and with the civil code in general. Unlike the situation a few years later, after the revolution, what we see here are not dictates, but rather an honest attempt to persuade the landowners and to secure agreement and compromise.

> The honorable deputy Tawfīq Khashba expressed the hope that the right of *shufʿa* would be extended, rather than reduced. *shufʿa* is a right drawn from the Islamic *Sharīʿa*, "and I cannot understand the logic that has led the government, in its proposed law, to define those eligible to *shufʿa* while excluding the neighbor, thus changing the content of the present (outgoing) code. We are an Eastern nation, with its own customs and traditions, and I believed that, in its new proposal, the government would actually remove the obstacles imposed on *shufʿa* in the present code, and would expand, rather than reduce, its scope."
>
> Khashba received a response from the honorable deputy ʾAḥmad Muḥammad Barīrī: "Only last week, I heard my colleague Khashba passionately defend the freedom of contracts . . . Yet this evening I cannot understand what reasons have led him to advocate the strangling of this freedom . . . There are two approaches in the *Sharīʿa* regarding the question of granting the possibility of *shufʿa* to a neighbor, a decisive opinion and a decided opinion. The minority opinion is that of ʾImām

[81] Landownership, p. 143.

ʾAbu Ḥanīfa, who alone, without the support of the remaining three schools, permitted a neighbor to enjoy *shufʿa* ... The three remaining schools did not permit this, for the reason that there is no need or benefit in such a measure. On the contrary, they saw that the interest was that owners should be free to sell to whomever they wish—to a neighbor or to any other person."

Honorable deputy Muḥammad Ḥamad Maḥshab: "But it is the school of ʾImām ʾAbu Ḥanīfa that is dominant in Egypt ..."

He received a reply from deputy Barīrī: "It is true that, in the past, Egypt tended toward the school of ʾAbu Ḥanīfa only. Today, however, we are not restricted to any particular school ... Thus far regarding the *Sharīʿa*. And as for the issue itself ... I shall address it here by means of a brief parable. Imagine that Mr. Tawfīq Khashba is the owner of 999 *fadān* of land in ʾAsyūṭ, while I own just one *fadān* adjacent to his land ... I wished to move from Asyūṭ to Cairo, and I have a brother, cousin or other relative who is the owner of one *fadān*, but unfortunately his *fadān* is not adjacent to mine. When I wished to sell my *fadān* to my relative, Mr. Khashba came and said: "Your *fadān* is adjacent to my land, and I wish to purchase it, so that I might have 1,000 *fadān*—a round number." Mr. Khashba wishes to coerce me to do this, and uses *shufʿa* to take my *fadān*, instead of my selling it to my brother or relative ..."

Honorable deputy Muḥammad Shawkat al-Tūnī: "Further to my colleague's comments, I would add that most legal experts regard *shufʿa* as a disliked right, such as divorce, since it embodies a form of fanaticism. My colleague Mr. Khashba spoke of the damage to neighborly relations, (but) this is a matter that has already ended, since in the past the population was small and a neighbor could injure his neighbor. Now, however, the number of residents has increased and people do not know their neighbors, but only those who live with them in the same building ..."

Honorable deputy Maḥmūd ʿAbd al-Qādir: "I support my colleague Tawfīq Khashba, although I believe that the basis for this legislation should not be the schools of the *Sharīʿa* (but rather logic and determination), just as the leaders of the schools themselves relied on logic and determination. Suppose that a man is the owner of land that is surrounded by the land of his good neighbor. The neighbor wishes to sell his land, and the man in our example is concerned lest the buyer not be someone who believes in good neighborly relations, or who is disturbing in terms of his standing or financial situation. Accordingly, out of his fear of what might happen and of potential damage, the owner in our example will purchase the land for sale by means of *shufʿa*. How can we deny him this right? After all, the man who sells his land suffers no damage (since there is no prohibition on him to sell)."

Honorable deputy ʿAlī al-Manzalāwī Bak: "I, too, support my colleague Tawfīq Khashba, since the right of *shufʿa* has been recognized in Egypt for a long time, and the law of 1901 (already restricted its scope). Who says that contractual freedom is impaired? After all, in any case the neighbor may sell his land. I would like to hear from the government what are the grounds for denying people this right, to which they have become accustomed over centuries."

The government representative (who is not named) replied: "The sages of Islamic law also stated that the right of *shuf'a* is a disliked right, and it was even permissible to resort to a ruse (*ḥīla*) in order to thwart its use. The law of 1901 also established restrictions in order to reduce the scope and use of this right. Nevertheless, we have seen cases, both in Mixed law and in *'ahlī* law, when this right has been abused for commerce and profiteering, and has caused endless problems and disputes. We have also seen that the Mixed and *'ahlī* court systems have been forced to resort to subterfuge in order to reject claims to apply *shuf'a*. Accordingly, it has been decided to restrict still further the application of the right of *shuf'a*: if, for example, any object, however small, stood between the owner's land and that of his neighbor, this will be sufficient to reject *shuf'a*."

Honorable deputy Fikrī 'Abāẓa Bak mentioned for the first time one of the true reasons for the landowners' opposition to the restriction of the neighbor's right of *shuf'a*: "The era of slavery and enslavement in land must end. We suffer grievously from this arbitrariness (*ta'assuf*) that collects all land in a single hand. It is the legislator's duty to seize every opportunity to prevent the (continued) expansion of the large estates and their seizure of small ones. If the poor Fikrī 'Abāẓa wishes to sell the sole *fadān* in his possession, his neighbor, the rich Khashba Bak, who owns hundreds of *fadān*, will offer him 120 pounds for a *fadān* worth 300 pounds. If I refuse to sell, he will threaten me with *shuf'a* (and then no-one will wish to buy from me, because they will be afraid of the *shuf'a*—G.B.), so that he usurps what little land I have and adds it to his extensive estate. In this way, the large ownerships expand and absorb smaller plots."

Honorable deputy Sayyid Jalāl: "I (also) oppose the position of Mr. Tawfīq Khashba, since we are living in an era in which we wish to put an end to the large ownerships, and to enable small ones to survive. I concur with my colleague Fikrī 'Abāẓa."

Honorable deputy Muḥammd Ḥamad Maḥsab: "With his renowned skill, Fikrī 'Abāẓa has turned this issue into a question of Capitalism and Bolshevism. The truth is that the person who wishes to sell his land will find before him the purchaser willing to pay the price, and, in addition, will find before him the *shafī'*, who is also willing to pay the price and expenses, and who is making a tangible offer... What damage, then, is there here to the seller? Our colleague 'Alī al-Manzalāwī questioned the wisdom of changing a situation to which we have become accustomed for many generations. Our colleague Mr. ('Abd al-Majīd) al-Sharqāwī replied that this is progress toward modern legislation. He informed us that the right of *shuf'a* has been eliminated in Sudan, but failed to inform us what is the situation in Syria and Iraq and other countries that follow Islamic legislation. (The opponents) told us that this right is unknown in France, but France does not have the Islamic *Sharī'a*, so how can we compare it to Egypt, a Muslim country that has become accustomed to the right of *shuf'a*, and an agricultural country three-fourths of whose capital is

> in farming land. They further stated that in modern times no attention is paid to a neighbor. This is true of the city-dwellers, but we in the villages still cling to our traditions, know out neighbors and act politely toward them. The truth is that I fail to see the wisdom in abolishing the neighbor's right of *shufʿa*."
>
> His Excellency the Minister of Justice intervened in the proceedings, noting that the problems caused by *shufʿa* impede the judicial system, "and the reason for these problems is that the neighbor wants his fellow's land to fall into his hands like a 'plump morsel' (*luqma sāʾigha*), after the purchaser has invested effort in searching for the land and in contacts with the seller. Accordingly, I welcome the amendment introduced by the committee, and agree that the neighbor should not have the right of *shufʿa* unless he held the right of *ʾirtifāq*, in order to free his land of this heavy burden of *ʾirtifāq*."
>
> The honorable deputy al-Manzalāwī bak again commented: "If you wish to amend the legislation, explain why and convince me of the grounds for this. If you wish to restrict large land ownerships—take what you wish from them and I shall welcome that. Take capitalism and demolish it; the curse of God upon it and upon those who love it. But here we are talking of legislation, and this should be justified—and we have heard no such justification."

A vote was held, and most of the deputies voted against eliminating the neighbor's right of *shufʿa* in the case of adjacent land. The neighbor's right was again included in the proposed law, passed in the Senate and became law. On this point the reform failed.[82]

4. Removing Obstacles in Society

In addition to the significant obstacles created in key points of social and economic activity by the *waqf* and by *shufʿa*—two mechanisms that relate to property law, which is of central importance in Egypt, and regarding which the Code claimed a special mission—it could be argued that this approach also represented an effort to remove additional obstacles at key junctions within Egyptian society, in the hope that this would enable free movement and encourage social progress and legal and economic mobility. This section examines these obstacles and the manner in which they were addressed by the Code. We shall illustrate our point using several examples relating to bankruptcy, the laws of inheritance and the assignment of debts and rights.

---

[82] Al-Qānūn al-Madanī, volume 6, pp. 373–383.

4.1 *Insolvency and Bankruptcy*

During the decades of protracted economic crisis and chronic inability of debtors to meet their required repayments, the number of cases of bankruptcy in Egypt rose dramatically. The former civil code, with its liberal approach, addressed this area only briefly; its provisions were contradictory and irregular, creating a state of complete chaos (*fawḍā*). Creditors were concerned that insolvent debtors would attempt to move money outside the bankruptcy arrangement; they were nervous of each other, lest one secure priority over the other in collecting the debt from the debtor, or seize preferential securities than those he held, thus leading to undesirable competition between them; debtors were also alarmed by the potentially arbitrary actions of their creditors, so that the institution of bankruptcy failed to meet the foundation of protection that is supposed to be one of its key hallmarks.[83] This situation resulted in constant tension and impaired commercial life and the national economy. As the economic situation deteriorated, so the level of damage increased.

As part of its goal of encouraging a form of legal and economic stability (insofar as this was possible, given its social goals) and of promoting healthy and honest competition in accordance with the principle of forgiveness (*ʿafū*), as discussed in the previous chapter, the New Code regulated the issue of bankruptcy for the first time in Egypt or any Arab country. "The interests of both parties were taken into account . . . in order to protect against the tyranny of the creditor and the distress of the debtor. (This dual approach) provides protection for both creditor and debtor."[84]

Defining clear boundaries for the institution of bankruptcy constituted an essential first step in the desired solution. The Code established that a debtor would be declared bankrupt if his assets were insufficient to pay his debts due for repayment. However, in accordance with the principle of judicial flexibility that characterizes the entire Code, such a declaration was not a merely mathematical procedure. The Code stated that the court must, in any case, taken into account the conditions relating to bankruptcy before making its ruling, whether these conditions were of a general or a specific nature. The court must take the future income of the debtor into account, as well as his personal

[83] Al-Wasīṭ, volume 1, pp. 72–73.
[84] Ibid., p. 73.

capability, the extent of his responsibility for the circumstances leading to bankruptcy, the interests of the creditors, and any other condition liable to influence his financial situation.[85]

After bankruptcy was declared and published in a special registry, the court was not required to present any future payment of the debtor for immediate repayment. On the contrary, the court enjoyed broad discretion in leaving future debts at their set dates, or to postpone repayment in order to facilitate the attempt by the debtor to remove his debts in the manner that was most convenient for him. Moreover, the Code went a step further toward the bankrupt individual, allowing him to sell parts of his assets even after bankruptcy, and against the creditors' wishes (in order to afford him a measure of control over his own fate, rather than obliging him merely to await the actions of his creditors). This was permissible if he sold assets at a proper price for the transaction in question, and the purchaser deposited the money in the court exchequers. The amount of money so received would be transferred for payment of the debtor's liabilities to his creditors.[86]

A further provision in favor of the bankrupt individual related to what the explanatory notes referred to as a 'humanitarian procedure' in order to provide the individual with money to cover his living expenses if his creditors had made his personal expenses subject to the arrangement. By request, the court could permit the bankrupt individual to receive living expenses from his income as seized by the creditors—a provision that had not been present in the previous civil code, and the absence of which caused great suffering to bankrupt individuals and their families.[87]

The New Code also protected the rights of creditors, unlike the outgoing civil code. Firstly, the registration of the demand to declare insolvency was sufficient to prevent any disposition by the debtor that might reduce his assets or increase his liabilities. If he took such action, this would be invalid from the creditors' standpoint. This situation freezes the debtor's actions and reassures the creditors. In order to reassure them still further, and, particularly, in order to prevent attempts by the debtor to move his assets outside the bankruptcy arrangement, the Code established that the debtor would be penalized if, after the judge

[85] The Egyptian Civil Code, articles 249, 251.

[86] Ibid., articles 255(2), 258; Al-Wasīṭ, volume 1, p. 73; Al-Qānūn al-Madanī, volume 2, p. 681.

[87] Al-Qānūn al-Madanī, volume 2, p. 685; The Egyptian Civil Code, article 259.

had declared his insolvency, he deceitfully concealed any of his assets from his creditors in order to prevent the execution of this declaration on these assets, or if he presented exaggerated or false debts in a manner intended to injure his creditors. "On the basis of what we have presented thus far, it would seem that the institution of bankruptcy as established by the New Code has undertaken to coordinate among all the opposing interests, protects the debtor from his creditors, protects creditors from their debtor, and protects the creditors from each other," summarized the interpretative comments in *Al-Wasīṭ*.[88]

4.2 *Removal of an Estate*

In the previous civil code, the question of the removal or distribution of an estate (*taṣfiyyat al-tarika*) among the inheritors had been left as a matter of personal status that depended on the religious community to which the deceased belonged.[89] This situation created confusion, since the different communities applied different legal rules. The old civil code included almost no references to the important issue of the removal of an estate, and estate debts were sometimes not paid before distribution began to the inheritors, so that the latter received their portions along with the debts of the estate. This created an intolerable situation whereby a person who purchased assets from the inheritors did not usually know, or could not know, of the existence of such debts. This confusion seriously impaired legal and economic stability and certainty. People were afraid to purchase from inheritors, and assets were sometimes left without buyers. Sanhūrī noted that the gravest problem facing the Egyptian judicial system was the lack of coordination between the basic principle of the Islamic *Sharīʿa*—*lā tarika ʾilā baʿd sadād al-dayn*—i.e. the allocation of the estate comes only after the removal of his debts—and the principle of French law that the inheritors assume both the rights and the liabilities of the bequeather.[90]

Once again, the New Code employed a principle from the *Sharīʿa*—that of *lā tarika ʾilā baʿd sadād al-dayn*—in order to resolve an issue that had caused difficulties for the Egyptian economy and for society at

[88] The Egyptian Civil Code, article 260; Al-Qānūn al-Madanī, volume 2, pp. 688–689; Al-Wasīṭ, volume 1, p. 73.

[89] The *ʾAhlī* Civil Code, article 54.

[90] The Explanatory notes of the code proposal, Al-Qānūn al-Madanī, volume 6, p. 200; Al-Wasīṭ, volume 1, p. 74; Wujūb, p. 85.

large. Indeed, the Code emphasized that it was employing an ancient Islamic legal principle in order to secure the progress it sought for its society, and it saw no contradiction in this. Did the Code adopt this principle due to the sacred nature of the *Sharīʿa* and its ostensibly special status? The Code attached importance to the idea that an estate should be divided only after the debts have been repaid, in order to restore certainty to the laws of inheritance and prevent damage to the economy. Once again, we may see how an arrow is placed in the wood, and the *Sharīʿa*—which, in this case, was consonant with the desire principle—was drawn around the arrow. To prove our point, we would argue that, had the *Sharīʿa* established the opposite principle, it may reasonably be assumed that it would not have been adopted, as we have seen in other areas that hampered economic certainly, such as the institution of the sale subject to a right of redemption, which was drawn from the *Sharīʿa*, and which was abolished by the New Code without any particular sentiments. The sanctity and status of the *Sharīʿa* were, therefore, recruited to serve the most mundane of causes. "The provisions for the removal of an estate as introduced in the New Code are certainly among the most important provisions innovated by this Code," Sanhūrī noted.[91]

Contrary to its predecessor, the New Code noted that, in the laws of inheritance, the Islamic *Sharīʿa* would apply to all citizens of Egypt, even if they were not Muslims. This provision emphasized the manner in which the Code regarded the element of *fiqh* in the *Sharīʿa*, as a tool for mundane law appropriate for the members of all the religious communities, regardless of any question of sanctity, unique morality or religious or ethnic status.[92]

For the first time in modern Egyptian legal history, the New Code established a stable, progressive and clear mechanism for the removal of an estate. An estate manager could be appointed by the bequeather or by the court; the estate, its liabilities and the liabilities of others toward it were all defined; the removal of the debts of the estate; and the transfer of what remained of the moneys of the estate to the inheritors, free of any debts.[93]

---

[91] Al-Wasīṭ, volume 1, p. 74.

[92] The Egyptian Civil Code, article 875; Al-Wasīṭ, volume 1, p. 74; *Fiqh al-Khilāfa*, p. 39.

[93] The Egyptian Civil Code, article 876; Al-Qānūn al-Madanī, volume 6, p. 201.

A further innovation, designed to protect economic stability, was the collective removal of the estate. This term, the explanatory notes to the Code clarified, meant that only the estate manager represented the estate, and the creditors could not take any legal proceeding otherwise than with reference to the manager. They could not seize possession of land belonging to the estate, and they could not execute any legal disposition prior to the completion of the removal of the estate. The explanatory notes to the proposed Code commented that the Code was thereby removing the creditors from the estate, preventing their taking any individual steps prior to the completion of the allocation. This ensured true equality among the different creditors, as we also saw in the case of bankruptcy. In this manner, all those involved should be satisfied: the creditors enjoyed equal status among themselves; their rights were protected, and a state of 'free for all' was avoided; the inheritors recognized that they would receive their portion free of any debt; and a third party purchasing assets from the inheritors knew that he had no cause to be concerned about hidden debts. "This will stabilize commerce in assets derived from inheritance" was the hopeful expectation expressed in the explanatory notes to the proposed Code.[94] The sale of movable and immovable property of an estate will be made by public auction unless all the heirs agree the sale will be carried out by negotiations or in any other way. If the estate is insolvent the approval of all the creditors is also necessary.[95]

A further ruling included in the Code in this context was that creditors who, for any reason, were not included in the allocation of debts would not enjoy any remedies with regard to a third party that purchased inherited assets in good faith. This was an important guarantee for economic security in Egypt: any person who purchased an asset from inheritors knew that he would never be required to face the burden of the debts of inheritance, even if this measure injured somewhat the rights of these creditors. Such creditors would, however, be entitled to file suit against the inheritors.[96] Finally, in order to stimulate the transferability of property the Code innovated that if a contract or a will contain clause stipulating the inalienability of a property, such a clause will be valid if based on a 'legitimate reason' and limited to a reasonable duration.[97]

[94] The Egyptian Civil Code, articles 883–884; Al-Qānūn al-Madanī, volume 6, p. 201.
[95] The Egyptian Civil Code, article 893(2).
[96] Ibid., article 897; Al-Qānūn al-Madanī, volume 6, p. 202.
[97] The Egyptian Civil Code, article 823(1).

4.3 *Assignment of a Debt and Assignment of a Right: Encouraging Horizontal Mobility*

The assignment of a debt from one debtor to another was not recognized in Egyptian law prior to the era of the New Code. The assignment of a right from one creditor to another did exist, but strangely required the authorization of the debtor, as we shall see below.

Assignment is of great importance in promoting economic mobility, since it permits not only restricted vertical activity between a specific creditor and debtor, but also horizontal mobility among creditors and among debtors. The frequency of use of such assignments may provide an indication of economic expansion and sophistication in an economy.

Sanhūrī noted that Egyptian society was in particular need of the tools of the assignment of a debt, since the main use of this tool was to sell mortgaged land. The debtor owned land which he sold, endorsing together with the land his debt to the mortgager to another debtor who took his place.

The main principle introduced by the New Code in this respect was that the right could be transferred to a new creditor without the agreement of the debtor, and the debt could be transferred to a new debtor without the agreement of the creditor. Thus the tool for the assignment of a debt or a right became particularly flexible.[98]

Assignment of a debt (*ḥawālat al-dayn*): The Code established a basic principle that the assignment of a debt was to take place by agreement between the debtor and a third party who would bear the debt instead of the original debtor. The dilemma that arose in this context was whether the assignment of the debt could be effected against the explicit or implicit wishes of the creditor.

The proposal, strongly supported by Sanhūrī, suggested an arrangement whereby the assignment would only bind the creditor if he authorized it; however, the creditor would not be permitted to reject the assignment if his rights were protected. The proposal added that if the creditor was tardy in giving his reply, this would be considered tantamount to rejection, "and, in this case, his refraining from replying or his refusal would be considered null, and the assignment would take place notwithstanding." Thus the proposed law created an imposed

98 Al-Wasīṭ, volume 1, p. 74. On the Assignment of a Debt see the Egyptian Civil Code, articles 315–322; on the assignment of a Right see article 303.

affinity between the action of assignment, which was permitted, and the element of the creditor's will.

The proposed Code based its grounds on the theory of the abuse of a right, which we encountered in the previous chapter, "since it is unfair that the creditors' rights be protected, yet he seek to prevent the assignment of the debt." In order to increase the chances of the adoption of this legal model by parliament, the explanatory notes mentioned that this norm was drawn from the Islamic *Sharīʿa* (according to the *Mālikī* school). It was also noted that the *Ḥanbalī* school of the *fiqh* also did not require the creditor's consent to assignment; if he refused, despite his not being damaged by the transaction, the judge could oblige him to concur.[99] However, the explanatory notes added that, as was well known, the position of the *Ḥanafi* school was the opposite: the creditor's consent was required as a condition for assignment, as was also the case in the Ḥanafī *Majalla*: "An assignment between the assigner and the assignee is bound and dependent on the acceptance of the assignee. He who says to his fellow, 'Accept by assignment the debt I owe to so-and-so', and the assigned accepts, the assignment is thereby bound, and it depends on the acceptance of the assignee—if he accepts—the assignment stands"[100] (clarification of the terms in the *Majalla*—the assigner is the debtor who makes the assignment; the assignee is the creditor; the assigned is the person who accepts the assignment).[101]

In the deliberations of the Civil Code Committee in the Senate, this proposal encountered opposition. The principle that assignment should be permitted was accepted, but the president of the committee, Muḥammad al-Wakīl, and another deputy, Ḥasan al-ʿAshmāwī, opposed the idea that the creditor should be obliged to consent to assignment, even if his rights were maintained thereafter. Sanhūrī referred them to the Islamic *Sharīʿa*, but they maintained their opposition. The two deputies could not oppose the *Sharīʿa*, given its lofty status, but they argued that the scope of application had changed in modern times, "and all has become dominated by evil and deceit (so that obliging the creditor to accept) will open a gate to numerous acts of deceit." Accordingly, they proposed that the end of the article, stating that the creditor could not reject the assignment if his rights were protected, be deleted, and

[99] Al-Qānūn al-Madanī, volume 3, p. 141.
[100] The Majalla, article 683.
[101] The Egyptian Civil Code, article 315; Al-Qānūn al-Madanī, volume 3, pp. 139–141; The code proposal, articles 444–447; The Majalla, articles 673–679, 683.

this was duly done. The committee accepted this argument, noting that it was the creditor's right to face a specific debtor of his choice, and not another—otherwise, he might suffer damage.[102]

Thus a complex legal situation emerged. As a general legal principle, the assignment of a debt continued to apply in any case. If approved by the creditor, the new debtor would replace the first one for all purposes. If the creditor did not approve, the assignment would still be valid, but it would not bind the creditor. For his purposes, he would continue to face the original debtor, while the new debtor would forward the sum of the debt to the original debtor, who would then pass this to the creditor.[103]

This was a typical example of the method of codification of the New Code: eschewing coercion, and favoring mutual persuasion and the acceptance of the majority decision. The intention was to secure as wide a common denominator as possible among all those involved in the process, so that the Code would secure the greatest possible measure of social legitimacy, and would hence be more effective and efficient. According to this logic, it was preferable that a particular reform be accepted only in part, but with broad consensus, rather than passing in its complete version, but at the price of lesser consensus and impaired legitimacy.

The assignment of a right (*ḥawālat al-ḥaqq*)—no particular problems emerged here during the legislative process, since this principle already appeared in the old Civil Code and was familiar in the Egyptian economy. Bizarrely, this right required the consent of the debtor to the endorsement of the creditor's debt, "which unnecessarily delayed commerce," as Sanhūrī noted. Accordingly, the Code now provided for the endorsement of a right without the need for the debtor's consent.[104]

---

[102] Al-Qānūn al-Madanī, volume 3, pp. 142–143.
[103] The Egyptian Civil Code, articles 317(1), 318(2).
[104] Al-Wasīṭ, volume 1, p. 76; The Egyptian Civil Code, article 303.

CHAPTER SIX

TOWARD A NEW *MODUS VIVENDI*: LEGAL FLEXIBILITY (*MURŪNA*) AS A SOCIAL INTEREST

"You are hereby accused of washing your clothes in the water channel."
"Your Honor, may God uplift you, are you imposing a fine on me for washing my clothes?"
"For washing them in the water channel."
"Then where should I wash them?"
The judge hesitated, pondered, and was unable to answer. He knew that these poor villagers did not have water pools with clean pipe water, yet they must obey a modern law imported from abroad. The judge looked at me and said:
"The prosecution?"
"The prosecution is not interested in discussing where a man should wash his clothes. What interests the prosecution is the application of the law."
The judge turned his head away from me, lowered it slightly, nodded, and then said quickly, like someone unfastening a heavy load:
"Fine twenty (qursh)... Next!"

Tawfīq al-Ḥakīm, *Diary of a Village Prosecutor* (*Yawmiyyāt Nā'ib fī al-'Aryāf*), 1937[1]

Our needs for the old exist, as do our needs for the new. The old represents permanence and stability; the new—flexibility and development.

Sanhūrī, 1949[2]

1. The Foundation of *Murūna*—The Theory

1.1 *Stone by Stone*

Having claimed above that the author of the New Code sought to achieve a balance between the polarized and conflict-ridden extremes

[1] *Tawfīq al-Ḥakīm, Al-Muallafāt al-Kāmila* (Beirut: Maktabat Lubnān Nāshirun, 1994) volume 1, pp. 369–370. In this story al-Ḥakīm depicts in literary way the gap between the Western legislation and the reality of the Egyptian peasant. In his story the legal system seems more occupied in its procedures and formalities than in creating justice. Al-Ḥakīm was the son of a judge, and he finished law school in 1924. His original ambition was to be a writer, but his father insisted on a more practical occupation. After completing his legal Ph.d in Paris and working for the Egyptian public prosecutor's office, he abandoned the legal field to become a famous novelist; Reid, pp. 108–109.

[2] Al-Jadīd wa al-Qadīm, pp. 6–8.

of Egyptian society—between poor and reach, the individual and the collective, the past and the future, and progress and tradition; and having described the manner in which this balance was manifested both in the New Code itself and during the legislative process, the question now arises as to how all these aspects may combine together to form a functioning and operative mechanism. What factor, if any, can connect all these components, and, indeed, is it even possible to bridge and connect them so that they do not contradict each other? The general principles described above for protecting the weaker members of society seem contradictory to the principles of encouraging the strong and achieving economic and social progress; the same is true for the tension between the individual and society.

Moreover, moral elements in particular and ideological elements in general introduced into the statute book may clash with the positivist and practical dimension of law, and questions of individual and social justice may clash with values that are important to any legal system, such as legal stability and commercial confidence.

In other words: what transforms these individual and apparently contradictory components into a dynamic legal formula capable of successful application in everyday life? This is a cardinal question, since the more complex the tasks taken on by the Code, the greater the apparent threat to its homogeneity and harmony, as Sanhūrī himself noted, reflecting his awareness of this growing problem.[3]

The element capable of connecting all these components is elusive and covert, and cannot easily be found through a positivist perusal of the articles of the Code. Nevertheless, its presence is evident and impressive. This element, the pulsing heart of the New Code, is what this book terms the foundation of flexibility (*murūna*).

I use the term *murūna* to refer to a philosophical state characterized by mutual concessions, compromise and conciliation, flexibility and elasticity, the bridging of distinct elements, pragmaticism and the eschewing of dogma, or, as the architect of the Code, ʿAbd al-Razzāq al-Sanhūrī, wrote in 1935:

> (Between the more and the less) I prefer the less. It has a completeness and purity that cannot be sullied. This is the practical interest—pragmatism (*al-brājmātiyya*).[4]

[3] Al-Wasīṭ, volume 1, p. 61.

[4] Diary, 17 August 1935, p. 268; Wujūb, p. 72.

This chapter argues that the principle of *murūna* is broad and comprehensive, and is supposed to be manifested in politics, in society and in law as a remedy for a polarized and tension-ridden society.

On the legal level, we have already seen evidence of this principle on various occasions relating to the legislative process, when the authors of the New Code sought to introduce normative elements, but to do so without a revolution and while attempting to secure broad legitimacy, even at the price of compromise. However, *murūna* in the legal realm cannot be divorced from the social, economic and political spheres, since the New Code sought to use law to achieve social, and perhaps even political, outcomes. Accordingly, this is a broad, horizontal foundation that cannot be confined to a specific discipline. We shall now examine the influence of this element on the content and spirit of the New Code, through the unique and sophisticated mechanisms it introduced.

The foundation of *murūna* is, above all, an essence of continuity and of a continuum of time and space on which the new is to be constructed. The new is built on the foundation of the old, but does not displace it. As Sanhūrī says: "The new is born of the old—without the old there is no new . . . What is new today will be old tomorrow, and tomorrow's old was new yesterday . . . Accordingly, there is no difference between new and old."[5] This continuity is not automatic, however, but one based on a critical dialogue between old and new. In his article 'The Old and the New', Sanhūrī poses a rhetorical question:

> What is civilization? Is it not a stable base of the old, on which we shall construct a building renewing over time? And what is science? Is it not the knowledge we have received from our ancestors, generation after generation; and each generation demolishes a crumbling stone in the building and replaces it with two new stones, so that the building becomes harmonious and rises to the edge of the sky? Does modern thought not clash with ancient thought, only to realize that the old can sometimes be like waste, but can sometimes also be like a rich fertilizer?[6]

In terms of scope, *murūna* relates to an adaptive and pragmatic approach that should be shown by *all* elements of society in order to ensure social reconciliation, and not merely by any specific sector of the population. This explains the importance Sanhūrī attached to ensuring the Code would apply to all sections of Egyptian society—locals and foreigners

[5] Al-Jadīd wa al-Qadīm, p. 6.
[6] Ibid., pp. 7–8.

and the members of the different religious communities. There were to be no extra-territorial sectors, as had hitherto been the case with foreigners and the members of some religious communities. Accordingly, Sanhūrī regretted the fact that the Egyptian New Code, unlike civil codes around the world, did not include the laws of personal status, contrary to his initial hopes.[7] In other words, his regret was not confined to the specific context of the laws of religious status, but also related to the comprehensive character of the Code as a unifying basis for all of Egyptian society. According to Sanhūrī's approach, the totality and integrity of civil law has a social value, permitting the establishment of the foundation of *murūna* among all sections of the population.

It might be added here that when Sanhūrī introduced into the Code norms drawn from the *Sharīʿa* and applied them to all the citizens and residents of Egypt—Muslims and non-Muslims alike—his perspective was centered not only on the religious component, but rather on the *Sharīʿa* as an ostensibly authentic local Eastern entity; a default source for society offering a broad cultural common denominator and capable of overcoming social slits and promoting a form of national reconciliation. Sanhūrī admitted his admiration of the Islamic *Sharīʿa*, including its strong component of *murūna*. As he noted, "It can take on the garb of the time in which it operates."[8]

Accordingly, *murūna* serves as the oil in the wheels of society, no less vital than progress and technology, since these cannot promote the desired social reconciliation. Sanhūrī wrote:

> The fundamental conditions for social reconciliation are maintaining consensus and coordination between citizens, interests and opinions. Reform and progress of any kind can be adopted only in an atmosphere of stable social reconciliation. Reform and progress alone cannot bring such social reconciliation.[9]

The development and emphasis of the foundation of *murūna* and its deliberate inclusion in the New Code, as we shall see further on, constitute a declaration on the part of the author of the Code that the intention is not only to issue a technical statute book, but also to develop a new, practical social formula for the functioning of Egyptian society;

---

[7] Wujūb, pp. 59–61.
[8] Diary, 27 June 1923, p. 93.
[9] Ibid., 15 July 1928, p. 180. Originally this was the remark of the French President, and Sanhūrī copied it with enthusiasm to his diary.

a new social contract centered on a new *modus vivendi* for Egyptian society, including mutual concessions and solidarity, including in the context of the relations between rich and poor:

> The social problem in Egypt is not how to take from the rich in order to give to the poor, but how to raise the standard of living for all, since the average per capita income in Egypt is incredibly low.[10]

The lack of dogmatism is reflected in the need for compromise or, at least, the need to assuage the tension that had accumulated in Egyptian society between East and West—between Eastern and Western legal tools, and between the different world views of these two normative worlds, between which Egyptian intellectual society, then as now, has tried to choose. Here, too, the foundation of *murūna* in the Code mandated compromise, drawing on the West for utilitarian purposes, in accordance with the functional tests of the benefit of the East. The West is not invalid *per se*, when it serves the interests of the East. Or as Sanhūrī commented in his personal diary in 1923:

> (There are two intellectual groups in Egypt). The first clings blindly to an Islamic past that does not develop with time—something that may produce hatred for the Islamic nation and harm the religious minorities that live in the Near East, who will therefore turn to Europe for protection, thus turning against us rather than combining their efforts with ours.
>
> On the other side, there is a group that seeks to cut the umbilical cord of the past in order to introduce European civilization in Egypt, making the country part of Europe, and without paying attention to the unique traditions and history of this country or to its Eastern temperament.
>
> Both groups present a danger for Eastern society. We must admit that we need Europe at the present; but this does not imply sacrificing our own national traditions and introducing a foreign civilization in our Eastern land . . . What binds us together forcefully is the past. A nation cannot rid itself of its past, unless this be a nation fumbling in the dark to find its way and unable to locate the path.[11]

We have indeed seen in the previous chapters that Islamic legal tools can be used in accordance with the required standard of functionality, just as Western legal tools can be employed. The focus of attention is the good of Egyptian society, and, according to this logic, it is unimportant what sources are used to this end. This is *murūna*, and one of its manifestations is the motif of *takhayyur*—selecting that which is

[10] Ibid., 13 January 1944, p. 293.
[11] Ibid., 31 October 1923, pp. 91, 125, 127.

good—a flexible and functional approach that has been perceived in the West as confused eclecticism.

What is the difference between *murūna* and *takhayyur*? The former is a broader term, describing a philosophical approach reflected in the legal, social and political spheres, whereas *takhayyur* is one of the practical tools employed to manifest such an approach.

This chapter argues that the pragmatic dimension of *murūna* has two contradictory meanings. On the one hand, it is the glue that binds together the legal components of the Code, as we shall see below. On the other, it is an opposite element that sometimes draws the different components apart in order to facilitate movement and efficiency. Which direction applies depends on the content, time and place of any given instance. It is, therefore, elastic and formless glue that adopts its desired form in accordance with the required functionality. This elastic duality in the foundation of *murūna* explains its importance and ensures its success.

The foundation of *murūna* is, therefore, intended to act as a glue in three different spheres, situated between law, society and time. The first is within the Code itself, as a legal component binding the various components into a holistic creation. It softens shocks, balances opposites and prevents friction. The second is the glue between the Code and society: the Code must be flexible enough to adapt to the polarized and rapidly-changing Egyptian society in order to help it and guide it to meet the objectives it sets. This dimension of flexibility is also required in order to provide the Code with legitimacy in the society in which it is introduced.

In the third sphere, the Code turns like the two-face god Janus to two different communities of time—contemporary Egypt, with all the flaws it sought to amend, and the future Egyptian society it sought to establish—the present and the future. The future community could be identical or similar to that of the present day, but it could also be a different Egypt, characterized by the solidarity and harmony that the Code would help develop over the years. The reform might be a success, or it might remain utopia; in any case, the Code was designed to be appropriate for all these societies—no easy task, and one that required a considerable measure of flexibility, since it had to adapt to any time and place, and be capable of changing as circumstances changed.

A further dilemma that explains the extensive use of the foundation of *murūna* is that the Code sought to avoid dismantling social frameworks or causing revolutions. It aimed to introduce change in order to maintain the existing social order, not in order to overthrow it. If the aim is to avoid dismantling existing frameworks, it is harder to address the ills of society, and particularly social polarization. This is the challenge of *murūna* and the challenge of the entire Code. The authors of the Code hoped that the flexibility of *murūna* would have a spiral quality enabling them to overcome this quandary: how to change without changing, and how to be flexible within an inflexible scope.

1.2 *Activating the Foundation of* Murūna

Given this complex dilemma, it could be argued that *murūna* as a central foundation in the New Code functions not only as a theory, but as a practical mechanism comprising several wheels of flexibility that operate simultaneously.

The first is the mechanism that renders the contract laws flexible, allowing them to function as social scales on which the various sectors of Egyptian society will be weighed, in the hope and intention of achieving balance among them; custom (*ʿurf*) is another important foundation of flexibility, manifested both within the New Code and between the Code and society; in addition to a series of legal criteria desired to introduce flexibility into the Code and its provisions; and all these are implemented with scrupulous discretion in order to ensure due balance.

These wheels of flexibility are scrutinized from above by the court, which is charged by the Code with the most important function in the process of legal and social mediation. This New Code granted the civil judge a normative status he had not previously enjoyed; he not only resolved disputes between the two parties, in which framework he also, to an extent, established general legal norms; the court was also expected to operate that new social order to which the Code aspired, and its success in so doing would depend on the measure of flexibility it showed. The court is charged with driving this socio-legal mechanism, and is the guarantee for its success.

In other words, the court is the mechanical dynamo that moves the system of flexibility in the Code, and hence the entire Code as a socio-legal machine. The function of the Code cannot be appreciated without understanding the decisive function of the court within the Code. We shall below discuss these components of flexibility.

2. Contractual Flexibility in Action

2.1 *The Restriction of 'Free Will' (Sultān 'al-'Irāda)*

As they came to draft the section of contract law in the New Code, the authors considered what approach to adopt in order to adapt this section to the general spirit of the Code. Should they follow the characteristic approach of Continental civil law in the eighteenth and nineteenth centuries, reflecting the Enlightenment philosophy which, as we have already seen in previous chapters, was based on the individual and saw the individual as the sum picture, and hence sanctified the individual's agreements and contractual freedom? Or should they prefer the contrary approach, which had emerged during the twentieth century—the sociological perspective that places society and its interests in the center, even at the expense of individual interests, and intervenes in the contractual freedom enjoyed by the individual? We have also seen that, as far as property and contract law is concerned, the New Code clearly followed the 'social function' of property law and the sociological doctrines of the contract, with the goal of transforming contracts into social tools for change. Despite this, however, it would also seem that the New Code struck compromises between the major philosophical schools of contract law, faithful to the pragmatic approach reflected in ideological terms in the foundation of *murūna*. The expression 'contract law as ideology' is not accidental; it was borrowed from the article of Feinman and Gabel, which reflected the changes that occurred in American case law and legal philosophy relating to contract law in the context of the changing socioeconomic perspectives of the past three centuries. In general terms, these transformations in American law mirror the dilemma faced by Egyptian law, between the nineteenth-century emphasis on the individual and the desire to create a more 'just' society that emerged during the first half of the twentieth century. However, American law played no role as a source of reference for Egyptian or Arab law, and this source is mentioned here solely as a methodological aside.[12]

The first approach, followed by the outgoing Egyptian civil code, founded the entire social system on the individual. The individual was the purpose, and the collective existed for his benefit. The personality

---

[12] J. Feinman, P. Gabel, "Contract Law as Ideology", in D. Kairys ed. *Politics of Law, a Progressive Critique* (New York: Pantheon Books, 1990), pp. 373–386.

of the individual becomes complete only when his motif of liberty is realized, and the external manifestation of this liberty is his autonomous free will. Sanhūrī emphasized that just as the French philosophers had made thought the epitome of personality (*cogito ergo sum*), so the legal experts who adhered to this school had lauded the foundation of will.[13] According to this approach, the individual is not subject to any obligations unless he has chosen this of his own free will. Exponents of this school claimed that their approach was consonant with natural law, which they saw as based on the obligation to respect individual liberty.

This approach was certainly attractive to the authors of the Egyptian New Code, who were familiar with it and with the accompanying economic approaches, such as the French theory of *Physiocrates*, which argued that if economic activity were completely free, competition would blossom and prices would be determined according to supply and demand rather than as instructed by the legislator. This test of supply and demand would eventually lead to stability in prices, which would also mean social stability. The ramification of this theory is that the economic sphere should be governed solely by free will, and contracts, *inter alia*, should be subject only to the will of the parties.[14]

According to the approach of the exclusive dominion of free will, obligations in general, and indeed the entire legal system, are essentially based on free will: ownership is rooted in free will, the rights of the family are based on the contract of marriage, i.e., on free will, and inheritance is based on the binding testament, which thus preserves free will even after death. According to this school, it is unacceptable to restrict the applicability of the contract on the grounds that discrimination has arisen (see the discussion of *ghabn* in Chapter Four) in the rights of one of the parties, provided that he chose to enter the contract in such a situation. Accordingly, the employee who signs a contract with an employer must perform whatever he has undertaken to do; the lack of balance between the parties to the contract is irrelevant. Factors such as 'social solidarity' (*taḍāmun ʾijtimāʿī*), 'the abuse of a right' and the elements of justice are secondary to the dominance of free will. Moreover, if a contract has been made through the agreement of the parties, it should only be amended with their joint consent, and the judge is not entitled to amend it or to add any new provision.[15]

---

[13] Al-Wasīṭ, volume 1, p. 153.
[14] Ibid., p. 156.
[15] Ibid., p. 158.

A second possible approach that developed during the twentieth century, again as the result of economic changes, was also well-known to the authors of the New Code. The development of industrialization, major corporations and workers' organizations led to a social perspective on contract law and, in particular, to an emphasis on the interests of the collective at the expense of the individual. Free will was overruled in favor of social interests, which were now perceived as of greater importance. Social considerations such as the stability of the contractual relationship, the development of trust between the parties to the contract, and the securing of social solidarity by legal means restricted the direction enjoyed by the individual within the legal totality, and emphasized the discretion of the collective.

The authors of the New Code, were aware of both these approaches. Since they perceived the use of contract law as a socio-legal manifesto and as an ideology, they decided to opt for the intermediate path of *murūna*. Sanhūrī wrote:

> The New Code adopted an intermediate position in defining free will. It did not injure it to the extent that it would be deferential to the judge or the legislator, and the legal basis is still the free will to associate; however, it did not allow it to run wild in defining contractual relations without attention to the public good and the requirements of justice.[16]

The explanatory notes to the proposed Code added that the Code did not position free will as the exclusive axis along which legal relations were to move, but rather gave it a mediating role as a bridge between individual liberty and the good of society.[17]

Indeed, the New Code restricted the free will of the party to an agreement both during the making of the contract and in its application. In the making (*takwīn*) of a contract, the Code expanded the framework of unfairness (*ghabn*), as we have already seen, and prevented one party from exploiting the levity or caprice of the other, even if the latter were satisfied and aware of his actions when signing the contract, since the element of his free will was not perfect (*ṣaḥīḥ*) in this situation, and accordingly was not to be taken into account. This is a clear example of the restriction of the free will of the parties to a contract—both that of the exploiter and that of the exploited.[18]

---

[16] Ibid., p. 90.

[17] Al-Qānūn al-Madanī, volume 1, p. 24.

[18] The Egyptian Civil Code, article 129; Al-Wasīṭ, volume 1, p. 90.

Further examples of restrictions in making a contract, as we have seen, included a restriction on the coercive force of a uniform contract (*ʿaqd al-ʾidhʿān*) and the theory of the abuse of a right. A prominent example of the restriction of the free will of a party in implementing an agreement is the theory of unforeseen circumstances, as discussed in detail in Chapter Four. Moreover, a party could pay financial compensation if it emerged that specific performance was very difficult; the Code established that "if specific performance were very difficult for the obliged party, it could pay financial compensation, if this would not cause substantive damage to the creditor."[19] Sanhūrī further noted that the New Code not only places the will of the legislator before that of the parties, but, in some cases, places the will of court before that of the parties. An example of this is when the Code states that

> If the parties have agreed to all the substantive matters in the contract, and reserved the option to agree the details at a later point, and did not include the stipulation that the contract would not be made in the absence of agreement between them, the contract will be considered as perfect and made. If a dispute emerges regarding details not agreed, these shall be determined by the court in accordance with the nature of the transaction, the provisions of the law, custom and equity.[20]

The obvious deviation in this article from the principle of free will aroused debate in an external seminar of jurists that accompanied the final stages of drafting the proposed Code. Judge Ṣādiq Fahmī commented that, in order for a contract to be completed, it was necessary to secure a full expression of the will of both parties in all the relevant subjects; if the expression of will was partial, the contract could not be made, and would, in his opinion, constitute a contract whose conditions had not been met. Another jurist, Dr. Ḥāmad Zakī of the Faculty of Law at Fouad University, criticized judicial intervention in filling in the details of the contract from a different angle: "The honorable Minister Sanhūrī Bāshā has perceived (the completion of the details of the contract) from the objective (*mawḍūʿī*) angle, whereas I believe that the details are personal and subjective matters that are substantive from the perspective of the parties to the agreement." He noted that, in accordance with this proposal, the judge was obliged to complete people's contracts (in keeping with custom, equity, etc.), even if this were contrary to their initial intention and will. Another participant in the deliberations, the

---

[19] The Egyptian Civil Code, article 203(2).
[20] Ibid., article 95.

Senate deputy Muḥammad Ḥilmī ʿĪshī Bāshā, determined that "It is already our usage (*ʿāda*) that, in the case of a lack of clarity in the text, the judge turns to the nature of the transaction, to case law, to custom (*ʿurf*) and to usage (*ʿāda*)."[21] The interpretation of the Code concluded that "in all these cases, there is a deviation from the principle of free will, but the New Code has sacrificed this principle in favor of loftier interests."[22]

The foundation of *murūna* may be seen here in two contexts. The first is the rejection of the 'tyranny' of absolute 'free will' in favor of the collective intervention with a desirable social goal: to protect the weak and to protect economic and social principles consonant with modern times. This is the first *murūna*.[23]

However, the New Code refrains from adopting a new dogmatic approach in place of the previous dogma, and, accordingly, it positions itself in the middle, between individual free will and the collective will. It balances these two elements while recognizing the conflict between them—and this is the second *murūna*.

In other words: the Code attributed a conscious social function to contract law, mediating and balancing individual will and collective will, leaning sometimes toward the former and sometimes toward the latter, depending on the circumstances. This process of weighing and adjustment may also be described in accordance with the social standard alone: contract law steers particular actions of the collective for some social purpose, while at the same time blocking other actions by society. Contract law is both a social accelerator and a braking mechanism, and this explains the high level of flexibility it must develop.

2.2 *Personal and Material Theories of Obligation*

The Code introduced an additional legal balance between two distinct schools current in the world of comparative law at the time, relating to the perception of the obligation (*al-ʾiltizām*). Faithful to the functional approach and to *takhayyur*, as discussed above, the Code once again combined both schools in order to secure the optimum result from its perspective. This balance showed not only the extent to which the

[21] Al-Qānūn al-Madanī, volume 1, pp. 73–76.
[22] Al-Wasīṭ, volume 1, p. 91.
[23] The explanatory notes of the code proposal used the term 'tyranny'. See Al-Qānūn al-Madanī, volume 2, p. 225.

authors of the Egyptian New Code were familiar with the changes taking place at the time in legal theory, but also the extent to which global legal discourse was part and parcel of internal Egyptian legal discourse. While this discussion of the obligation relates to a legal distinction, it nevertheless has social significance.

Two principal schools applied in the legal perception of an obligation. The personal (*shakhṣiyya*) school saw the essence of the definition of an obligation as relating to the personal relations created between a specific creditor and a specific debtor; this approach is essentially characteristic of Latin law.[24]

By contrast, the material (*maddiyya*) school sees the subject of the obligation as the central factor in the relationship, and attributes secondary importance to the personal relationship. According to this school, an obligation is essentially a material rather than a personal relationship. This is the traditional approach of German law.[25] In accordance with this approach, if the personal connection is less central, then the entire question of will, and, particularly, the mental and moral defects in the expression of will, are less significant. The focus is on the subject of the transaction rather than on those who perform the transaction.

Accordingly, the material school explains in logical terms that the obligation remains valid even if the parties involved change—for example, in the assignment of a right the creditor is replaced, and in the assignment of a debt the debtor is replaced, yet the obligation remains intact. According to the personal school, as the parties to the transaction change, the obligation is dissolved. The *maddiyya* school also explained that an obligation may be created without a debtor, in an obligation in favor of an undefined or absent person; for example, in an obligation to award a prize; in a condition in favor of a third party; or in the obligation of a person who has signed a bearer's certificate. The *maddiyya* school argued that if the obligation were no more than the personal relationship between creditor and debtor, there would be no obligation in the absence of either of these parties.

The material school is the more sophisticated in legal and economic terms. This was recognized by the Latin codes of the twentieth century, which accepted some of its applications, recognizing the assignment of

---

[24] Al-Wasīṭ, volume 1, p. 93.
[25] Ibid., pp. 93–94.

a right (but not the assignment of a debt; this was the case, for example, with the outgoing Egyptian civil code) and a bearer's certificate. Conditioning in favor of a third party was extended to include a condition in favor of an undefined person. Some Latin codes went still further, recognizing the assignment of a debt.

In the framework of the perception of contract law as a socioeconomic ideology aspiring to encourage dynamism, it may be seen that the New Code was uncertain which path to take. It was undoubtedly attracted by the more sophisticated theoretical perception of obligation, with its concomitant elaboration of contract law. The Code strove to be as modern and progressive as possible, in order to encourage progress in Egyptian society and economic life, and it might be argued that it was reluctant to relinquish the chance to adopt sophisticated legal tools. On the other hand, we have also seen the importance it attached to the mental dimension, since this permitted it to introduce considerations relating to justice and morality and offered an opportunity to direct and control processes. As always in the New Code, this apparent contradiction would have to be resolved by way of compromise.

Accordingly, Sanhūrī, as the architect of the New Code, noted that "the New Code has adopted an intermediate position: it has not dived to the depths of the material school, but it does reflect the developments that have been seen in this field in the Latin codes under the influence of German law."[26] In other words, the Code remained within the sphere of Latin law, in order to protect the personal context of the obligation, which it considered an important foundation; but it placed itself in the sector of progressive Latin law, which had already accepted some of the principles of the *maddiyya* school.

Consequently, the New Code continued to view the obligation as a personal relationship between individuals who had expressed a common will to associate; this will permits the entry of the mental and moral factors. Naturally, this must be without bias, coercion or exploitation, error or deception. Even an involuntary relationship (*ʾiltizām ghayr ʾirādī*) is seen by the New Code as a relationship between specific parties; for example, a creditor who sues for compensation for mental suffering, cannot transfer this right to his inheritors, unless the obligation acquired the form of an agreement between himself and the person causing the

[26] Ibid., p. 94.

damage, or unless he demanded this right from the court. In *Al-Wasīṭ*, Sanhūrī noted that this example embodies the clear recognition by the Code of the personal dimension in non-contractual obligations.[27]

At the same time, however, the Code readily accepted the innovations of the *maddiyya* school of obligation. Firstly, it retained the small number of applications of this school that were already included in the outgoing Egyptian code and in case law; within this framework, and as already noted, it recognized and even extended the rules for the assignment of a right.[28] It also permitted conditioning in favor of a future person or in favor of a party or interest who were undefined at the time of making the contract. The conditioning in favor of a third party could be effected in favor of a future person or institution, or in favor of a person or institution that was undefined at the time of making the contract, subject to the provision that it would be possible to define such persons or institutions when the outcomes of the contract would become valid, in accordance with the conditioning.[29]

The Code also introduced the most recent developments in the progressive Latin codes of the period, particularly those from the proposed Franco-Italian civil code of 1928, which later became the Italian civil code, just as these codes had adopted the *maddiyya* school. For example, in addition to the assignment of a right, the Code added the assignment of a debt, or an explicit provision stating that a person who presented to the public an undertaking to award a prize in return for specified work would be required to award the prize, even if the work were undertaken without direct affinity to the promise of the prize, or even without knowledge thereof—a classic position of the material school.[30]

2.3 *Internal Will and External Will*

A further balance addressed by the contract law of the New Code was that between two additional legal theories that were current in contemporary European law: the theory of the internal or covert will

[27] The Egyptian Civil Code, article 222; Al-Wasīṭ, volume 1, p. 95; Al-Qānūn al-Madanī, volume 2, pp. 566–567.
[28] The Egyptian Civil Code, articles 303–314.
[29] Ibid. article 156.
[30] Al-Wasīṭ, volume 1, p. 95; The Egyptian Civil Code, articles 315–322, 162.

(*naẓariyyat al-ʾirāda al-bāṭina*) and external or overt will (*naẓariyyat al-ʾirāda al-ẓāhira*).[31]

The theory of internal will, which generally characterizes Latin law, is based on the element of mental will, i.e., on the actual intention of the party to the agreement. The concrete manifestation of this will is no more than a presumption (*qarīna*) that may be contradicted. The second theory, of external will, typifies the German school, and emphasizes the external manifestation of will, which it considered as will itself, since this manifestation is the social appearance of will, and law is generally interested in the social appearance rather than the internal and mental appearances.

The dilemma faced by the authors of the New Code was which school to follow. This decision had practical significance: choosing the school of external will might stabilize commerce and enhance the security of those engaging in various types of transactions. The internal school, by contrast, does not emphasize security in transactions, but rather the ability of the court to intervene in the civil sphere through the mental foundation, to clarify the true intention of the party to an agreement and to protect this intention from error, deception, fraud, coercion or usurping. Having come to recognize the sense of responsibility the New Code felt to protect those who required protection, emphasizing the role of the court as the guardian of the new civil constitution, we might reasonably expect that the Code would remain in the realm of the internal theory, and this was indeed the case. However, we have also seen the flexibility adopted throughout the Code, and here, too, a compromise position was maintained.

"For our purpose, it is important that the Code remain within the sphere of the Latin codes," the explanatory notes to the proposed Code and Sanhūrī remarked, "so that the principal attention is to the covert will... This is true will, as far as this may be clarified, free of error, coercion, exploitation or pressure... The Code has fathomed the depths of the covert goals of the element of will, for example, when it addressed motivating factors, such as the element of remuneration, which the Code has activated in full." However, the Code followed the approach of twentieth-century Latin codes, which were influenced by the theory of external will, including several clauses that support this theory, mainly "for a legitimate purpose, namely the stability of economic life."[32]

---

[31] Al-Wasīṭ, volume 1, pp. 95–99.
[32] Ibid., p. 98.

We shall see below some examples of the theory of external will as adopted by the New Code, in which a distinction can be seen between the true will of the party making the offer and his overt will, before returning to the theory of internal will.

For example, in a case when an individual received a legal offer and agreed to it, but later changed his mind, but the person making the offer heard of the other party's acceptance before he learned of the withdrawal thereof, the contract will be based not on the true will (as reflected in the amendment), but on the basis of overt will.[33]

Elsewhere, the Code established that "if a person who expressed his will died or became legally incapacitated before the manifestation of this will became effective (i.e., before the proposal met with acceptance—G.B.), then (the death or loss of legal capacity) do not prevent the effectiveness when this reaches the knowledge of someone to whom it was addressed. . . ."[34] In other words, the expression of will was disconnected from the person who made it and became independent to execute its purpose, in accordance with the theory of overt will, even if the person expressing this will had since died or become legally incapacitated. Such a proposal by a person who had since died could still create a binding contract.

The explanatory notes added that since the expression of will is the criterion in the New Code, rather than the internal, personal will, the expression of will would, once dispatched, be binding on the heirs of the person making the proposal, or persons coming in his stead.[35] This change constituted nothing short of a revolution in Egyptian law, and indeed a revolution that was difficult to accept, since prior to the New Code Egyptian case law had determined that the death or legal incapacity of a person making an offer led to the nullification of the offer.[36]

As with other problematic innovations in the proposed Code, the authors sought legitimacy for this change in Islamic law. The explanatory notes to the proposed Code stated that the Malakite school of Islamic law supported such a separation between the expression of will and personal will, although the Ḥanafī school opposed it.[37]

---

[33] The Egyptian Civil Code, article 91.
[34] Ibid., article 92.
[35] Al-Qānūn al-Madanī, volume 2, p. 31.
[36] Ibid.
[37] Ibid., p. 30.

This distinction between personal and overt will aroused widespread opposition among the judges of the Egyptian Supreme Court—a body that often emerged as particularly conservative during the deliberations. They argued that this approach was contrary to the accepted position in both Egypt and France, and that this separation would injure commerce and thus cause real damage. They proposed an alternative formula for this clause in the spirit of the legal situation pertaining prior to the New Code, stating that the effectiveness of the expression of will would terminate with the death or legal incapacitation of the person expressing this will, if the expression of will had not yet reached the knowledge of a person to whom it was addressed.[38]

In other words, if the expression of will had not managed to reach the knowledge of the person to whom it was addressed, the latter could no longer respond by acceptance. The Code, by contrast, established a contrary position, such that if the expression of will had not yet managed to reach the person for whom it was intended, that person could still accept and thus transform it into a valid and binding contract.

The representative of the Ministry of Justice asked to reject the judges' proposal, claiming that the proposed law actually ensured a greater measure of commercial stability. Sanhūrī explained that, contrary to the old theory, which argued that will is a mental foundation that dies with the death of the person expressing it, the overt theory states that will does not die and is not invalidated by the death of this person.

After discussion, the Civil Code Committee in the Senate decided to reject the judges' objection. It explained its decision by noting that contractual interests embody a measure of importance by comparison with which the death of the person making the proposal is insignificant. Moreover, the proposed Code included greater protection of stability in commercial life and protection of the interests of the parties.[39]

A further example: the New Code stated that a substantive error by either party would not create grounds for nullifying the contract, unless the other party to the contract had also fallen victim to the same error, known thereof or had a good possibility to discern it.[40] Accordingly, if the first party made an error, and the other party did not make this error and did not and could not have notice it, the contract will be valid, based

[38] Ibid., pp. 34–35.
[39] Ibid., pp. 34–35.
[40] The Egyptian Civil Code, article 120.

not on the real will of the first party, since a substantial error in estimation or fact occurred therein, but on the basis of his will as expressed, on which the other party relied. The stability of the transaction is more important here than the integrity of the element of will.[41]

The New Code also established that if fraud (*tadlīs*) were committed by a third party, as, for example, in the case of a mediator who caused the defrauding of one of the parties to the contract, the defrauded party does not have the right to request the nullification of the contract unless he proves that the other party to the contract knew or should have known of the fraud.[42]

The Code created a similar situation regarding the element of coercion (*ʾikrāh*): if coercion was applied by a third party, the coerced party does not have right to request nullification of the contract unless he proves that the other party to the contract knew of the coercion, or unless it could have been assumed with certainty that he knew of this coercion. In such a case, the contract will be valid not on the basis of the true will of the first party, since this will was 'defaced' by the coercion or deception, but on the basis of his overt will, on which the other party to the contract relied.[43]

Al-Wasīṭ noted that in interpreting contracts there were also cases in which preference was given to the theory of overt will—again, in order to strengthen contractual stability in these cases.

A good example of the preference for the stability of transactions in certain cases is the interpretative approach applied regarding contracts whose verbal manifestation is clear. The Code established that "if the language of the agreement is clear, the interpretation should not deviate therefrom in order to fathom the will of the parties." Sanhūrī noted that this is an 'indirect' borrowing from the theory of overt will. He explained that while the clear language of the agreement was indeed perceived as evidence of the true will of the parties, and that adhering to this manifestation ostensibly constitutes attention to true will and not only to overt will. However, the fact remains that we deduce the true will from the overt will, and, in effect, what we adhere to is the overt will, even if we do so in disguise (*taḥt sitār*), claiming that this is the true will.[44]

---

[41] Al-Wasīṭ, volume 1, p. 97; Al-Qānūn al-Madanī, volume 2, p. 140.

[42] The Egyptian Civil Code, article 126; Al-Qānūn al-Madanī, volume 2, p. 174.

[43] The Egyptian Civil Code, article 128; Al-Wasīṭ, volume 1, p. 97.

[44] The explanatory notes of the code proposal, Al-Qānūn al-Madanī, volume 2, p. 296; The Egyptian Civil Code, article 150(1); Al-Wasīṭ, volume 1, pp. 97–98.

Sanhūrī added that the Code found it convenient to state that a contract is made between two parties who exchange a mutual *expression* of their common will, thus transforming the concrete expression of will into a tool permitting us to know the wills and the correlation between them.[45]

However, as we have already noted, it is the theory of internal will that guides the Civil Code as a whole. Moreover, the theory of overt will was introduced only in a number of specific and defined issues, due to the fear of the 'tyranny' of this school.[46] In order to soften this tyranny and position internal will as the yardstick for contract law, the Code developed the element of causativeness in accordance with Latin law, thus introducing a mental and moral factor into the Code.

The explanatory notes stated that the significance of this approach was the focus on the cause of the obligation rather than the cause of the contract. The cause of the obligation is an integral part of the making of a contract; it is the genuine mental foundation that underlies a given action. Accordingly, formalistic grounds will not lead to the nullification of the contract, and attention must always be given to the covert, true reason. In other words—it is not necessarily the reason stated in the contract that automatically determines the obligation, but rather the reason behind the obligation, which the court must investigate and discern. Accordingly, we may now understand the provision in the Code that "if there were no reason for the obligation, or if the reason is contrary to public order or morality, the contract is void.[47]

The theory of covert will also dominated the interpretation of the contract in the Code in cases where the wording of the contract was unclear, which is true of the majority of cases that reach the courts. The Code established that "if the need arises to interpret the contract, the common intention (*nīyya*) of the parties should be sought, beyond the literal meaning, while seeking guidance from the nature of the transaction and the extent of the trust that should prevail between the parties, and in accordance with the custom (*ʿurf*) practiced in commerce."[48]

Sanhūrī noted that the principal task in the interpretation of a contract is, therefore, the search for the common intention of the parties,

---

[45] The Egyptian Civil Code, article 89; Al-Wasīṭ, volume 1, p. 98.
[46] The explanatory notes of the code proposal, Al-Qānūn al-Madanī, volume 2, p. 225.
[47] The Egyptian Civil Code, article 136; Al-Qānūn al-Madanī, volume 2, p. 226.
[48] The Egyptian Civil Code, article 150(2); Al-Wasīṭ, volume 1, p. 98.

i.e., the search for true will; if the Code established objective criteria for investigating and fathoming this true will, such as 'the nature of the transaction' or 'the custom practiced in commerce', these criteria provided effective tools for reaching the true will of the parties under an element of reliable control.[49]

In other words: Sanhūrī intended that these factors provide a stable foundation within a fluid and subjective expanse. It may, however, be asked whether the Code was not indirectly returning to the theory of overt will, employing these objective tests of the nature of the transaction and commercial custom. Sanhūrī did not deny this logical contradiction. His response was that in some cases, internal will acquires a concrete form and becomes overt will—in accordance with the requirements of commercial stability. It is then based on the foundation of the 'trust' created between the parties. Sanhūrī was alluding here to an intermediate theory, between internal will and external will, that appears in the German and Swiss civil codes, and is known as the theory of trust (*thiqa, Vertrauenstheorie*). This theory supports internal will, but deduces this will in accordance with objective criteria, as manifested in the Egyptian New Code in this article. Overt will is a means (for knowing and investigating internal will), but it is not a goal in its own right, Sanhūrī explained, in an effort to solve the logical contradiction. *Al-Wasīṭ* quoted a study published by Dr. ʾAḥmad Zakī al-Shītī in 1949 by the Institute of Comparative Law in the University of Paris, which argued that the Egyptian civil code indeed employed the above-mentioned theory of trust.[50]

3. Custom (*'Urf*) as a Foundation of Flexibility

French civil law was inclined to view custom (*la coutume*) as an evasive element that varies from region to region without clear justification. Accordingly, the French jurist considered custom to be inherently illogical. René David noted that "Even today, French lawyers and students consider it obvious that Codification means improvement (and that) legislation is a source of law superior to custom."[51] The French Code

[49] Al-Wasīṭ, volume 1, p. 99.
[50] Ibid., footnote number 1.
[51] David, pp. 156, 170–178.

Civil does not include a definition of custom. Article 7 of the law of 21 March 1804, which presented the Code Civil, noted that general or local customs must defer to the civil code as a source of authority. However, during the twentieth century, the *Cour de Cassation* ruled that a judge must take custom into account, if he is aware of its presence, so that one could argue that French case law moderated the extreme position of the code regarding the institution of custom.[52]

In accordance with the classic French approach, and in the footsteps of the Napoleonic Code, the position of custom (*ʿurf*) in the outgoing Egyptian civil code was also highly restricted. Although the law for the establishment of the *ʾahliyya* courts mentioned usages (*ʿādāt*) as a source for filling a lacuna in the outgoing code, this was restricted to commercial *ʿādāt*.[53] However, it may be asked whether this restriction of custom in the outgoing code was consonant with the prevailing social reality of Egyptian society regarding the institution of *ʿurf?*

Jasper Brinton, the American judge in the Mixed Courts, made the following comment regarding the relationship between custom (he preferred to use the term usage) and law during the period of the previous Egyptian code:

> In a peculiarly real sense it could be said that in Egypt usage is law. Usage was present as a living force in every detail of the system. The codes contain many specific references to it. The decisions of the courts, too, are replete with references to usage, both general and local, in almost every field . . . Thus the Mixed Courts themselves developed a large body of usage . . . usage constantly supplemented and often, in fact, actually modified, in matters of procedure, the written law.[54]

Custom is indeed an official source of Arab civil law, ranked in second place in Egypt and Iraq, even before the principles of the Islamic *Sharīʿa*, and in third place in Libya (Article 1 of the various civil codes).

The Egyptian jurist ʿAbd al-Jawād Muḥammad defined custom as "an unbroken chain of behavior of human beings in a particular field, whereby they believe that this behavior has become binding for them". Usage (*ʿāda*), meanwhile, is a collective action that does not meet the tests of custom, and is hence of lower status in terms of binding normativity. When asked to define the foundations of custom, he proposed two:

---

[52] Dadomo, pp. 37–39.

[53] The Law of establishing the *ʾAhlī* courts, article 29.

[54] Brinton, p. 90.

acceptability (*iʿtiyad*) is the material (*māddī*) foundation, and coercion (*ʾilzām*) is the mental foundation.[55]

Regarding the first foundation, the practice of people must be general (*ʿām*); it must be ancient, i.e., enough time must have passed in order to permit us to state that we have a stable custom; and consistent (*muṭṭarrad*), i.e., that it is not abandoned and then readopted by people. In addition, this custom must not contradict general law and order. In some Arab countries, for example, the court would consider the blood feud to be an existing custom, but not a binding one, since murder is contrary to general law and order.

As for the mental foundation, a usage may meet the criteria of a custom, but still not be recognized as a custom by law, if people are not convinced that there is an obligation to observe such a custom, and that those who do not observe it injure society and social interests and must therefore be punished. In the absence of the mental foundation, this is merely usage, which positivist law does not recognize as binding.[56]

It is doubtful whether the Islamic *fiqh* made the distinction between custom and usage that is applied in modern Arab law. For the Ḥanafī and Mālikī Islamic jurists, for example, both categories may constitute a binding legal source.[57] Indeed, the *Majalla*—the Ḥanafī Ottoman codification, employs both terms interchangeably. Article 36 of the *Majalla* states that the "usage is an arbitrator" (*al-ʿāda muḥakima*); Article 43: "A matter recognized by custom, it is as if it had been conditioned' (*al-maʿrūf ʿarfān kal-mashrūṭ sharṭan*); Article 44: "a matter recognized by merchants is regarded as being a contractual obligation between them" (*al-maʿrūf bayn al-tujjār kal-mashrūṭ baynahum*); and, lastly, Article 45: "A matter established by custom is like a matter established by law" (*al-taʿyīn bil-ʿurf kal-taʿyīn bil-naṣṣ*).[58]

Custom appears in Egyptian law as the second source for filling a lacuna if the civil code is silent on the question. In practice, however,

---

[55] Muḥammad ʿAbd al-Jawwād Muḥammad, *ʾUsūl al-Qānūn Muqāranatan bi-ʾUsūl al-Fiqh* (Alexandria: Munshāh al-Mʿārif, 1991), pp. 138–139.

[56] Ibid., pp. 139–140.

[57] B. Hakim, "The Role of ʿUrf in Shaping the Traditional Islamic City", in C. Mallat ed. *Islam and Public Law: Classical and Contemporary Studies* (London: Graham & Trotman, 1993); R. Shaham, *Family and the Courts in Modern Egypt, a Study Based on Decisions by the Shariʿa Courts, 1900–1955* (Leiden: Brill, 1997), pp. 230–231.

[58] Muḥammad ʿAbd al-Jawwād Muḥammad, pp. 145–146; Muḥammad Saʿīd al-ʿAshmāwī, *Al-Sharīʿa al-ʾIslāmiyya wa al-Qānūn al-Miṣrī* (Cairo: Maktabat Madbūlī al-Saghīr, 1996), p. 33.

a positivist legal system was reluctant to use this source due to three key defects of which Arab law was also aware: custom can be vague and unclear, since it is unwritten; customs can change from country to country and from region to region; there can be no certainty that the custom is indeed one that has been consolidated in light of the criteria outlined above, and this can lead to disputes between the parties, impairing the credibility of the legal system.[59] In any case, the Arab legal system recognizes custom as a legal social foundation to be taken into consideration.

The gulf created between the previous civil code and social reality was a source of concern for the Mixed Courts, and, as we have seen in the writings of the judge Brinton, this led them to adopt case law that sometimes even contradicted written law in procedural matters. In the native *ʾahliyya* courts, this gulf was seen in its full severity, since these courts tended to be less creative than the Mixed Courts, and remained faithful to the classic French approach that was hostile to custom.

Thus a form of dissonance emerged between custom, which dictated the rhythm of Egyptian society, and positivist Egyptian civil law, which used custom sparingly. It is reasonable to assume that this gulf impaired the legitimacy of the previous civil code, emphasizing its alien and imported character.[60]

For example, Sanhūrī noted the provision in the previous civil code drawn from French law, in accordance with which a woman might pay alimony to her husband, or even to her father-in-law's wife. He described this as a 'strange provision', which most Egyptian courts regarded as a 'dead letter' and refrained from implementing.[61]

This gulf was particularly evident since the *Sharīʿa*—which enjoyed considerable religious, moral and cultural authority in Egyptian society—managed to coexist with custom in all matters relating to civil law, to the point that it was eventually difficult to gauge the distance, if any, between custom and *Sharīʿa*.[62] "This *Sharīʿa* has permeated the

---

[59] Muḥammad ʿAbd al-Jawwād Muḥammad, pp. 142–143; According to the Jordanian civil code of 1976, article 2(3) the custom is a legal source only if it general (ʿām), ancient (*qadīm*), stable (*thābit*) and sequential (*muṭrid*). In addition it should not oppose the positive law, public order and morality.

[60] On the alleged foreignness of the old Code see Laṭīfa Sālim, Al-Niẓām al-Qaḍāʾī, 1982, p. 44.

[61] The *ʾAhlī* Civil Code, articles 155–156; Wujūb, p. 31.

[62] About the custom as an integrated source in the Islamic *Fiqh*, see G. Libson, "On the development of Custom as a Source of Law in Islamic Law", *Islamic Law and Society* 4(1997), p. 131.

Egyptian environment to a great extent," chairperson Al-Wakīl noted in the deliberations of the Civil Code Committee in the Senate, "and the honorable gentlemen are aware that life in the country has remained in its old framework, and it (*Sharīʿa*) has penetrated their customs and thoughts . . ."[63] Hill even argued that the judicial interpretation that relates to the *ʿurf* in the code actually relates to Islamic law.[64] On questions of personal status, the *Sharīʿa* courts (*al-maḥākim al-sharʿiyya*) in Egypt granted priority, in most cases, to the *Sharīʿa* rulings over custom, if there were a tension between the two.[65] However, since civil law was generally outside the judicial authority of *al-maḥākim al-sharʿiyya* in Egypt, this tension between custom and *Sharīʿa* was not usually particularly evident in civil matters.

This situation was reversed in the New Code. Custom not only gained a prominent place in the list of legal sources of the Code, but was even brought forward, as a source for filling lacunae in the Code, and positioned before *Sharīʿa*, in second place immediately after the written form of the Code. This change reflected a recognition of the popular normative status of the *ʿurf* in a country such as Egypt.[66] The Code also included the *ʿurf* in many other articles, particularly as an objective criterion serving a an accepted and quantifiable gauge in society.

The explanatory notes to the New Code sought to interpret in a broad manner the term *al-ʿādāt al-tijāriyya*, i.e., commercial usage, as appears in Article 29 of the law for the establishment of the *ʾahlī* courts. They argued that the reference there to *ʿurf* was not supposed to be restricted to the commercial sphere, but merely to emphasize this sphere. They added:

> *ʿUrf* is the well-rooted popular source that is connected directly to society. It is considered as a natural means of action for society in cases in which there is no solution in written law. Accordingly, this source is and will remain a complementary source, alongside legislation, and its scope is not limited solely to transactions of a purely commercial character, but also includes the transactions of the civil code and the other sections of private and public law.[67]

The coupling of the Code and custom is ostensibly successful. The Code embraced custom as a flexible foundation that could provide social

---

[63] Al-Qānūn al-Madanī, volume 1, p. 92.
[64] Hill, p. 80.
[65] R. Shaham, *Family and the Courts in Modern Egypt*, pp. 230–231.
[66] The Egyptian Civil Code, article 1(2); Al-Qānūn al-Madanī, volume 1, p. 187.
[67] Al-Qānūn al-Madanī, volume 1, p. 188.

legitimacy, and custom found its place in positivist written law. What, though, were the considerations that were to guide the Code and the courts in introducing a given custom rather than another one? What mechanism would be used to ensure cooperation between these two institutions, which usually find themselves in conflict?

During the 1980s, the sociological and anthropological research of law developed a paradigm of 'legal pluralism'.[68] This approach argued that several legal systems could coexist within a single social unit, and indeed claimed that in every society differ rent legal systems actually operate simultaneously.

This paradigm struggled against the hegemonic perception of 'legal centralism', which relates exclusively to the sovereign state as the source of the normative system ("the notion that the state and the system of lawyers, courts and prisons is the only form of ordering").[69] This approach also commented on the tension it believed was created between custom law, which predated the colonial system, and the essentially Western law imposed by colonialism on the society it dominated. It even argued that custom law, which in various societies was presented as an antithesis to the law of the state, was not a genuine or original remnant of an ancient traditional legal system, but rather the result of the relationship between occupiers and occupied. This approach was rightly criticized for the excessive emphasis it placed on the perception of custom law as a means for consolidating a unique identity in the face of the state, or as a means of opposition to the colonial occupier. Even if we give credence to this criticism, however, this paradigm may still help us analyze the situation in which the *ʿurf* was introduced into the New Code.

As with the principle of *takhayyur*, which was activated with regard to the legal sources included in the Code, this same principle was applied regarding *ʿurf*: Not every *ʿurf* was included in the Code, and not every *ʿurf* should be involved in its application, but only those aspects the court felt to be appropriate and consonant with the spirit of the law. Thus this is an *ʿurf* that has been processed in accordance with the ideology of the Code and the court, and, in keeping with the paradigm of legal-pluralism, this not merely the expropriation of parts of custom, but also the removal from the legal field of other customary elements.

---

[68] S. E. Merry, "Legal Pluralism", *Law and Society Review* 22(1988), pp. 869–896; J. Griffiths, "What is Legal Pluralism", *Journal of Legal Pluralism* 24(1986), p. 1; S. Engle Merry, "Legal Pluralism", *Law and Society Review* 22(1988), p. 869.

[69] S. E. Merry, p. 874.

From this point on, the Code would not only define what was law, but also define what was custom, and to what extent this was legitimate and acceptable to it. Thus the mutual relations were crystallized: custom grants legitimacy to the Code, and the Code grants legitimacy to sections of the custom it finds convenient. Whereas the previous code rejected custom, a dialogue was now created between the New Code and the judges who applied it—and the element of custom. This dialogue did not impair the legal centralism of the Code, and possibly even reinforced it.

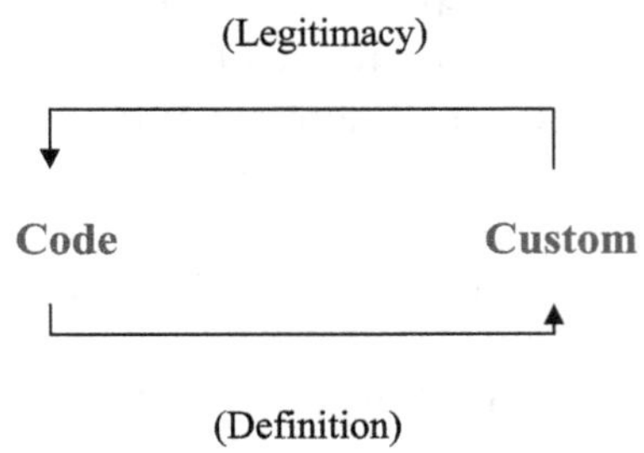

However, the foundation of custom is more flexible than other legal sources introduced through the principle of *takhayyur*. Whereas these principles were introduced and frozen, becoming an integral part of the Code, custom is not a principle, but permission to activate a principle, and hence it is fluid, changing and elastic. This is precisely what the Code sought: a factor that could facilitate the combination of its various parts, sufficiently fluid yet also sufficiently stable, since the *ʿurf* is an objective factor that can serve as a standard for a particular action.

Accordingly, the prominent inclusion of the *ʿurf* in Article 1 of the Code may, paradoxically, be considered both as exceptional flexibility and as inflexible dogmatism. It is inflexible in so far as Sanhūrī applied here a form of legal centralism that determines what is law, who are its authorized manufacturers, what methods it should use and what is its desired scope. It is flexible due to the changing character of the institution of the *ʿurf* across time, place and space.

4. Tools or Shackles?

Having examined the manner in which the Code developed contract law and prioritized the institution of *ʿurf* as part of the principle of *murūna*, we shall now turn to examining the manner in which the Code provided judges with flexible and sophisticated tools enabling a wide measure of judicial discretion, thus replacing what the Code saw as the rigid legal tools of the previous code. Sanhūrī spoke of placing 'tools in the hands of the judge' (*'adā fī yad al-qāḍī*) rather than the 'shackles of justice' (*'aghlāl al-qānūn*) which, he claimed, restricted judicial discretion under the old code.[70]

As we shall see below, this is a type of *murūna* that is dispersed throughout the Code, and whose importance lies in the expansion and quantification of judicial discretion. In this last sentence we already discern a contradiction, since the Code did not extend judicial discretion indiscriminately, but rather established limits for this discretion in the form of the measurable quality of these tools. This was designed not only to serve judicial discretion, but also to control and supervise it, and to create an element of public expectation regarding the field of license enjoyed by the judge.

"Of the elements of development in the Code, the most important are the flexible criteria developed in place of the rigid rules found in the old Egyptian civil code," Sanhūrī noted,[71] adding that these rigid rules provide a single solution for legal problems and do not change as circumstances change. In some instances, there was no alternative but to leave intact the rigid rules inherited from the previous code, such as the *ghabn* in the sale of the land of a legally incapacitated person. This was applied on at least one-fifth of the value of the land, and in this case the seller who had usurped the legally incapacitated person was required to complete the shortfall up to four-fifths of the value of similar land.[72] In other words, the previous code had established an immutable arithmetic test, with no flexibility in light of changing circumstances.

Other cases in which the New Code 'reluctantly', as Sanhūrī put it, maintained rigid tests were legal and consensual interest, for which maximum values were determined;[73] the abolition of the voluntary distribution of joint assets, if one of the dividing partners proved that his right had been usurped in an amount greater than one-fifth of the value at the time of distribution,[74] and so on.

---

[70] Al-Wasīṭ, volume 1, pp. 24 , 104.
[71] Ibid., p. 102.
[72] The Egyptian Civil Code, article 425.
[73] Ibid., articles 226–227; Al-Wasīṭ, volume 1, p. 102.
[74] The Egyptian Civil Code, article 845; Al-Wasīṭ, volume 1, p. 102.

These are rigid tools, the architect of the New Code explained, and flexible criteria that respond to changing circumstances are preferable. He clarified his point by offering an example of a rigid rule in the previous code that was replaced in the New Code. The old civil code mentioned the possibility of nullifying the sale of objects sold in a single group (e.g., a pile of crops, fabric, wood) if it emerged that the quantity was greater or smaller than originally agreed—i.e., where it emerged that there was a discrepancy between the agreed situation and the actual situation. The old code added that the purchaser was permitted to nullify the sale in such cases "only if the error amounted to half of one-tenth (i.e., one-twentieth) of the established price".[75]

The New Code replaced this arithmetic rule, which specifies the amount involved, with a flexible creating, noting that "the purchaser is not to be permitted to nullify the contract due to the deficiency (*naqṣ*) of the sold item unless he has proved that this is a grave deficiency (*min al-jasāma*) such that he known thereof (in advance) he would not have entered into the contract."[76]

This is the first time that we encounter one of the important criteria adopted by the New Code, namely the extent of gravity (*jasāma*) as a quantifiable criterion. Thus, we see that the Code speaks of an error and a grave error; a risk as opposed to a grave risk; fraud as opposed to grave fraud, and so on. Whereas, in Islamic law, the definition of *jasāma* was arithmetic—for example, gross fraud is defined as an error of half of one-tenth or more in tools, one-tenth or more in livestock, and one-fifth or more in real estate assets[77]—the importance of the definition of *jasāma* in the New Code is precisely that it is undefined. The judge is to decide what is the desirable measure, based on the totality of his general and specific considerations. It should be noted that the New Code was aware of the arithmetic definitions in the *Majalla* and in the Ḥanafī codification of *Murshid al-Ḥayrān*, and hence aware of the standard for *jasāma*; however, it chose not to adopt this definition.[78]

Sanhūrī noted that this new criterion of *jasāma* was preferable to the previous rule, since the judge could adjust it to the conditions of each case and find an appropriate legal solution for that case. Accordingly,

---

[75] The *ʾAhlī* Civil Code, articles 291–293.

[76] The Egyptian Civil Code, article 433(1); Al-Qānūn al-Madanī, volume 4, p. 59.

[77] The Majalla, article 165.

[78] Al-Qānūn al-Madanī, volume 2, p. 172.

there might be situations where the lack or surplus in the group were more or less than one-tenth, respectively, yet the judge would refuse to order the nullification of the contract, according to the circumstances of the case.[79]

This standard of gross severity, *jasāma*, was also employed in additional cases, for example in the criterion for the 'substantive error' (*ghalaṭ jawharī*). The Code established that an error would be substantive (and hence create the possibility of the nullification of a contract) if it amounted to the level of *jasāma*, i.e., if the misled party would not have entered into the contract had this error not been present—in other words, the error was an incentive to the agreement.[80] Whereas the previous code relate solely to 'an error in the matter', i.e., in the subject of the transaction, the explanatory notes to the proposed Code emphasized that the error could be related both to the subject of the transaction itself and to the identity of the associating party, or to any element that the party claiming an error subjectively considered to be an error. The latter criterion is a subjective criterion examined by an objective test—the measure of fairness (*nazāha*) in commerce.[81]

Another example is the standard of grave fraud (*tadlīs jasīm*). The Code established that a contract may be nullified on account of fraud if the ruse perpetrated by one of the parties, or by someone acting on their behalf, amounted to the level of *jasāma*, so that without this ruse, the other party would not have made the contract.[82] The explanatory notes added that fraud would be considered to have occurred if one of the parties planned to perpetrate a ruse. This differs from the criminal definition of fraud; in civil law, a fault on the part of the party to the contract, such as silence regarding a substantive fact, is sufficient to establish fraud.[83]

A further example is that of fear (*al-rahba*). The New Code established that a contract could be nullified on the grounds of coercion (*ʾikrāh*) if one party associated in the contract due to a justified sense of fear (*rahba qāʿida ʿala ʾasās*) leveled against him unlawfully by the other party.[84] If, in the circumstances of the matter, the party arguing coercion believed

---

[79] Al-Wasīṭ, volume 1, p. 103.

[80] The Egyptian Civil Code, article 121(1); Al-Qānūn al-Madanī, volume 2, p. 143; Al-Wasīṭ, volume 1, p. 103.

[81] Al-Qānūn al-Madanī, volume 2, p. 143.

[82] The Egyptian Civil Code, article 125(1).

[83] Al-Qānūn al-Madanī, volume 2, p. 172.

[84] The Egyptian Civil Code, article 127; Al-Wasīṭ, volume 1, p. 103.

that he was subject to grave danger (*khaṭar jasīm*), endangering him or another person mentally, physically or in matters of honor or finance, then his sense of fear was justified. Typically in cases when judicial discretion in applying a given criterion was perceived as excessively broad, as in this case, the Code attached instructions to the judge stating that in evaluating such coercion, the court should consider the gender, age, social status and state of health of the party that had fallen victim to coercion, as well as any other circumstance likely to influence the gravity of the coercion.[85] This legal combination is also a type of balance and *murūna*.

An example of another flexible legal tool is that of 'due justification' (*al-ʿadhr al-maqbūl*). The Code permitted a person who made a gift to another person to ask the court to permit him to recoup the gift (effectively in cases when the recipient refused to return it). There is no blanket prohibition on the return of a gift, but there must be due justification for this measure—a flexible term subject to the discretion of the court. However, in accordance with the double-edged principle mentioned already, the court's discretion is not absolute. Alongside the open judicial discretion as to the presence of 'due justification', the Code emphasized 'in particular' cases of such due justification, i.e., objective criteria that envelop the subjective discretion and render it relative. These cases included a situation whereby the recipient of the gift was not required to commit a breach of trust and act with ingratitude toward the giver, and the provision that the giver should not be required to lower his standard of living in the context of his social status.[86]

Lastly, the Code developed a further tool that encourages *murūna* and testifies to the effort by the Code to provide a legal and commercial response to what were defined in the previous chapter as the obstacles facing Egyptian economic and social life. This further tool is the principle that a debtor may pay financial compensation to his creditor if it emerges that specific performance (i.e., the actual performance of a particular act) entails considerable difficulty for the debtor, and provided the financial compensation will not cause the creditor substantive damage. This central principle, which applies to property and contract law in the New Code, reflects the character of this civil statute book—pragmatic, never needlessly obstinate, and flexible. Why insist on specific

[85] The Egyptian Civil Code, article 127(3).
[86] The Egyptian Civil Code, articles 500–501; Al-Wasīṭ, volume 1, pp. 104, 109.

performance, which may sometimes be complicated, involved and fraught with passions, if a dispute can be ended through a financial exchange? Here we may see both the effort by the Code to help the weak and the effort to remove the obstacles that blocked proper social life.[87]

"In this case, the judge must balance the interests of the parties to the matter," the explanatory notes to the proposed Code emphasized, "and refrain from imposing a heavy burden (of specific performance—G.B.) on the debtor due to minor damage."[88] We have already seen, in our discussion of property law, that this alleviating principle was applied in the highly complex property law of Egypt, for principled reasons of flexibility and alleviation. The Code established, for example, that a person who deviated from the restrictions imposed on construction on his land would be liable to sanctions and required to amend the deviation in practice (for example, by means of demolition). However, the court could require the violator to pay financial compensation, if it considered this to be justified.[89]

5. *Perpetuum Mobile* between Society and the Court

The gatekeeper at the court was in the custom of announcing aloud the names of the witnesses outside the court room, and he would do so with a particular pronunciation, in a nasal and sing-song voice, akin to the melodious chants of the itinerant peddlers.

One of the judges notice this once, and asked him: "Ya Sha'bān, are you announcing the trials of offenses and crimes or sweet potatoes and fresh dates in the market?" The gatekeeper replied: "Offenses and crimes or fresh dates—it's all a livelihood."

Tawfīq al-Ḥakīm, *Diary of a Village Prosecutor*
(*Yawmiyyāt Nā'ib fī al-'Aryāf*), 1937[90]

5.1 *Inherent Duality*

Having argued above that the principle of *murūna* supervises the New Code and shapes it in the image of a new social order, a form of *modus vivendi* for the values of a new partnership in the Egyptian community, this philosophical, social and legal theory now reaches its zenith. Having been woven throughout the Code like Ariadne's thread, the heart of

[87] The Egyptian Civil Code, article 203(2); Al-Wasīṭ, volume 1, p. 92; Al-Qānūn al-Madanī, volume 2, p. 509.
[88] Al-Qānūn al-Madanī, volume 2, p. 511.
[89] The Egyptian Civil Code, article 1018(2).
[90] P. 369.

the component of *murūna* lies in the court, the judicial system and the judge. This is the engine that is meant to drive the entire New Code and, accordingly, it is also supposed to be the driving force behind the new social order. Without *murūna*, the flexible mechanisms of the Code could not function, and would become empty and sterile vessels; and, according to the same logic, without this foundation, the new perception of the Egyptian collective could not function. In accordance with the ideology of the New Code, the court could be likened to an orchestra: it blends the individual principles and tools into a single, harmonious piece of music, with its own unique rhythm, a beginning and an end.

In other words, the court is not supposed merely to supervise and activate the Code and the legal tools it includes, but, through this action, is also supposed to provide normative guidance and direction for society at large. "Egyptian jurisdiction is the best manifestation of the needs of the country," states the explanatory notes to the proposed Code.[91]

The affinity between court and society is not one-way, but may be characterized as mutual and two-way; and this mutuality is the source of the New Code's strength. Accordingly, one might argue that it establishes here a form of *perpetuum mobile* that moves from its own energy, between the court and society. The judge is the representative of society, to which he owes allegiance; the judge activates the Code, which guides society toward the desired social goals; society recognizes the importance of the judicial enterprise and grants its judges authority and legitimacy; the judges must be honest and fair, and owe a debt of loyalty to society—and so on.

To this, one should add the fields of liberty and restriction in the relations between judge and Code, within the framework of the *perpetuum mobile* that should pertain between the Code and society. As early as 1923, Sanhūrī noted that he would like to transform the judicial system into the supreme power in the state, "inspecting and supervising" the other two powers.[92] It should be recalled that the discourse that underlay the drafting of the New Code was that of Continental law, which argues that law relates to the entire population, since it establishes the essentials of social order and instructs the citizens as to how they should behave in light of the social and philosophical ideas of the period.[93]

[91] Al-Qānūn al-Madanī, volume 1, p. 18.
[92] Diary, 2 January 1923, pp. 82–83.
[93] David, p. 73.

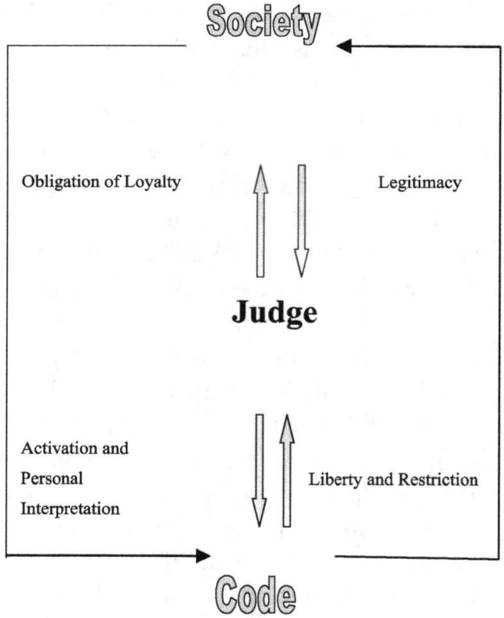

Prior to the adoption of the New Code, its authors and advocates considered two possible models for the involvement of the court in society and in the community: the model of French law in general, and of the well-established Code Civil in particular, and that of the 'new' Swiss civil code of 1912 (enacted in 1926 in modern Turkey as its civil law). The question essentially related to the perception of the function of the judge—should this follow the classic French model, or that which emerged after the teleological development described in Chapter Three and manifested in concrete terms in the Swiss code?

According to the classic French approach, the judge has only that granted him by the legislator. French law, in its substance, is not the creation of judges, but of legal scholars. Classic French law abhorred the Anglo-Saxon practice, and the judge was not responsible for establishing legal rules. According to the French model, the judge ostensibly merely implements a 'judicial rule' (*régle juridique*) that already exists in the articles of the Code, regardless of how general these articles may be.

In Anglo-Saxon law, a sudden change in a judicial decision can be a serious matter: if a rule accepted in the past is now rejected, what will become of stability in legal relations? And what is to prevent the modification or rejection of other rules? Renè David noted that in France, by contrast, changes in the position of the court relate only to the interpretation of an existing legal rule, and, accordingly, the danger to the systems of legal relations is limited, and there is little reason to fear that law as a whole will be destabilized. Legal rules are perceived as superior to judicial decisions, and they create a stable framework that limits the impact of changes in the position of the court or of jurists.[94]

The position of the judge in the Swiss code was different. In 1936, before the legislative process of the New Code began, Sanhūrī wrote: "Attention should be given to the courageous step taken by the Swiss legislator in honestly recognizing the broad discretion of the judge, not only in interpreting the law, but also in its very shaping."[95]

Sanhūrī's comment referred to the first article in the Swiss civil code, which established that "if the judge does not find a text for application in the Code, he will rule in keeping with custom, and, if he finds no customs, the judge will rule in accordance with the rules that he would establish *were he a legislator* (*s'il avait à faire acte de législateur*), receiving guidance therefore from the doctrines of law and from jurisprudence."

"The courageous nature of this article lies in its honesty," Sanhūrī noted. "If the judge does not find a solution in the formula of the law or in custom, he will turn to judicial legislation, aided by the theory of law and by case law. In practice, this is what any judge does (in such as situation), Swiss or not. The importance of the Swiss Code lies in the fact that it honestly states what other codes do not state, due to their concern that judges might apply excessively broad interpretative discretion and become legislators." Is this what Sanhūrī would wish to see in the future Egyptian Code?

In 1936, the year Sanhūrī made these comments, and before he immersed himself in drafting the Code, he evidently preferred to leave this question unanswered. "We shall confine ourselves to drawing the attention of our learned scholars to the wording of this important article (in the Swiss code). We would not (at this stage) wish to form a position as to the appropriateness of transferring this to our own New Code".[96]

As befits its guiding spirit of *murūna*, the New Code adopts an intermediate position between the two approaches described above regarding the normative status of the court. It expanded judicial discretion

---

[94] Ibid., pp. 77, 80–81.
[95] Wujūb, p. 95.
[96] Ibid., p. 96.

beyond the limit of classic French law, but restricted it relative to the approach of the Swiss code.

The explanatory notes to the proposed Code explicitly stated that the proposal did not wish to imitate the Swiss civil code, which permits the judge to apply the provisions he would have enacted had he been a legislator. The explanation offered was that the Swiss code indeed granted the judge the possibility of judicial legislation, "but his action should be confined solely to implementing provisions."[97] "The Egyptian Code stopped at logical limits, preventing the blending of fields between legislative authority and judicial authority," Sanhūrī added in *Al-Wasīṭ*.[98]

Two explanations may be offered for this intermediate position, one legal and the other social. In the legal sphere, the New Code reflects the approach that the court relates solely to what it has been granted by the legislature. The court lives within the scope defined by the law, and, according to the New Code, this scope is particularly broad relative to the restricted scope of the code under the previous Egyptian civil code. Nevertheless, the court is still limited by the framework of the law, from which it cannot deviate. Such deviation, as permitted by the Swiss code, is ostensibly impossible in accordance with the New Code.

On the social theory level, the court operates not only a legal code, but also social order. However, it is the operating engine, not the initiating mind. The latter lies in the Code and acts in accordance with its spirit. Accordingly, it is unthinkable that the engine that activates the social framework could at the same time change and shape this framework as it sees fit. It is entitled and obliged to adapt and adjust this framework in pace with changing times, and the Code permits it to do so—but not to change its substance. The framework is the legal rule, and the court merely applies this rule. The Code repeatedly reminds the judge that he does not stand above the social framework it establishes, but is part of it, and a part cannot change a whole. The judge can ensure the coherence of the various parts of the Code, and of the relations between them, but cannot nullify or amend them in their entirety. Moreover, breaching the existing framework could have a destructive impact on the fabric of society and on the legitimacy this framework provides for the court and the Code.

---

[97] Al-Qānūn al-Madanī, volume 1, p. 188.
[98] Al-Wasīṭ, volume 1, p. 104.

Accordingly, the Code adopted an ambiguous approach here, as described above. It granted broad authority to the court in order to operate *murūna* and to operate the Code, but at the same time restrained the court from creating judicial legislation that would impair the Code and the contract it sought to establish in society.

This inherent duality might strengthen the principle of *murūna* that guides the judge in ruling on civil issues and the mechanism of *perpetuum mobile* discussed above, since it could be argued that, in accordance with the New Code, the judge has a dual loyalty: on the one hand, to society, which grants him his power and authority; and on the other, to the Code, which grants him his judicial discretion within defined limits. These two sides do not always move in tandem; tension between the Code and society, if it emerges, requires the judge to adjust, weigh and balance his steps. The success of the Code depends on the extent of this interplay, and on the extent of adjustment between its differing inherent norms. If the court is successful in this complex act of adjustment, the desired social order may emerge. If the court in unsuccessful in its task, social order may be no more than a dead letter.

5.2 *The Skills of the Judge: 'A Sacred Mission'*

The tenuous link between his local legal system—and particularly the Egyptian law schools—and society, was a source of concern for Sanhūrī. He argued that law studies in Egypt were excessively theoretical and divorced from the true problems of society. One of his arguments was that the lecturers who taught law in Egypt were themselves disconnected from society and from the reality of the courts where law and society met. Accordingly, and before drafting the Code, he proposed that these lecturers should work as judges in the courts, "thus enabling them to prepare their students for practical life in a more successful manner than is presently the case."[99]

As for the New Code's image of the judge: since he bore a heavy burden as the activator of the mechanisms in the Code, and hence of the social order it embodied, he must be conscious of its complex purpose. In other words, he must realize that, in addition to the judicial discretion granted by the New Code, his function was to act as an engine in the activation of the Code, and to provide a connection

[99] Diary, 15 January 1923, p. 85.

point between the Code and society. Accordingly, Sanhūrī argued as early as 1923 that "in order for the judge to have the tools to be suited to his function, he is required not to confine himself to the study of laws and justice, but to add to these the social sciences, economics and finance, and he must study these areas scientifically." Twenty seven years later, as the Code took effect, he added: "Judges should be chosen from amongst those who have the appropriate character and talent to meet this sacred mission."[100]

Once again, this approach carries echoes of the French perception of law as a field that cannot be isolated from intellectual disciplines, and which must encompass the study of political and social science, economics and public administration.[101] According to the logic of the New Code, the judge must be a multi-faceted expert, and this is of the utmost importance, since if he wishes to perform the intended process of bilateral adjustment between the Code and society, he must be familiar with the affairs, mores and problems of society, just as he is familiar with the law and statutes. It goes without saying that the judge must maintain honesty, fairness and impartiality (*nazāha*).[102]

Understanding the serious function he must perform, "the judge should beware of introducing his personal opinions relating to social justice ... The judge should adopt a general school acceptable to society as a whole, and not a specific and personal principle," as emphasized in the explanatory notes to the Code.[103] Each specific judge should form part of the totality of the new social contract, and, as such, he must act in accordance with the measure of *murūna* required of him in the spirit of the Code. Any deviation from this, for example by emphasizing his personal views in a manner that is unacceptable to the collective, thus harms not only the specific judicial proceeding, but also the overall harmony that is planned by the Code.

---

[100] Diary, 29 September 1923, p. 108; ibid., 23 March 1950, p. 265.
[101] Dadomo, p. 12.
[102] Diary, 2 January 1923, p. 83.
[103] Al-Qānūn al-Madanī, volume 2, p. 223; Al-Wasīṭ, volume 1, p. 436.

5.3 *Expanded Judicial Scope*

From our analysis of the idea of *murūna* it would be apparent that the New Could would considerably expand the scope of judicial discretion. The explanatory notes to the proposed Code were emphatic on this point, stating: "Let no one imagine that a judge who rules in accordance with a frozen basis and whose hands are shackled by a narrow text can adapt the legal provisions for just application in changing circumstances. For he will then either bring justice, but break the shackles of the law, or remain committed to the limits of the law, and bring only partial justice." The explanatory notes added that it had already been proven that a frozen legal base quickly broke under the pressure of practical requirements; accordingly, it was preferable to provide flexible criteria that anticipated future development and change. Sanhūrī added in *Al-Wasīṭ* that the provisions of the Code became tools in the hands of the judge "so that he can develop the Code on an ongoing basis, and, with the help of these tools, meet changing circumstances and conditions."[104]

We shall examine several situations in which the discretion of the court was expanded in the New Code. These situations will be divided into three categories, according to a progressive increase in the extent of intervention of the court in the contractual relationship: The implementation of judicial rules in accordance with what is fitting and appropriate; the completion of aspects missed or ignored by the parties; and the changing by the court of an aspect that was already agreed by the parties.

First situation

5.3.1 *Modalities of execution of obligations*—The Code granted considerable scope for discretion by the court in evaluating compensation: the judge is to determine the form of compensation according to the nature of the case, and the compensation must be just and financially valuable. According to the circumstances of the matter, the judge may, at the request of the injured party (*maḍrūr*), order the restitution of the situation to its former state.[105] The explanatory notes to the proposed Code

[104] Al-Qānūn al-Madanī, the Explanatory notes of the code proposal, volume 1, p. 23; Al-Wasīṭ, volume 1, p. 104.

[105] The Egyptian Civil Code, article 171; Al-Wasīṭ, volume 1, p. 105.

stated that this prerogative originates in the *Majalla*, which grants the injured party a choice. For example, if someone unlawfully demolishes property belonging to another, such as a house or shop, the injured party may choose to leave the demolished site to the other party and collect the value of the building as constructed, or, if he prefers, he may deduct the value of the debris from its constructed value, collect the balance and take the debris. If the demolisher rebuilt the building in its former state, he is exempt.[106]

The Code granted discretion to the judge in evaluating the compensation due for damage caused by one person to another when that person was in a state of legitimate defense (*difāʿ sharʿī*) of his life or property, or the life or property of another (and hence is exempt), unless he exceeded the extent necessary for his defense, in which case he would be required to pay compensation in accordance with the extent of the damage[107] (the explanatory notes referred to the principle in the *Sharīʿa* of "necessity permits that which is forbidden" and "necessity is evaluated within its confines," which are pertinent to this instance).[108] In this context, a person who causes damage to another in order to prevent greater damage will be liable only to such compensation as the judge considers fitting. Again, the explanatory notes to the proposed Code referred to the principles of the *Sharīʿa*: "The greater injury is removed by a lesser one," and "the lesser of two evils is committed in order to avoid the greater."[109]

The judge is also entitled to determine, in the absence of a specific provision on the matter in law, when a moral obligation (*wājib ʾadabī*) will become a 'natural obligation'. This is an interesting innovation in the Code, referring to cases when there is no legal obligation, despite their legal character, for example due to formal defects. Examples of this situation would include a contract signed by legally incapacitated persons without the approval of their guardians; a will that fails to meet the formal legal requirements; a limitation of debt, and so on. This judicial decision creates a relationship between the parties, but in declaring that a moral obligation is a natural obligation, the judge is

[106] The Majalla, Article 918.
[107] The Egyptian Civil Code, article 166; Al-Wasīṭ, volume 1, p. 105.
[108] The Majalla, articles 21–22.
[109] The Egyptian Civil Code, article 168; The Majalla, articles 27–28.

restricted by public order, whose conditions must be met by a natural obligation.[110]

Moreover, the judge can determine the appropriate date for implementation of the obligation if this was not defined, "while taking into account the current and future resources of the obliged party, and in accordance with the test of the person who scrupulously maintains the execution of his undertaking". In exceptional cases, if the law does not prevent this and assuming that no grave (*jasīm*) damage was caused to the creditor, the judge may also award the debtor a postponement in executing his undertaking until a logical date.[111]

5.3.2 *The decisive oath*—an interesting form of discretion granted to the judge in the New Code for the first time relates to the institution of the decisive oath (*al-yamīn al-ḥāsima*) as an evidential element in court.

The institution of the oath is a central evidential element in Islamic law (and the explanatory comments in the Code indeed explicitly referred to the *Majalla*). The oath emphasizes the religious nature of this legal system, its holistic character and the blurring between religion and state and between law and morality (the separation of these concepts, of course, is a Western idea, whereas in Islam it is evident that religious law relates to all human affairs in their totality). Accordingly, in the legal theory of a system that forms part of religion and of religious morality, the assumption is that a person will not dare to commit perjury and will not dare to take the name of his God in vain.

According to the Ḥanafī school, when a plaintiff was unable to prove his claim, he could demand that the defendant be required to take an oath.[112] When a litigant is sworn in, he swears in the name of the Almighty, saying 'By God'.[113] The oath has concrete legal relevance, since, if a person refuses to swear an oath (explicitly or by silence) after being required to do so by the other party, the judge will consider this an evidential element to be taken into account in determining the verdict.[114]

[110] Al-Qānūn al-Madanī, volume 2, pp. 495–496; The Egyptian Civil Code, articles 201–202. The examples were taken from footnote number 2 in the English translation of the Egyptian New Code, Translation by Perrott, Fanner & Sims Marshall, Lawyers, Cairo, 1952, p. 38.

[111] The Egyptian Civil Code, articles 272, 346(2).

[112] The Majalla, article 1742.

[113] Ibid., article 1743.

[114] Ibid.

Institution of the oath was included in the previous Egyptian civil code without any element of judicial discretion, and this seems to have led to a widespread phenomenon of perjury, since the explanatory comments to the New Code discuss such occurrences, as we shall see below.[115]

The New Code established, by contrast, that the judge could prevent one party from demanding that the other swear an oath, if the former party acted in a manner that was offensive or vexatious toward the party being asked to swear.[116] In other words, the demand for an oath was now dependent on the court's discretion. The explanatory notes to the proposed Code explained that involving the judge in the subject of swearing an oath was tantamount to a declaration that the oath does not relate solely to the parties and their arbitrary decisions, but is connected with the entire legal regime; this is a negative connection, and one that is to be restricted. 'The proposal seeks to warn against the dangers of perjury in an oath when it is perceived an evidential element of proof," since it is not an appropriate form of proof, "but returns in its original form to the conscience, the laws of morality and equity." Moreover, the judge should reject an oath if it were dishonest, and he will be aware of this if there is proof from another source about the fact regarding which it is requested that the oath be made."[117] Thus the role of the oath in the New Code was restricted, and, at the same time, judicial discretion was extended. The New Code has a strong down to earth perspective, despite its use of and references to the *Sharīʿa*; as we have seen, the considerations it applied were often substantive and dispassionate. It had little sentiment for the morality and the religious legal perspective that formed the foundation of the institution of the oath, but was concerned solely with the functionality this institution provided when this was considered appropriate.

5.3.3 *Mixing of chattels*—if two assets comprised of chattels (*ʾiltiṣāq manqūlān*) belonging to two different owners were mixed to the point that they could not be separated without sustaining damage, and there were no agreement between the parties, the court would determine the matter in accordance with the principles of equity, taking into account the damage caused, the state of affairs and the good faith of each party. While

---

[115] Ibid., articles 1742–1743; The *ʾAhlī* Civil Code, article 224; The Egyptian Civil Code, articles 410–417.

[116] The Egyptian Civil Code, article 410.

[117] Al-Qānūn al-Madanī, volume 3, pp. 443–444.

this norm is drawn from the old civil code,[118] it reflects the essence of the unique function attributed to the court by the Code. If we examine this question of mixed chattels as a social symbol, the message is that even if the situation is difficult and apparently insoluble, with blurred perceptions, social confusion and the emergence of conflict and crisis, it is the court—the Core of the approach embodied in the Code—that is called on to resolve the crisis and stabilize the situation.[119]

Second situation

This category refers, for example, to an article we have already encountered in a different context, which states that if a dispute emerges regarding details not agreed upon in a contract, the court may complete these details in accordance with the nature of the transaction, the legal provisions, custom and equity.[120] This is a key article, and it is positioned immediately after the basic article presenting the essence of making a contract through proposal and acceptance. Indeed, in the re-examination committee headed by Sanhūrī, disagreement emerged. Some participants argued that the distinction between substantive matters and details in the contract was a marginal one, and it was therefore undesirable to leave this decision to the judge, out of fear that he might rule arbitrarily. It was eventually decided (evidently under the influence of Sanhūrī, who exercised control of the re-examination committee) that the article would be left intact, with minor amendments.[121] A similar debate emerged during the deliberations of the Civil Code Committee in the Senate. Dr. Ḥamad Zākī, a lecturer in civil law, adopted his customary stance of an opponent to Sanhūrī's proposals, arguing that this article represented an excessively broad extension of judicial authority. As usual, Zakī was unsuccessful in his argument with Sanhūrī, and the article was approved.[122]

A further example: The Code established that power of attorney (*wikāla*) was to be made without remuneration, unless otherwise agreed, or unless the contrary could be understood from the character of the power of attorney. Even if payment to the accredited party were agreed, this was still subject to the judge's evaluation, unless payment were

[118] The *ʾAhlī* Civil Code, article 67.
[119] The Egyptian Civil Code, article 931.
[120] Ibid., article 95.
[121] Al-Qānūn al-Madanī, volume 2, p. 47.
[122] Al-Qānūn al-Madanī, volume 2, pp. 47–48.

made voluntarily after the implementation of the power of attorney. The explanatory notes commented that "if the parties made an error in evaluating the payment for the power of the attorney, the judge could correct this. It is true that this (judicial intervention) contradicts the freedom of contractual association, but this (intervention by the court) is already a traditional norm in the laws of *wikāla* as adopted by the present code from French case law.[123]

Third situation

The New Code created a precedent by establishing that a contract binds the parties not only in terms of what is explicitly included, but also in terms of what is implicit, given the nature of the obligation, the law, custom and equity.[124] This is a general article that significantly extends the discretion of the court, including reference to sources outside the contract made between two parties. Needless to say, opposition was voiced to this provision in the Civil Code Committee of the Senate. Two members, ʿAshmawī and ʿĪshī, opposed the article, among other reasons due to their claim that it granted the judge a 'dangerous mandate', since he could henceforth add to the parties' undertakings as he saw fit, something that was inconsonant with the principle of the sanctity of the contract—a principle that appears in the article immediately before the one in question.[125]

The Code also granted this discretion to the judge in nullifying a contract. For example, if part of the contract were nullified or demanded nullification, that part alone would be nullified, unless it emerged that the contract would not have been signed without this particular part, in which case the entire contract would be nullified.[126] Another example is particularly interesting: if the contract were nullified or prone to nullification, and sufficient foundations of another contract were found in it, the contract would be valid within the confines of the new contract as created, if the court found that the parties' intention was to create such a type of different contract. This situation was referred to in the interpretation of the New Code as the theory of the transformation of a contract (*taḥawwul al-ʿaqd*).[127]

---

[123] The Egyptian Civil Code, article 709(2); Al-Wasīṭ, volume 1, p. 106; Al-Qānūn al-Madanī, volume 5, p. 222.

[124] The Egyptian Civil Code, article 148(2).

[125] Al-Qānūn al-Madanī, volume 2, pp. 288–289.

[126] The Egyptian Civil Code, article 143; Al-Wasīṭ, volume 1, p. 105.

[127] The Egyptian Civil Code, article 144; Al-Wasīṭ, volume 1, pp. 545–551.

The explanatory notes pointed out that this principle was drawn from Article 140 of the German civil code,[128] which allowed the judge to put himself in the place of the parties and transform their old contract, which had been nullified or disqualified for whatever reason, into a new contract. A condition for this was that the original contract was nullified or could be nullified; in addition, all the conditions of the new contract must appear in the original contract. The judge did not have the authority to include new conditions in the new contract that did not appear in the original, and it must be evident to him that the parties have intention and interest in such a new contract. The explanatory notes added that these conditions show that the judge's discretion in this transformation is not arbitrary (*taḥākkumī*). It was noted that these three conditions place restrictions on the judge's discretion in order to draw the assumed intention of the parties as close as possible to their real intention. The proposal noted that the honor of a bill (*kambiyāla*) is one of the main applications of this article, for example, when the bill fails to meet some formal requirement but the parties have a real desire in its honor.[129]

As we would expect, this proposal also met with opposition in the Civil Code Committee in the Senate. Deputy Ḥilmī ʿĪshī expressed concern that this article would be interpreted as granting the judge total power to oblige the parties to accept a specific contract. The president of the committee reassured him that, in accordance with this article, the judge could not make a new contract if the parties did not so intend.[130]

Further examples of this situation we have already encountered include: The theory of unforeseen circumstances, where the judge actively amends the agreement between the parties; the amendment of discriminatory conditions in a uniform contract; the ruling of financial compensation although the parties agreed on compensation in kind, if specific implementation was burdensome for the debtor; or the reduction of the level of agreed compensation stated as a punitive condition in a contract if this was excessive.[131]

---

[128] Al-Wasīṭ, volume 1, p. 546.
[129] Al-Qānūn al-Madanī, volume 2, p. 264.
[130] Al-Qānūn al-Madanī, volume 2, pp. 265–266.
[131] The Egyptian Civil Code, articles 149, 203(2), 224(2).

5.4 *Restricted Judicial Scope*

In direct continuation to the principle of *murūna*, implying compromise and uncontroversial statements, albeit ones not devoid of innovation, while the judge was indeed granted broad freedom to act in the space between society and the law, the same Code also restricted this judicial scope, so that "the judge almost becomes a legislator in this flexible space . . . but he is a legislator limited by the morality of his period, the fundamental arrangements of his nation and its general interests," as Sanhūrī noted.[132]

We have already seen that the New Code emphasized that it did not imitate the Swiss civil code, which permits the judge to apply the provisions he would have established had he himself been a legislator. "The Egyptian Code stopped at logical limits, preventing the blending of fields between legislative authority and judicial authority."[133]

Accordingly, it could be argued that the Code employed two tools in implementing this restriction: The imposition of objective criteria (*maʿāyir mawḍūʿiyya*), with which the Code is replete, and what Sanhūrī referred to as 'objective bridles' (*ḍawābiṭ mawḍūʿiyya*), which were attached to subjective criteria and viewed judicial discretion as worthy of supervision or guidance. Just as the bridle attached to a horse's mouth is intended to direct it on its way, so the objective bridle is intended to guide the judge in applying his subjective discretion, steering him in the direction the Code considered proper. Indeed, the application of such objective bridles to particular issues is evidence of the sensitivity shown to those issues by the Code, and its interest in ensuring a minimum level of stability in court rulings and in the level of expectations among the general public.[134]

Objective Criteria—The objective criterion is a legal index, a test or a level of relativity, and it conveys a certain sense of stability; it may be grasped and sensed, estimated or compared to another accepted index. "Objectivity (which is the partner of external will) is one of the important factors in stability, and it is particularly characteristic of the New Code," Sanhūrī claimed.[135] The following are some examples of objective criteria:

---

[132] Al-Wasīṭ, volume 1, p. 437.
[133] Ibid., p. 104.
[134] Ibid., pp. 107–108.
[135] Al-Qānūn al-Madanī, volume 2, pp. 280–281.

In the very first article of the Code, the article presenting the legal foundations from which the judge could derive interpretation, the proposed Code consciously sought to introduce an objective criterion in order to guide the judge. "The proposal did not wish to refer the judge to the general principles of law in the country (as in Article 3 of the new Italian civil code), or to legal principles in general (Article 1 of the Chinese code), but rather referred to 'natural law and equity' (*al-qānūn al-ṭabīʿī wal-ʿadāla*). It is true that modern codes attribute a measure of vagueness to these terms, but, in reality, this obliges (the judge) to rely on general objective foundations rather than on private subjective thought . . ."[136]

A very prominent objective criterion in the Code is the test of the reasonable person (*ʿināyat al-shakhṣ al-muʿtād*), i.e. the standard to be used by the judge relating not to a specific person whose case is pending legal deliberation, but assuming what an imaginary person, acting in accordance with the accepted social norm on that matter, would have done. It should be pointed out that this imaginary reasonable person is also a figment of the judge's spirit and thought; nevertheless, the judge will be obliged to root the behavior of this reasonable person in accepted and familiar public norms. This test restricts judicial discretion and binds the judge to a particular and accepted reality.

For example, if, as part of his obligations, an obliged party was required to protect or manage some object, or to take cautionary steps, and he acted as a reasonable person would have acted, even if failing to secure the desired goal, then he would have met his obligations.[137] Thus, for example, a partner in a partnership contract must protect the interests of the partnership as if they were his own, unless he were a paid director, in which case his responsibility would be examined in accordance with the responsibility of a reasonable person (i.e., the test of a reasonable person is stricter than that of the test of the management of personal affairs, which is subjective in character);[138] or a lessee in a lease contract might be obliged to invest the attention of a reasonable person in protecting the property let to him;[139] the borrower in a lending contract (*ʿaqd al-ʿāriya*) must protect the object he has borrowed a he would protect his own property, and not less than the attention of

---

[136] Al-Wasīṭ, volume 1, p. 106.
[137] Ibid.
[138] Al-Qānūn al-Madanī, volume 1, p. 188.
[139] The Egyptian Civil Code, article 211; Al-Wasīṭ, volume 1, p. 107.

a reasonable person;[140] the employee in a work contract must execute the work with the attention of a reasonable person;[141] and an appointed representative, if the power of attorney were without remuneration, must invest the intention he would invest for his personal affairs, and not more than the attention of a reasonable person. If the appointed representative received remuneration, he must meet the test of the reasonable person;[142] the same is true of the rules for a guardian in accordance with a guardianship contract (*ʿaqd al-wadīʿa*);[143] or the guardian in 'legal guardianship' (*ḥirāsa qaḍāʾiyya*) (when both parties in a legal proceeding deposit the asset in legal dispute between them with a thirty party for guardianship and management; he then forwards the asset to the party that wins the suit), in which case the test of the reasonable person will always apply.[144] Or the case of the officious (*fuḍūlī*)—a person who voluntarily undertakes to care for the commercial or other affairs of another person or in his name, without his being obliged to do so. In the *Majalla*, such a person is defined as someone who acts in the assets of another without legal permission. In the New Code, the *fuḍūlī* must always meet the test of the reasonable person.[145]

Another example, on the subject of unforeseen circumstances, the explanatory notes stated that excessive judicial liberty might impair stability and economic expectations; accordingly, the Code:

> Granted a material and objective tone to this question, manifested in the definition of the unexpected factor and the evaluation of due compensation in such a case. The Code did not leave the court to evaluate this in accordance with subjective or personal criteria, as did the Polish code, which left this to the discretion of the court in accordance with the level of 'need' that arose. Rather, the proposed Code noted that this was to be done 'if justice so demanded' (this phrase was omitted from the final wording of the law—G.B.), and this is a reference to an objective criterion. Similarly, if the judge decided to reduce the obligations of a party injured by an unexpected event, he must do so up to 'the logical limit'—a further restriction of a material and objective tone that has no parallel in the Polish code.[146]

[140] The Egyptian Civil Code, article 521(2); Al-Wasīṭ, volume 1, p. 107.
[141] The Egyptian Civil Code, article 583(1).
[142] Ibid., article 641(1).
[143] Ibid., article 685(1).
[144] Ibid., article 704.
[145] Ibid., article 720.
[146] Ibid., 734(1).

It could be argued that these 'bridles', in the form of the level of objective certainty applied in specific cases, cannot exist without the judicial scope of the judge; equally, this judicial scope will develop in the wrong direction and be liable to criticism if it fails to take account of the objective criteria. "We have seen that the New Code has frequently established flexible criteria that encourage development," Sanhūrī noted, "and we now see that most of these criteria are objective rather than subjective. Thus a type of balance is created between development and progress, on the one hand, and stability, on the other. By its nature, the objective criterion is one that promotes development while at the same time seeking stability . . . In this way, the New Code sought to restrict the severity of the subjective tendency that is the hallmark of the Latin codes."[147]

Are these objective tools granted to the judge, or are they more akin to shackles placed on his hands? From the perspective of the judge, the answer in accordance with the New Code would seem to be ambiguous: These criteria and bridles were indeed intended to guide him in his search for the answer to a judicial dilemma, but at the same time—to guard his path, ensuring that he would follow the desired route for the Code, and reminding him that there are limits to his judicial scope; that he, too, forms part of the social system the Code sought to establish. By the same measure, these were also intended for public eyes: to ensure a minimum measure of commercial and legal stability, while at the same time clarifying to the public, as part of the educational function of the Code, that the judge is not above the law, and that he, too, is restricted by the social function of the Code.

It could be argued that these messages are of great importance if the model of *perpetuum mobile* discussed above is to be able to function safely. The court maintains a minimum of legal and commercial stability, thus securing public legitimacy within the framework of its duty of trust toward society. Equally, when strengthened by such legitimacy, it will be easier for the court to cope with social, economic and legal problems as part of its duty of trust toward the public—and vice versa. This is a delicate balance, with a value-based and central character that must be appreciated by the judges if they wish to understand and apply the formula of legal engineering created by the Code.

---

[147] The Majalla, article 112; The Egyptian Civil Code, article 192.

Subjective criteria with objective brakes—Sanhūrī noted that when the Code adopted a subjective approach, it did not do so in a pure manner, but applied to it objective brakes or bridles.[148] For example: in interpreting a contract, the joint intention of the parties is to be sought, and this is a subjective criterion that requires the court to examine the subject intention of the parties associating in the contract, beyond its literal meaning. However, the article further established that the judge "should seek guidance (*ʾistihdāʾ*) in this test in the nature of the transaction, in accordance with the extent of trust that should apply between the two parties, and in accordance with commercial custom"—and these are objective brakes.[149]

Or the definition of 'proper justification' in order for a person to rescind the granting of a gift, as we have already seen above. This is a subjective criterion that is wrapped in objective brakes: For example, the recipient of the gift must not break trust and act with ingratitude toward the granter or the gift or one of his relatives, and the granter of the gift must not reduce his standard of living, relative to his social status, or when the person making the gift has a new child and is still alive at the time that the gift is rescinded.[150]

A further example—the assumption of knowledge. When a person was aware of something, this is a subjective criterion; when he should have been aware of it, this is an objective brake. This legal structure appeared several times in the Code, for example on the issue of the power of attorney, error, deception, coercion[151] and elsewhere. Regarding an error, the Code established that a party to a contract who made an error could not exploit this error in a manner contrary to the principles of good faith; Sanhūrī considers this a subjective criterion. The person who made the error would continue to be bound by the contractual relationship, if the other party showed that he were willing to implement the contract—this is the objective brake.[152]

Clearly, balance and flexibility were included throughout the Code, even in its most detailed rules and articles. Accordingly, the principle of *murūna* was not seen by the Code as a merely theoretical heading, but

---

[148] Al-Wasīṭ, volume 1, p. 106.

[149] The Egyptian Civil Code, article 150(2); Al-Wasīṭ, volume 1, pp. 108–109.

[150] The Egyptian Civil Code, article 501; Al-Wasīṭ, volume 1, p. 109.

[151] The Egyptian Civil Code, articles 104, 106, 120, 126, 128 (respectively); Al-Wasīṭ, volume 1, p. 109.

[152] The Egyptian Civil Code, article 124; Al-Wasīṭ, volume 1, p. 109.

as a practice that permeated the smallest articles and details, ensuring balance and adjustment. It should be recalled that this is an expansive civil code employed every day by thousands of citizens, whose rights and obligations as citizens and as individuals are shaped by its norms. For each citizen, his own case constitutes an entire world, in accordance with which he will examine the Code as a whole, the legal system and current social order.

CHAPTER SEVEN

THE LESSER EVIL

The issue for the Lawmakers, however, was not how to reform the structure, but how to save it from meaningful change.

R. Stanley, *Dimensions of Law in the Service of Order*[1]

1. Other Faces of the Egyptian Parliament

The social context of the Code, with its restrictions on the right of property and its protection for the weaker members of society, raises a question that has remained unanswered in this book. How can we explain the fact that the members of both houses of the Egyptian parliament—the Lower House (*majlis al-nuwwāb*) and the Upper House (the Senate or *majlis al-shuyūkh*)—raised their hands to approve the proposed Code, and why did this happen at this particular timing? It is commonly accepted that the representatives in the Egyptian parliament came from the privileged sections of society, and we may therefore ask why they approved a code that might ostensibly impair their preferential status, as manifested in the introduction, of relativist land laws and the motif of justice and morality in law. Logic would suggest that the members of parliament would have a strong interest in opposing such reforms, which could limit the privileges they enjoyed in Egypt.

The members of parliament, and certainly the members of the committees that discussed the Code in both houses, were well aware of its intention to protect the weak strata and to adopt a more relativist and restrict approach to property laws—the rights that gave them their status, money and social privileges. The President of the Civil Code Committee in the Upper House, for example, offered full details on the 'social justice orientations' of the Code at a plenum session held

[1] Robert Stanley, *Dimension of Law in the Service of Order* (Oxford: Oxford University Press, 1993), p. 112.

on June 8, 1948. The expression 'social justice orientations' was his, as will be discussed below.[2]

Over many months, the committee members examined article after article in the proposed Code, in its many drafts, showing surprising patience and attention to detail. Had they so wished, they would have had no difficulty overturning the proposed Code. Indeed, until the last moment it was unclear whether or not the Code would be adopted. On May 30, 1948, a symposium was held for those involved in the legislative process of the Code—parliamentarians, jurists, officials from the bar, religious figures and others; it remained unclear whether the Code would be passed. The meetings of the Senate Civil Code Committee continued through June 1948, and it was still not certain whether the Code would be accepted by parliament.[3]

This dilemma is all the more acute since mainstream historical research has tended to depict the Egyptian parliament as almost completely impervious to social pressure, and as a body that blocked any serious attempt at social or economic reform. This traditional approach is exemplified, *inter alia*, by Mayfield, who wrote:

> In the late 1940s agricultural conditions were widely reported in the press, but series of proposals for social and economic reform were defeated in a landlord-dominated Parliament.[4]

A similar description of the late 1940s was offered by Beinin and Lockman:

> The large landowners who dominated both the *Wafd* and the opposition political parties clung tenaciously to their privileges, and were unwilling to concede even the minimal reforms in the vital areas of land tenure, ground rent, and the taxation of agricultural property...
>
> The Egyptian industrial bourgeoisie and its representation in Parliament, often identified with the Saʿadist party, acknowledged the need for agrarian reform, more equitable distribution of wealth, and accelerated industrial development, though in practice, because the industrialists were so closely linked to large landowning interests by family and social ties... they shared the same social conservatism and fear unleashing

[2] The text of his speech: Al-Qānūn al-Madanī, volume 1, pp. 140–167.

[3] Al-Qānūn al-Madanī, volume 1, pp. 81, 117.

[4] J. B. Mayfield, "Agricultural Cooperatives: Continuity and Change in Rural Egypt", *Egypt from Monarchy to Republic*, Shimon Shamir ed. (Boulder: Westview press, 1995), p. 85; G. Baer, *A History of Landownership in Modern Egypt, 1800–1950* (Oxford: Oxford University Press, 1962), p. 204.

> the anger of the impoverished rural urban masses. Many proposals for economic and social reform were blocked by this fear.[5]

Nevertheless, both houses of parliament approved the Civil Code—the second-most important act of legislation after the Constitution. This is an historical fact; we must now attempt to explain it.

Before answering this question, we should consider who sat in the Egyptian parliament. The parliament was established within the framework of an experimental parliamentary constitutional regime that lasted from the adoption of the independent Egyptian Constitution in 1923 until the Free Officers' Revolution in 1952. Both houses of parliament were dominated by the major landowning elite and industrialists who emerged from these circles, together with leading establishment and social figures. One-fifth of the members, including the president, were appointed directly by the king; these members were privileged social figures who enjoyed power and wealth. As Beinin, Lockman, Bear and Safran have already noted, this was a pluralistic group in political terms, but relatively homogenous socially, despite the bitter political disputes that erupted between the various political factions.

It has been argued that the common interests of these representatives led them to work as a single bloc against the unprivileged section of society. Bear, for example, noted that the agrarian platforms of the various parliamentary parties were almost identical. While Marīt Buṭrus Ghālī, who was considered a 'conservative', proposed that limits should be established in the future for land ownership, the Wafd, which was considered a movement of the people as a whole, fiercely opposed this idea.[6]

In broad terms, these same people might be described as those with most to lose from the destabilization of the existing social order. Gabriel Bear emphasized that it was no coincidence that the members of the Upper House (the Senate) were major landowners—this was a condition for their acceptance to the institution:

> The 1923 constitution, in force except for a few years until the military coup of 1952, laid down, as one of the qualifications for membership of the Senate, ownership of land on which not less than EL 150 was paid in tax.

---

[5] J. Beinin, Z. Lockman, *Workers on the Nile: Nationalism, Communism, Islam and the Egyptian Working Class, 1882–1954* (Princeton N.J.: Princeton University Press, 1987), p. 395.

[6] Landownership, p. 146; Safran, p. 187.

> Since land tax averaged between EL 0.9 and EL 1 per feddan per year at the time, it is clear that only a large landowner, with at least 150 feddans could seek appointment to the Senate. About thirty of the large land owning families were represented in either the Lower or the Upper House between 1942 and 1952 (in many cases by more than one member of the family).[7]

A related manifestation of this situation was that all the members of the Civil Code Committee in the Senate carried the Ottoman honorific titles Bāshā and Bak: Muḥammad Ḥilmī ʿĪshī (*Bāshā*), Muḥammad Ḥasan al-ʿAshmāwī (*Bāshā*), ʾAḥmad Ramzī (*Bak*), Jamāl al-Dīn ʾAbāẓa (*Bak*), Muḥammad ʿAlī ʿAlūba (*Bāshā*), Sābā Ḥabbashī (*Bāshā*) and Khayrat Rāḍī (*Bak*). All these figures were former politicians, ministers and officials close to the Royal Court, financiers and the owners of estates.

As an aside, it may be noted that Sanhūrī (who himself bore the title Bāshā by virtue of his ministerial post) was less than enthusiastic about the members of the Egyptian parliament. In his personal diaries he wrote that the people reject their elected representatives. He even described the parliamentary representatives as closing themselves off from society in a fortress. In a type of sarcastic poem, he wrote in his diary:

> The deputies of this people arraigned their armies and closed themselves off behind their swords and bayonets;
> Why are they so scared, as if they had not entered the building through its front gates?
> Do they close themselves off with their armies to be safe from the plotting of the people against whom they have so successfully fought?
> The people reject them;
> Is there no honest man who will come to protect the people from its representatives?[8]

Sanhūrī had little confidence in the parliamentary deputies, possibly fearing that they would spoil the coherent nature of his proposed Code, thus damaging its status and message ("Members of parliament are first and foremost politicians, and they do not generally have the expertise required for such an important technical process as codification").[9] Accordingly, Sanhūrī wrote as early as 1936 that parliament should approve the Code as a single entity, without dismantling its various components. If it wished to introduce amendments, the proposed

[7] Landownership, 143.
[8] Diary, 22 June 1931, p. 184.
[9] Wujūb, p. 66.

Code would be returned to the committee of jurists that had prepared the original draft—the parliamentary deputies themselves would not introduce the changes.[10]

As this book has shown, this was not the case in practice. The politicians in parliament did not forego their right of intervention, although, for the most part, Sanhūrī's essential messages were maintained.

As for the timing of the adoption of the New Code, it should be recalled that the process of drafting and ratification lasted twelve years, from 1936 through 1948, while the intention was that the Code would take effect on October 15, 1949. On this date, the post-capitulation regime (granting privileges to foreigners), which was perceived by Egyptian nationalists as humiliating and injurious to Egyptian independence, was abolished forever, and the gates of the Mixed Courts were closed. This was an uplifting day for Egyptian nationalism, carrying hopes of renewal.

The date of the end of capitulation was an opportune moment, ostensibly offering a historic opportunity to change ancient orders in order to benefit the homeland; to seize this historic national moment in order to benefit Egyptian society and economic life. The New Code was indeed presented from a national angle as an authentic Egyptian legal creation. In 1946, the Civil Code Committee in *Majlis al-shuyūkh* made the following comments in its final report recommending the ratification of the Code:

> Now, after the nation has restored its legislative sovereignty, and as the last shadows of the capitulation regime (*'imtīyāzāt*) fade away, it is an honor for the Committee to express its great satisfaction at the fact that the New Civil Code will constitute a faithful Egyptian manifestation of this sovereignty, since, after the Constitution, this Code represents the most important act of legislation adopted by the Egyptians themselves...
>
> In this final stage, the proposed Code is submitted before the members of the House of Representatives... If the *Egyptian* Civil Code (emphasis in original—G.B.) passes this stage, it will become a fact. The coming generations will be proud, recalling Egypt's misfortunate suffering due to defective legislation, yet Egypt diligently struggled until it brought out this new act of legislation from itself and for itself.[11]

This approach led scholars such as Enid Hill to argue that the central motif in the manner of enactment of the Civil Code was the national

[10] Ibid., p. 69.
[11] Al-Qānūn al-Madanī, volume 1, pp. 122–123.

one, or, to borrow her term—Egyptization. "From its inception to its promulgation (the Code) was inspired by concerns of nationalist politics", she noted.[12] In fact, however, the national aspect seems to have been less central, both in the social and ideological perception of the Code itself and in its legislative stages. At most, the national motif was secondary to the social considerations—means rather than a goal in its own right. The 'national' moment was an opportunity to achieve something internally, for Egyptian society. Yet this national consideration does not answer the question posed at the beginning of this chapter.

2. Dynamic Stability

The willingness of the parliamentary deputies to ratify the New Code seems to have been based on their concern as a small, ruling and threatened elite—concern that grew during the period 1936–1948, years of social polarization, economic difficulties, political violence and assassinations in the street, challenges by extra-parliamentary groups, and a sense among the parliamentarians that they were losing power. The deputies were already well aware of all these processes.

Their fear was that excessive social polarization might eventually lead to the collapse of the existing social order, which could lead them to lose everything. They were also afraid of the extra-parliamentary and social movements, particularly Socialism, workers and labor movements, the Communists and others who were openly calling for revolution, the overthrowing of privileged circles and fundamental change in Egypt. The deputies felt that existing social order was threatened, and perceived the law in general, and this Code in particular, as one potential way of avoiding the worst possible scenarios, from their perspective. Accordingly, cautious reform was preferable to imminent revolution. Such voices could certainly be heard within the discourse of intellectual Egyptian society.

In the introduction to his book *The Agrarian Reform*, published in 1945, Mirrīt Buṭrus Ghālī (a scion of the Coptic Ghālī family, which held an important position in the cotton industry) stated that there was a need for calculated land reform: "We do not believe that we are taking a path that no one has hitherto taken, since many countries have intro-

---

[12] Hill, p. 83.

duced agrarian reform in varying forms and conditions." Ghālī went on to list numerous examples from around the world. "Regarding the Russian experience, this is a violent revolution rather than healing and development. As such, it does not, we feel, offer much from which we could extract benefit for our purpose . . . What is important in all this is that we want repair and changes, not revolution and upheaval . . ."[13] Ghālī, who was considered an essentially conservative figure, added:

> What is important is that the reform should come promptly, for otherwise much of its value will be lost. It is important . . . that it should not come after public opinion will feel that reform and development are no longer sufficient, and will demand revolution and rebellion.[14]

The writer and publicist ʾIbnat al-Shāṭī (ʿAisha Bint ʿAbd al-Raḥmān) wrote in her book *The Problem of the Fallaḥ*: "We would do better to begin now a balanced and sensible reform, before the *fallaḥ* senses his poverty and demands his rights."[15]

We may now examine how these fears found their manifestation in the context of the New Code. Our examination will be confined to the members of the Egyptian parliament, as the group that ratified the Code.

First and foremost, the members of parliament sought to promote stability, in order to prevent the collapse of an already-sensitive social system. A leading deputy in the Senate, Minister Muḥammad ʿAlī ʿAlūba (himself a representative of one of the main landowning families),[16] expressed concern during the debates that the New Code would break the connection between the past and the present, constituting "an upheaval in the situation to which we have become accustomed."[17]

Sanhūrī, with his concept of *murūna*, understood the concerns of his colleagues and sought to alleviate these worries. Several times during the legislative process, he commented:

> I should like to state that three-fourths or four-fifths of the provisions in this Code are based on the rulings of the Egyptian courts and on the current code.[18]

---

[13] Landownership, pp. 203–204.
[14] Ibid., 210–215.
[15] Qaḍīyat al-Fallaḥ (Cairo, 1938–1939).
[16] Landownership, p. 143.
[17] Al-Qānūn al-Madanī, volume 1, p. 34.
[18] Ibid., p. 70.

Indeed, the concluding report of the Senate Civil Code Committee, which recommended the ratification of the New Code, noted with satisfaction:

> The Committee concluded its study with two key conclusions. Firstly, that the proposed Code does not deviate from the legal traditions that have developed in the nation since the introduction of the codification system with the establishment of the Mixed Courts in 1867 and the National Courts in 1883, and, in this respect, it does not break the continuum between past and present... And, as for the second conclusion: This derives from the first, and it is that the application of the new provisions in the proposal will not impair the commercial norms to which people have become accustomed—on the contrary, it helps these norms through a reform for which we have waited for so long.[19]

From the perspective of the members of parliament, however, the demand was no longer for stability insofar as this suggested stagnation and inertia. The growing social threat led them to adopt the Code as a form of dynamic stability—not seeking to destabilize the existing social order, but to strengthen and preserve it by adopting greater social sensitivity, with the social and political pragmatism of *murūna*. "The New Code is not a harbinger of revolution and does not produce revolution," Sanhūrī emphasized in April 1952—as already noted, this comment was ironically made just three months before the revolution of the Young Officers.[20] Deputy Muḥammad Ḥasan al-ʿAshmāwī made the following comment in the first session of the Civil Code Committee in the Senate:

> The question arose as to whether we should complete (what is lacking in) the existing civil code or draft an entirely new code. The latter possibility was preferred to the former, the reason being the unreasonable deficiency in the current code. This deficiency was not addressed in legislation, and it was therefore left to the judiciary and jurists to fill it. This situation entails great danger... since the judiciary is supposed to interpret existing articles, not create new legislation. Accordingly, it is essential to draft a new code that will address this deficiency so that matters might stabilize... (Moreover) the new code does not disconnect the link with the past, since it has established the past as its base.[21]

In this respect, these parliamentarians shared Sanhūrī's vision: it was right and proper that the upper floor should be responsible for the

[19] Ibid., pp. 119–120.
[20] Al-Wasīṭ, volume 1, p. 6.
[21] Al-Qānūn al-Madanī, volume 1, p. 36.

welfare of the lower floor, and vice versa, in accordance with the model of the *ʿuluww* and *sufl* (which we argue was presented by the Code), yet these would still remain an upper and a lower floor—social classes would still prevail, with a clear distinction between them.

The deliberately minor tone in which the New Code was drafted, the principle of flexibility and the covert social objectives it contains eased its acceptance by the Egyptian legislators. It was in keeping with their broad direction. After all, the Code did not mandate an agrarian reform that would explode in the faces of the landowning parliamentarians. Indeed, it did not even promise thorough reform favoring the exploited peasant or laborer. This was a subtle reform, a Code with covert social goals, that avoided creating antagonism from any direction and had a practical rather than a declarative tone. The Code sought to create a *process* toward a healthier society—not an *act* with immediate results. The legislators hoped that this Code would indeed encourage long-term processes that could mitigate social polarization. Sanhūrī offered them an ideal of social solidarity without their being required to pay a price, and this appealed to them. They could only win from such a situation, which they saw as the lesser evil.

Muḥammad al-Wakīl, president of the Senate Civil Code Committee (and himself a representative of a landed family),[22] made a speech to a plenum session of the Senate on June 8, 1948. He discussed the issues of social justice introduced in the New Code (a sensitive point for the deputies). After his speech, the Senate ratified the Code:

> The proposed Code follows contemporary trends in its social and economic goals, striking a balance between individual liberty and the interests of society. There are numerous examples of this in the Code, from the doctrine of the abuse of a right, through the protection of the weak, the interpretation of a uniform contract in favor of the exploited party, the guarantees in a work contract, the protection of a debtor against unforeseen circumstances, and the reduction of the right of *ʾikhtiṣāṣ* . . . The proposed Code faithfully reflects the modern trends of social justice, within logical borders (*fī ḥudūd maʿqūla*).[23]

In supporting the Code, the deputies did not, therefore, aim to introduce change, just as Sanhūrī himself did not seek social upheaval, but rather the reinforcement of the status quo, avoiding drastic change in the form of collapse or even revolution. Robert Stenley, whose

[22] Landownership, p. 143.
[23] Al-Qānūn al-Madanī, volume 1, p. 156.

comments appear at the head of this chapter, analyzed a similar situation in the USA in the late nineteenth century (1881–1894), when the upper classes sought to preserve their social hegemony through the tax laws. In this way, they sought to prevent anarchy and halt the growth of Socialism. Under their domination, legislation provided a platform and a remedy for preventing the threat of revolution and change.[24] As in the Egyptian parliament, the class unity of the American parliamentarians outweighed their political differences.

Adoption of the New Code was also advanced, as we have seen, through a process of professional consultations (*'istiftā'*) and broad social discourse. This process, which crossed different social strata, was important to the parliamentarians, as a narrow and threatened landowning class. The process of political dialogue and consent among different elements of society strengthened the sense of legitimacy of this class and solidarity, *inter alia* in the face of religious forces. In this respect, the legislative process of the Code constituted a source of legitimacy for the members of parliament, and thus increased the prospects that the Code would ultimately be adopted.

A colloquy was held in May 1948, attended by the members of Senate, leading academics and jurists, Ḥasan al-Huḍaybī (one of the leaders of the Muslim Brothers, who would be appointed leader of the movement a year after the meeting, following the assassination of its founder, Ḥasan al-Bannā), and senior figures from the Al-'Azhar religious academic establishment. The colloquy was extremely important, and it positioned Sanhūrī as a national mediator. The event was important for the Code, in its mission to establish a new social order, and for the members of parliament themselves. As the minutes show, it is true that the Grand Mufti of Egypt left the colloquy in a rage, but he tacitly accepted the adoption of the Code, or, at least, did not protest against it.[25] The discussions of the Code showed the participants that they shared a minimum common denominator, with the potential for even greater agreement. This was a methodology based on innovation with a foundation for optimism.

We may now also understand the true significance of the deputies' support for the Code. Their support was not only for the sake of Egyptian society, but above all for their own sakes. While the Code,

[24] Stanley, pp. 100–135.
[25] Al-Qānūn al-Madanī, volume 1, p. 116.

with its new social orientation, might have seemed opposed to their interests, according to this logic it was actually consonant with, and even strengthened, these interests.

The parliamentarians' fear of social collapse does not appear in the protocols that accompanied the legislative process of the Code, and which were collated in the seven-volume collection *Al-Qānūn al-Madanī*, published by the Egyptian Ministry of Justice (presumably, once again, with the goal of legitimizing the Code and those who discussed it). It would seem that the major landowners in parliament did not permit themselves to discuss their true fears openly, since this would be tantamount to acknowledging the threat to their status. Accordingly, the detailed discussions of the New Code in the Senate were formal and legalistic in tone, seemingly divorced from the questions that were of concern to society as a whole, and presumably also to the deputies.[26] The parliamentary deputies thus manifested their clear position on this issue through their support for the proposed Code and its passage into law.

A review of Sanhūrī's diaries from this period shows that he was certainly perturbed by the social and political threats facing Egypt. His diaries were not intended for publication, and were published partly some two decades after his death. Accordingly, they are important as an authentic source reflecting his personal thoughts during this period. On February 7, 1950, he wrote the following warning:

> The usurping and arbitrariness of rulers leads only to the humiliation of the ruled. And if such ruled individuals gather their courage and fight against usurping and arbitrariness, the suffering they will face due to such opposition will seem, to them, preferable to the suffering they faced due to tyranny.[27]

During the same period, he made the following comment, reflecting his fear of extremism—both Communism and capitalism:

Communism is a disease—but capitalism is also a disease. The worst thing about capitalism is that its defects gave birth to Communism.[28]

---

[26] For example: Al-Qānūn al-Madanī, volume 1, pp. 39–118.
[27] Diary, p. 264.
[28] Ibid. 3 June 1951, p. 273.

3. A Different Vision

The sense of the parliamentary deputies that the Code was the lesser evil also reflected their sense that they were still able to develop the Code by themselves, preparing a form of new social contract and directing it as they saw fit—as if there were no new vocal class of *ʾaffandiyya*, demanding their place within the national decision-making process; as if there were no waves of Islamic and nationalist fervor outside parliament, not merely threatening social disorder but seeking to take the reigns of society. As if we were still in the relative calm of the 1920s, when social processes were still controlled by the major landowners, and not in the tempestuous 1940s.

In this respect, Sanhūrī's vision differed from that of the parliamentarians. His emphasis was on the outcome: the creation of a new and improved Egyptian society. They also sought this goal, but their emphasis seems to have been more on process: their desire to lead and direct this change exclusively. Moreover, Sanhūrī essentially envisioned an Egyptian society in which the future plated a key role in shaping other parameters. As we have already seen, the past and its traditional tools were defined by the parameters of current and future needs. Through his vision, Sanhūrī sought to take Egyptian society forward.

By contrast, the legislators envisioned an Egyptian society in which the past would play a determining role. They sought to return Egyptian society to what they perceived as a stable, secure and promising past. However, thanks to Sanhūrī's principle of flexibility, which was maintained in terms of the relations between past, present and future, the legislators were able to accept his version as presented in the Civil Code and consent to it. The *murūna* of the Civil Code could even bind together two ostensibly opposed visions such as these.

We shall now examine how the legal approach of the parliamentary deputies and their desire to direct and shape the New Code were manifested after Sanhūrī had already drafted the proposed legislation. These comments relate to two key periods—the process of *ʾistiftāʾ*, or consultation, with leading figures in the nation, whose comments were forwarded to Sanhūrī's re-examination committee, and the deliberations of the parliamentary committees relating to the Code, in a last effort to delete certain provisions and make changes.

The re-examination committee (*lajnat al-murājaʿa*), headed by Sanhūrī, indeed introduced a fair number of changes into the proposed Code after the process of *ʾistiftāʾ*—the consultation with jurists, administrative officials and financial experts. However, an examination of these changes shows that few of them were sensitive in social terms.

By way of example, the original proposal included an article that was eventually omitted by Sanhūrī's re-examination committee before reaching parliament. This article stated that the owner of land adjacent to a main road must permit the public to pass through his land, if passage were difficult or impossible, provided that such passage would be effected in a logical manner, with compensation to the owner from the administrative authority responsible for roads, if necessary.[29] This was apparently perceived as too grave an infringement of property rights, and was therefore deleted.

Some articles were accepted by the re-examination committee but blocked in the Senate. Such instances were relatively few, however, once the principle of reform had been accepted. On certain specific points, the members of the Senate moderated the damage from their perspective.

For example, the proposed Code sought to include the phrase 'social function' in the context of land and property laws, as we saw in Chapter Three. Muḥammad al-Wakīl, president of the Civil Code Committee in the Senate, opposed this proposal, for no apparent reason. The committee thus declined to include this phrase in the Egyptian statute book.[30] The proposed Code noted that this term was drawn from the new Italian civil code (which was drafted on the basis of the proposed Franco-Italian code). However, the deputies were probably aware that this phrase relating to the potential social function of land law also appeared in the first article of the Soviet civil code—a fact that, in itself, would have been sufficient to cause its rejection. The deputies were not opposed to the principle itself, but to the use of a term that had Communist undertones and which might one day be interpreted in such a manner, or in another Socialist context. The Soviet code stated that "citizens' rights are protected by law, with the exception of cases in which they are exercised in a manner contrary to their socioeconomic purpose."

A further example: The proposed Code stated that the 'owner of a thing' (i.e., the owner of a property right) was the owner of all its

[29] The Egyptian Civil Code proposal, article 1180; Al-Qānūn al-Madanī, volume 6, p. 49.
[30] Al-Qānūn al-Madanī, volume 6, p. 15.

substantive parts that could not be separated from the thing without its being destroyed, defaced or changed, "in accordance with custom." This reference to custom (*ʿurf*) was deleted by the Senate committee, since property rights were too important to be left in the hands of such a seemingly unstable legal element as custom.[31]

Another example: The proposed Code established that a landowner must permit any interested party to enter or pass through his land in order to undertake repair or development work required by that person, to return lost items, or for any other lawful purpose, provided that he did not cause grave damage to the land he entered, and in return for just compensation, if required.[32] This article was also deleted in its entirety and excluded from the Code, after various arguments were leveled against it by the members of Senate. One deputy argued that there was no need for an explicit provision on this matter, since such cases were subject to judicial discretion. Another claimed that the central doctrines of the Code, such as the restriction of property rights and the principle of the abuse of a right, were sufficient to deal with this specific instance.[33] A similar provision restricting ownership rights was also deleted following intervention by Senate deputies: the provision prohibited an owner from preventing another person from entering his land if this entry were essential to prevent a sudden danger.[34]

These amendments and changes introduced by the deputies were relatively minor; as already noted, they did not prevent the substantive reforms of the Code—the restriction of ownership rights and the protection of the weak. It was not easy to convince the members of parliament, and particularly the deputies in the Senate, to adopt the central reform proposed by Sanhūrī, but they eventually consented, recognizing that this might develop in their favor, and that what yesterday they had considered to be a threat might tomorrow prove to be in their interests.

As we have seen, opposition emerged in the Senate to the adoption of one of the most important doctrines in the Code—that of unfore-

[31] The Egyptian Civil Code proposal, article 871(1); Al-Qānūn al-Madanī, volume 6, p. 18.

[32] The Egyptian Civil Code proposal, article 883; Al-Qānūn al-Madanī, volume 6, p. 48.

[33] Al-Qānūn al-Madanī, volume 6, p. 49.

[34] The Egyptian Civil Code proposal, article 876; Al-Qānūn al-Madanī, volume 6, p. 29.

seen circumstances.[35] Sanhūrī was forced to work hard to convince the members of the committee, even though the article had already been amended by this stage, and now related only to general events, and not personal ones. Eventually, however, the members of the Egyptian elite approved article after article, even though these tended to favor the wretched peasants who worked their land.

This book has also shown that the Egyptian legislators were less than enthusiastic about another principle of justice that supports the weak—the doctrine of exploitation (*'istighlāl*); once again, though, this was ultimately accepted.[36] The same applied to the inclusion of the principle of good faith in the Code, imposing restrictions on contractual freedom, and again the principle was eventually approved.[37]

Ultimately, after examining the actions of the parliamentary deputies in approving the New Code, it could no longer be stated that the Egyptian parliament blocked any manifestation of reform. It may be that the parliament was excessively tardy in adopting reform, and it may be that it did so mainly for the sake of the social class to which its members belonged. It could also be argued that the reform was excessively cautious, restricted and limited in scope. Yet the fact remains that the New Code, as an act of legal, economic and social reform embodying the possibly utopian vision of ʿAbd al-Razzāq al-Sanhūrī and his desire to forge a better Egyptian society, was adopted by parliament in October 1948 and went into force one year later. Despite the turbulent events that have followed and attempts to attack the Code, it has continued to serve as the foundation of Egyptian and Arab civil law into the twenty-first century.

Shortly before the New Code took effect, Sanhūrī recorded his feelings in his diary regarding the long period he had invested in this enterprise. He stated with satisfaction:

> In this Code, I marked the end of one era (in the nation's history) and began a new one. I have brought glory to my beloved homeland and built fame for it.[38]

---

[35] Al-Qānūn al-Madanī, volume 2, p. 286.
[36] Ibid., p. 195.
[37] Ibid., p. 289.
[38] Diary, p. 260.

BIBLIOGRAPHY

Arabic

ʿAlūba, M. A., "Fī al-Waqf", *Al-Muḥāmā*, Volume 7(4)(1927), p. 309.

Mabādīʾ fī al-Siyāsa al-Miṣriyya (Cairo: Dār al-Kutub al-Miṣriyya, 1942).

ʿAshmāwī, M. S., *Al-Sharīʿa al-ʾIslāmiyya wa al-Qānūn al-Miṣrī*, (Cairo: Maktabat Madbūlī al-Ṣaghīr, 1996).

ʿAṭiyya, M. L., "Taṭawwūr Qānūn al-ʿUqūbāt fī Miṣr min ʿAhd ʾInshāʾ al-Maḥākim al-ʾAhliyya" in *Al-Kitāb al-Dhahabī lil-Maḥakim al-ʾAhliyya, 1883–1933* (Cairo: Al-Maṭbaʿa al-ʾAmīriyya, Bulāq, 1938), Volume 2, p. 5.

Egyptian Government, Ministry of Justice, *Al-Qānūn al-Madani, Majmūʿat al-ʾAʿmāl al-Taḥḍiriyya* (Cairo: Maṭbaʿat al-Kitāb al-ʿArabī, 1949).

Fazārī, H., *ʾāthār al-Ẓurūf al-Ṭariʾa ʿala al-ʾIltizām al-ʿAqdī, Dirāsa Taʾsiliyya wa Taḥlīliyya li-Nazariyyat al-Ẓurūf al-Ṭariʾa fī al-Qānūn wa al-Sharīʿa al-Islāmiyya* (Alexandria: Matbaʿat al-Gīza, 1979).

Ḥakīm, T., *Yawmiyyāt Nāʾib fī al-ʾAryāf* in *Tawfīq al-Ḥakīm, Al-Muallafāt al-Kāmila* (Beirut: Maktabat Lubnān Nāshirun, 1994), volume 1, pp. 369–370.

Ḥasān, A. A., ʿAbd al-Hādī, F., *Mawsūʿat al-ʾAwqāf, Tashrīʿāt al-ʾAwqāf, 1895–1997* (Alexandria: Munshāh al-Maʿārif, 1999).

Luṭfī al-Sayyid, A., *Mushkilat al-Ḥuriyya* (Beirut: 1959).

Qiṣṣat Ḥayātī (Cairo: 1960).

Māzin, M. S., "Al-Maḥākim al-ʾAhliyya Baʿda ʾInshāʾiha" in *Al-Kitāb al-Dhahabī lil-Maḥākim al-ʾAhliyya, 1883–1933* (Cairo: Al-Maṭbaʿa al-ʾAmīriyya, Bulāq, 1938) Volume 1, p. 151.

Muḥammad, M. A. J., *ʾUsūl al-Qānūn Muqāranatan bi-ʾUsūl al-Fiqh* (Alexandria: Munshāh al-Maʿārif, 1991).

Qadrī, M., *Kitāb Murshid al-Ḥayrān ʾila Maʿrifat ʾAḥwāl al-ʾInsān fī al-Muʿāmalāt al-Sharʿiyya ʿala Madhhab al-ʾImām al-ʾAʿẓam ʾAbi Ḥanīfa al-Nuʿmān Mulāʾiman fī al-Diyār al-Miṣriyya wa Sāʾir al-ʾUmam al-ʾIslāmiyya* (Cairo: Ḥusayn Ḥasanin Ṣāḥib al-Maktaba al-Miṣriyya, 1338 h.).

Sālim, L. M., *Al-Niẓām al-Qaḍāʾī al-Miṣrī al-Ḥadith, 1875–1914* (Cairo: Markaz al-Dirāsāt al-Siyāsiyya wa al-ʾIstrātijiyya bil-ʾAhrām, 1982).

Al-Niẓām al-Qaḍāʾī al-Miṣrī al-ḥadith, 1914–1952 (Cairo: Markaz al-Dirāsāt al-Siyāsiyya wa al-ʾIstrātijiyya bil-ʾAhrām, 1986).

Sanhuri, A. R.

Majmūʿat Maqālāt wa ʾAbḥāth al-ʾUstādh ʿAbd al-Razzāq al-Sanhūrī (Cairo: Maṭbaʿat Jāmiʿat al-Qāhira, 1992).

"Al-Dīn wa-al-Dawla fī al-ʾIslām", *Majmūʿat Maqālāt wa ʾAbḥāth al-ʾUstādh ʿAbd al-Razzāq al-Sanhūrī*, volume 1, p. 9.

"Al-ʾInḥirāf fī ʾIstiʿmāl al-Sulṭa al-Tashrīʿiyya", in *Majmūʿat Maqālāt wa Abḥāth al-ʾUstādh ʿAbd al-Razzāq al-Sanhūrī*, volume 1, pp. 423, 476–477.

"Al-Jadid wa al-Qadīm", al-Hilāl (1949), Special Edition, p. 6.

"Al-Taʿāwūn al-Thaqāfī wa al-Tashrīʿī Ma Bayna al-Bilād al-ʿArabiyya", in *Majmūʿat Maqālāt wa ʾAbḥāth al-ʾUstādh ʿAbd al-Razzāq al-Sanhūrī*, volume 1, p. 327.

"Al-Taʿbīr ʿan Raʾy al-ʾUmma" *al-Hilāl* 46(April 1938), pp. 601–603.

Al-Wajīz fī Sharḥ al-Qānūn al-Madanī al-Jadīd (Cairo: Dār al-Nahḍa al-ʿArabiyya, 1997).

Al-Wasīṭ fī Sharḥ al-Qānūn al-Madanī (Cairo: Dār al-Nahḍa al-ʿArabiyya, 1988).
Fiqh al-Khilāfa wa Taṭwirhā Litaṣbaḥ ʿUṣbat ʾUmam Sharqiyya (Cairo: Al-Hayʾa al-Misriyya lil-Kitāb, 1993).
"Min Majallat al-ʾAḥkām al-ʿAdliyya ila al-Qānūn al-Madanī al-ʿIrāqī wa-Ḥarakat al-Taqnīn al-Madanī fī al-ʿUṣūr al-Ḥadītha", *Majmūʿat Maqālāt wa-ʾAbḥāth al-Sanhūrī*, volume 2, p. 3.
"Taqrīr ʿan al-Muʾtamar al-Dawlī lil-Qānūn al-Muqārin bi-Lāhāy fī ʾIjtimāʿihi al-ʾAwal Sanat 1932", *Majmūʿat Maqālāt wa ʾAbḥāth al-ʾUstādh ʿAbd al-Razzāq al-Sanhūrī*, volume 1, pp. 23–29.
"Wujūb Tanqīḥ al-Qānūn al-Madanī al-Miṣrī wa ʿAala ʾAy ʾAsās Yakūn Hadha al-Tanqiḥ", in *Majallat al-Qānūn wa-al-ʾIqtiṣād* 6(1936), p. 3.

Sanhūrī, N., Al-Shāwī, T., ed., *ʿAbd al-Razzāq al-Sanhūrī min ḥilal ʾAwrāqihi al-Shakhṣiyya* (Cairo: al-Zahrāʾ lil-ʿAllām al-ʿArabī, 1988.
Sayyid, ʿA. F., Mursī, M. K., *Majmūʿat Qawānīn al-Maḥākim al-ʾAhliyya wa al-Sharʿiyya* (Cairo: Maṭbaʿat al-Raʿaʾib bi-Miṣr, 1921).
Sharabīnī, ʿA. M., *Al-Mawsūʿa al-Shāmila li-Aḥkām al-Maḥkama al-Dustūriyya al-ʿUlya* (Cairo: publisher and year not mentioned), volume 1.
Shawāzī ʿA. Ḥ., ʿUthmān, U., *Munāzaʿāt al-ʾAwqāf wa al-Ḥikr* (Alexandria, 1997).
Shiḥāta, T., *Taʾrīkh Ḥarakat al-Tajdīd fī al-Nuzum al-Qānūniyya fī Miṣr* (Cairo: Dār ʾIḥyāʾ al-Kutub al-ʿArabiyya, 1961).
Slimān, M., "Bi-ʾAy Sharʿ Naḥkumu", *L'Egypte Contemporaine* 27(1936), p. 289.

English and French

Aluba, M. A., "Le Probléme du Wakf", *L'Egypte Contemporaine* (1927), pp. 501–524.
Anderson, B., *Imagined Communities: Reflections on the Origin and Spread of Nationalism* (London: Verso, 1991).
Anderson, J. N. D., "Law Reform in Egypt: 1850–1950", in P. M. Holt, *Political and Social Change in Modern Egypt* (London: Oxford University Press, 1968), p. 209.
—— "The Shariʿa and Civil Law", *Islamic Quarterly* 1(1)(1954), p. 29.
—— *Law Reform in the Muslim World* (London: University of London, 1976).
Atiyah, P. S., *The Rise and Fall of Freedom of Contract* (Oxford: Clarendon Press, 1979).
Badr, G., "The New Egyptian Civil Code and the Unification of the Laws of Arab Countries", *Tulane Law Review* 30(1955–56), pp. 299–304.
Baer, G., *A History of Landownership in Modern Egypt, 1800–1950* (Oxford: Oxford University Press, 1962).
Bälz, K., "Sharīʿa and Qanun in Egyptian Law: A Systems Theory Approach to Legal Pluralism", in E. Cotran, C. Mallat eds., *Yearbook of Islamic and Middle Eastern Law* 2(1995), p. 37.
Barnes, J., ed. *The Complete Works of Aristotle*, ed., (Princeton: Princeton University Press, 1984).
Bechor, G., "To hold the Hand of the Weak: The Emergence of Contractual Justice in the Egyptian Civil Law", *Islamic Law and Society* 8(2001), p. 179.
Beinin, J., Lockman, Z., *Workers on the Nile: Nationalism, Communism, Islam and the Egyptian Working Class, 1882–1954* (Princeton N.J.: Princeton University Press, 1987).
Bell, J. S., *French Administrative Law* (Oxford: Clarendon Press, 1993).
Berman, H. "The Historic Foundation of Law", *Emory Law Journal* 54(2005), p. 13.
Berque, J., *Egypt: Imperialism and Revolution* (London: Faber & Faber, 1972).
Biscardi, A., "Epieikeia and Aequitas: History of Law", in A. M. Rabello, *Aequitas and Equity: Equity in Civil Law and Mixed Jurisdiction* (Jerusalem: the Hebrew University of Jerusalem, 1997), 8–11.

Bourdieu, P., "The Force of Law: Towards a Sociology of the Judicial Field", *The Hastings Law Journal* 38(1987), p. 814.
Brinton, J. Y., *The Mixed Courts of Egypt* (New Haven: Yale University Press, 1968).
Brown, N., "Brigands and State Building: The Invention of Banditry in Modern Egypt", *Comparative Studies in Society and History* 32(1990), p. 258.
——, "Law and Imperialism: Egypt in Comparative Perspective", *Law and Society Review* 29(1995), p. 103.
——, "Shari'a and State in the Modern Middle East", *International Journal of Middle East Studies* 29(1997), p. 359.
——, *The Rule of Law in the Arab World: Courts in Egypt and the Gulf* (Cambridge: Cambridge University Press, 1998).
Burman, S. B., Harrell-Bond, B. E., eds. *The Imposition of Law* (New York: Academic Press, 1979).
Cannon, B., *Politics of Law and the Courts in Nineteenth-Century Egypt* (Salt Lake City: University of Utah Press, 1988).
Cattan, H., "The Law of Waqf", in M. Khadduri, H. Liebesny eds. *Law in the Middle East* (Washington D.C.: Middle East Institute, 1955), p. 203.
Chehata, C., "La Théorie de l'Abus des Droits ches les Jurisconsultes Musulmans", *Revue Internationale de Droit Comparé* 4 (1952) p. 217.
——, "Les Survivances Musulmanes dans la Codification du Droit Civil Égyptien", *Revue Internationale de Droit Comparé* 17(1965), p. 839.
——, "Volonté Réelé et Volonté Declaré dans le Nouveau Code Civil Égyptien", *Revue Internationale de Droit Comparé*, 6(1954), p. 241.
Christelow, A. C., *Muslim Law Courts and the French Colonial State in Algeria* (Princeton: Princeton University Press, 1985).
Cohen, R., *Culture and Conflict in Egyptian-Israeli Relations* (Bloomington: Indiana University Press, 1990).
Cohn, B. S., "Law and the Colonial State in India", in J. Starr and J. Collier eds. *History and Power in the Study of Law* (Ithaca, NY: Cornell University Press: 1989).
Cotterrell, R., "The Sociological Concept of Law", *Journal of Law and Society* 10(1983) p. 241.
Crépeau, P. A., "Abuse of Rights in the Civil Law of Quebec", in A. M. Rabello, *Aequitas and Equity: Equity in Civil Law and Mixed Jurisdiction* (Jerusalem: The Hebrew University of Jerusalem, 1997), p. 582.
Cuno, K., *The Pasha's Peasants, Land Society and Economy in Lower Egypt, 1740–1858* (Cambridge: Cambridge University Press, 1992).
Dadomo, C., Farran, S., *The French Legal System* (London: Sweet & Maxwell Ltd., 1993).
David, R., *French Law: Its Structure, Sources and Methodology*, trans. M. Kindred, (Baton Rouge: Louisiana State University Press, 1972).
Davis, E., *Challenging Colonialism: Bank Misr and Egyptian Industrialization, 1920–1941* (Princeton N.J.: Princeton University Press, 1983).
Deeb, M., *Party Politics in Egypt: The Wafd & its Rivals, 1919–1939* (London: Ithaca Press, 1979).
Dicey, A. V., *Lectures on the Relations between Law and Public Opinion in England during the Nineteenth Century* (London: Macmillan, 1962).
Dubber, M. D., "Historical Analysis of Law", *Law and History Review* 16(1998) pp. 160–161.
Durkheim, E., *The Division of Labor in Society*, W. D. Halls trans. (London: Macmillan, 1984).
Dworkin, R., "Law as Interpretation", *Texas Law Review* 60(1982), p. 527.
Eccel, C. A., *Egypt, Islam and Social Change: Al-Azhar in Conflict and Accommodation* (Berlin: K. Schwarz, 1984).
Ellickson, R. C., "Property in land", *The Yale Law Journal* 102(1993), p. 1315.

Engle Merry, S., "Legal Pluralism", *Law and Society Review* 22(1988), p. 869.

Erlich, H., *Students and Universities in Twentieth Century Egyptian Politics* (London: F. Cass, 1989).

Ewick, P., Silbey, S., "Subversive Stories and Hegemonic Tales: Toward a Sociology of Narrative", *Law and Society Review*, 29(2) (1995), p. 198.

Feinman, J., Gabel, P., "Contract Law as Ideology", in D. Kairys ed. *Politics of Law, a Progressive Critique* (New York: Pantheon Books, 1990), p. 373.

Fuller, L. L., "Human Interaction and the Law", *American Journal of Jurisprudence* 14(1969), p. 24.

——, *The Principles of Social Order* (Durham, N.C.: Duke University Press, 1981).

Gambaro, A., "Abuse of Rights in Civil Law Tradition", in A.M. Rabello, *Aequitas and Equity: Equity in Civil Law and Mixed Jurisdiction* (Jerusalem: The Hebrew University of Jerusalem, 1997), p. 632.

Geertz, C., *Local Knowledge*, (New York: Basic Books Publishers, 1983).

Gershoni, I., Jankowski, J., *Egypt, Islam, and the Arabs: The Search for Egyptian Nationhood, 1900–1930* (Oxford: Oxford University Press, 1986).

——, *Redefining the Egyptian Nation, 1930–1945* (Cambridge: Cambridge University Press, 1995).

Gordon, J., *Nasser's Blessed Movement* (Oxford: Oxford University Press, 1992).

Griffith, J., "What is Legal Pluralism", *Journal of Legal Pluralism* (1986), p. 1.

Hakim, B., "The Role of 'Urf in Shaping the Traditional Islamic City", in C. Mallat ed. *Islam and Public Law: Classical and Contemporary Studies* (London: Graham & Trotman, 1993).

Hallaq, W. B., *A History of Islamic Legal Theories: An Introduction to Sunni Usul al-Fiqh* (Cambridge: Cambridge University Press, 1997).

—— "On the Authoritativeness of Sunni Consensus", *International Journal of Middle East Studies*, 18(1986), p. 427.

Harris, C., *Nationalism and Revolution in Egypt: The Role of the Muslim Brethren* (The Hague: Mouton 1964).

Hedly, S., "Superior Knowledge or Revolution: An Approach to Modern Legal History", *Anglo-American Law Review* 18 (1989), p. 199.

Herget, J., Wallace, S., "The German Free Law Movement as the Source of American Legal Realism", *Virginia Law Review* 73(1987), p. 399.

Hill, E., "Islamic Law as a Source for the Development of a Comparative Jurisprudence, The 'Modern Science of Codification': Theory and Practice in the life and work of 'Abd al-Razzaq Ahmad al-Sanhuri (1895–1971)" in A. al-Azmeh (ed.), *Islamic Law: Social and Historical Contexts* (NY: Routledge, 1988), p. 146.

——, *Al-Sanhuri and Islamic Law*, Cairo Papers in Social Science, Vol. 10 Monograph 1 (Cairo: The American University in Cairo Press, 1987).

——, *Mahkama! Studies in the Egyptian Legal System, Courts & Crimes, Law & Society* (London: Ithaca Press, 1979).

——, "Majlis al-Dawla, The administrative Courts of Egypt and Administrative Law", in C. Mallat (ed.) *Islam and Public Law: Classical and Contemporary Studies* (London: Graham & Trotman, 1993), p. 207.

Horwitz, M., *The Transformation of American Law 1780–1860*, (Cambridge, Mass.: Harvard University Press, 1977).

——, *The Transformation of American Law, 1870–1960, The Crisis of Legal Orthodoxy*, (New York: Oxford University Press, 1992).

Hourani, A., *Arabic Thought in the Liberal Age, 1798–1939* (Cambridge: Cambridge University Press, 1983).

Hoyle, M., *Mixed Courts of Egypt* (London: Graham & Trotman, 1991).

Issawi, C., *Egypt at Mid Century* (Oxford: Oxford University Press, 1954).

Jhering, R., *Law as a Means to an End*, trans. I Husik (New York: A. M. Kelley, 1968).

Josserand, L. *De l'Abus des Droits* (Paris: Rousseau, 1905).

—— *De l'Esprit des Droits et de Leur Relativité*, 2e éd. (Paris: Dalloz, 1939).
Jwaideh, Z., "The New Civil Code of Iraq", *George Washington Law Review* 22(1953), p. 176.
Kedouri, E., *The Chatham House Version and the Middle-Eastern Studies* (London: Weidenfeld and Nicolson, 1970).
Kelly, J. M., *A Short History of Western Legal Theory* (Oxford: Clarendon Press, 1999).
Kerr, M. H., *Islamic Reform, the Political and Legal Theories of Muhammad 'Abduh and Rashid Rida* (Berkeley: University of California Press, 1966).
Khadduri, M., "From Religious to National Law", in R. N. Anshen, ed. *Mid-East: World Center, Yesterday, Today and Tomorrow* (New York: Harper, 1956), p. 220.
——, *Political Trends in the Arab World: The Role of Ideas and Ideals in Politics* (Baltimore: Johns Hopkins Press, 1970).
Lambert, E., *La Fonction du Droit Civil Comparé*, (Paris: V. Giard et E. Brière, 1903).
Landau, P., "'Aequitas' in the 'Corpus Iuris Canonict'", in A. M. Rabello, *Aequitas and Equity: Equity in Civil Law and Mixed Jurisdiction* (Jerusalem: The Hebrew University of Jerusalem, 1997), p. 128.
Liebesny, H. J., *The Law of the Near and Middle East, Readings, Cases and Materials* (Albany: State University of New York Press, 1975).
Lord Lloyd of Hampstead, M. D. A. Freeman, *Lloyd's Introduction to Jurisprudence* (London: Stevens, 1985).
Lutfi al-Sayyid Marsot, A., *Egypt's Liberal Experiment: 1922–1936* (Berkeley: University of California Press, 1977).
Mann, K., Roberts R., eds., *Law in Colonial Africa* (Portsmouth: Heinemann,1991).
Mayer, P., "Équité in Modern French Law", in A. M. Rabello (ed.) *Aequitas and Equity: Equity in Civil Law and Mixed Jurisdictions*, p. 365.
Mayfield, J. B., "Agricultural Cooperatives: Continuity and Change in Rural Egypt", *Egypt from Monarchy to Republic*, Shimon Shamir ed. (Boulder: Westview press, 1995), p. 85.
Meron, Y. "Le Droit Allemand en Israël", *Revue International de Droit Conparé* 43(1991), p. 127.
Messick, B., *The Calligraphic State: Textual Domination and History in a Muslim Society* (Berkeley: University of California Press, 1993).
Mitchell, T., *Colonising Egypt* (Cambridge: Cambridge University Press, 1988).
Newman, R., *Equity and Law, a Comparative Study* (New York: Oceana Publications, 1961).
Nicholas, A., *The French Law of Contract* (Oxford: Clarendon Press, 1992).
Özsunay, E., "Abuse of Rights under Turkish Civil Law" in A. M. Rabello, *Aequitas and Equity: Equity in Civil Law and Mixed Jurisdiction* (Jerusalem: the Hebrew University of Jerusalem, 1997), p. 645.
Posner, R. A., "Legal Narratology Law's Stories: Narrative and Rhetoric in the Law" *University of Chicago Law Review* 64(1997), pp. 737–748.
Powers, D. S., "Orientalism, Colonialism, and Legal History: The Attack on Muslim Family Endowments in Algeria and India", *Comparative Studies in Society and History* 31(1989), p. 535.
Qasem, A. "The Unlawful Exercise of Rights in the Civil Codes of the Arab Countries of the Middle East", *The International and Comparative Law Quarterly* 39(1990), p. 396.
Reid, D. M., *Lawyers and Politics in the Arab World* (Minneapolis/Chicago: Bibliotheca Islamica, 1981).
Rosen, L., *The Anthropology of Justice: Law as Culture in Islamic Society*, (Cambridge: Cambridge University Press, 1989).
Sadat, A., *In Search of Identity: an Autobiography* (New York: Harper & Row, 1977).
Safran, N., *Egypt in Search of Political Community: An Analysis of the Intellectual and Political Evolution of Egypt, 1804–1952* (Cambridge, Mass.: Harvard University Press, 1961).

Saleh, N., "Civil Codes of Arab Countries: The Sanhuri Codes", *Arab Law Quarterly*, 8(1993), p. 161.

——, *Unlawful Gain and Legitimate Profit in Islamic Law: Riba, Gharar and Islamic Banking* (Cambridge: Cambridge University Press 1986).

Sanhoury, A. R., "L'Universite Egyptienne au Congrès International de Droit Comparé de la Haye", *Majmū'at Maqālāt wa 'Abḥāth al-'Ustādh 'Abd al-Razzāq al-Sanhūrī*, volume 1, p. 525.

—— *Le Califat: Son Évolution vers une Société des Nations Orientale* (Paris: Librairie Orientaliste, Paul Geuthner, 1926).

—— *Les Restriction Contractuelles à la Liberté Individuelle de Travail dans la Jurisprudence Anglaise* (Paris: Marcel Biard, 1925).

Schmidhauser, J., "Power, Legal Imperialism, and Dependency", *Law and Society Review* 23(1989), p. 857.

Sfeir, G., *Modernization of the Law in Arab States* (San Francisco, London, Bethesda: Austin and Winfield Publishers, 1998).

Shaham, R., *Family and the Courts in Modern Egypt, a Study Based on Decisions by the Sharī'a Courts, 1900–1955* (Leiden: Brill, 1997).

Shamir, S., "Liberalism: From Monarchy to Postrevolution", in Shamir ed. *Egypt, from Monarchy to Republic* (Boulder: Westview Press, 1995), p. 195.

Sharabi, H., "Impact of Class and Culture on Social Behavior: The Feudal-Bourgeois Family in Arab Society", in L. Brown and N. Itzkovitz eds. *Psychological Dimension of Near Eastern Studies* (Princeton: The Darwin Press, 1977), p. 246.

Smith, C. D., "The Crisis of Orientation: The Shift Of Egyptian Intellectuals to Islamic Subjects in the 1930's", *International Journal of Middle East Studies* 4(1973), p. 409.

Stanley, R., *Dimension of Law in the Service of Order* (Oxford: Oxford University Press, 1993).

Starr J., Collier J., eds. *History and Power in the Study of Law* (Ithaca NY: Cornell University Press, 1989).

Sturm, F., "Abuse of Rights in the Swiss Law, A survey of Recent Jurisprudence", in A. M. Rabello, *Aequitas and Equity: Equity in Civil Law and Mixed Jurisdiction* (Jerusalem: The Hebrew University of Jerusalem, 1997) p. 672.

Sugarman, D., (ed.) *Law in History: Histories of Law and Society*, Vol. 1 (Aldershot: Dartmouth, 1996).

Tignor, R., *Capitalism and Nationalism at the End of Empire* (Princeton N.J.: Princeton University Press, 1998).

——, *State, Public Enterprise and the Economic Change in Egypt 1918–1952* (Princeton N.J.: Princeton University Press, 1984).

Turner, J. H., *The Structure of Sociological Theory* (Homewood: Dorsey Press, 1978).

Winter, M., "Islam in the State: Pragmatism and Growing Commitment", in S. Shamir ed. *Egypt from Monarchy to Republic*, p. 44.

Yadlin, Y., "The Seeming Duality: Patterns of Interpersonal Relations in Changing Environment", in S. Shamir ed. *Egypt from Monarchy to Republic*, p. 151.

Ziadeh, F. J., *Lawyers, the Rule of Law and Liberalism in Modern Egypt* (Stanford Calif.: Hoover Institution, 1968).

——, *Law of Property in the Arab World: Real Rights in Egypt, Iraq, Jordan, Lebanon and Syria* (London: Graham and Trotman, 1978).

INDEX

www.ingramcontent.com/pod-product-compliance
Lightning Source LLC
LaVergne TN
LVHW010640300926
849161LV00005B/994